T5-ARJ-045

[redacted] LIBRARY
[redacted] UNIVERSITY

Literary Influence and African-American Writers

WELLESLEY STUDIES IN CRITICAL THEORY, LITERARY HISTORY AND CULTURE
VOLUME 10
GARLAND REFERENCE LIBRARY OF THE HUMANITIES
VOLUME 1849

Wellesley Studies in Critical Theory, Literary History and Culture

William E. Cain, *General Editor*

Making Feminist History
The Literary Scholarship of Sandra M. Gilbert and Susan Gubar
edited by William E. Cain

Teaching the Conflicts
Gerald Graff, Curricular Reform, and the Culture Wars
edited by William E. Cain

American Women Short Story Writers
A Collection of Critical Essays
edited by Julie Brown

Alternative Identities
The Self in Literature, History, Theory
edited by Linda Marie Brooks

The Canon in the Class-room
The Pedagogical Implications of Canon Revision in American Literature
edited by John Alberti

Genetic Codes of Culture?
The Deconstruction of Tradition by Kuhn, Bloom, and Derrida
William Roger Schultz

The New Criticism and Contemporary Literary Theory
Connections and Continuities
edited by William J. Spurlin and Michael Fischer

Regionalism Reconsidered
New Approaches to the Field
edited by David M. Jordan

Rereading Modernism
New Directions in Feminist Criticism
edited by Lisa Rado

Literary Influence and African-American Writers
Collected Essays
edited by Tracy Mishkin

Literary Influence and African-American Writers

Collected Essays

Edited by
Tracy Mishkin

Garland Publishing, Inc.
New York and London
1996

Copyright © 1996 by Tracy Mishkin
All rights reserved

Library of Congress Cataloging-in-Publication Data

Literary influence and African-American writers : collected essays / [edited by] Tracy Mishkin.
p. cm. — (Wellesley studies in critical theory, literary history and culture ; vol. 10. Garland reference library of the humanities ; vol. 1849.)
Includes bibliographical references (p.).
ISBN 0-8153-1724-7 (alk. paper)
1. American literature—Afro-American authors—History and criticism. 2. Influence (Literary, artistic, etc.) 3. Afro-Americans in literature. 4. Harlem Renaissance. 5. Intertextuality. I. Mishkin, Tracy. II. Series: Garland reference library of the humanities ; vol. 1849. III. Series: Garland reference library of the humanities. Wellesley studies in critical theory, literary history and culture ; vol. 10.
PS153.N5L48 1996
810.9'896073—dc20 95-19543
CIP

Printed on acid-free, 250-year-life paper
Manufactured in the United States of America

to my parents

Contents

Contemporary

Preface

The idea for this collection of essays came in part from my dissertation research: As I examined evidence of positive interactions between African-American and Irish writers during the Harlem Renaissance—a time when African and Irish Americans were hardly on good terms—I became interested in the theories and the realities of literary influence, especially as they affect African-American writers. I asked myself several questions:

> How do black writers feel about literary influence?
>
> Is Harold Bloom's model of "the anxiety of influence" unnecessarily negative?
>
> What influences have African-American writers had on writers from other cultures?

These questions might have lain dormant but for a timely letter from Bill Cain, General Editor of Garland's series Wellesley Studies in Critical Theory, Literary History and Culture. I would like to thank him for his confidence in me when I was a graduate student and his ongoing encouragement and advice. Phyllis Korper, Senior Editor at Garland, has also proved most helpful and patient with this first-time author.

I would also like to thank my dissertation co-directors at the University of Michigan, George Bornstein and Rafia Zafar, who have always supported my work and offered constructive criticism. I can say the same of my colleagues at Georgia College who read and commented on my contributions to this volume. The college itself provided the funding for me to deliver an earlier version of the introduction at the 1994 National Association of African-American Studies (NAAAS) meeting, a very helpful experience.

Finally, I need to thank my husband, George Kelley, for imparting to me his finely-tuned sense of the balance between work and leisure.

Tracy Mishkin
Georgia College

General Editor's Introduction

The volumes in this series, Wellesley Studies in Critical Theory, Literary History and Culture, are designed to reflect, develop, and extend important trends and tendencies in contemporary criticism. The careful scrutiny of literary texts in their own right of course remains a crucial part of the work that critics and teachers perform: this traditional task has not been devalued or neglected. But other types of interdisciplinary and contextual work are now being done, in large measure as a result of the emphasis on "theory" that began in the late 1960s and early 1970s and that has accelerated since that time. Critics and teachers now examine texts of all sorts—literary and non-literary alike—and, more generally, have taken the entire complex, multi-faceted field of culture as the object for their analytical attention. The discipline of literary studies has radically changed, and the scale and scope of this series is intended to illustrate this challenging fact.

Theory has signified many things, but one of the most crucial has been the insistent questioning of familiar categories and distinctions. As theory has grown in its scope and intensified in importance, it has reoriented the idea of the literary canon: There is no longer a single canon, but many canons. It has also opened up and complicated the meanings of history, and the materials and forms that constitute it. Literary history continues to be vigorously written, but now as a kind of history that intersects with other histories that involve politics, economics, race relations, the role of women in society, and many more. And the breadth of this historical inquiry has impelled many in literary studies to view themselves more as cultural critics and general intellectuals than as literary scholars.

Theory, history, culture: these are the formidable terms around which the volumes in this series have been organized. A number of these volumes will be the product of a single author or editor. But perhaps even more of them will be collaborative ventures, emerging from the joint enterprise of editors, essayists, and respondents or commentators. In each volume, and as a whole, the series will aim to highlight both distinctive contributions to knowledge and a process of exchange, discussion, and debate. It will make available new kinds of work, as well as fresh approaches to criticism's traditional tasks, and indicate new ways through which such work can be done.

William E. Cain
Wellesley College

Literary Influence and African-American Writers

Theorizing Literary Influence and African-American Writers

Tracy Mishkin

Any writer takes what he needs to get his own work done from wherever he finds it.

Ralph Ellison

Tradition is a source of life and renewal rather than a dead, oppressive weight.

Edward Lobb

In recent years, the term "literary influence" has not had a particularly positive connotation. It is often perceived as old-fashioned by the proponents of intertextuality, who envision texts rather than authors interacting and associate influence studies with obsessive source-hunting. Indeed, when I began this project, a colleague suggested using the term "intertextuality" in the title instead of "literary influence" in order that it sound up to date. Further, when literary influence is accepted as a scholarly subject, it is often associated with Harold Bloom's theory of "the anxiety of influence," in which metaphors of illness and mutilation figure prominently, hardly an upbeat approach. As Robert Weisbuch writes,

> [w]e live at a moment in critical history that belatedly has adopted the demonic worldview of much of our century's literature. We are given to credit compulsion and hatred and to discount freedom and gratitude. (xvi)

Because of the prominence of intertextuality and "the anxiety of influence" as ways of reading literary interaction, one rarely hears of admiring or respectful relationships between writers and their precursors. For reasons I will discuss later, this is at least as true for African-American writers as for those of European descent. However, literary influence has not always been seen in a negative light.

Writers borrowed openly from their fellows for many more centuries than otherwise. Linda Hutcheon cites several examples:

> I am thinking of the Classical practice of citing from the great works of the past—in order to lend prestige and authority, of course—but also to internalize literary models. I am also thinking of the Medieval and Renaissance revivals of this practice, of, for instance, Dante's use of Virgil—which was intended to show both the poet's respect for and knowledge of the tradition in which he operated, and also the new possibilities he saw in his particular redistribution of those traditional formal elements. (235)

In teaching a rapidly paced Western world literature course in which one reads Homer, Virgil, and Dante in swift succession, I have found the borrowings and reworkings to be striking. No culture that privileged originality could produce authors like these.

The mid-eighteenth century saw a new concern with originality and a concomitant change of attitude towards influence. Writers began to feel that all original subject matter was exhausted and that their work would merely repeat what had gone before (Bate 46). Influence was perceived as something a precursor did *to* one, a passive, unavoidable experience rather than the byproduct of actively seeking one's own voice or an homage to a venerated predecessor. Jay Clayton and Eric Rothstein write that

> In such a climate, it was only natural for critics, bent on evaluation, to look for influences that lessen an author's claim to genius and for poets, bent on immortality, to guard against such influences by searching for the new in both style and subject matter. (5)

At this time Shakespeare was held up as the exemplary "natural genius," one who "imitated nature rather than art" (5)—ironic, in light of today's widely held belief that Shakespeare's genius lies in his ability to rework popular and historical sources.

As originality gained prominence and influence grew suspect, the first works by African Americans were appearing in print. Black authors had even more at stake than white ones when it came to being declared original because the intellectual capacity of blacks—and their humanity—was often judged on the basis of their writings. Those whites in favor of slavery justified their beliefs by terming these works imitative or derivative, the products of sub-human minds.[1] Thus, African-American writers were proving not only their personal merit but their racial merit as well.

Over the next two centuries, the interest in source-hunting among critics remained strong, although the concern with originality softened enough by the early twentieth century that T. S. Eliot could criticize those who

> dwell with satisfaction upon the poet's difference from his predecessors, especially his immediate predecessors [and] endeavour to find something that can be isolated in order to be enjoyed. Whereas if we approach a poet without this prejudice we shall often find that not only the best, but the most individual parts of his work may be those in which the dead poets, his ancestors, assert their immortality most vigorously. (38)

Eliot argued that the best writers surrender to "the consciousness of the past" and allow the tradition to speak through them, an emotionally neutral depiction of the relationship between authors (40). Edward Lobb summarizes the approach to literary influence during Eliot's lifetime as follows: "The unstated paradigm was that of growing up and moving away from home . . . that a writer achieved self-hood in literature as he achieved it in life. Recognizably his parents' child, he was nevertheless his own man" (68). It was this belief in a capacity for originality that Harold Bloom would so strenuously critique as "idealism" in several works, beginning with *The Anxiety of Influence* in 1973, giving literary influence the negative associations it largely retains today (*Anxiety* 5, 31).

Bloom's vision of influence is one of mortal combat acted out in texts. Indeed, one of the recurring images in *The Anxiety of Influence* is of the older author castrating the younger as the latter fights for his poetic voice, purposely misreading his precursor's works in his own to clear the way for himself: "[t]he history of fruitful poetic influence . . . is a history of anxiety and self-saving caricature, of distortion, of perverse, willful revisionism without which modern poetry as such could not exist" (30). When the metaphor is not combat, it is disease. Bloom even refers to influence as "*Influenza*" (95).

In addition to being negative in connotation, Bloom's perception of literary influence is limited in scope; after all, to be castrated, one must be male. Bloom's imagery casts writers and their precursors as sons and fathers enacting an Oedipal drama with canonical status as the prize. Women writers are not included in his early work on influence, where the only female presence is the Muse. His most recent work, *The Western Canon*, admits women and, marginally, some non-white writers to the discussion, but generalizes about their attitudes towards influence:

> feminist cheerleaders proclaim that women writers lovingly cooperate with one another as quilt makers, while African American and Chicano literary activists go even further in asserting their freedom from any anguish of contamination: each of them is Adam early in the morning. (7)

The only thing more reductive than this statement is Bloom himself, who for twenty-one years has revelled in a vision of violence and contamination. In truth, literary influence engenders every emotion from hate to uncertainty to respect to love.

Feminist theorists have critiqued Bloom and given their own accounts of literary influence and women writers. In *The Madwoman in the Attic: The Woman Writer and the Nineteenth-Century Literary Imagination*, Sandra Gilbert and Susan Gubar suggest that because most of a female writer's precursors are male, she faces a different struggle with them, an "even more primary 'anxiety of authorship'—a radical fear that she cannot create" (48–49). Gilbert and Gubar posit that the woman writer therefore seeks out "a *female* precursor who, far from representing a threatening force to be denied or killed, proves by example that a revolt against patriarchal literary authority is possible" (49). Like most feminist revisionists of Bloom, Gilbert and Gubar accept the negative and over-generalized "anxiety of influence" model for male writers and attempt to construct an alternate model for female writers, sometimes a more positive one, but not necessarily.[2] Indeed, the affirming relationship between the woman writer and her female precursor is called into question in Gilbert and Gubar's sequel, *No Man's Land: The Place of the Woman Writer in the Twentieth Century*:

> On the one hand, as some feminist critics have suggested and as we ourselves have argued, female artists, looking for literary mothers and grandmothers whose achievements certify the female imagination, have been delighted to recover the writings of their ancestresses. On the other hand, we are now convinced that female artists, looking at and revering such precursors, are also haunted and daunted by the autonomy of these figures. (195)

Even for those bent on revising Bloom's paradigm, it seems difficult to avoid his negativity, his "anxiety." When Gilbert and Gubar refer to the relationship between a female writer and her precursors as being "inexorably contaminated," one can't help but feel that the perception of literary influence has been contaminated as well (195).

One way to skirt this problem is intertextuality, an alternative to influence coined by Julia Kristeva in the late 1960s and fleshed out by her, Roland Barthes, and Michel Foucault in the years that followed. With intertextuality, the author is displaced—as in Barthes's provocative title "The Death of the Author"—and the text itself is made central. Without human players, there is no need for anxiety. The individual work takes its place in a network of texts, literary and non-literary, all of which can potentially play off each other, and all of which are theoretically created equal, unlike in Bloom's construct, which privileges canonical texts. For example, William Andrews describes "antebellum black folk culture, Joel Chandler Harris' Uncle Remus tales of the 1880s, and the conjure stories of Charles W. Chesnutt in the 1890s. . . ." (300) all growing out of the network that was Southern culture in the nineteenth century. As Andrews notes, it is difficult to document black writers influencing white ones, but intertextuality allows him to study the cultural interaction that most certainly occurred (299–300).[3]

Susan Stanford Friedman suggests that American theorists of intertextuality have added an important modification: they have refused to abandon the author. In Nancy Miller's image, they keep the concept of the network, or web, of interacting texts, but they bring back the spider (Friedman 158). With a spider building the web, its connections are many but not infinite. Miller's is a useful modification of the theory of intertextuality, for it acknowledges that the author is alive and well, which is important to many disempowered groups who are understandably unwilling to give up this central figure. It also retains, yet contains, the notion of communicating texts, which allows for study of the rich interplays such as that noted by Andrews. These modifications, says Friedman, are not popular with the originators of intertextuality because, ironically, they suffer from an anxiety of influence, being unwilling to acknowledge the importance of the author, a key component of their theory's precursor (150). Literary influence and intertextuality are, however, complementary theories, for they can identify each other's weaknesses—the source-fixation of influence and the authorlessness of intertextuality—thereby enhancing the study of literary interaction.

In addition to Andrews, other African Americanists have also found intertextuality useful in theorizing about black literature. Houston Baker Jr. writes in the Introduction to *Blues, Ideology and Afro-American Literature* that

> Afro-American culture is a complex, reflective enterprise which finds its proper figuration in blues conceived as a matrix. . . . The matrix is a point of ceaseless input and output, a web of intersecting, crisscrossing impulses always in productive transit. Afro-American blues constitute such a vibrant network. (3–4)

Like intertextuality, Baker's blues theory is less author-specific, more oriented towards milieu, towards atmosphere. However, critics of Baker have pointed out that his perception of intertextuality is as limited as Bloom's of influence. His matrix of the blues does not seem to include black women or whites of either gender.

While some African Americanists have made use of intertextuality, others have taken up a Bloomian approach to literary influence. Henry Louis Gates Jr.'s *Signifying Monkey: A*

Theory of Afro-American Literary Criticism contains several examples of antagonistic relationships between black writers in which they "signify" on each other, repeating and reversing the master's (read literary precursor's) discourse (52).[4] Gates states that "[m]uch of the Afro-American literary tradition can be read as successive attempts to create a new narrative space for representing the recurring referent of Afro-American literature, the so-called Black Experience" (111). He cites the example of Charles Chesnutt, who decided in his journals that William Wells Brown was not good enough to be considered the first black novelist so that Chesnutt could claim that honor himself. "Try as one might not to use the term, one must conclude," says Gates, "that there is some *anxiety* here, an anxiety that is revealed much more convincingly when one realizes the degree to which Chesnutt revised tropes from Brown's fiction" (117). Gates does emphasize that "signifyin(g)" is not necessarily a negative activity, but his negative examples far outweigh his positive ones. The positive examples he gives are also termed unusual: he calls Alice Walker's love for Zora Neale Hurston "an act of literary bonding quite unlike anything that has ever happened within the Afro-American tradition" (244).

But Walker's attitude towards Hurston, which is similar to the model of influence advanced by Gilbert and Gubar in *Madwoman in the Attic,* is not as unusual as Gates suggests. As Walker writes in *In Search of Our Mothers' Gardens*:

> The absence of models . . . is an occupational hazard for the artist, simply because models in art, in behavior, in growth of spirit and intellect—even if rejected—enrich and enlarge one's view of existence" (4).

For Walker, unlike Bloom and his followers, the danger is not in being influenced but in having no one to be an influence. When she says, of her black female precursors, "I was in need of something that only one of them could provide," (9) one hears influence not as "influenza," but as its cure.

Similarly, for novelist Terry McMillan, the discovery of black writers was enabling, not disabling. In the introduction to *Breaking Ice: An Anthology of Contemporary African-American Fiction*, she describes how she came to be a writer and to edit her collection of fiction. McMillan states that "[a]s a child, I didn't know that African-American people wrote books" (xv). Even as a college student anticipating the first day of a class entitled Afro-American Literature, McMillan wondered, "[d]id *we* really have enough writers to warrant an entire class?" (xvi). McMillan found not an anxiety of influence but a source of inspiration in African-American literature. When one grows up feeling one has few (or no) literary ancestors, the benefits of a theory which sets author and ancestor at odds are minimal.

However, one does not have to be a black woman to share Walker and McMillan's positive attitude about literary influence: writers of other races and genders can and do have more positive relationships with their precursors than many theorists suggest. Even Ralph Ellison, often portrayed as irredeemably hostile to Richard Wright, was reacting more to the assumptions of a critic than to Wright when he remarked that Hemingway was his literary ancestor and Wright merely a relative (140). In fact, like Ellison, many African-American writers cite non-black authors as influences. To give just one example, in *The Big Sea*, Langston Hughes wrote, "I think it was [Guy] de Maupassant who made me really want to be a writer and write stories about Negroes, so true that people in far-away lands would read them—even after I was dead" (34). Hughes did not see any contradiction between being influenced by de Maupassant and writing "stories about Negroes"; in fact, his interest in the French writer showed him that a writer could have an international appeal. Despite the facts of imperialism and racism, black writers can identify with white writers on an individual level, can see them as people. Scholars need to do the same when discussing literary influence: it is time to stop taking overgeneralized, negative approaches for granted and, instead, to listen to what the authors have to say.

Every writer is influenced by somebody or something, and the theorist of literary influence is no exception. Bloom asserts that he was correcting the overly idealistic work of earlier scholars. Many feminist critics have felt it necessary to rework Bloom's theory to fit women writers. Gates also has the influence of Bloom to contend with: although he never says why, he seems uncomfortable with Bloom's term "anxiety" in his account of Chestnutt and Brown. Earlier in *The Signifying Monkey*, when defining his terms, Gates directly "signifies" on Bloom: he creates a chart matching Bloom's Greek terms (Clinamen . . . Askesis . . .) to their Black English and Yoruba equivalents (Signifying . . . Naming . . . Rìran . . . Afiwè . . .) (87). As Baker notes, Gates seems to experience an anxiety of influence of his own regarding Bloom's impact on his titular "theory of Afro-American literary criticism" (*Blues* 111).

Bloom, Gates, and the other theorists I have mentioned all become my influences as I undertake formulating my own theory of literary influence. Several of the essays gathered here demonstrate the positive relationship between author and precursor. Reggie Young's essay is unique to this collection in that it involves a novelist exploring his own work in relation to a literary tradition. Young asserts that slave narratives, broadly defined, constitute the bulk of African-American literature, and sees his own first novel as a contemporary example of the genre. He considers the acquisition of literacy, a theme which dominates many slave narratives, of paramount importance to African-American youth and ascribes to it his own escape from a spiritually and materially impoverished life. Like McMillan, Young describes feeling empowered, not dismayed, by his discovery of African-American literature.

Several essays extend this positive relationship between writers across racial lines. In an excerpt from her recent book *Was Huck Black? Mark Twain and African-American Voices*, Shelley Fisher Fishkin suggests that black culture, as well as specific African Americans, influenced Twain, sparking his interest in the vernacular. She compares the critical silence on this issue to the history of resistance to the notion that blacks have influenced white speech. Fisher Fishkin also examines Twain's influence, in turn, on African-American writers, focussing on Ralph Ellison, who has emphasized both his debts to Twain and Twain's to black culture. She concludes that our understanding of American literature needs to be revised to account for the rich cross-cultural interactions which have occurred throughout American literary history. Along similar lines, Mark Jeffreys writes that Sterling Brown openly acknowledged both black and white writers as his influences. He focusses on Brown's relationship with Robert Frost, whom he suggests showed him a way to write dialect poetry which does not condescend to its subjects. Jeffreys shows that although Brown wrote a very different type of poetry from Frost and he sometimes disagreed with the older man's politics, he was still able to make use of his ideas. These cross-cultural interactions are not limited to blacks and whites: Helen Jaskoski examines Richard Wright's influence on the Filipino-American writer Carlos Bulosan. She demonstrates how their similar experiences with the acquisition of literacy and with prejudice may have led Bulosan to reflect the themes and language of Wright in his autobiography, *America Is in the Heart,* which, like *Black Boy,* blurs the boundary between fiction and autobiography. Rather than repeating and reversing, in Gates's phrase (*Monkey* 52), Bulosan repeats and revises Wright to fit his own situation: Bloom's notion of a deliberate misreading is not evident, perhaps because Bulosan does not perceive himself to be competing with Wright.

The remarkable connections between black and Irish writers also come under the heading of positive influence. I have collected in this volume essays by the three scholars, including myself, who I know have written about the relationship between Irish and African-American literature. Brian Gallagher has been a Hurston to my Walker: at the time I wrote my dissertation, *Black/Irish: Comparing the Harlem and Irish Renaissances,* his was the only work I could find on the subject, and it strengthened my resolve. He focusses on the similarities between the Harlem and Irish Renaissances, examining language, heritage, and cultural institutions. Gallagher argues that despite some differences black literature and Irish literature have more in common than the traditional divisions of English and American literature allow, and he asks scholars to set these boundaries aside. My research was also supported and assisted by my dissertation co-director, George Bornstein. During my years at Michigan, we worked together, sharing sources, and explored various aspects of African American and Irish interaction. His essay examines the connections between the two cultures made by their nineteenth-century political leaders, the sentimental and stereotypical representations of the two peoples, and the resolve of black and Irish writers during the late nineteenth and early twentieth centuries to change those representations. He compares two Renaissance dramas, John Synge's *Playboy of the Western World* and Zora Neale Hurston and Langston Hughes's *Mule Bone,* finding similarities of theme and audience response, and concludes, as do many of the authors in this volume, that cross-cultural interaction should be considered the rule, not the exception. My own contribution explores the literary and political connections between the Harlem and Irish Renaissances in more detail and examines some of their problematic aspects. I assert that although the black/Irish comparisons were sometimes based on inadequate information or stereotypes, they nonetheless inspired writers, helping them to better understand their own situations.

Although in this introduction I have posited a model of literary influence more positive than most, I acknowledge that some black writers do have an ambivalent relationship with their precursors. Several essays in this collection address these more adversarial relationships, which, like the other type, occur throughout African-American literary history. Richard Yarborough describes the impact of *Uncle Tom's Cabin* on early black novelists. He characterizes Stowe's work as a sympathetic portrayal which nevertheless fell into stereotypes and appealed to emotions to the detriment of its political agenda. Early African-American novelists, Yarborough asserts, appreciated that the novel could help them politically but resented both the ending, in which George and Eliza move to Africa, and Stowe's portrayal of Uncle Tom. Despite their ambivalence, black writers of the time were influenced by *Uncle Tom's Cabin*. They challenged some of the stereotypes, yet reinforced others, such as the color hierarchy; they had trouble creating heroic characters instead of passive, forgiving Uncle Tom's; and they, like Stowe, sought to make white audiences sympathetic to the plight of African Americans more than they portrayed realistic responses on the part of their characters to various racial tensions. Peter Caccavari also writes about a member of the generation which first reacted to Stowe's work, but he chooses to discuss a black writer's relationship with a white novelist all but unheard of today, Albion Tourgée. Caccavari suggests that Charles Chesnutt admired Tourgée's work, but felt that as an African American he could create more believable black characters than the white author. He argues that in *The Conjure Woman* Chesnutt signifies on Tourgée's novel *A Fool's Errand*, which is also the story of a naive white Northerner who moves to the South. Caccavari adopts Gates's terminology but gives it a less antagonistic cast, emphasizing Chesnutt's respect for Tourgée.

Moving into the twentieth century, Pierre Walker takes up the familiar argument that Ralph Ellison executes a Bloomian rewriting of Richard Wright in *Invisible Man*.[5] However, he uses Barbara Herrnstein Smith's theory of "value" to further the parameters of the Ellison influence discussion. Walker suggests that in addition to being influenced by Wright, Ellison has influenced our acceptance of contemporary literary theory. He calls Ellison's view of social history "proto-Foucauldian," noting how it focusses on the marginal and rejects the linear, and he states that Ellison's valorization of folk or "low" culture has also become a part of contemporary academic culture, namely cultural studies. Alicia Ostriker also discusses both the influences by and on a writer, in this case the contemporary poet Lucille Clifton. She explores the spiritual complexity of this minimalist poet, showing how she rewrites Biblical stories to tell her own tales. Ostriker also addresses her own ambivalence about Clifton's influence on herself: she is drawn to Clifton's work and identifies with her speakers, but she is painfully aware of her own whiteness and where that locates her in Clifton's poems—as the outsider. Walker and Ostriker allow us to see literary influence as the multi-directional phenomena it truly is.

Peter Erickson and Richard Hardack examine the ambivalence of African-American authors toward different renaissances, the English and the American. Erickson explores Gloria Naylor's use of Shakespeare in her four novels, arguing, like Caccavari, that she values Shakespeare but feels a need to rewrite him. Erickson shows how Naylor dramatizes the tension between older and newer literary traditions, represented here by Shakespeare and Toni Morrison. He concludes that Shakespeare needs to be decentered but not dismissed not only by Naylor and other black writers but by scholars in all areas of literature. Hardack argues that Reed parodically rewrites the American Renaissance— namely Emerson and *Uncle Tom's Cabin*—but that Reed is not sure whether he is a child of the American or the Harlem Renaissance because he draws his central figure, Jes Grew, from both nineteenth-century American pantheism and Egyptian (read *black*) mythology. Hardack looks at the conflict in Ishmael Reed's *Mumbo Jumbo* between claiming to be a self-created artist and acknowledging one's sources, and he explores Reed's delicate balancing act between satirizing Western culture and belonging to it. Hardack ultimately urges him—like Naylor—to continue to question but not discard.

The call for papers for this anthology requested essays addressing any and all of the possible ethnic combinations of author and precursor, yet the majority of submissions discussed the influence of white writers on black ones, and the make-up of this volume reflects that. Although some, like Katherine J. Mayberry, suggest that this results from "cultural arrogance," (A48) I feel the essays in this collection which explore white on black influence speak for themselves, demonstrating the liminality of American cultures, not racism.

Despite evidence which shows that writers of African descent have been influenced—whether ambivalently or not—by white authors, some African Americanists are not comfortable with this claim. Almost as long as there has been black literature, there has been an effort to create a black canon, and this effort has only intensified in the past generation as African-American literature has become an acceptable field of study at predominately white universities. But canon building often means restricting oneself to the study of internal influences, even if that affords a limited perspective. In an early work, *Long Black Song*, Baker argued that black American culture was radically "separate and distinctive" (10) from white culture; ironically, a few pages earlier he mentioned the white writers he had enjoyed reading as a boy.

The desire to have African-American literature be a thing apart from white culture continues today. When I presented a version of this introduction at the National Association of African-American Studies (NAAAS) conference in 1994, some of the younger African-American participants told me afterwards that despite their interest in the subject, they felt threatened by my discussion of interracial literary influence because they did not feel they had finished building a canon of their own. As Gates puts it,

> When I was a student in the 1960's, my professors still thought of the great American tradition as white and male. . . . Then, from the late 1960's on, some of us began to analyze a self-contained black tradition as a corrective. (Winkler A7)

However, from here Gates concludes, "Now people are beginning to look at cultural contact." Perhaps the next generation of African Americanists will follow his lead, becoming more comfortable with the type of cross-cultural influences which appear in this collection and accepting that interracial influence means not that a black canon is not self-sufficient but that it did not grow in a vacuum. In addition, after seeing how writers can have positive relationships even across racial divides, perhaps theorists of literary influence will also change, depicting a more balanced view of the many types of interactions between authors, adding cooperation to castration, innervation to enervation.

Notes

1. Gates, *Figures in Black,* 4. The first chapter of this work contains an excellent discussion of this phenomenon.

2. Other feminist revisions of Bloom include Joanne Feit Diehl, "'Come Slowly—Eden': An Exploration of Women Poets and Their Muse" and Annette Kolodny, "A Map for Rereading: Gender and the Interpretation of Literary Texts."

3. Other works on black and white intertextuality include Shelley Fisher Fishkin, *Was Huck Black? Mark Twain and African-American Voices,* excerpted in this collection; Ann duCille, *The Coupling Convention: Sex, Text, and Tradition in Black Women's Fiction;* Aldon L. Nielsen, *Writing Between the Lines: Race and Intertextuality;* Eric Sundquist, *To Wake the Nations: Race in the Making of American Literature;* Wendy Harding and Jacky Martin, *A World of Difference: An Inter-Cultural Study of Toni Morrison's Novels;* Kenneth Warren, *Black and White Strangers: Race and American Literary Realism;* and Toni Morrison, *Playing in the Dark: Whiteness and the Literary Imagination.*

4. In his 1987 work *Figures in Black: Words, Signs, and the "Racial" Self,* Gates referred to signifying as an intertextual theory, one which "allows us to understand literary revision without resource to . . . Oedipal slayings at the crossroads" (49), but *The Signifying Monkey* (1988) does indeed explore the feelings of specific authors.

5. For a discussion of Wright and Ellison, see Joseph T. Skerritt Jr., "The Wright Interpretation: Ralph Ellison and the Anxiety of Influence."

Works Cited

Andrews, William L. "Inter(racial)textuality in Nineteenth-Century Southern Narrative." *Influence and Intertextuality in Literary History*. Eds. Jay Clayton and Eric Rothstein. Madison: University of Wisconsin Press, 1991. 298–317.

Baker, Houston, Jr. *Blues, Ideology and Afro-American Literature*. Chicago: University of Chicago Press, 1984.

———. *Long Black Song: Essays in Black American Literature and Culture*. Charlottesville: University Press of Virginia, 1972.

Barthes, Roland. "The Death of the Author." *Image-Music-Text*. Trans. Steven Heath. New York: Hill and Wang, 1977. 142–48.

Bate, Walter Jackson. *The Burden of the Past and the English Poet*. Cambridge: Harvard University Press, 1970.

Bloom, Harold. *The Anxiety of Influence*. New York, Oxford University Press, 1973.

———. *The Western Canon: The Books and School of the Ages*. New York: Harcourt, Brace, 1994.

Clayton, Jay, and Eric Rothstein. "Figures in the Corpus: Theories of Influence and Intertextuality." *Influence and Intertextuality in Literary History*. Eds. Jay Clayton and Eric Rothstein. Madison: University of Wisconsin Press, 1991. 3–36.

Diehl, Joanne Feit. "'Come Slowly—Eden': An Exploration of Women Poets and Their Muse." *Signs* 3 (1978): 572–87.

duCille, Ann. *The Coupling Convention: Sex, Text, and Tradition in Black Women's Fiction*. New York: Oxford University Press, 1993.

Eliot, T. S. "Tradition and the Individual Talent." *Selected Prose of T. S. Eliot*. New York: Harcourt Brace Jovanovich, 1975. 37–44.

Ellison, Ralph. *Shadow and Act*. New York: Random House, 1964.

Fishkin, Shelley Fisher. *Was Huck Black? Mark Twain and African-American Voices*. New York: Oxford University Press, 1993.

Friedman, Susan Stanford. "Weavings: Intertextuality and the (Re)Birth of the Author." *Influence and Intertextuality in Literary History*. Eds. Jay Clayton and Eric Rothstein. Madison: University of Wisconsin Press, 1991. 146–80.

Gates, Henry Louis, Jr. *Figures in Black: Words, Signs, and the "Racial" Self*. New York: Oxford, 1987.

———. *The Signifying Monkey: A Theory of Afro-American Literary Criticism*. New York: Oxford University Press, 1988.

Gilbert, Sandra, and Susan Gubar. *The Madwoman in the Attic: The Woman Writer and the Nineteenth-Century Literary Imagination*. New Haven: Yale University Press, 1979.

———. *No Man's Land: The Place of the Woman Writer in the Twentieth Century. Vol. 1. The War of the Words.* New Haven: Yale University Press, 1988.

Harding, Wendy, and Jacky Martin. *A World of Difference: An Inter-Cultural Study of Toni Morrison's Novels*. Westport, Conn.: Greenwood Press, 1994.

Hughes, Langston. *The Big Sea.* New York: Hill and Wang, 1940.

Hutcheon, Linda. "Literary Borrowing . . . and Stealing: Plagiarism, Sources, Influences, and Intertexts." *English Studies in Canada* 12 (1986): 229–39.

Kolodny, Annette. "A Map for Rereading: Gender and the Interpretation of Literary Texts." *The New Feminist Criticism: Essays on Women, Literature, and Theory*. Ed. Elaine Showalter. New York: Pantheon-Random, 1985. 46–62.

Lobb, Edward. "The Dead Father: Notes on Literary Influence." *Studies in the Humanities* 13:2 (1986): 67–80.

Mayberry, Katherine J. "White Feminists Who Study Black Writers." *Chronicle of Higher Education*, 12 October 1994: A48.

McMillan, Terry. Introduction. *Breaking Ice: An Anthology of Contemporary African-American Fiction*. New York: Penguin, 1990. xv–xxiv.

Morrison, Toni. *Playing in the Dark: Whiteness and the Literary Imagination.* Cambridge: Harvard University Press, 1992.

Nielsen, Aldon L. *Writing Between the Lines: Race and Intertextuality.* Athens: University of Georgia Press, 1994.

Skerritt, Joseph T., Jr. "The Wright Interpretation: Ralph Ellison and the Anxiety of Influence." *Speaking for You: The Vision of Ralph Ellison*. Ed. Kimberly Benston. Washington: Howard University Press, 1987. 217–30.

Sundquist, Eric. *To Wake the Nations: Race in the Making of American Literature.* Cambridge: Belknap-Harvard University Press, 1993.

Walker, Alice. *In Search of Our Mothers' Gardens.* New York: Harcourt Brace Jovanovich, 1983.

Warren, Kenneth. *Black and White Strangers: Race and American Literary Realism.* Chicago: University of Chicago Press, 1993.

Weisbuch, Robert. *Atlantic Double-Cross: American Literature and British Influence in the Age of Emerson.* Chicago: University of Chicago Press, 1985.

Winkler, Karen J. "A Scholar's Provocative Query: Was Huckleberry Finn Black?" *Chronicle of Higher Education*, 8 July 1992: A7-8.

The Nineteenth Century

Strategies of Black Characterization in *Uncle Tom's Cabin* and the Early Afro-American Novel

Richard Yarborough

Poor Uncle Tom,
The faithful, honest, brave
Poor Uncle Tom!
The patient captive slave,
Poor Uncle Tom!

"Poor Uncle Tom!", a song from *The Uncle Tom's Cabin Almanack*

Mrs. Stowe has *invented* the Negro novel.

George Eliot

In lectures, journals, pamphlets, newspapers, and sermons throughout the first half of the nineteenth century, pro- and antislavery forces debated not only the place of the black in the United States but also the very physical and psychological nature of the transplanted Africans. When the abolitionist journal *National Era* began the serial publication of a tale by Harriet Beecher Stowe called *Uncle Tom's Cabin; or, Life among the Lowly* in June 1851, fiction immediately became a major weapon in the arsenals of both sides. Appearing in two-volume book form in March 1852, Stowe's novel set off an astounding public response unique in the history of American publishing. Frederick Douglass reported that the first edition of 5,000 was gone in four days ("Literary Notices") and that in one year *Uncle Tom's Cabin* sold more than 300,000 copies ("Work"). This figure is particularly astonishing when one considers that out of a population of roughly 24 million in the United States, much of the South has to be excluded from any serious estimation of Stowe's readership—both because of the huge slave population and because the novel was banned in many communities. Furthermore, one must forget neither the degree of illiteracy in mid-nineteenth-century America nor the widespread practice of passing books from hand to hand. Another indication of the reading public's infatuation with Stowe was the reception accorded *The Key to Uncle Tom's Cabin* (1853), a ponderous compilation of the factual material she claimed to have used in composing her bestseller: in the space of a month, roughly 90,000 copies were sold.

Uncle Tom's Cabin was the epicenter of a massive cultural phenomenon, the tremors of which still affect the relationship between blacks and whites in the United States. Articulating most contemporaneous arguments regarding the Afro-American and endorsing a response to the race problem that has haunted black thinkers for over a century, Stowe's novel has had a particularly powerful artistic impact as well. As the black critic William Stanley Braithwaite observes, not only was *Uncle Tom's Cabin* "the first conspicuous example of the Negro as a subject for literary treatment," but it also "dominated in mood and attitude the American literature of a whole generation" (30). In so doing, Stowe's work played a major role in establishing the level of discourse for the majority of fictional treatments of the Afro-American that were to follow—even for those produced by blacks themselves. This is not to underestimate the crucial prototypical role the slave narratives played in shaping the Afro-American fiction tradition, especially through their impact upon white abolitionist writers (like Stowe), who, in turn, influenced black authors. A further important intergeneric connection can be discerned in the work of the ex-slaves William Wells Brown and Frederick Douglass, both of whom published narratives before turning to fiction. Finally, as Benjamin Quarles points out, "the vast audience that responded to [Stowe's] classic tale of Uncle Tom . . . had already been conditioned and prepared by the life stories of runaway slaves" (67). Nonetheless, the lasting effect of Stowe's masterwork on popular American culture dwarfs that of the slave narratives. With its extraordinary synthesizing power, *Uncle Tom's Cabin* presented Afro-American characters, however derivative and distorted, who leaped with incredible speed to the status of literary paradigms and even cultural archetypes with which subsequent writers—black and white—have had to reckon. The grandeur of Leslie Fiedler's claim that "for better or worse, it was Mrs. Stowe who invented American Blacks for the imagination of the whole world" (26) does not belie its essential truth.[1]

Although Stowe unquestionably sympathized with the slaves, her commitment to challenging claims of black inferiority was frequently undermined by her own endorsement of racial stereotypes. And it could hardly have been otherwise, for as Thomas Graham contends, "the Negro remained an enigma to her" (616). Of necessity, Stowe falls back upon popular conceptions of the Afro-American in depicting many of her slave characters. As one result, the blacks she uses to supply much of the humor in *Uncle Tom's Cabin* owe a great deal to the darky figures who capered across minstrel stages and white imaginations in the antebellum years. The black pranksters Sam and Andy, for instance, provide a comic counterpoint to the melodramatic flight of Eliza and Harry from the slave trader Haley. And although the two slaves play a critical role in Eliza's escape by leading the white man astray, they ultimately seem little more than bumptious, giggling, outsized adolescents. Further, Stowe never attributes their trickster-like manipulation of Haley to any real desire to help the fugitives to freedom. Rather, Sam and Andy realize that Mrs. Shelby does not want Eliza captured; eager to please their mistress, they are only too glad to oblige. Stowe's attitude toward these slaves is also revealed in Sam's other appearances, which are wholly comic. Primarily concerned with his own image, he is a pompous, philosophizing amateur politician, and his speeches are fraught with the tortured syntax and strained malapropisms that Stowe intends to be amusing.[2]

Other frequent sources of humor for Stowe are the slave children, whom she evidently viewed as part of the quaint furnishings below the Mason-Dixon line. If we take *Uncle Tom's Cabin* literally, "little negroes, all rolled together in the corners," could be found in slaves' quarters, big-house kitchens, and barrooms throughout the South.[3] Most closely resembling wild, boisterous puppies bent on driving the adults to distraction, these black children generally appear in tumbling heaps and bundles rather than as individuals. The only one whom Stowe seriously attempts to characterize is "poor, diabolic, excellent Topsy" (5), as George Sand called her; consequently, this figure embodies in particular detail the traits the author felt to be endemic to the undomesticated African.

Stowe introduces Topsy as the stereotypical pickaninny, with teeth gleaming, hair in bristling braids, eyes round and sparkling. A quick-witted, hyperactive child of eight or nine, she acts entirely from impulse and perversely flouts the accepted rules of polite white society, particularly those championed by the chilly, puritanical New Englander, Miss Ophelia. Inured to whipping and recalcitrant in the extreme, Topsy claims no natural origin—or, to be more precise, she offers a now-famous explanation of her own conception in such outrageously "natural" terms that it approaches the atheistic absurd: "I spect I grow'd. Don't think nobody never made me." She also justifies her destructive prankishness with a despairing resignation that exasperates Ophelia to no end: "Cause I's wicked,—I is. I's mighty wicked, any how. I can't help it." Despite her mistress's best efforts, Topsy's behavior remains quirkily schizoid. Assigned to clean Ophelia's room, she either does so flawlessly or else unleashes a "carnival of confusion"; she learns to read and write "as if by magic" but refuses to master sewing (Chap. 20).

Stowe also hints at an eerie, otherworldly side to the "goblin-like" Topsy. In one of the more memorable scenes, the child responds to her owner's whistle like a pet displaying a favorite trick:

> The black, glassy eyes glittered with a kind of wicked drollery, and the thing struck up, in a clear shrill voice, an odd negro melody, to which she kept time with her hands and feet, spinning round, clapping her hands, knocking her knees together, in a wild, fantastic sort of time, and producing in her throat all those odd guttural sounds which distinguish the native music of her race; and finally, turning a summerset or two, and giving a prolonged closing note, as odd and unearthly as that of a steam-whistle, she came suddenly down on the carpet, and stood with her hands folded, and a most sanctimonious expression of meekness and solemnity over her face, only broken by the cunning glances which she shot askance from the corners of her eyes.

Although this incredible passage incidentally reveals the author's rather odd and yet, for many whites of the time, entirely typical perception of Afro-American folk music and dance, of paramount importance is the emphasis Stowe places on the grotesque freakishness of Topsy's performance, for she identifies this darkly magical and faintly sinister quality of the "sooty gnome" with her unredeemed African nature. With her irrepressible penchant for "turning a summerset" and the mesmerizing power "her wild diablerie" maintains over Eva St. Clare and the other youngsters, Topsy is the imp child whose undisciplined devilish spirit must be controlled (Chap. 20).

Her scenes with Eva bring Topsy's allegedly innate African traits into sharpest relief. If Eva is the "fair, high-bred child, with her golden head, her deep eyes, her spiritual, noble brow, and princelike movements," Topsy is her "black, keen, subtle, cringing, yet acute neighbor." Eva, "the Saxon," and Topsy, "the Afric," are both "representative of their races," and the moral struggle that ensues between them constitutes an important motif in *Uncle Tom's Cabin* (Chap. 20). On one side stands the precocious, cherubic Eva, whom Stowe describes as "an impersonation in childish form of the love of Christ" (*Key* 51). On the other is Topsy, who embodies an innocent but still dangerous lack of self-control and restraint. And although fascinated by Topsy "as a dove is sometimes charmed by a glittering serpent" (the religious symbolism here is obvious), Eva holds the key to the black child's conversion as she tries to touch her "wild, rude heart" with "the first word of kindness" (Chap. 20). Initially, Topsy resists, linking her hopeless spiritual condition with her race: "Couldn't never be nothin' but a nigger, if I was ever so good.... If I could be skinned, and come white, I'd try then.... There can't nobody love niggers, and niggers can't do nothin'! *I* don't care." However, Eva's response—"Oh, Topsy, poor child, *I* love you!"—pierces her defenses. Prostrated by the gentle force of selfless love, Topsy breaks down, with Eva bending over her like "some bright angel stooping to reclaim a sinner" (Chap. 25). In Stowe's world, to be born black is to be born a pagan, but paradoxically close to a state of grace; once a character's heathen African nature is controlled, redemption becomes a possibility.

Stowe's depiction of Legree's henchmen, Sambo and Quimbo, reiterates this same formulation. Although easily the most immoral black characters in the novel, the two slaves have, Stowe hastens to point out, no real predisposition to cruelty. Their mocking of Uncle Tom and their participation in Legree's satanic, drunken revels result directly from their infamous master's example and instruction, for he "had trained them in savageness and brutality as systematically as he had his bull-dogs" (Chap. 32). In a subsequent discussion of African psychology, Stowe claims that blacks "are possessed of a nervous organisation peculiarly susceptible and impressible" (*Key* 45).[4] Not only does this trait explain Sambo and Quimbo's degraded condition on the Legree plantation but, from a Christian perspective, it entails what we can term an infinite capacity for conversion. Like Topsy, Sambo and Quimbo simply need more positive influence in order to be saved. Thus, witnessing Tom's agony brings about an immediate change, and they shed tears of repentance and grief when exposed to the Holy Word. Because of the impressionability and the innate fascination with things spiritual that allegedly typify the African race, Stowe's blacks, when apparently evil, are but misguided and always receptive to Christian rehabilitation.

Throughout *Uncle Tom's Cabin*, Stowe draws important distinctions in personality and behavior between full-blood and mixed-blood blacks. In her portrayal of the former—Sam, Andy, Topsy, Sambo, and Quimbo—she emphasizes the racial gifts she saw as innately African. The traits of her mulatto figures, however, resemble those conventionally associated with whites. This is why, for example, Stowe stresses their physical attractiveness and why, in contrast to the dialect (or at least rough colloquialisms) of the full-blood blacks, the speech of the mulatto slaves is generally "correct." Nonetheless, the dash of African blood insures that many of these mixed-blood characters will never be more than poor approximations of genteel bourgeois whites. That is, when we laugh at the dandified, spoiled slave Adolph St. Clare as he tosses his head, fingers his perfumed hair, and waves his scented handkerchief, we are laughing at a boy mimicking adult affectations. And in their obsession with showy displays of manner and finery, the servants Jane and Rosa are but two girls pretending to be grown ladies. In each case, the style is ill-fitting and the "clothes" too large. The humor in these house slaves' futile attempt to be white gives way to pathos, however, when they are sold after their owner's death. Their helpless, hysterical reaction to the harsh realities of chattel enslavement pitifully dramatizes what Stowe contends is one of the greatest evils of the institution—the domestic insecurity of even the most pampered slaves. The dark-skinned St. Clare cook, Aunt Dinah, describes their true status with pithy directness: "Don't want none o' your light-colored balls . . . cuttin' round, makin' b'lieve you's white folks. Arter all, you's niggers, much as I am" (Chap. 18).

On the one hand, the tragic experiences of the two most important mixed-blood black characters, Eliza and George Harris, also derive from their status as relatively well-treated slaves who are suddenly confronted with unjust treatment. On the other hand, they have precious little else in common with Adolph, Jane, and Rosa. In particular, Eliza and George rival any white in the novel in nobility of character and fineness of sensibility. That in a sense they *are* white suggests that they represent not only Stowe's attempt to have her target audience identify personally with the plight of the slaves but also her inability to view certain types of heroism in any but "white" terms.

A literate, polite Christian woman, the quadroon Eliza embodies the mid-nineteenth-century ideal of bourgeois femininity. In an attempt to counter claims that female slaves lacked maternal instincts, Stowe especially emphasizes the obsessive strength of Eliza's love for her son, Harry. Indeed, it is only this motherly devotion that leads to her frenzied, desperate flight from slavery, for her sheltered life and religious upbringing have taught her to accept her lot: "I always thought that I must obey my master and mistress," she says early in the novel, "or I couldn't be a Christian" (Chap. 3). Unfortunately, her maternal dedication and unshaken piety constitute virtually the entire range of her characterization; we see little real psychological depth or intellectual vigor.

In contrast, Eliza's husband, George, more fully engages Stowe's imagination, and his personality is rendered in greater detail as she dramatizes the fall into atheism that she feared would afflict the ill-treated, thoughtful slave. George's rational questioning of his condition marks the first stage in this process. Here, he argues that by white society's own standards, he deserves freedom as much as, if not more than, his owner:

> My master! and who made him my master? That's what I think of—what right has he to me? I'm a man as much

> as he is. I'm a better man than he is. I know more about business than he does; I am a better manager than he is; I can read better than he can; I can write a better hand,—and I've learned it all myself, and no thanks to him,—I've learned it in spite of him; and now what right has he to make a dray-horse of me? (Chap. 3)

George soon asserts his independence without qualification: "I've said Mas'r for the last time to any man. *I'm free*!" (Chap. 11). This defiance, however, begins to undercut his belief in God. At one point, he confesses to his wife, "I an't a Christian like you, Eliza; my heart's full of bitterness; I can't trust in God. Why does he let things be so?" (Chap. 3). Later, in rejecting the hackneyed religious sentiments of a white acquaintance named Wilson whom he meets during his escape, George restates his doubts: "*Is* there a God to trust in? . . . O, I've seen things all my life that have made me feel that there can't be a God" (Chap. 11).

Stowe clearly appreciates George's position; nevertheless, she cannot let his corrosive anger and potentially violent self-assertiveness sabotage her Christian conception of true heroism. Consequently, two chapters after his conversation with Wilson, he finds refuge in an utopian Quaker settlement, where a mixture of religious integrity, domestic security, and democratic egalitarianism quickly assuages his spiritual malaise:

> This, indeed, was a home,—*home*,—a word that George had never yet known a meaning for; and a belief in God, and trust in his providence, began to encircle his heart, as, with a golden cloud of protection and confidence, dark, misanthropic, pining atheistic doubts, and fierce despair, melted away before the light of a living Gospel. (Chap. 13)

Although still determined to fight for his own freedom and that of his wife, George now manifests a spirit softened, tranquilized by a reborn religious faith; he promises Eliza, "I'll try to act worthy of a free man. I'll try to feel like a Christian" (Chap. 17). His behavior in a heated battle with some slave hunters exemplifies this new attitude. After George shoots one of them, he, Eliza, and other escaping slaves help the wounded man to a

Quaker household where he is nursed back to physical and spiritual health.

Stowe's treatment of Harris reveals her deep reluctance to portray the pent-up rage of an intelligent, strong-willed male slave without marbling it with a Christian restraint that entails the eschewing of violence. No such qualification is necessary in the case of Uncle Tom, who stands in antithetical juxtaposition to the aggressive, embittered George. If Harris is the articulate mulatto, correct in speech, rational, and initially impatient with religion, Tom is the passive, full-blood black, simple in expression, solicitous of all around him, gentle, and rarely shaken in his Christian faith. In fact, about the only traits the two slaves share are a willingness to die for their beliefs and a disconcerting lack of a sense of humor. Otherwise, they inhabit different worlds, parallel dimensions that never intersect. A full-blood Clark Kent and a mulatto Superman, they are never on stage at the same time. One can imagine that, like matter and antimatter, if they were forced into contact, the result would be an explosion of immeasurable force that would leave only Tom, for he, not George, is Stowe's real hero. It is Tom, not George, who so quickly entered the stock of American cultural archetypes; it is Tom, to paraphrase Faulkner, who "endured."

We first hear of Uncle Tom when his master, Mr. Shelby, describes to a skeptical Haley how his most reliable slave elected not to escape while conducting business for him in Cincinnati. This steadfast refusal to violate a trust is one of Tom's most important traits. Whereas George rejects his master's attempt to control his life and runs away with a clear conscience, Tom cannot do so. Despite the urging of his wife after his sale, he still maintains, "Mas'r always found me on the spot—he always will. I never have broke trust, nor used my pass no ways contrary to my word, and I never will" (Chap. 5). In fact, Tom mentions that he wants to be free just three times in the novel. In the first case, Augustine St. Clare has already made plans to manumit him. Even then, after exclaiming that "bein' a *free man*" is "what I'm joyin' for," Tom vows that he will remain by his owner until "Mas'r St. Clare's a Christian"—an eventuality on which one would certainly not stake one's life (Chap. 28). During Tom's trials on the Legree plantation, the issue is raised again, this time by Cassy, who asks, "Tom, wouldn't you like your liberty?" He replies, "I shall have it, Misse, in God's time" (Chap. 38). The only occasion when he himself broaches the subject is after St. Clare's tragic death. With the utmost tact and humility, Tom approaches Ophelia and asks that she intervene for him with his master's widow, who feels no compunction whatsoever at reneging on her husband's promise to free him. Unfortunately, Stowe chooses not to present the scene in which Ophelia reports back to Tom, so we can only imagine the prayers he no doubt mutters under his breath when given the bad news.

Grounded in neither fear of recapture and subsequent punishment nor any explicit satisfaction with his enslaved condition, Tom's principled refusal to strike out aggressively for his freedom grows out of his unimpeachable personal integrity and his staunch faith in Providence. In her attempt to make Tom the ideal Christian, however, Stowe deprives him of most of his imperfect human nature; he becomes, as St. Clare observes, "a moral miracle" (Chap. 18). Not only does he exhort his fellow blacks to refrain from hating slave traders, but he also finds it in himself to bless "Mas'r George" after Shelby has sold him. Even the indulgent, resolutely cynical St. Clare is subject to Tom's tearful, teetotaling ministrations. Consequently, by the time he falls into Legree's clutches, Tom has become more of a saint than a man. His religious study having been "confined entirely to the New Testament," Tom approaches the Christlike in his passivity, piety, and resigned refusal to challenge the apparent will of God (Chap. 12). When he helps two old slave women, he does so in the spirit of Christian kindness, not from any sense of racial solidarity. And when he defies Legree, it is because the man is attacking his religion, not because the villain holds no rightful claim to him: "Mas'r Legree, as ye bought me," Tom pledges, "I'll be a true and faithful servant to ye. I'll give ye all the work of my hands, all my time, all my strength; but my soul I won't give up to mortal man. I will hold on to the Lord" (Chap. 36). Even his brief struggle with religious doubt and fear during his epic battle with Legree resembles Christ's momentary questioning of his fate shortly before his crucifixion more than it does Job's all-too-human response to his overwhelming misery.

Tom's relationship with Cassy, Legree's erstwhile mistress, best exemplifies his effect on other blacks. A proud, willful, mixed-blood woman who has been driven to infanticide by broken promises, sexual exploitation, and horrible suffering, Cassy resists her enslavement more fiercely and actively than any black character besides George Harris. It is Cassy who openly defies and steals money from Legree, and it is Cassy who plans her and Emmeline's elaborate escape. However, as he does with almost every lost soul he encounters, Tom soothes her intense bitterness and rights her unbalanced mind. In the face of Cassy's despair, Tom reminds her, "The Lord han't forgot us,—I'm sartin' o' that ar'. If we suffer with him, we shall also reign, Scripture says; but, if we deny Him, he also will deny us" (Chap. 34). Later, after refusing to help her murder Legree, Tom urges Cassy to give herself not to hatred and vengeance, but to love. Her furious contention that love for "*such* enemies . . . isn't in flesh and blood" receives a predictably earnest response from Tom: "No, Misse, it isn't . . . but *He* gives it to us, and that's the victory" (Chap. 38). At this point, Stowe apostrophizes the African race in the explicitly redemptive terms of sacrificial martyrdom: "And this, O Africa! latest called of nations,—called to the crown of thorns, the scourge, the bloody sweat, the cross of agony,—this is to be *thy* victory" (Chap. 38). An echo of Christ's final words, Tom's prayer just before his death completes the image: "Into thy hands I commend my spirit!" (Chap. 40).

The debate between Tom and Cassy dramatizes an important issue in *Uncle Tom's Cabin*, the key, in fact, to Stowe's social vision. From the outset, Stowe outlines a conflict in human nature, of which slavery's lamentable effect upon the moral condition of the United States was but the most immediately visible evidence: on one side stands the "feminine" side of human personality; on the other, the "masculine." The former is loving, warm, maternal, usually passive, and often childlike in its free expression of feeling; the latter is hard, chilly, aggressive, skeptical, analytical, and sometimes violent. In religious terms, the first tends toward New Testament Christianity, the second toward worldly cynicism and even atheism.

Given Stowe's commitment to this scheme, it is not surprising that the most admirable figures among the whites are generally female. Notable exceptions include the Quaker males, who have consciously acquiesced to the supremacy of what Stowe would term the feminine side of their personality. Another is the sensitive, indulgent Augustine St. Clare, whose proximity to this saving femininity gives him the limited moral strength he possesses. Unfortunately, he cannot totally renounce the paralyzing skepticism that prevents him from following his instincts. In contrast, his wife, Marie, has betrayed her own feminine nature by abdicating her maternal responsibilities, an especially grievous sin for Stowe. One need only compare Marie's reaction to her daughter Eva's return home to that of Mammy to discern who is the child's true mother (Chap. 15).

With Eliza and George, the conventional gender roles are righted as Eliza desperately attempts to mollify the destructive force of her husband's rational, violently male rejection of slavery. In her discussion of the popular conception of the bourgeois woman's place in nineteenth-century America, Barbara Welter argues that an indispensable component of the "cult of true womanhood" was piety: "Religion belonged to woman by divine right, a gift of God and nature" ("Cult" 152). Consequently, her moral duty was to bring "an erring man back to Christ" (153) or, as Theodore Parker put it, "to correct man's tastes, mend his morals, excite his affections, inspire his religious faculties" (qtd in Welter, "Tale," 11). Stowe's endorsement of such ideas partially explains why George's embodiment of traditionally male traits precludes her unqualified approval of his behavior, no matter how apparently heroic and manly it is.

With Uncle Tom, the gender inversion occurs once again, for it is Tom, first with Aunt Chloe and then with Cassy, who provides the religious forbearance, indiscriminate love, and intuitive faith conventionally associated with women. Indeed, as Elizabeth Ammons has pointed out, "Stowe makes him a heroine instead of a hero" ("Heroines" 162). In addition to displaying the feminine qualities that Stowe felt the African innately possessed, Tom also exemplifies another important race trait: a child's innocence and purity of spirit. Thus, with "the soft, impressionable nature of his kindly race, ever yearning toward the simple and childlike," Tom can relate to Eva as a virtual peer (Chap. 14). In *The Key to Uncle Tom's Cabin*, Stowe presents this idea more explicitly, conflating concepts of race, gender, age, and religion into the extraordinary redemptive amalgam that is Uncle Tom: "The negro race is confessedly more simple, docile, childlike, and affectionate, than other races; and hence the divine graces of love and faith, when in-breathed by the Holy Spirit, find in their natural temperament a more congenial atmosphere" (41). Together, Tom and Eva form the moral center of the novel, and their deaths reflect

Stowe's sad belief that the slave South cannot endure those who approximate overmuch the divine.

* * *

Northern readers embraced *Uncle Tom's Cabin* with such fervor that proslavery advocates could no longer dismiss abolitionist sentiment as a phenomenon restricted to New England negrophiles. Accordingly, the South and its allies reacted fiercely and immediately, and Stowe's novel became, as Langston Hughes put it, "the most cussed and discussed book of its time" (Ammons 102). James D. Hart reports that a Mobile, Alabama, bookseller was run out of town for stocking it (111). Stowe herself received countless threats and even an ear cut from a slave's head. In the course of a review of *The Key to Uncle Tom's Cabin*, William Gilmore Simms took time to attack Stowe personally, noting that her "daguerreotype . . . is such as to damage the reputation of any female writer under the sun" (221). This ungentlemanly thrust typifies the condemnation of many disapproving commentators who argued that Stowe had compromised her femininity by producing such a work. Other writers decided to reply to Stowe's fiction in kind; Sterling Brown notes, "In the three years following the appearance of *Uncle Tom's Cabin* (1852), there were at least fourteen proslavery novels published" (21). One such fictive response was *Aunt Phyllis' Cabin; or Southern Life as It Is* (1852), in which the Mammy figure holds center stage. In the case of John W. Page's *Uncle Robin in His Cabin in Virginia and Tom Without One in Boston* (1853), the title accurately summarizes the novelist's message.

Some critics attacked Stowe for her treatment of Southern whites and for her depiction of the quotidian workings of the slave system. The more perceptive of them, however, saw *Uncle Tom's Cabin* as an attempt to posit a conception of the Afro-American that would undercut the basic assumptions upon which proslavery defenses were built. Desperately desiring to counter this particularly pernicious threat to Southern interests, several commentators found two major chinks in Stowe's abolitionist armor.

The first is her treatment of the mixed-blood blacks. In a review of *Uncle Tom's Cabin*, the Southern critic Louisa S. C. McCord identifies the problem:

> Look again at the wonderful accumulation of instances she offers of *quadroons* and *mulattoes,* so fair as to be almost mistaken—frequently, quite mistaken—for white; with glossy brown curls, fair soft hands, &c., &c. Indeed, seeming to forget that her principal task is the defence of the negro, decidedly the majority of the persecuted individuals brought forward for our sympathy, are represented as whites, of slightly negro descent, not negroes. (113)

She continues,

> The real unfortunate being throughout her work is the mulatto. . . . and we confess that, in fact, although far below her horrible imaginings, his position is a painful one. . . . Raised in intellect and capacity above the black, yet incapable of ranking with the white, he is of no class and no caste. (117)

McCord here exposes the roots of Stowe's treatment of near-white slaves in the tradition of the tragic mulatto, a motif based on the assumption that mixed-blood blacks are somehow more self-aware, more sensitive to their oppressed condition than full-blood blacks. To concede the existence of major racial or genetic (and not merely environmentally-determined) distinctions between mixed-blood and full-blood blacks does little, McCord contends, to support claims that Afro-Americans are equal to whites and thus deserving of equal treatment.

In *The Key to Uncle Tom's Cabin,* Stowe explicitly reveals her adherence to contemporary concepts of race: "It must be remembered that the half-breeds often inherit, to a great degree, the traits of their white ancestors" (117). She refers here specifically to George Harris, and it is upon her characterization of this mixed-blood figure that Simms bases an attack not dissimilar to that leveled by his compatriot, McCord. Sarcastically terming Harris "the genius, the mulatto Apollo," Simms rather pruriently suggests that, evidenced in Stowe's "most voluptuous portrait," the slave's "good looks and locks seem to have worked very happily upon her imagination" (232). Disputing the attribution of great intelligence to Harris, Simms argues, with a somewhat suspect logical flourish, that once one establishes

> that the negro intellect is fully equal to that of the white race . . . you not only take away the best argument for keeping him in subjection, but you take away the possibility of doing so. *Prima facie*, however, the fact that he *is* slave, is conclusive against the argument for his freedom, as it is against his equality of claim, in respect of intellect. . . . Whenever the negro shall be fully fit for freedom, he will make himself free, and no power on earth can prevent him. (221–22)

Simms then lands a more telling blow by questioning Stowe's conception of racial heredity and black intelligence: "The genius of George is Caucasian, not Ethiopian; and the argument for intellectual equality falls prone, headlong to the ground" (223). Stowe sets herself up for this attack when she describes George's ability to pass as white in the following terms:

> George was, by his father's side, of white descent. . . . From one of the proudest families in Kentucky he had inherited a set of fine European features, and a high, indomitable spirit. From his mother he had received only a slight mulatto tinge, amply compensated by its accompanying rich, dark eye. (Chap. 11)

It is also evident that when Stowe comments upon the childlike qualities of blacks or upon their grotesque music and passionate religious services, she is hardly referring to Eliza or George. We can no more envision these two slaves singing a spiritual or turning a "summerset" than we can Stowe herself.

The second crucial weakness in Stowe's argument involves Uncle Tom, and here she found herself in a most precarious position. As Simms points out, Southerners could accept her portrait of Tom easily:

> That such a negro should grow up under the institution of slavery, is perhaps sufficiently conclusive in behalf of the institution. The North has no such characters. We shall not deny Uncle Tom. He is a Southron all over. He could not have been other than a Southron. We have many Uncle Tom's. (234)

The Northern, proslavery novelist Nehemiah Adams puts it this way:

> SLAVERY MADE UNCLE TOM. Had it not been for slavery, he would have been a savage in Africa, a brutish slave to his fetishes, living in a jungle, perhaps; and had you stumbled upon him he would very likely have roasted you and picked your bones.

Thus, conceding the accuracy of her depiction of Tom, Stowe's critics proceed to offer him as proof that slavery, in Adams's words, "is not an unmixed evil" (135).

That one can view Tom as a positive product of slavery raises some troubling questions regarding the extent of Stowe's condemnation of the institution: would Eliza have run away if Shelby had not sold her son, Harry? And would George Harris have fled if his owner had not jealously removed him from his position in the factory? Put more generally, can blacks ever be truly satisfied in their enslaved condition and slavery therefore condoned? Given that the expressed desire for freedom on the part of Stowe's black characters results exclusively from harsh or inhumane treatment, her answer to this last question must be a qualified "yes"—if one could regulate the disposition of slaves through sale and thereby guarantee the security of the family unit. Stowe contends that the slaveholders could never meet this condition; her Southern critics vehemently disagree.

In other words, although *Uncle Tom's Cabin* is a powerful attack on the evil effects of the chattel slave system, Stowe does not consistently argue the immorality of all social institutions based on the presumption of one group's innate superiority over another. In rejecting what one scholar calls "the domestic metaphor of proslavery thought" (Duvall 3–22), Stowe endorses in its place a benevolent Christian maternalism best exemplified by the arrangement young George Shelby works out with his slaves at the end of the novel, an arrangement Harold Beaver aptly describes as the transformation of "a slave plantation to a mid-Victorian landed estate" (95). Further, Stowe's desire that "the white race shall regard their superiority over the coloured one only as a talent intrusted for the advantage of their weaker brother" (*Key* 56) bears an uncomfortable resemblance to Louisa McCord's characterization of slavery as "a Godlike dispensation, a providential caring for the weak, and a refuge for the portionless" (118). The basic assumptions about race underlying the two statements are, for all practical purposes, identical, and they buttressed not only proslavery arguments but also countless justifications of U. S. imperialism from the mid-nineteenth century to the present.

* * *

Although most white Northerners fell hopelessly and uncritically in love with *Uncle Tom's Cabin*, there were a number of dissenting voices. Like their Southern counterparts, some Northern critics noticed the distinctions Stowe draws between mixed-blood and full-blood slaves. Others questioned the consistency of Stowe's commitment to nonviolence, especially given her relatively sympathetic treatment of the more rebellious mulattoes. For example, while praising the novel as "eminently serviceable in the tremendous conflict now waged for the immediate and entire suppression of slavery," William Lloyd Garrison wondered whether Stowe was "a believer in the duty of non-resistance for the white man, under all possible outrage and peril, as well as for the black man" (Review 50). In contrast to Garrison, who ultimately saw Stowe's hero as an embodiment of "real moral grandeur of character and the spirit of unconquerable goodness," the abolitionist Charles Whipple had more difficulty approving of Tom's response to his enslavement. In a general discussion of violence as an antislavery weapon, Whipple sets forth "the laws which are to regulate our action against evil-doers":

> LOVE YOUR NEIGHBOR AS YOURSELF!
> LOVE EVEN YOUR ENEMIES!
> OVERCOME EVIL *WITH GOOD*! (6)

With particular regard to the slaves, he explains that "the wrong-doing of the master to the slave does not in the slightest degree release the slave from *his* duties to God, and his obligation to obey God's law of love" (20). Nonetheless, Whipple does not endorse passive resignation:

> His [the slave's] first duty of good-will to the slaveholder is utterly to refuse any longer to be a slave! to put a stop . . . to a relation in which the slaveholder

> was sinking himself deeper and deeper in sin and in manifold evil. . . .
>
> Quiet, continuous submission to enslavement is complicity with the slaveholder. . . . It is the duty of a man and a Christian not only to protest against this, but, if he is able, acting in the right way, to put a stop to it. . . . And circumstances must decide whether this duty shall be performed in the most satisfactory manner, by a firm, manly, open declaration made to the face of the slaveholder, or by the attempt to escape. (21–22)

As a result, Whipple concludes, "I do not consider 'Uncle Tom' to be *the highest* type, either of the manly character or the Christian character, in the relation he bore to various slaveholders" (21).

Not only did the abolitionist Henry C. Wright agree with this judgment of Tom, but he further suspected that the public outpouring of sympathy represented an attempt to escape difficult moral questions, not to grapple with them. "I wonder not at the unprecedented popularity of Uncle Tom's Cabin," he wrote in 1852. "The conscience of this nation is lashed to madness by uncompromising Anti-Slavery. Uncle Tom's Cabin comes as a quietus, to some extent. Thousands will be satisfied by reading and praising it" (111). Wright could easily have added, "and by crying over it," because among the most telling testimonials to the novel's power were the frequent accounts of its bringing grown men to their emotional knees. Indeed, any attempt to understand Stowe's strategy must begin with the recognition that from the outset she was aiming more for the heart than for the head. Her explicit goal was, in her words, "to awaken sympathy and feeling for the African race, as they exist among us; [and] to show their wrongs and sorrows, under a system so necessarily cruel and unjust as to defeat and do away the good effects of all that can be attempted for them by their best friends." Thus, her utilization of the sentimental novel—a literary mode of expression grounded in the presumption that emotion is superior to reason, sensibility to logical ratiocination, and feminine to masculine—represents an entirely appropriate conjunction of fictive form and ideological function.

Unfortunately, the debt *Uncle Tom's Cabin* owes to both the novel of sentiment and that of sensibility also limited the degree to which it could effect radical political change. Characterized chiefly by "emotional exaggeration" and "the implicit argument that persistent purity eventually overcomes vigorous vice" (57), the early nineteenth-century sentimental novel soon spawned a closely related form—the novel of sensibility, which at its most indulgent "allowed one to feel deeply about any situation without having compunctions that something must be done to rectify it" (60). Including aspects of both forms, *Uncle Tom's Cabin* elicited a series of public responses that tend to justify Henry Wright's cynicism. Not only was a children's version of *Uncle Tom's Cabin* issued in 1853 called *A Peep into Uncle Tom's Cabin*, but within a year there also appeared "Uncle Tom and Little Eva," a parlor game "played with pawns that represented 'the continual separation and reunion of families'" (112). In fact, Stowe's best-seller inspired a veritable flood of Uncle Tom poems, songs, dioramas, plates, busts, embossed spoons, painted scarves, engravings, and other miscellaneous memorabilia, leading one wry commentator to observe, "[Uncle Tom] became, in his various forms, the most frequently sold slave in American history" (Hart 311). Finally, the more maudlin and broadly humorous strains in Stowe's novel lent themselves particularly well to the influential dramatic treatments of *Uncle Tom's Cabin* that were soon produced. It apparently bothered audiences not at all that these "Tom Shows" presented greatly adulterated versions of the novel—for example, adding bloodhounds to the scene of Eliza's escape over the ice where originally there were none, incorporating entirely irrelevant comic and musical minstrel interludes, and depicting Uncle Tom as a weak, white-haired, old darky despite the fact that in the book he is a "large, broad-chested, powerfully-made man" in, or at most just past, the prime of life (Chap. 4).[5]

Stowe's appeal to sentiment had another flaw as well. Just after the publication of *Uncle Tom's Cabin*, Frederick Douglass confidently predicted that "the touching portraiture she has given of '*poor Uncle Tom*,' will, of itself, enlist the kindly sympathies, of numbers, in behalf of the oppressed African race, and will raise up a host of enemies against the fearful system of slavery" (2). The direct correlation Douglass assumes between arousing the "kindly sympathies" of the readers and successfully mobilizing that audience into an antislavery force also underlies the answer Stowe provides for the most important question raised by her novel—"But, what can any individual do [about slavery]?":

> There is one thing that every individual can do—they can see to it that *they feel right.* An atmosphere of sympathetic influence encircles every human being; and the man or woman who *feels* strongly, healthily and justly, on the great interests of humanity, is a constant benefactor to the human race. See, then, to your sympathies in this matter! (Chap. 45)

Apparently, Stowe did not foresee that the "sympathies" of many of her critics could lead them to disagree with her. As a "Southern lady" put it in an open letter to British women who supported the abolition effort:

> We can think as women, and feel as women, and act as women, without waiting for the promptings of your appeals, or of Mrs. Stowe's imaginative horrors. It seems to us, that you should receive it as a strong proof of how much you have mistaken our system, that so many millions of women . . . have contentedly lived in the midst of it [slavery], and yet the common woman-heart among us has not risen up to call it *cursed*. (260)

"Our system," she asserts, "abhorrent as it seems to your ladyships, has the sanction of our hearts and heads" (279). That this writer could so easily share Stowe's language and assumptions about the female sensibility without reaching Stowe's conclusions regarding slavery demonstrates the danger of any attempt to tie moral judgment to emotional response.

Stowe's adherence to what George Frederickson terms the "romantic racialist" (103) view of the Afro-American weakened her argument as well. This conception of the African personality held that the black was a "natural Christian" whose soft emotionalism and gentle passivity were destined to temper the harshness of Anglo-Saxon culture. Behind this apparently positive depiction of the Afro-American, however, was what Frederickson describes as "the inability of the abolitionists to ground their case for the black man on a forthright and intellectually convincing argument for the basic identity in the moral and intellectual aptitudes of all races" (127). Like most white writers of her day, Harriet Beecher Stowe was not especially committed to (or equipped to present) a complex, realistic depiction of blacks. For example, she describes Africans as "an exotic race, whose ancestors, born beneath a tropic sun, brought with them, and perpetuated to their descendants, a character so essentially unlike the hard and dominant Anglo-Saxon race, as for many years to have won from it only misunderstanding and contempt" ("Preface" v). Rather than rejecting such stereotypes directly, Stowe tries to effect, in Jean Fagan Yellin's terms, a "Christian transvaluation" of "what the world sees as the curse of racial inferiority and cultural deprivation" (136). Unfortunately, to offer such a radical reconceptualization does not at all guarantee that it will be shared, especially in a society in which hardness and dominance were increasingly perceived to be prerequisites for success. Further, Stowe's tragic failure of imagination prevented her from envisioning blacks (free or slave, mulatto or full-blood) as viable members of American society, so she deports the most aggressive, intelligent, "acceptable" ones to Africa to fill the same role there that she assigns to women in the United States. Thus, the outrage of many black abolitionists at her apparent endorsement of colonization resulted less from a disagreement over tactics than from an accurate recognition of the limitations of Stowe's utopian social vision: heavenly salvation might indeed be possible for blacks; but a truly just interracial society was inconceivable.

Finally, a close reading of *Uncle Tom's Cabin* suggests that Stowe's fiercest critique was not directed at the patriarchal slave system at all, but rather at male domination in American society generally. Storming the fortress of masculine privilege under the cover of a Trojan Horse named Uncle Tom worked against her most subversive agenda, however, for Tom's melodramatic story proved so captivating and her exposé of the abuses of slavery so moving that her wholesale attack on male hegemony went largely unnoticed. Moreover, regardless of her approach, positing the spiritual superiority of women and blacks was hardly likely to disrupt the status quo, for despite lip service to the contrary, many Americans—especially males—simply did not share Stowe's pietistic, eschatological priorities. In examining Stowe's "gospel of womanhood" (1), Gayle Kimball argues that she "wanted spiritual power for women rather than political power" (71) and that "the legacy of this praise [of the moral superiority] of women was disastrous . . . [because] women had made the mistake of asking for their civil rights, not on the grounds of equal adulthood, but on the basis of moral superiority" (177). Kimball's analysis applies with equal force to Afro-Americans as well. That is, both blacks and women were tolerated if they kept out of the white male sphere of direct political action. Ultimately, Stowe's challenge to the racial and gender hierarchies in American society was bounded by the same assumptions which helped support the superstructure she strove to topple.[6]

* * *

Who has not wept as he has stood at the deathbed of poor old Uncle Tom, who, though a slave in body, was a philosopher in mind, a saint at heart, and a martyr in death.

Mary Church Terrell

Blest be the hand that dared be strong to save,
And blest be she who in our weakness came—
Prophet and priestess! At one stroke she gave
A race to freedom and herself to fame.

"Harriet Beecher Stowe," Paul Laurence Dunbar

Uncle Tom's Cabin grappled in the mire of Southern slavery and lifted a despised and helpless race into living sympathy with the white race at the North.

Sutton E. Griggs

The controversy over *Uncle Tom's Cabin* did not die out with the emancipation of the slaves and the military defeat of the South. Not only did late-nineteenth-century Southern writers like Thomas Nelson Page and Thomas Dixon feel obliged to respond to Stowe's novel in their own fiction, but also "it was still possible at the beginning of the century," Edmund Wilson reports, "for a South Carolina teacher to make his pupils hold up their right hands and swear that they would never read *Uncle Tom*" (4). Most Southern critics in Stowe's day would have applauded the novelist Margaret Mitchell when she wrote in 1938, "It makes me very happy to know that 'Gone with the

Wind' is helping refute the impression of the South which people abroad gained from Mrs. Stowe's book" (217). And they would have fully understood the hostility underlying William Faulkner's contention that "*Uncle Tom's Cabin* was written out of violent and misdirected compassion and ignorance of the author toward a situation which she knew only by hearsay" (Fant and Ashley 104).

Likewise, Afro-Americans have struggled with the implications of Stowe's work well into the twentieth century. In 1946, for example, *Negro Digest* asked groups of blacks and whites, "Is 'Uncle Tom's Cabin' Anti-Negro?" (Lee 68). Although it was a controversial stage production that occasioned the poll, that the vast majority of whites said "no" in contrast to the three out of every five blacks who responded "yes" suggests the degree to which the characters Stowe set loose in the American imagination still appealed to whites and, at the same time, elicited a troubled, divided response from blacks. Several years earlier, Richard Wright had entitled his first collection of stories *Uncle Tom's Children*, as if to stress the generational gap between Stowe's protest fiction and his own, while simultaneously acknowledging a familial relationship. In describing the genesis of his next book, however, he repudiates all connection with Stowe and, most importantly, with her sentimental appeal for white sympathy:

> I had written a book of short stories which was published under the title of *Uncle Tom's Children*. When the reviews of that book began to appear, I realized that I had made an awfully naive mistake. I found that I had written a book which even bankers' daughters could read and weep over and feel good about. I swore to myself that if I ever wrote another book, no one would weep over it; that it would be so hard and deep that they would have to face it without the consolation of tears. (xxvii)

Wright's transformation of Uncle Tom into Bigger Thomas marks a watershed in the relations between black authors and the most popular American novel on the race question ever written. Nonetheless, James Baldwin's subsequent critique, "Everybody's Protest Novel" (1949), and Ishmael Reed's satiric jousting with Stowe's ghost in *Flight to Canada* (1976) suggest that the dialogue will continue as Afro-American writers strive to distance themselves from all that *Uncle Tom's Cabin* represents.

Most free Northern blacks in the 1850s, however, saw *Uncle Tom's Cabin* as a godsend destined to mobilize white sentiment against slavery just when resistance to the Southern forces was urgently needed. Hailing Stowe's novel as the greatest weapon ever brought to bear in the abolitionist battle, blacks memorialized its author in print and from pulpits and convention platforms. William Wells Brown, the first Afro-American novelist, celebrated the publication of Stowe's book in a letter to the *Liberator*: "Uncle Tom's Cabin has come down upon the dark abodes of slavery like a morning's sunlight, unfolding to view its enormities in a manner which has fastened all eyes upon the 'peculiar institution,' and awakening sympathy in hearts that never before felt for the slave" (87). The poet and future novelist Frances Ellen Watkins [Harper] was inspired to compose a poem about Eliza's escape (4), and the participants of the Colored National Convention in Rochester in 1853 resolved that *Uncle Tom's Cabin* was "a work plainly marked by the finger of God, lifting the veil of separation which has too long divided the sympathies of one class of American people from another" (*Proceedings* 40).

With this sanguine view of the practical role *Uncle Tom's Cabin* could play in their struggle for justice, understandably few blacks publicly quarreled with her depiction of the slave experience. Nonetheless, several Afro-American readers did express serious reservations with regard to Tom's passivity. The son of a slave who died trying to escape, Reverend J. B. Smith seconded the sentiments of Whipple in his belief that "resistance to tyrants was obedience to God, and hence, to his mind, the only drawback to the matchless Uncle Tom of Mrs. Stowe was his virtue of submission to tyranny—an exhibition of grace which he . . . did not covet" (Nell 199). William G. Allen, a free black teacher, also raised the issue:

> Uncle Tom was a good old soul, thoroughly and perfectly pious. Indeed, if any man had too much piety, Uncle Tom was that man. I confess to more of "total depravity." More shame to me, possibly, but nevertheless, such is the fact. My non-resistance is of the Douglass, Parker, and Phillip's [sic] school. I

> believe ... that it is not light the slaveholder wants, but *fire*, and he ought to have it. I do not advocate revenge, but simply, resistance to tyrants, if it need be, to the death" (3)

The eagerness with which Afro-American leaders greeted the opportunity for blacks to prove their courage in the time-honored arena of warfare a decade later suggests that despite their support for Stowe's best-seller, they in no way rejected traditional measures of male worth, measures by which Uncle Tom fell considerably short of the mark.

The most controversial aspect of Stowe's book and the one that many blacks felt they could not afford to let pass uncriticized was her apparent endorsement of emigration when she depicts George Harris relocating his family to Liberia in search of "an African *nationality*" (Chap. 33). (The reformed Topsy also ends up in Africa, where she is reportedly teaching in a missionary station.) To blacks like Allen and George T. Downing, Harris was "the only one that really betrays any other than the subservient, submissive, Uncle Tom spirit, which has been the cause of so much disrespect felt for the colored man" (3). For Stowe to have him despair of ever attaining his rights in the United States seemed to undermine the already precarious position of many free blacks who had opted to stay in this country and fight. One writer in an Afro-American newspaper vehemently protested, "Uncle Tom must be killed, George Harris exiled! Heaven for dead Negroes! Liberia for living mulattoes. Neither can live on the American continent. Death or banishment is our doom, say the Slaveocrats, the Colonizationists, and, save the mark—Mrs. Stowe!!" (qtd in Quarles 220). Stowe reportedly regretted her decision, explaining that she would end the novel differently if given the opportunity to write it over again. However, her popularity and increasing influence as a world-famous abolitionist probably did most to quell the protests.[7]

Describing a pilgrimage he made to Stowe's home, Frederick Douglass reported, without a shred of irony, how her Andover residence had come to be known locally as "Uncle Tom's Cabin" ("Day" 2). In addition to reflecting the nature of fads in American culture, Douglass's observation hints at the power to shape reality that Stowe's fiction quickly attained, a power that blacks could not help but acknowledge. Some were more than willing to play along: the ex-slaves Lewis Clarke and Josiah Henson, for example, promoted themselves as the prototypes of George Harris and Uncle Tom, respectively. Henson, in fact, drove the black critic Benjamin Brawley to complain that "any student of [his] career is likely to be exasperated by his tendency to exploit himself" (66). Stowe's prefaces to the 1858 edition of Henson's slave narrative and to Frank J. Webb's novel, *The Garies and Their Friends* (1857), further suggest the weight her imprimatur carried in establishing the credibility of black writers.[8] Inevitably, other Afro-Americans responded to Stowe and the immense power she wielded as an interpreter of black life with frustration and resentment. We find the most dramatic evidence of such hostility in a public exchange of letters between Frederick Douglass and Martin R. Delany.

In March 1853, Douglass explained in his newspaper that he had recently visited Stowe in order "to consult with the authoress, as to some method which should contribute successfully, and permanently, to the improvement and elevation of the free people of color" ("Day" 2). Delany's angry response to this admission comes within a month: "I beg leave to say, that she *knows nothing about us*[;] . . . neither does any other white person" (Letter 2). Douglass's bristling retort reflects the heated nature of this debate: "The assertion that Mrs. Stowe 'knows nothing about us,' shows that Bro. Delany knows nothing about Mrs. Stowe; for he certainly would not so violate his moral, or common sense if he did" ("Remarks" 2). Predictably, the discussion soon encompasses Stowe's major contribution to the Afro-American cause. In a letter entitled "Uncle Tom," Delany sarcastically argues that because Stowe and her publishers were profiting so substantially from the book, it would be only right for Josiah Henson, the "real *Uncle Tom*," to receive compensation. Proceeding then to link some of Stowe's characters with their real-life counterparts, Delany delivers an impassioned, scathing attack upon the passivity embodied by Tom:

> I have always thought that George and Eliza were Mr. Henry Bibb and his first wife, with the character of Mr. Lewis Hayden, his wife Harriet and little son, who also effected their escape from Kentucky. . . . I say the *person* of Bibb with the *character* of Hayden; because, in

> personal appearance of stature and color, as well as circumstances, Bibb answers precisely to George; while he stood quietly by, as he tells us in his own great narrative[,] . . . with a hoe in his hand, begging his master to desist, while he *stripped his wife's clothing off (!!!)* and lacerated her flesh, until the blood flowed in pools at her feet! To the contrary, had this been Hayden—who, by the way, is not like Bibb nearly *white*, but *black*—he would have buried the hoe deep in the master's skull, laying him lifeless at his feet.

Delany closes with the rather unconvincing claim that his familiarity with *Uncle Tom's Cabin* is due solely to "*my wife* having *told* me the most I know about it" (3).

Delany's skirmish with Douglass, whom he terms Stowe's "attorney" ("Letter of Delany" 3) continues the following week, with the two black leaders bickering over Stowe's view of Haiti, the apparent endorsement of colonization in *Uncle Tom's Cabin*, and the proposed use of white instructors in the industrial school that Stowe and Douglass were discussing. By this point, however, it is clear that the debate between these two dedicated black men involves not just emigration, educational policy, or even the nature of Uncle Tom's heroism. Rather, the differences between them are both ideological and deeply personal. At the time, Delany was looking outside of the United States and, indeed, outside of white society's sphere of influence for a solution to the dilemma confronting Afro-Americans; Douglass endorsed an integrationist position and saw no reason to "find fault with well-meant efforts for our benefit" (2). These stances necessarily entailed antithetical attitudes toward cooperation with sympathetic whites in general and especially with Stowe, considering her preeminent role as a literary and inevitably ideological authenticator of the black experience. When Delany tautly declares, "[N]o enterprize, institution, or anything else, should be commenced *for us*, or our general benefit, without *first consulting us*" ("Position" 3), he is demanding the right of self-determination, a right that he felt Stowe was violating and one that blacks, in Douglass's mind, were too "disunited and scattered" (2) to exercise effectively. In a broad sense, their argument is an early manifestation of a disagreement among Afro-American thinkers over tactics—both literary and political—that still persists.[9]

* * *

Regardless of their feelings toward Stowe herself or toward her creation, early Afro-American fiction writers inevitably wrote in her wake. This is not to suggest that most black authors consciously modeled their work upon *Uncle Tom's Cabin*. To do so would be to give the book, as great an impact as it had, more credit than it deserves. Rather, Stowe's best-seller embodied a whole constellation of preexisting, often conflicting ideas regarding race, powerfully dramatized them in a sentimental fashion, presented them with an unabashedly didactic reformist message, and, finally, proceeded to sell like the dickens. Black writers could not help but be convinced that if enough of the right ingredients were combined in the right proportions under the right conditions, they too could concoct deeply political novels that might tap the same mass audience that Stowe did and thereby shape the attitudes of whites toward the black minority in the United States.

In bequeathing to Afro-American protest novelists writing after her a literary form and stance as well as a white audience with certain strong expectations, Stowe also helped to establish a range of character types which served to bind and restrict black authors for decades. As a result, *Uncle Tom's Cabin* was an abiding, at times daunting, paradigmatic influence for most early Afro-American fiction writers, casting its shadow over their diverse attempts to define realistically the black capacity for heroic action while not alienating the white audience that they felt they absolutely had to hold in order to bring about political change. William Stanley Braithwaite puts it this way: "The moral gain and historical effect of Uncle Tom have been an artistic loss and setback. The treatment of Negro life and character, overlaid with these forceful stereotypes, could not develop into artistically satisfactory portraiture" (30–31). For example, many Afro-American writers tacitly endorsed the incipient class and color hierarchies underlying Stowe's treatment of mixed-blood and full-blood black characters in her fiction. It is, in fact, a short step from Stowe's depiction of full-blood field hands as "low," often comic figures to the emphasis in many Afro-American novels on the alleged distinctions in behavior, education, speech, and appearance between generally light-skinned, bourgeois characters and dark-skinned, lower-class blacks.

Thus, although James H. W. Howard's *Bond and Free: A True Tale of Slave Times* (1886) is ultimately as much an antidote to Stowe's oversentimentalized depiction of slavery as it is to the work of the racist plantation tradition writers, it is also marred by the use of stereotypical black characterizations. For example, his portrayal of the slave Eloise reveals her to be kin to Topsy:

> Eloise was very fat, very round, and very ugly, with a face like a butter ball, and eyes that sat in her head like two holes burnt into a blanket. Her hair stood out straight from her head like the quills upon a porcupine. In addition to this, she was black, sly, . . . had a[n] insatiable desire for mischief, and was as near being uncivilized as a human being can be without being actually so. (118)

Even more grotesque is his treatment of a servant named Alanthe. The only acrobatic, cartoonish, black imp figure in the novel, she "might have been taken for a boy from the scarcity of hair on her head, and the coat-like garment she wore reaching down to her knees, exposing a pair of very black and very thin legs, [and] very large feet whose toes stood apart with perfect individuality" (190). In a bit of gratuitous darky humor, Howard explains how, when sent on an errand, Alanthe "bounded from the room, turning a somersault through the window, and landing on the portico" (192–93).

Less crude but equally revealing endorsements of class and color distinctions are evident in the often ambivalent attitudes of nineteenth-century Afro-American writers toward black folk culture, something that, if not entirely foreign to their own experience, many of them would just as soon leave behind. In *Iola Leroy, or Shadows Uplifted* (1892), for example, Frances Ellen Watkins Harper undercuts the tragic mulatto motif by presenting light-skinned blacks who, although able to pass, refuse to do so. Further, like George and Eliza Harris, these figures meet or surpass every white criterion for beauty, intelligence, respectability, and training. To depict such characters who are above white reproach on any count does indeed serve to prove that hostile portraits of Afro-Americans are neither fair nor completely valid. However, their unrelenting, high-minded propriety often subverts the verisimilitude Harper is struggling to establish, and the accompanying implied condemnation of black folkways does little to counter the suggestion that Afro-Americans need not be treated as equals until they become "white." Harper merely argues that such a cultural, if not racial, transmogrification is possible. Although both *Bond and Free* and *Iola Leroy* generally succeed as revisionist blows against the appalling array of antiblack novels, histories, and pseudoscientific studies that flooded the literary marketplace in the post-Reconstruction period, they also serve to perpetuate limited patterns of characterization which first received widespread currency in fiction through *Uncle Tom's Cabin*.

The most crucial aspect of the "artistic loss and setback" Braithwaite mentions involves Stowe's depiction of the appropriate black response to oppression. It is not merely that she makes Uncle Tom the major heroic figure in the text. Rather, it is that her contrasting portraits of Tom and George Harris posit a specific ethical basis for acceptable black behavior. If, as Richard Wright contends, "oppression spawned among them [blacks] a myriad variety of reactions, reaching from outright blind rebellion to sweet, other-worldly submissiveness" (xii), then Stowe obviously places a greater moral value on the latter, on a willing victimization that receives its reward in the hereafter. Struck by the forthright militance of George Harris, the modern reader might be tempted to conclude that Stowe sees this character as embodying a brand of heroism at least as attractive as Uncle Tom's. However, to interpret her locating George within an American patriotic tradition as a blanket endorsement of his stance is, I would argue, to misread her position. Many commentators have noted how adherents to the philosophy of nonresistance expressed ambivalence toward and occasionally even condemnation of the violent means used by American colonists to win their independence. In a speech in 1837, for example, William Lloyd Garrison declared, "This nation is destined to perish, because in wading through blood and carnage to independence, *it at the outset discarded the Prince of Peace, and elected George Washington to be its Saviour*" (123). Although Stowe is hardly so doctrinaire in her pacifism that she cannot find Harris's behavior appealing, her staunch New Testament Christianity forces her to view his urge toward rebellion as of questionable morality, for it can entail disobedience and, more importantly, a willingness to use violence.

Stowe renders a similar judgment in her depiction of Cassy, whose militance must also be diluted. Unlike Harris, however, whose vehement resistance to slavery struck many readers (and, at some level, even Stowe herself) as manly, Cassy is a far more dangerous figure, for there was no readily available paradigm for acceptable female heroism which would safely permit her insurgence to stand unqualified by her apparent emotional derangement. That is, it is Eliza and not Cassy who meets the criteria of the mid-nineteenth century sentimental heroine; and given the extraordinarily dehumanizing racist image of the black slave woman held by most whites at the time, Eliza does indeed represent a step forward. Nonetheless, although Cassy's successful exploitation of Legree's guilt and fear exemplifies an indirect form of resistance through which slave women ensured their own survival and that of their families, Stowe provides no validation of the more direct, aggressive rebellion of the numerous female slaves who struck back and even killed rather than endure their oppression any longer. Clearly, Afro-American writers who sought to depict nonsentimental heroic female figures had to challenge not just racial stereotypes but gender stereotypes as well.

The novella *Aunt Lindy, A Story Founded on Real Life* (1892) by the black journalist and community worker Victoria Earle [Matthews] reveals in stark, disconcerting images the psychological cost of this Uncle-Tomish abjuration of violence on the part of the female protagonist. In this short melodrama, an ex-slave named Aunt Lindy takes in a white victim of a disastrous fire. While nursing him back to health, she discovers that he is her old master who had sold away her children. Before her urge for revenge can explode into action, however, she hears the sound of an "olden-time melody" (15) from a prayer meeting located conveniently nearby, and she relents. The totally incredible resolution comes when we learn that the new black preacher in the neighborhood is Lindy's long-lost firstborn.

Although *Aunt Lindy* superficially resembles the mawkish plantation tradition tale of the ex-slave who saves the life of his or her former white owner, Earle's characterization of Lindy differs radically from the black images in the works of writers like Thomas Nelson Page and Joel Chandler Harris. It also represents an important motif in the development of the black fictive protagonist: the struggle to incorporate the human emotion of anger into a figure the author wishes the white audience to view favorably. Here Earle's description of Aunt Lindy's rage is undeniably powerful, albeit overwritten:

> Demoniac gleams of exultation and bitter hatred settled upon her now grim features; a pitiless smile wreathed her set lips, as she gazed with glaring eyeballs at this helpless, homeless "victim of the great fire," as though surrounded by demons; a dozen wicked impulses rushed through her mind—a life for a life. . . . Her blood was afire, her tall form swayed, her long, bony hands trembled like an animal at bay. (14–15)

This moment soon passes, however, for in Earle's world (as in Stowe's), religion proves a palliative for such a near loss of control. In a real sense, Lindy is "saved" from herself.

When black fiction writers more ambitious and technically adept than Earle turn away from the relative moral straightforwardness of the slavery issue and try to confront ethically complex contemporary racial problems, they encounter even greater difficulties in their characterizations. In particular, the majority of them fall prey to the most pernicious and yet indispensable of Stowe's tactics: the use of black victimization as an emotional lever to move white readers to pity and even a sense of guilt. Although such an approach ensures the moral superiority of the Afro-American figure, in approximating the Christlike, the black martyr leaves the realm of the human.

Two black Detroit journalists, Walter H. Stowers and William H. Anderson, adopt this strategy in *Appointed* (1894). Late in the novel, John Saunders, a fair-skinned, college-trained Afro-American, accidentally collides with a white man in a Southern city. In the resultant scuffle, the Northern-bred Saunders instinctively defends himself against his white assailants and is arrested. The authors' depiction of this middle-class young black man as he moves from violent rage through a determination to hide his fear of the gathering lynch mob to final grief is quite effectively rendered. Unfortunately, before Saunders dies at the hands of that mob, he finds enough breath to exclaim melodramatically, "Oh, my country! What scenes of carnage and strife, of woe and sorrow, will take place if these unworthy ideas and wild passions are allowed to hold such full sway." He then gives Seth Stanley, his white friend and the true protagonist of the novel, the message that Stowers and Anderson are doubtless directing to their white audience as well: "Stir up and create a public opinion and cease not, until it is so aroused that justice, waking from her long sleep, will demand equal protection and liberty, for all citizens of the Republic. God will be with you" (350). In *Appointed,* the authors present the literal annihilation of the black hero in the hope that his martyrdom will inspire in the receptive white reader a new understanding of and sympathy for the plight of the Afro-American. That Stowers and Anderson never convincingly endorse a Christian view of Saunders's fate indicates the desperate nature of the attempt to elicit a favorable white response. Unlike Uncle Tom's death, which, to Stowe, represents in itself the real victory—the entry into a heavenly afterlife—the significance of Saunders's martyrdom depends upon the subsequent actions of Stanley and, the authors hope, of the white reader.

The Afro-American writer most sensitive to the ethical dilemma raised by the attempt to depict blacks both as victims and as heroes is Charles W. Chesnutt. In *The Marrow of Tradition* (1901), he details the painful, inevitable conflict between antithetical strategies for coping with the virulent racism that made life so treacherous for Afro-Americans at the turn of the century. On one side stands William Miller, the bourgeois mulatto physician whose response to prejudice is patience, rationalization, and a desperate hope that justice will win out. On the other stands Josh Green, the violent black laborer whose fierce pride and belief in his own self-worth motivate his suicidal posture of militant resistance. By the end of the book, Josh Green is dead, having given his life to defend the property of blacks from a destructive white mob; Miller's son has been killed by a stray bullet during the riot; and Major Carteret, the white editor responsible for instigating the tragedy, has come to beg Miller to save his own sick child. Like George Harris, Cassy, Aunt Lindy, and John Saunders, Miller initially responds to his predicament with an explosive, righteous anger seen all too rarely in early Afro-American fiction. He quickly yields, however, to the pleas of Mrs. Carteret and allows Janet, his wife and Mrs. Carteret's half-sister, to make the final decision. Predictably, she agrees to send him, and the book ends as he rushes out the door on his errand of mercy.

Here, in the last scene of this powerful novel, Chesnutt gallantly attempts to recapitulate in a post-Reconstruction context the entire moral thrust of *Uncle Tom's Cabin*. Unlike Stowe and the authors of *Appointed*, however, Chesnutt does not sacrifice his main black character. Instead, he offers up the Millers' child—and a great deal of their credibility as characters—on the altar of racial conciliation. As we see in a number of nineteenth-century Afro-American novels, rage, bitterness, and a desire for revenge on the part of positively portrayed black figures must be curbed in order to establish them as self-controlled, all-forgiving, and eminently acceptable candidates for membership in the American mainstream. However, Chesnutt was not so blind to the realities of his time that he can show his characters' repudiation of their anger as the result of any genuine, unqualified acceptance by whites. That is, Mrs. Carteret's plea to the Millers is a far cry from the Quakers' bringing George Harris and his family into the charmed circle of their loving household. Nor is Chesnutt so committed to an explicitly Christian view of social change that he can, like Stowe, justify the behavior of his characters in solely religious terms. Thus, the moral superiority of the Millers is important for primarily extraliterary reasons: it becomes a weapon Chesnutt uses to hammer away at the hard hearts and iron-clad consciences of white readers, who, he knows, are not thoroughly convinced that Afro-Americans are really human. It is both ironic and understandable that Chesnutt hoped that *Marrow* would "become lodged in the popular mind as the legitimate successor of Uncle Tom's Cabin."[10]

Underlying much of the fiction produced by Afro-Americans before World War I is not a desire to render black life as accurately and honestly as possible but rather a willingness to dissemble, to overemphasize, even to misrepresent—that is, to write with the aim of eliciting sympathy from the white reader. And evoking the appropriate response from that reader was no easy task, for unlike many black writers during the 1840s and 1850s, Afro-American novelists after Reconstruction could not count at all on the existence of a supportive white audience. As a result, in reading these texts today, one is sometimes struck in the course of a paragraph, a page, a chapter, or indeed an entire novel by the realization that the particular work of literature is not primarily about black people but rather designed to guide stock, inadequately developed characters through the motions of an empty ritual that had long since lost significance and to which the artists themselves, their protests to the contrary notwithstanding, could not wholeheartedly commit themselves.

In terms of genre, many nineteenth-century Afro-American writers simply could not effectively reconcile their urge toward realism with the antithetical desire to appropriate the emotional appeal of the sentimental novel, a genre grounded in a Christian conception of social redemption and, as a tool of political protest, best exemplified by *Uncle Tom's Cabin*. Stowe fortuitously tapped both a religious and a secular millennial ideology that would view the Civil War as divine retribution, Appomatox as the brave new world reborn, and Lincoln as the Christlike sacrificial lamb. Unfortunately for many of the writers who followed Stowe, although her images maintained their power—indeed, became more vivid and persistent as time passed—abolitionism may have been the last successful reform movement in the United States fueled largely by a progressive Christianity. If the salvation of the Union did not sufficiently release the tensions Stowe's novel had helped to screw tighter, then the accelerating secularization of American culture that accompanied the industrial and commercial explosion of the Gilded Age served to make moral appeals for change nearly irrelevant. The rise of Social Darwinism reinforced this trend by providing not only the terms racist theorists needed to justify the oppression of blacks but also the Sumnerian *laissez-faire* social policy that saw almost any reform at all as a futile violation of the inexorable evolutionary sorting of the fit from the unfit. Even some of the staunchest friends of the freed slaves manifested this tough, new pragmatism; for example, Booker T. Washington's famous mentor, General Samuel C. Armstrong, once observed drily, "The whole darky business has been in the hands of women and sentimentalists" (Toll 52). In the final analysis, post-Reconstruction Afro-American writers who desired to duplicate Stowe's success found themselves addressing an audience that could no longer be made to feel guilty and for whom a quasi-Christian appeal had lost much of its moral force. Few, if any, realized that, as the black poet Albery A. Whitman put it in 1885, "all 'Uncle Toms' and 'Topsies' ought to die. *Goody goodness* is a sort of man worship:

ignorance is its inspiration, fear its ministering spirit, and beggary its inheritance" (8). Few, if any, seemed to realize that they were courageously but futilely assailing what the turn-of-the-century black author James D. Corrothers called "the closed gates of justice" (272) with weapons dulled by time and rendered obsolete by inevitable social change.

Notes

This essay was previously published in *New Essays on Uncle Tom's Cabin*, edited by Eric Sundquist. It has been reprinted with the permission of Cambridge University Press. Funding from the National Endowment for the Humanities, the U.C.L.A. College Institute, the U.C.L.A. Academic Senate Research Committee, and the U.C.L.A Institute of American Cultures supported my work on this essay. I am also indebted to the U.C.L.A. Center for Afro-American Studies and to the staffs of the libraries at Fisk University, Harvard University, Howard University, and U.C.L.A.

1. My essay was written before the publication of Thomas F. Gossett's *Uncle Tom's Cabin and American Culture* (Dallas, Texas: Southern Methodist University Press, 1985). In discussing Stowe's racial attitudes and the public responses to her novel, we draw upon some of the same sources.

2. For discussions of how the minstrel show shaped white conceptions of the Afro-American, see Van Deburg 39–49 and Toll.

3. Harriet Beecher Stowe, *Uncle Tom's Cabin; or, Life among the Lowly*, ed. Kenneth Lynn (1852; rpt. Cambridge, Mass.: Harvard University Press, 1962), chap. 11. Subsequent references to this edition of *Uncle Tom's Cabin* will be indicated parenthetically in the text by the chapter number.

4. The following remark, made by F. W. Boreham over a century after the publication of *Uncle Tom's Cabin*, attests to the persistence of this idea: "Shipped as savages from Africa, the coloured people brought virgin minds and vacant hearts to the new world" (15).

5. Stowe's conclusion to the serialized version of *Uncle Tom's Cabin* reveals the degree to which she aimed the novel at young readers: "Dear children, you will soon be men and women, and I hope that you will learn from this story always to remember and pity the poor and oppressed. When you grow up, show your pity by doing all you can for them. . . . Farewell, dear children, until we meet again" (564).

6. Perhaps Constance Rourke was the first to suggest that "it was Uncle Tom . . . with whom Mrs. Stowe most identified herself, covering him with a pity akin to self-pity, endowing

him with a mild faith which she had struggled so long to attain" (108).

7. George Downing alludes to Stowe's change of heart in his letter. In addition, the white abolitionist Louis Tappan claimed that he "wrote to have it [the reference to emigration in *Uncle Tom's Cabin*] omitted; but it was too late; otherwise she would have done so" (Douglass, "American," 2). Thomas Graham points out, however, that "in her next antislavery novel *Dred*, she again wrote favorably of colonization" (621).

8. In a discussion of the authenticating strategies of ex-slave writers, Robert Stepto points out that in dedicating his narrative to Stowe, Solomon Northup calls it "another *Key to Uncle Tom's Cabin*" (11).

9. For one of the earliest contacts between Stowe and Douglass, see her letter of July 9, 1851. In it, she admits that she disagrees with Douglass's position on two subjects—"the church and African colonization."

10. Charles W. Chesnutt to Houghton Mifflin and Co., October 26, 1901. For a broader discussion of the treatment of emotion by Afro-American novelists, see Hedin.

Works Cited

A Southern Lady. "British Philanthropy and American Slavery." *DeBow's Review* 14 (March 1863). 258–80.

Adams, Nehemiah. *The Sable Cloud: A Southern Tale, with Northern Comments.* Boston: Ticknor and Fields, 1861.

Allen, William G. Letter. *Frederick Douglass' Paper* 20 May 1852. 3.

Ammons, Elizabeth, ed. *Critical Essays on Harriet Beecher Stowe.* Boston: G. K. Hall, 1980.

———. "Heroines in *Uncle Tom's Cabin.*" *American Literature* 49 (May 1977). 161–79.

Baldwin, James. "Everybody's Protest Novel." *Partisan Review* 16 (June 1949): 578–85.

Beaver, Harold. "Time on the Cross: White Fiction and Black Messiahs." *Yearbook of English Studies* 8 (1978). 40–53.

Boreham, F. W. *The Gospel of Uncle Tom's Cabin.* London: Epworth Press, 1956.

Braithwaite, William Stanley. "The Negro in American Literature." *The New Negro.* Ed. Alain Locke. 1925. New York: Atheneum, 1975.

Brawley, Benjamin. *The Negro Genius.* New York: Dodd, Mead, 1937.

Brown, Sterling. *The Negro in American Fiction*. 1937. New York: Atheneum, 1969.

Brown, William Wells. Letter. *The Liberator* 3 June 1853. 97.

Chesnutt, Charles W. Letter to Houghton Mifflin and Co. 26 October 1901. Charles Waddell Chesnutt Collection. Erastus Milo Cravath Memorial Library. Fisk University.

Corrothers, James D. "At the Closed Gate of Justice." *Century* 86 (June 1913). 272.

Delany, M. R. Letter. *Frederick Douglass' Paper* 1 April 1853. 2.

———. "Mrs. Stowe's Position." *Frederick Douglass' Paper* 6 May 1853. 3.

———. "Uncle Tom." *Frederick Douglass' Paper* 29 April 1853. 3.

[Douglass, Frederick]. "A Day and a Night in 'Uncle Tom's Cabin.'" *Frederick Douglass' Paper* 4 March 1853. 2.

———. "American and Foreign Anti-Slavery Society." *Frederick Douglass' Paper* 27 May 1852. 2.

———. "A Year's Work." *Frederick Douglass' Paper* 22 April 1853. 2.

———. "The Letter of M. R. Delany." *Frederick Douglass' Paper* 6 May 1853. 2.

———. "Literary Notices." *Frederick Douglass' Paper* 8 April 1852. 2.

———. "Remarks." *Frederick Douglass' Paper* 1 April 1853. 2.

Downing, George T. Letter. *Frederick Douglass' Paper* 22 December 1854. 3.

Dunbar, Paul Laurence. "Harriet Beecher Stowe." *Lyrics of the Hearthside*. New York: Dodd, Mead, 1899.

Duvall, Severn. "*Uncle Tom's Cabin*: The Sinister Side of the Patriarchy." *New England Quarterly* 36 (March 1963): 3–22.

Earle, Victoria. *Aunt Lindy; A Story Founded on Real Life*. New York: J. J. Little, 1893.

Eliot, George. Review of *Dred; A Tale of the Great Dismal Swamp*, by Harriet Beecher Stowe. *Critical Essays on Harriet Beecher Stowe*. Ed. Elizabeth Ammons. Boston: G. K. Hall, 1980.

Fant, Joseph L. III, and Robert Ashley, eds. *Faulkner at West Point*. New York: Random House, 1964.

Fiedler, Leslie A. *The Inadvertent Epic: From "Uncle Tom's Cabin" to "Roots."* New York: Simon & Schuster, 1979.

Frederickson, George M. *The Black Image in the White Mind: The Debate on Afro-American Character and Destiny, 1817–1914*. New York: Harper Torchbooks, 1971.

Garrison, William Lloyd. "Fourth of July in Providence." *The Liberator* 28 July 1837. 123.

———. Rev. of *Uncle Tom's Cabin*, by Harriet Beecher Stowe. *The Liberator* 26 March 1852. 50.

Gossett, Thomas F. *Uncle Tom's Cabin and American Culture*. Dallas: Southern Methodist University Press, 1985.

Graham, Thomas. "Harriet Beecher Stowe and the Question of Race." *New England Quarterly* 46 (December 1973). 614–26.

Griggs, Sutton E. *The Hindered Hand; or, The Reign of the Repressionist*. 1905. Miami: Mnemosyne, 1969.

Hart, James D. *The Popular Book: A History of America's Literary Taste*. 1950. Berkeley: University of California Press, 1963.

Hedin, Raymond. "The Structuring of Emotion in Black American Fiction." *Novel* 16 (Fall 1982): 35–54.

Hirsch, Stephen A. "Uncle Tomitudes: The Popular Reaction to *Uncle Tom's Cabin*." *Studies in the American Renaissance* (1978). 303–30.

Howard, James H. G. *Bond and Free; A True Tale of Slave Times*. Harrisburg, Pa.: Edwin K. Myers, 1886.

Hughes, Langston. Introduction to *Uncle Tom's Cabin. Critical Essays on Harriet Beecher Stowe.* Ed. Elizabeth Ammons. Boston: G. K. Hall, 1980.

Kimball, Gayle. *The Religious Ideas of Harriet Beecher Stowe.* New York: Edwin Mullen Press, 1982.

L.S.M. [Louisa S. C. McCord]. Rev. of *Uncle Tom's Cabin*, by Harriet Beecher Stowe. *Southern Quarterly Review* 23 (January 1853). 81–121.

Lee, Wallace. "Is 'Uncle Tom's Cabin' Anti-Negro?" *Negro Digest* 4 (January 1946). 68.

Mitchell, Margaret. Letter to Alexander L. May. 22 July 1938. *Margaret Mitchell's "Gone with the Wind" Letters, 1936–1949.* Ed. Richard Harwell. New York: Macmillan, 1976.

Nell, William C. "The Colored Citizens of Boston." *The Liberator* 10 December 1852. 199.

"Proceedings of the Colored National Convention, Held in Rochester, July 6th, 7th and 8th, 1853." *Minutes of the Proceedings of the National Negro Conventions, 1830–1864.* Ed. Howard Holman Bell. New York: Arno, 1969.

Quarles, Benjamin. *Black Abolitionists.* New York: Oxford University Press, 1969.

Reed, Ishmael. *Flight to Canada.* New York: Random House, 1976.

Rourke, Constance Mayfield. *Trumpets of Jubilee.* New York: Harcourt, Brace, 1927.

Sand, George. Rev. of *Uncle Tom's Cabin*, by Harriet Beecher Stowe. *Critical Essays on Harriet Beecher Stowe.* Ed. Elizabeth Ammons. Boston: G. K. Hall, 1980.

[Simms, William Gilmore]. Rev. of *The Key to Uncle Tom's Cabin*, by Harriet Beecher Stowe. *Southern Quarterly Review* 24 (July 1853). 214–54.

Stepto, Robert B. *From Behind the Veil: A Study of Afro-American Narrative.* Urbana: University of Illinois Press, 1979.

Stowe, Harriet Beecher. *The Annotated Uncle Tom's Cabin.* Ed. Philip Van Doren Stern. New York: Paul S. Eriksson, 1964.

———. *The Key to Uncle Tom's Cabin.* 1853. New York: Arno, 1968.

———. Letter to Frederick Douglass. 9 July 1851. *The Life and Letters of Harriet Beecher Stowe.* Ed. Annie Fields. Boston: Houghton Mifflin, 1970.

———. Preface to *Uncle Tom's Cabin; or, Life among the Lowly.* 1852. New York: New American Library, 1966.

———. *Uncle Tom's Cabin; or, Life among the Lowly*. Ed. Kenneth Lynn. 1852. Cambridge: Harvard University Press, 1962.

Stowers, Walter H., and William H. Anderson [pseud. Sanda]. *Appointed*. 1894. New York: AMS Press, 1977.

Terrell, Mary Church. *Harriet Beecher Stowe: An Appreciation*. Washington, D. C.: Murray Brothers, 1911.

Toll, Robert C. *Blacking Up: The Minstrel Show in Nineteenth-Century America*. New York: Oxford University Press, 1974.

Toll, William. *The Resurgence of Race: Black Social Theory from Reconstruction to the Pan-African Conferences*. Philadelphia: Temple University Press, 1979.

The Uncle Tom's Cabin Almanack, or Abolitionist Memento. London: John Cassell, 1853.

Van Deburg, William L. *Slavery and Race in American Popular Culture*. Madison: University of Wisconsin Press, 1984.

Watkins, Frances E. "Eliza Harris." *Frederick Douglass' Paper* 23 December 1853. 4.

Welter, Barbara. "The Cult of True Womanhood." *American Quarterly* 18 (September 1966). 151–74.

———. "The Merchant's Daughter: A Tale from Life." *New England Quarterly* 42 (March 1969). 3-22.

Whipple, Charles K. *The Non-Resistance Principle: With Particular Application to the Help of Slaves by Abolitionists*. Boston: R. F. Wallcut, 1860.

Whitman, Albery A. Preface to *Twasinta's Seminoles; or, Rape of Florida*. Rev. ed. 1885. Upper Saddle River, New Jersey: Gregg Press, 1970.

Wilson, Edmund. *Patriotic Gore: Studies in the Literature of the American Civil War*. New York: Oxford University Press, 1962.

Wright, Henry C. "Uncle Tom's Cabin—Objectionable Characteristics." *The Liberator* 9 July 1852. 111.

Wright, Richard. "How 'Bigger' Was Born." *Native Son*. 1940. New York: Harper & Row, Perennial Classics, 1966.

Yellin, Jean Fagan. *The Intricate Knot: Black Figures in American Literature, 1776–1863*. New York: New York University Press, 1972.

Break Dancing in the Drawing Room: Mark Twain and African-American Voices

Shelley Fisher Fishkin

> The Negro looks at the white man and finds it difficult to believe that the "grays"—a Negro term for white people—can be so absurdly self-deluded over the true interrelatedness of blackness and whiteness.
>
> Ralph Ellison[1]

> The more come in with a free good will, make the band seem sweeter still.
>
> African-American spiritual, sung by Fisk Jubilee Singers

The range of models critics cite when they probe the sources of Mark Twain's *Adventures of Huckleberry Finn* is wide. It includes the picaresque novel, the Southwestern humorists, the Northeastern literary comedians, the newspapers Twain contributed to and read, and the tradition of the "boy book" in American popular culture.[2] Twain himself weighed in with a clear statement about the roots of his main character, claiming that Huck Finn was based on Tom Blankenship, a poor-white outcast child Twain remembered from Hannibal, and on Tom's older brother Bence, who once helped a runaway slave.[3] These sources may seem quite different. On one level, however, they are the same: they all give Twain's book a genealogy that is unequivocally white.

Although commentators differ on the question of which models and sources proved most significant, they tend to concur on the question of how *Huckleberry Finn* transformed American literature. Twain's innovation of having a vernacular-speaking child tell his own story *in his own words* was the first stroke of brilliance; Twain's awareness of the power of satire in the service of social criticism was the second. Huck's voice combined with Twain's satiric genius changed the shape of fiction in America.

In this essay I will suggest that Twain himself and the critics have ignored or obscured the African-American roots of his art. Critics, for the most part, have confined their studies of the relationship between Twain's work and African-American traditions to examinations of his depiction of African-American folk beliefs or to analyses of the dialects spoken by his black characters.[4] But by limiting their field of inquiry to the periphery, they have missed the ways in which African-American voices shaped Twain's creative imagination at its core.

Compelling evidence indicates that the model for Huck Finn's voice was a black child instead of a white one and that this child's speech sparked in Twain a sense of the possibilities of a vernacular narrator. The record suggests that it may have been yet another black speaker who awakened Twain to the power of satire as a tool of social criticism. This may help us understand why Richard Wright found Twain's work "strangely familiar," and why Langston Hughes, Ralph Ellison, and David Bradley all found Twain so empowering in their own efforts to convert African-American experience into art.[5]

As Ralph Ellison put it in 1970, "*the black man [was] a co-creator of the language that Mark Twain raised to the level of literary eloquence*" ("America" 109, italics mine). But his comment sank like a stone, leaving barely a ripple on the placid surface of American literary criticism. Neither critics from the center nor critics from the margins challenged the reigning assumption that mainstream literary culture in America is certifiably "white."

I suggest that we need to revise our understanding of the nature of the mainstream American literary tradition. The voice we have come to accept as the vernacular voice in American literature—the voice with which Twain captured our national imagination in *Huckleberry Finn,* and that empowered Hemingway, Faulkner, and countless other writers in the twentieth century—is in large measure a voice that is "black."

Mark Twain was unusually attuned to the nuances of cadence, rhythm, syntax, and diction that distinguish one language or dialect from another, and he had a genius for transferring the oral into print.[6] Twain, whose preferred playmates had been black, was what J. L. Dillard might have called "bidialectal"; as an engaging black child he encountered in the early 1870s helped reconnect Twain to the cadences and rhythms of black speakers from Twain's own childhood, he inspired him to liberate a language that lay buried within Twain's own linguistic repertoire and to apprehend its stunning creative potential. Twain, in turn, would help make that language available as a literary option to both white and black writers who came after him. As Ellison put it in 1991, "he made it possible for many of us to find our own voices"(Fishkin interview).

Mark Twain helped open American literature to the multicultural polyphony that is its birthright and special strength. He appreciated the creative vitality of African-American voices and exploited their potential in his art. In the process, he helped teach his countrymen new lessons about the lyrical and exuberant energy of vernacular speech, as well as about the potential of satire and irony in the service of truth. Both of these lessons would ultimately make the culture more responsive to the voices of African-American writers in the twentieth century. They would also change its definitions of what "art" ought to look and sound like to be freshly, wholly "American."

Am I suggesting that the sources and influences that scholars have documented over the last hundred years are not important to our understanding of Twain's career as a whole? No. Southwestern humor, for example, clearly played a key role in shaping Twain's art, particularly in such early works as *Innocents Abroad* and *Roughing It.* But there is something about *Huckleberry Finn* that sets it off from Twain's earlier work and makes it seem less a continuation of the art he had been developing and more of a quantum leap forward; its unrivaled place in both the Twain canon and in the American literary canon reflects this special status.[7] In *Huckleberry Finn* something new happened that would have an enormous impact on the future of American literature. That "something new" has never been adequately accounted for. My suggestion is this: here, more than in any other work, Twain allowed African-American voices to play a major role in the creation of his art. This fact may go a long way toward clarifying what makes this novel so fresh and so distinctive.[8]

Twain's responsiveness to African-American speaking voices should come as no surprise to us, for the intense and visceral nature of his response to African-American *singing* voices has been widely documented. After entertaining the Fisk Jubilee Singers in his home in Lucerne, Switzerland, in 1897, Twain wrote,

> Away back in the beginning—to my mind—their music made all other vocal music cheap; and that early notion is emphasized now. It is utterly beautiful, to me; and it moves me infinitely more than any other music can. I think that in the Jubilees and their songs America has produced the perfectest flower of the ages; and I wish it were a foreign product so that she would worship it and lavish money on it and go properly crazy over it.[9]

Twain acknowledged his admiration for the beauty and power of these songs and their singers in the publicity blurb he wrote for the Fisk Jubilee Singers on their European tour: "I do not know when anything has so moved me as did the plaintive melodies of the Jubilee Singers." Calling their music "eloquent" (underlining the close connection in his mind between speech and song), Twain wrote, "I heard them sing once, and I would walk seven miles to hear them sing again. You will recognize that this is strong language for me to use, when you remember that I never was fond of pedestrianism."[10]

Katy Leary, a servant of the Clemens family, reports that one evening as a group of guests were sitting in the music room looking out at the moonlight at the home of Charles Dudley Warner, a neighbor in Hartford, Twain "suddenly got right up without any warning" and began to sing "negro Spirituals." He sang "low and sweet," Leary recalled, and "became kind of lost in it." When he came to the end of the song, "to the Glory Halleluiah, he gave a great shout—just like the negroes do—he shouted out the Glory, Glory, Halleluiah!" Those who were there said that "none of them would forget it as long as they lived" (Lawton 212–13).

As his voice projected in song black voices from his childhood, Twain's bearing would become strangely transformed. Drawing on accounts by guests who were present,

Justin Kaplan describes an evening at Twain's Hartford home in 1874:

> After dinner, with a log fire blazing in the red-curtained drawing room, he sang "Swing Low, Sweet Chariot," "Golden Slippers," "Go Down, Moses". . . . He swayed gently as he stood; his voice was low and soft, a whisper of wind in the trees; his eyes were closed, and he smiled strangely. Through the sadness and exultation of these songs which he had known through boyhood, he transported himself far from the circle of polite letters and from the New England snowscape, and he found it difficult to go back. . . . (174)

Twain could often be found singing his favorite African-American spirituals when he was farthest from home—in Liverpool in 1873, as well as in Florence in 1904, the night his wife, Livy, died (Kaplan 172, 174). William Dean Howells recalled the "fervor" and "passion" with which Twain's "quavering tenor" sang these songs during his last visit to Twain's home in Redding, Connecticut, shortly before Twain's death (*My Mark Twain* 99). Twain identified with these songs in ways that went to the core of his being; they spoke uniquely to a part of himself that no other art could touch.

African-American speaking voices played much the same role, on a subliminal level, in Twain's consciousness.[11] Twain never expressed his admiration for the power of African-American speaking voices as publicly as he expressed his admiration for the Fisk Jubilee Singers, but many such voices made deep impressions on him during the years preceding *Huckleberry Finn.* During his childhood, Twain had stood in awe of the storytelling powers of a slave named Uncle Dan'l, whom he remembered from summers spent on his uncle's farm in Florida, Missouri. In his autobiography, when Twain described "the white and black children grouped on the hearth" listening to Uncle Dan'l's folk tales, he recalled "the creepy joy which quivered through me when the time for the ghost story of the 'Golden Arm' was reached and the sense of regret, too, which came over me for it was always the last story of the evening."[12]

In the late 1860s and 1870s, Twain was impressed by the narrative skills of black speakers like Frederick Douglass and

Mary Ann Cord (a servant at the Clemenses' summer home in Elmira, New York). In 1869, the "simple language" in which Douglass told a story in the course of social conversation struck Twain as so remarkably "effective" that he described it in detail in a letter to his future wife:

> Had a talk with Fred Douglas, *[sic]* to-day, who seemed exceedingly glad to see me—& I certainly was glad to see *him,* for I do so admire his "spunk." He told the history of his child's expulsion from Miss Tracy's school, & his simple language was very effective. Miss Tracy said the pupils did not want a colored child among them—which he did not believe, & challenged the proof. She put it at once to a vote of the school, and asked "How many of you are willing to have this colored child be with you?" And they *all* held up their hands! Douglas added: "The children's hearts were right." There was pathos in the way he said it. I would like to hear him make a speech. . . .[13]

And in 1874, the "vigorous eloquence" with which former slave Mary Ann Cord told the story of her reunion with her son after the Civil War inspired Twain's first contribution to the esteemed *Atlantic Monthly;* a quarter-century later, Twain would still recall her stunning "gift of strong & simple speech."[14] Twain wrote that he found the story she told a "curiously strong piece of *literary work* to come unpremeditated from lips untrained in the literary art," showing his awareness of the close relationship between speaking voices and "literature." "The untrained tongue is usually wandering, wordy & vague," Twain wrote; "but this is clear, compact & coherent—yes, & vivid also, & perfectly simple & unconscious."[15] Throughout his career as a lecturer and as a writer, Twain aspired to have the effect upon his listeners and readers that speakers like Frederick Douglass and Mary Ann Cord had upon *him.*[16]

Ernest Hemingway declared that "All modern American literature comes from one book by Mark Twain called *Huckleberry Finn* (22). William Faulkner called Twain "the father of American literature" (quoted in Jelliffe 88). The African-American roots of Twain's art, however, have never been fully recognized or explored. In 1987 Toni Morrison issued a call for critics to examine "literature for the impact Afro-

American presence has had on the structure of the work, the linguistic practice, and fictional enterprise in which it is engaged" ("Unspeakable" 19). This work is a response. My goal is to foreground the role previously neglected African-American voices played in shaping Mark Twain's art in *Huckleberry Finn.* Given that book's centrality in our culture, the points I make implicitly illuminate, as well, how African-American voices have shaped our sense of what is distinctively "American" about American literature.[17]

* * *

In his pathbreaking 1970 essay, "What America Would Be Like Without Blacks," Ralph Ellison wrote,

> If we can resist for a moment the temptation to view everything having to do with Negro Americans in terms of their racially imposed status, we become aware of the fact that for all the harsh reality of the social and economic injustices visited upon them, these injustices have failed to keep Negroes clear of the cultural mainstream; Negro Americans are in fact one of its major tributaries. (108)

One important dimension of the "cultural mainstream" that African Americans have shaped, Ellison noted, is the language. "The American nation," he wrote,

> is in a sense the product of the American language, a colloquial speech . . . that began by merging the sounds of many tongues, brought together in the struggle of diverse regions. And whether it is admitted or not, much of the sound of that language is derived from the timbre of the African voice and the listening habits of the African ear. (109)

Ellison called *"the black man a co-creator of the language that Mark Twain raised to the level of literary eloquence. . ."* (109, italics mine). My research and interpretations clearly support this assertion.

"The spoken idiom of Negro Americans," Ellison declared,

> its flexibility, its musicality, its rhythms, freewheeling diction, and metaphors, as projected in Negro American

> folklore, were absorbed by the creators of our great nineteenth-century literature even when the majority of blacks were still enslaved. Mark Twain celebrated it in the prose of *Huckleberry Finn;* without the presence of blacks, the book could not have been written. No Huck and Jim, no American novel as we know it. (109)

Ellison's intuitions were stunningly correct—in general terms, and in particular terms as well. Rather than reflecting a consensus of twentieth-century scholarly opinion, however, Ellison's insights stick out like a car headed the wrong way down a one-way street.

The role of "the spoken idiom of Negro Americans" in shaping the language of Southerners was doggedly denied by scholars throughout most of this century. Their comments echoed the dismissive tone Thomas Jefferson had used when describing African-American speech. "Never yet could I find a black had uttered a thought above the level of plain-narration," Jefferson wrote; he found the imagination of African-Americans to be "dull, tasteless and anomalous."[18]

In a 1924 article entitled "The English of the Negro" in the *American Mercury,* George Krapp wrote that "it is reasonably safe to say that not a single detail of Negro pronunciation or Negro syntax can be proved to have other than English origins."[19] And in 1928 H. P. Johnson announced that "... Negroes have made only one contribution to the language of the English speaking world. They have given it the word, buckra, which means white man" (381).

As J. L. Dillard, a leading authority on the subject, observed in 1972,

> Without evidence, but loyal to a commitment to the British origins theory, dialect geographers have assumed that the Negro got his dialect from the Southern white—that the influence has been almost exclusively unidirectional. (*Black English* 186)

According to Dillard, scholars often "disallowed" evidence to the contrary. They preferred to believe in theories that

> will not allow for the spread of Negro dialect features to the white Southern population, except in very restricted

> areas adjacent to Gullah territory. Orthodox works like Cleanth Brooks's *The Relation of the Alabama-Georgia Dialect to the Provincial Dialects of Great Britain* (1935) have been specifically aimed at dispelling the heretical notion of Negro influence on white speech which was propounded in L. W. Payne's article "A Word List from East Alabama." . . .[20]

Payne had written, in the 1905 article Dillard cites,

> The ordinary southerner would scoff at the idea that it is the negro dialect of his section that has largely molded its own speech. For my own part, after a somewhat careful study of East Alabama dialect, I am convinced that the speech of the white people, the dialect I have spoken all my life and the one I have tried to record here, is more largely colored by the language of the Negroes than by any other single influence. (279)

Although Brooks's position generally found favor among twentieth-century scholars,[21] many casual eighteenth- and nineteenth-century observers often made comments similar to Payne's. In 1746, for example, a visitor to the United States observed in the *London Magazine* that the American planters gave their children too much freedom "to prowl amongst the young Negroes, which insensibly causes them to imbibe their Manners and broken Speech."[22] Fanny Kemble, in *A Journal of Residence on a Georgia Plantation in 1838–39*, observed, ". . . The children of the owners, brought up among [the slaves] acquire their Negro mode of talking" (quoted in Dillard, *Black English*, 192). And in 1864, Thomas L. Nichols noted *in Forty Years of American Life* that

> Southern speech is clipped, softened, and broadened by the Negro admixture. The child learns its language from its Negro nurse, servants, and playmates, and this not unpleasant patois is never quite eradicated. (1:385)

John Bennett recalled in 1909 that among the Charleston aristocracy of his day, "It is true that, up to the age of four, approximately, the children of the best families, even in town, are apt to speak an almost unmodified *Gullah,* caught from brown playmates and country bred nurses. . . ."[23]

While some twentieth-century scholars like Brooks resisted the idea, innumerable observers throughout the nineteenth century felt that "the ever-present Negro had more influence on the speech of the Southern white than the far-away East Anglian—or the occasional Scotsman or Irishman" (Dillard, *Black English,* 216).

This perception turns out to be largely correct. W. J. Cash, C. Vann Woodward, and Melville Herskovits concur with Dillard on this point.

As W. J. Cash noted,

> . . . in this society in which the infant son of the planter was commonly suckled by a black mammy, in which gray old men were the most loved story-tellers . . . in this society in which by far the greater number of white boys of whatever degree were more or less shaped by such companionship, and in which nearly the whole body of whites, young and old, had constantly before their eyes the example, had constantly in their ears the accent of the Negro, the relationship between the two groups was, by the second generation at least, nothing less than organic. Negro entered into white man as profoundly as white man entered into Negro. (51)

C. Vann Woodward noted the "lamentations of the [nineteenth-century] planters that *their children talked like Negroes,* sang Negro songs, preferred Negro music at their dances, and danced like Negroes" ("Clio" 17, italics mine).

And Melville Herskovits averred that

> *[It] is not only phonetically that Southern speech has been influenced by the Negro.* It is trite to point out how "musical" is Southern speech. Cadenced more than any other American dialect, it may almost be said to have melodic line, and it is not insignificant in this connection that a basic aspect of West African speech is the presence of what linguists call "significant tone" [meaning] that to pronounce a word—a phonetic combination—in different tonal registers gives it different meaning. ("Africa" 93, italics mine)

For much of the twentieth century, however, this perspective was rarely voiced, or, when it was voiced, it was attacked vociferously. A 1935 essay entitled "Southern Speech" by William Cabell Greet is a case in point. Greet opined that while in America's "songs and dances [the negro] has added zest,"

> He has in the main used language to so little purpose that there I cannot find he has contributed anything at all.[24]

As late as the 1960s folklorists and ethnographers still found resistance to the idea that "the terms *OK, wow, uh-huh* and *unh-unh*" were African-American contributions to the American language (Abrahams and Szwed 1–2).

> "Prior to the Emancipation," as Ernest F. Dunn observes, most well-to-do [white people in the South] tolerated the Black speech patterns in their children only up to a certain age. The formal educational experience was designed, in part, to extricate out of the child the linguistic and behavioral patterns he or she had acquired under the tutelage of her "mammy" and the "plantation playmates."[25]

After the war, Southern whites of all classes came to view "the influence of black speech patterns" as "a stigma with which [they] did not wish to be marked."[26] Part of the tenacity with which Southern whites clung to segregation might be linked, in Dunn's opinion, to these linguistic legacies: "The process of white education could not succeed in the presence of Blacks since part of the purpose of that education was to put aside Black influence" (118). Thus while educators struggled to suppress linguistic habits white children had acquired naturally living in an environment shaped by black as well as white speech patterns, numerous scholars labored tenaciously to deny any evidence of black influence on Southern white speech (117).

If linguists were so resistant to recognizing the influence of African-American speech patterns on both Southern speech and American speech in general, it is not surprising that their colleagues in literature were content to ignore the influence of

African-American traditions on mainstream texts. It may be one thing to acknowledge the black sources of the dialect spoken by black characters in a novel, or a white novelist's use of black folktales and folk beliefs. But it is quite another to explore the ways in which African-American vernacular traditions may have shaped mainstream American literature at its core.

Ellison is virtually alone in making this claim. As he put it in 1969, "I recognize no American culture which is not the partial creation of black people. I recognize no American style in literature, in dance, in music, even in assemblyline processes, which does not bear the mark of the American Negro" (quoted in McPherson 44). Art historian Robert Farris Thompson voiced a variation on this theme in a lecture on "The Kongo Atlantic Tradition" in 1992: "To be white in America is to be very black. If you don't know how black you are, you don't know how American you are." Or, as C. Vann Woodward put it in 1969, "so far as their culture is concerned, all Americans are part Negro" ("Clio" 17).

In "Going to the Territory," Ellison elaborated on the process by which "America" became "American."

> American culture is of a whole, for that which is essentially "American" in it springs from the synthesis of our diverse elements of cultural style. . . . [I]n the days when our leaders still looked to England and the Continent for their standards of taste, the vernacular stream of our culture was creating itself out of whatever elements it found useful, including the Americanized culture of the slaves. . . . Ironically, it was the vernacular which gave expression to that very newness of spirit and outlook of which the leaders of the nation liked to boast. (142)

Ellison makes a strong case for why the vernacular is so central to our definitions of who and what we are:

> . . . on the level of culture no one group has managed to create the definitive American style. Hence the importance of the vernacular in the ongoing task of naming, defining and creating a consciousness of who and what we have come to be. (143)

Mark Twain, according to Ellison, played a key role in making the vernacular as important as it is to our sense of how we think of ourselves as a nation. Twain

> . . . transformed elements of regional vernacular speech into a medium of uniquely American literary expression and thus taught us how to capture that which is essentially American in our folkways and manners. For indeed the vernacular process is a way of establishing and discovering our national identity. (140)

It is easy to assemble a diverse litany of attestations to Twain's centrality as the quintessentially "American" artist. H. L. Mencken, for example, called Twain "the true father of our national literature, the first genuinely American artist of the blood royal" (69–70). Louis Budd noted that the story *Reader's Digest* ran during the *Huckleberry Finn* centennial

> quoted Charles Kuralt as speaking for the "feelings of millions of the book's admirers" when he declared on TV: "if I had to say as much about America as I possibly could in only two words, I would say these two words: 'Huck Finn.'" ("Recomposition" 195)

Budd reports that ". . . a supposedly scientific poll showed that 96% of college faculty now put *Huckleberry Finn* at the very head of the reading list for entering freshmen," and a feature article in the *Washington Post* in January 1986 deemed *Huckleberry Finn* "the greatest work of art by an American, the Sistine Chapel of our civilization" (195).

Budd finds these attitudes in earlier periods as well. He cites William Lyon Phelps's declaration in the 1920s that *Huckleberry Finn* "is not only the great American novel. It is America." In 1940 Clifton Fadiman dubbed Twain "'our Chaucer, our Homer, our Dante, our Virgil' because *Huckleberry Finn* 'is the nearest thing we have to a national epic. Just as the Declaration of Independence . . . contains in embryo our whole future history as a nation, so the language of *Huckleberry Finn* (another declaration of independence) expresses our popular character, our humor, our slant'" (Budd, "Recomposition," 195). As David Sloane has noted, "with over 150 editions in print, selling over a quarter of a million copies a year, if American sales are added to the panoply of foreign translations in German, French, Russian and other major world languages, *Huckleberry Finn* is one of the most steadily experienced projections of America and the American spirit."[27] By 1976, 696 foreign editions of the novel had been published.[28]

In the thousands of books and articles written on *Huckleberry Finn*, however, the role of African-American oral traditions in shaping Twain's achievement gets virtually no attention.[29] Ellison was certain about that influence despite the fact that he adduced no specifics to support his theory. In a 1976 interview in *Pulp*, for example, Ellison claimed that "the American vernacular culture out of which what we identify as American writing arose was very much influenced by the oral lore, the oral literature of the Afro-American. This appears in Mark Twain" (quoted in Sage 12). Ellison's conviction on this point dates back to his high school days, when it occurred to him that

> what some of my "teachers" were calling "white literature" was not really *white* at all. . . . Part of the music of the language, part of the folklore which informed our conscious American literature came through the interaction of the slave and the white man, and particularly so in the South. ("Initiation" 47–48)

Much as the observations of lay commentators on black and white speech patterns in the nineteenth century resemble theories that are at the cutting edge of dialect study today, Ellison's intuitive understanding of the dynamics of Twain's culture and of our own resonates with insights that frame perfectly the ideas explored here.

* * *

"Materially, psychologically, and culturally," Ellison wrote, "part of the nation's heritage is Negro American, and whatever it becomes will be shaped in part by the Negro's presence. . ." (America 111). As he put it elsewhere, "American culture is part Afro-American culture, and that's especially true in music, in literature, in dance. . ." (quoted in Sage 11). These statements are neither radical nor extravagant; yet Ellison knew that they would meet with strong resistance.

> . . . by ignoring such matters as the sharing of bloodlines and cultural traditions by groups of widely differing ethnic origins, and by overlooking the blending and metamorphosis of cultural forms which is so characteristic of our society we misconceive our cultural identity. It is as though we dread to acknowledge the complex, pluralistic nature of our society, and as a result we find ourselves stumbling upon our true national identity under circumstances in which we least expect to do so. ("Territory" 125)

I had not yet stumbled upon the specific African-American speakers who shaped *Huckleberry Finn* when I interviewed Ralph Ellison in July 1991.[30] But months later, as I listened to the tape of our two-hour conversation and read the notes I had taken on Ellison's work in preparation for the interview, I realized that Ellison had played an important role in preparing and shaping my awareness of the role of African-American voices in Twain's art.

Ellison told me he first encountered Mark Twain when he was around eight years old and promptly nicknamed his brother Herbert, "Huck." He returned to *Huckleberry Finn* when he started to write. "When I began to think consciously about writing naturally I went back to it." What was it that spoke to him in Twain's work as a writer? Were there things that it taught him that he valued when he began writing himself?

Ellison responded,

> Well, for one thing, Mark Twain, as against so many other writers, knew more about the country. He knew something of its geographical and cultural variety. And being from the section of the country from which he came, he knew something about my own people. The other thing to say here is that as a newspaperman and as a writer he was interested (at least certainly aware of, maybe not at first consciously—but he became so) in the vernacular language, which was so very important in conveying the essence of people, the spoken speech. He didn't always do it so well, but he was a pioneer.

Did Twain make Ellison aware of some of the possibilities of vernacular speech?

> Oh yes. His attempts to render the speech of Southern negroes—it was very important to see the efforts, and to see what he grasped in the personalities behind the speech.

At what point did Ellison begin to understand that Twain was doing more than just writing a boys' book? At what age did he understand that it was a book that he could learn from as someone who aspired to using satire himself? Ellison says it must have been in his twenties, when he "read a lot, and after I got into Hemingway I went back to Twain." In Hemingway (who said all "modern American literature comes from . . . *Huckleberry Finn*"), Ellison was struck by

> the use of vernacular speech, the rhythms, the ability to use understatement, which again, I have a connection with through my own folk tradition: so much is said, implied, in negro folk songs, negro folklore, and so on.

Ellison was aware of Twain's presence as well in the work of William Faulkner, who also acknowledged a strong debt to Twain.

> . . . And of course, when I began to read Faulkner—I didn't really begin to read Faulkner until the forties, but I read it before he was rediscovered—there, reading a Southern writer who had lived very closely with Southern negroes, and who was closer to Slavery through his own family and so on, and through the manners which still obtained, again, I went back to Twain to make comparisons and to try to trace influences.

Ellison believes the vernacular is as shaped by African-American voices today as it was in Twain's day. "Today's slang is always influenced by what comes from the Afro-American background. Just as the music is influenced by jazz, by the blues—you wouldn't have an American music without it." No one would attempt to write a segregated history of American music, but the history of American literature has, for the most part, been a segregated enterprise: white writers come from white literary ancestors, black writers from black ones. It is time to acknowledge the very mixed literary bloodlines on both sides. Ellison found Twain's "free-wheeling appropriation of the vernacular, his transforming it into an agency of literature," exhilarating and inspiring. His influence on Ellison's own work—both direct and indirect—and on the work of other African-American writers, was profound. As Ellison put it in our interview, *"he made it possible for many of us to find our own voices."*

The implications of this statement are provocative and intriguing. In what ways—conscious and unconscious, direct and indirect—might Twain have empowered black writers? Charles W. Chesnutt kept a bust of Twain in his library.[31] Ralph Ellison has a photo of Twain over his desk.[32] Other twentieth-century African-American writers, such as Langston Hughes, David Bradley, and Richard Wright, have paid eloquent homage to Twain. What did they learn from him?

In our interview, Ellison credited Twain with having been a "pioneer" in opening up new possibilities for the literary use of African-American vernacular. Ellison also appreciated Twain's use of comedy to "allow us to deal with the unspeakable," as he put it. In Ellison's view, the unspeakable that Twain addressed was "the moral situation of the United States and the contrast between our ideals and our activities," the ways in which the realities of American race relations always so sharply rebuked our national ideals, a subject that has remained central to twentieth-century African-American fiction.

Did he return to Twain at all when he was writing *Invisible Man?* "Not consciously," Ellison responded,

> but what reading does for a writer . . . [is] that you build up a bank within your unconscious. You might not even realize at the time you're putting stuff down that you're being influenced. . . .

His language is curiously reminiscent of Twain's, on a similar subject.

Did Twain shape Ellison's writing in *Invisible Man?* Some of Trueblood's lyrical descriptions have always struck me as evoking Huck's language and angle of vision. Trueblood says, for example,

> . . . I'd be awake lookin' at the lights comin' up from the water and listenin' to the sounds of the boats movin' along. . . . I'd be layin' there and it would be quiet and I could hear it comin' from way, way off. Like when you quail huntin' and it's getting dark, and you can hear the boss bird whistlin' tryin' to get the covey together again, and he's coming toward you slow and whistlin' soft 'cause he knows you somewhere around with your gun.[33]

Was Huck lurking in the background? Ellison said he "couldn't deny it." Twain's influence on him, he suggested, may have been unconscious, but it was there.[34]

Could some of the things Ellison learned from Twain be things Twain himself learned from the rhetorical performances of African-Americans? Ellison responded, "*I think it comes full circle.*"

Richard Wright, too, saw in Twain's work some potent echoes of his own childhood that he found "strangely familiar." David Bradley asked a stunned audience in Hartford in 1985 whether, even though Sam Clemens was white, Mark Twain might have been black? He then proceeded to make a case for Twain as a key figure in the development of African-American fiction ("The First 'Nigger' Novel"). Given Ellison's own debt to Twain, it is possible that some African-American writers in the twentieth century may have been influenced by Twain as mediated *through* Ellison;[35] others may have encountered him on their own.

Almost as little attention has been paid to Twain's influence on African-American voices as to the influence of African-American voices on Twain. One notable exception to this general pattern of neglect, however, is Arnold Rampersad's important 1984 essay, "*Adventures of Huckleberry Finn* and Afro-American Literature."[36] Rampersad cites some key ways in which Twain's novel "differs from the bulk of black American fiction." These include (1) Twain's use of a first-person narrator (the autobiographical voice being largely absent from African-American fiction until very recent times); (2) Twain's use of dialect (dialect did not play a central role in black fiction until the 1930s); (3) Twain's decision to entrust his story to a child (something "the black writer has been reluctant until recently" to attempt); (4) the book's status as a work "of adult fiction readily accessible to young readers" (virtually unheard of in black fiction); (5) Twain's use of humor to explore the subject of race (a generally taboo combination in black fiction—with notable exceptions, like that of Charles Chesnutt); (6) Twain's "'twinning' of white and dark-skinned characters to suggest an ideal American hero who combines the best qualities of the white and some darker race in a merger of complementary abilities and values" (an approach to characterization rejected by black fiction writers); and (7) Twain's focus on "the great question of Nature and its relationship to humanity," which Rampersad takes "to be at the heart of Mark Twain's depiction of the river" in the novel (a theme that has been largely unimportant in African-American fiction) (217–24).

However, Rampersad observes, the differences between *Huckleberry Finn* and African-American fiction narrow in the twentieth century. In 1943 Langston Hughes

> began building perhaps the best achievement in the fictional use of dialect by a black author when he created in the *Chicago Defender* his extremely popular character Jesse B. Semple, or "Simple." . . . The books that resulted between 1950 and 1965 (*Simple Speaks His Mind, Simple Takes a Wife, Simple Stakes a Claim, Simple's U.S.A.,* and *The Best of Simple*) were all very well received by critics, who persisted in pointing out, to the Missouri-born Hughes's great satisfaction, the similarities between his work and that of Mark Twain. (219)

"I'd not thought of it before myself," was Hughes's response when the resemblance was pointed out to him, "but am glad if there's something of the same quality there, naturally" (quoted in Rampersad, *Life, Volume II,* 223). Rampersad cites as "examples in recent black fiction of the combining of autobiography and dialect in Twain's manner," Alice Childress's *A Hero Ain't Nothin' but a Sandwich* (1973), "whose thirteen-year-old narrator is Huck's age and even of his temperament" and Al Young's *Sitting Pretty* (1976), "whose hero has more than once been compared with Huck by reviewers." Rampersad also believes that in Alice Walker's best-seller *The Color Purple,* the "heroine, Celie, whether or not Walker herself would like the notion, is definitely a black country cousin of Huck Finn."[37]

Twain's awareness of what Rampersad calls "the subversive power of comedy" on the subject of race is echoed not only in Ellison's *Invisible Man*, but in "some of the writing of Chester Himes and . . . the most innovative recent black fiction—that of Ishmael Reed in particular, as in *Mumbo Jumbo* (1972), and of William Melvin Kelley, as in *dem* (1967)" (222).

And his depiction of "a moral dilemma, or moral inversion, as being at the heart of Southern, and by inference American society," prefigures the existential alienation of protagonists like Richard Wright's Bigger Thomas *(Native Son)* or Cross Damon *(The Outsider)*, James Baldwin's Richard and Rufus (*Go Tell It on the Mountain* and *Another Country)*, and Ellison's "wildly disoriented hero in *Invisible Man*." Rampersad concludes,

> In his stress on folk culture, on dialect, and on American humor, Mark Twain anticipated Dunbar, Hughes (who lauded Twain in an introduction to *Pudd'nhead Wilson*), Hurston, Fisher, Thurman, Ellison, Gaines, Childress, Reed, and Alice Walker; in his depiction of alienation in an American context, prominently including race, Twain anticipates other aspects of most of these writers' work and also that of Richard Wright, Chester Himes, Ann Perry, James Baldwin, and Toni Morrison. (227)

To Rampersad's list of the areas of influence one might add Twain's recognition of the intimate connection between oral culture and literature. In 1984, Toni Morrison noted that she tries to incorporate into her fiction "one of the major characteristics of Black art,"

> the ability to be both print and oral literature: to combine those two aspects so that the stories can be read in silence, of course, but one should be able to hear them as well. . . . To make the story appear oral, meandering, effortless, spoken . . . is what's important. (quoted in Trudier Harris 1)

When black and white writers looked for literary models in their efforts to translate oral culture into print, Mark Twain was available as a potential guide. He served that function for Ralph Ellison, David Bradley, Ernest Hemingway, William Faulkner, Sherwood Anderson, and many others—including Morrison herself, who acknowledges that she probably returned to Twain and reread him when she began honing her own skills as a writer (personal communication). Although such writers as Ellison and Morrison were able to hear on their own the black voices that had shaped America's past and present, Twain provided a model for some of the ways in which they could translate those voices into print. Twain helped his fellow writers learn, in very practical ways, how to write books that "talked."[38]

If Twain sometimes showed prescience about the kinds of issues and aesthetic strategies that would preoccupy black writers in the twentieth century, black writers sometimes expressed extraordinary insight into the difficulties of being Mark Twain. Perhaps the most perceptive one-sentence summary of Twain's struggle as a man and as a writer comes from Richard Wright: "Twain hid his conflict in satire and wept in private over the brutalities and the injustices of his civilization."[39]

Potential parallels, prefigurings, echoes, influences, and other links between Mark Twain and African-American writers deserve more attention than they have received. A number of unpublished fragments left by Twain, for example, curiously prefigure work by Frances E. W. Harper, Pauline Hopkins, James Weldon Johnson, Nella Larsen, W. E. B. Du Bois, and Amiri Baraka. The possibility that Twain and these writers may have been responding to some of the same dimensions of our culture in similar ways is intriguing.[40]

And although Arnold Rampersad is undoubtedly right that there is no counterpart in black fiction to "the presence of the river" in *Huckleberry Finn* (with all its moral and symbolic implications), I cannot help wondering whether fellow Missourian Langston Hughes, who found "a first reading of *Adventures of Huckleberry Finn* so thrilling that he remained a lifelong admirer of Mark Twain" (Rampersad, *Life, Volume 1*, 19) might not have had Twain's river somewhere in the back of his mind when he wrote, "I've known rivers. . . . "[41]

* * *

Charles T. Davis noted in 1973 that "a double history" informs "every black work."

> We have, of course, the tradition of American letters, that continuity in form and ideas that contributed much, say, to the shape of Chesnutt's art, as it did to that of his contemporaries, Howells, Cable, Aldrich. But beyond this there is the hidden tradition, the rich and changing store of folk forms and folk materials, the advantages of a dialectical tongue, with a separate music of its own, and the background of rituals, learned responses, and wisdom that grew from a community given an amount of homogeneity through isolation and oppression.[42]

Could many "white works," as well, also be said to have "a double history," one intimately shaped, whether or not their creators were consciously aware of the fact, by black "folk materials and folk traditions"?[43]

With some notable exceptions, scholars of American literature have been curiously reticent about addressing, in all their rich concreteness, the mixed literary bloodlines of American fiction.[44] As Werner Sollors put it, "Do we have to believe in a filiation from Mark Twain to Ernest Hemingway, but not to Ralph Ellison (who is supposedly descended from James Weldon Johnson and Richard Wright)?"[45] Sollors insists that we need to probe "the pervasiveness of cultural syncretism in America" if we are to get beyond reductive descent-based readings of our culture ("Critique" 256).

His point resonates with an observation made by Charles Johnson in *Being and Race:*

> Our lives, as blacks and whites, we come to realize, are a tissue of cross-cultural influences. One can say as much about this book, written by a black American . . . on paper invented by the Chinese and printed with ink evolved out of India and from type developed by Germans using Roman symbols modified from the Greeks, who got their letter concepts from the Phoenicians, who had adapted them partly from Egyptian hieroglyphs. (43–44)

As Ellison put it in 1976,

> you can learn from [other groups]; you can make their contributions your own by the simple act of respect and showing a willingness to understand the human implications of [their traditions]. (quoted in Sage 10)

Maxine Hong Kingston is surprised when readers in China insist on a direct line between her book *The Woman Warrior* and the Chinese classic *Dream of the Red Chamber*, for, when she is asked to name her literary ancestors, the ones that first come to mind are Walt Whitman and William Carlos Williams (Fishkin, "Interview," 784, 790). David Bradley's models were Herman Melville, Robert Penn Warren, and Robert Heinlein.[46] Tillie Olsen claims W. E. B. Du Bois as a key literary forebear.[47]

I would not want my research to be interpreted as suggesting that black writers in the twentieth century were attracted to Twain simply because his work was so shaped by African-American influences. Black writers like Ellison and Wright and Bradley may well have been attracted to Twain for other reasons entirely, reasons having to do with art and genius, with well-crafted sentences, and with his ability to evoke brilliantly recognizably human traits.[48] White writers—like Faulkner, for example—may have been attracted to Twain not despite the influence of African-American voices on his art but because of them.[49]

America's long history of racism has made addressing "cultural syncretism" across racial lines particularly problematical. But as these barriers gradually give way, we can begin to see a vision of our culture that is infinitely richer and more complex than any we had before. Stephen Foster's "Camp-Town Races," a song recognized throughout the world as "uniquely American,"[50] turns out to be a tune sung by Yoruba mothers to their children (Lorenzo Turner, cited in John A. Davis 77). Harriet Beecher Stowe's *Uncle Tom's Cabin* influenced slave narratives and fiction by African Americans (Yarborough "Strategies" and Stepto). African motifs, organizational principles, and aesthetic values may have shaped the American patchwork quilt (Leon). Tones of the Jewish *shofar* may have made their way into Louis Armstrong's trumpet riffs (Sage 10). Walt Whitman empowered June Jordan to make poetry out of her experience as a woman of color.[51] The cultural conversation turns out to be jazzy and improvisational, unpredictable and serendipitous, dynamic and tricky.

Toni Morrison's landmark essay in the *Michigan Quarterly Review*, "Unspeakable Things Unspoken: The Afro-American Presence in American Literature," and her important book *Playing in the Dark: Whiteness and the Literary Imagination*, as well as books on race and literature currently being written by a number of outstanding scholars, substantiate and amplify Henry Louis Gates Jr.'s trenchant insight that segregation "is as difficult to maintain in the literary realm as it is in the civic one."[52]

Although the mixing of races and the mixing of cultures has been going on from the start, our country's legal system and our society's cultural narratives long accepted the fiction that it was possible to draw sharp lines of demarcation between the races. The fiction of "racial purity"—the notion that it was, in fact, possible to divide the society into "white" and "black"—justified the elaborate system of segregation statutes created in the 1890s and not dismantled until the middle of the twentieth century.

We may no longer segregate trains, schools, water fountains, waiting rooms, bibles for witnesses in courtrooms, parks, residences, textbooks, telephone booths, ticket windows, ambulances, hospitals, orphanages, prisons, morgues, and cemeteries. But segregation is alive and well among literary historians, who persist in affirming that white writers come from white literary ancestors, and black writers from black ones.[53]

The laws against miscegenation have been struck from the books. But unwritten laws prevent critics from acknowledging how fully black and white voices and traditions have mingled to create what we know as "American" culture. "The Negro looks at the white man," Ralph Ellison wrote, "and finds it difficult to believe that the 'grays'—a Negro term for white people—can be so absurdly self-deluded over the true interrelatedness of blackness and whiteness" ("Change" 55). In this essay I have attempted to deconstruct some of those delusions.

Toni Morrison observed, in 1992,

> There seems to be a more or less tacit agreement among literary scholars that, because American literature has

> been clearly the preserve of white male views, genius, and power, those views, genius, and power are without relationship to and removed from the overwhelming presence of black people in the United States. . . . The contemplation of this black presence is central to any understanding of our national literature and should not be permitted to hover at the margins of the literary imagination. (*Playing* 5)

David Bradley put it more bluntly. "American criticism today," he wrote in 1989, "remains both segregationist and racist."[54]

When the segregation statutes were eliminated in the middle of the twentieth century, much of American society had to alter its habits of travelling, residing, eating, learning, playing, and burying its dead. Acknowledging and understanding what Bradley has called "an integrated American Literature" ("Foreword" xviii) might well entail equally disruptive changes in familiar practice in the classroom, in the training of teachers, in institutions, and in scholarship.

A shift in paradigm is in order. Understanding African-American traditions is essential if one wants to understand *mainstream* American literary history. And understanding mainstream literary history is important if one wants to understand African-American writing in the twentieth century. We can no longer deny the mixed literary bloodlines on both sides.

Acknowledging the African-American roots of Twain's art in *Huckleberry Finn* does not make the novel any easier to teach; on the contrary, it may raise more questions than it answers. What correlation is there between listening carefully and appreciatively to African-American voices and recognizing the full humanity of the speakers to whom those voices belong? What connection is there between seeing beyond "race" to qualities that are at root simply "human," and actively challenging the racist social and political mechanisms that prevent large numbers of people in one's society from fulfilling their human potential? Can satire play a catalytic role in shaping people's awareness of the dynamics of racism, or do satire's inherent ambiguities invite too much evasion and denial?

Some of Twain's contemporaries—George Washington Cable comes immediately to mind—launched full frontal attacks against racism in the 1880s. Twain did not. Twain's attacks were more subtle, less risky, less courageous. They are also more lasting. Cable's polemics, *The Silent South* and "The Freedman's Case in Equity," for all their forceful directness, are forgotten, except among a handful of scholars. *Huckleberry Finn,* on the other hand, remains one of the most widely read and taught works by an American writer. Has it lasted despite or because of its capacity to be simultaneously all things to all people? Do its complexities contain the power of its social critique or unleash that power?

These questions remain to disturb and provoke us.[55] The research presented here suggests that *Huckleberry Finn* may be more subversive, ultimately, than we might have suspected. For Twain's imaginative blending of black voices with white ones (whether conscious or unconscious) effectively deconstructs "race" as a meaningful category. "Race," for Mark Twain, far from being the "ultimate trope of difference,"[56] was often simply irrelevant. The problem of racism, on the other hand, was for Twain, and continues to be for us, undeniably real.

How will Americans respond to the news that the voice of Huck Finn, the beloved national symbol and cultural icon, was part black? Will they react with the astonishment that the citizens of Dawson's Landing showed in *Pudd'nhead Wilson* when they learned that the pretentious blue-blood, Tom Driscoll, was really a mulatto? Will the forces of reaction demote Huck from his place of honor in the culture and relegate him to a lesser role in the national consciousness—the equivalent of selling him down the river, the fate that awaited Tom Driscoll? Or will Huck become an emblem of a society that is now, and has always been, as multiracial and multicultural as the sources of the novel that we have embraced as most expressive of who we really are?

* * *

Early in *Huckleberry Finn,* Huck complains about the food at the Widow Douglas's:

> When you got to the table you couldn't go right to eating, but you had to wait for the widow to tuck down her head and grumble a little over the victuals, though there warn't really anything the matter with them. That is, nothing only everything was cooked by itself. In a barrel of odds and ends it is different; things get mixed

> up, and the juice kind of swaps around, and the things go better. (2)

Twain's imagination was closer to Huck's barrel than to the Widow Douglas's separate pots. As he "mixed up" black voices with white ones, the flavors "swapped around" deliciously. America's taste in literature would never be the same.

Notes

From *Was Huck Black? Mark Twain and African-American Voices* by Shelley Fisher Fishkin. Copyright © 1993 by Shelley Fisher Fishkin. Reprinted by permission of Oxford University Press.

1. Ralph Ellison, "Change the Joke and Slip the Yoke," 55.

2. See, for example, Robert Alter, *Rogue's Progress: Study in the Picaresque Novel;* Alexander Blackburn, *The Myth of the Picaro;* Hugh A. Harter, "Mark Twain y la tradicion picaresca"; John B. Hughes, "*Lazarillo de Tormes* y *Huckleberry Finn*"; Kenneth S. Lynn, *Mark Twain and Southwestern Humor;* James M. Cox, *Mark Twain: The Fate of Humor;* Walter Blair, *Mark Twain and "Huck Finn";* Henry Nash Smith, *Mark Twain: The Development of a Writer;* Pascal Covici Jr., *Mark Twain's Humor;* David E. E. Sloane, *Mark Twain as a Literary Comedian;* M. Thomas Inge, ed., *The Frontier Humorists;* Leo Marx, "The Vernacular Tradition in American Literature"; Shelley Fisher Fishkin, *From Fact to Fiction: Journalism and Imaginative Writing in America;* Edgar Marquess Branch, *The Literary Apprenticeship of Mark Twain* and "Mark Twain: Newspaper Reading and the Writer's Creativity"; and Alan Gribben, "'I Did Wish Tom Sawyer Was There': Boy-Book Elements in *Tom Sawyer* and *Huckleberry Finn.*"

3. Twain said, "'Huckleberry Finn' was Tom Blankenship" (*Autobiography*, 73). See also notes on Tom and Bence Blankenship in Dahlia Armon and Walter Blair, "Biographical Directory," 302–3.

4. The notable exceptions to this rule are William Andrews ("Mark Twain and James W. C. Pennington: Huckleberry Finn's Smallpox Lie"), David Bradley ("The First 'Nigger' Novel"), Ralph Ellison ("What America Would Be Like Without Blacks"), Lucinda MacKethan ("*Huck Finn* and the Slave Narratives"), and Arnold Rampersad ("*Adventures of Huckleberry Finn* and Afro-American Literature").

For critical discussions of the speech of Twain's African-American characters, see Lee A. Pederson, "Negro Speech in *The Adventures of Huckleberry Finn*"; James Nathan Tidwell, "Mark Twain's Representation of Negro Speech"; Sally Boland, "The Seven Dialects in *Huckleberry Finn*"; Curt Morris Rulon, "The Dialects in *Huckleberry Finn*"; and David Carkeet, "The Dialects in *Huckleberry Finn.*" The best-known consideration of

African-American folk beliefs in Twain's work is Daniel G. Hoffman, "Black Magic—and White—in *Huckleberry Finn*."

Critics have also approached *Huckleberry Finn* in terms of the roles played by Twain's black characters, and Twain's racial attitudes. See Ralph Ellison, "Change the Joke and Slip the Yoke" and "Twentieth-Century Fiction and the Black Mask of Humanity"; Arthur G. Pettit, *Mark Twain and the South;* Philip Foner, *Mark Twain: Social Critic;* Louis J. Budd, *Mark Twain: Social Philosopher;* Louis Rubin Jr., "Southern Local Color and the Black Man"; Catherine Juanita Starke, *Black Portraiture in American Fiction;* Thomas Weaver and Merline A. Williams, "Mark Twain's Jim: Identity as an Index to Cultural Attitudes"; Sterling A. Brown, *The Negro in American Fiction;* Sterling Stuckey, "True Huck"; Forrest Robinson, "The Characterization of Jim in *Huckleberry Finn*"; Sloane, "*Adventures of Huckleberry Finn*": *American Comic Vision;* Sherwood Cummings, "Mark Twain's Moveable Farm and the Evasion"; Rayford W. Logan, *The Negro in American Life and Thought: The Nadir, 1877–1901;* Leslie A. Fiedler, "Come Back to the Raft Ag'in, Huck Honey"; Guy Cardwell, *The Man Who Was Mark Twain;* and Shelley Fisher Fishkin, "Racial Attitudes" (in *The Mark Twain Encyclopedia*). For additional references, see "For Further Reading" by Thomas A. Tenney, in *Satire or Evasion?*

By far the most important publications on Twain's racial attitudes and on the portrayal of black characters in his work are the 1984 special issue of the *Mark Twain Journal*, "Black Writers on *Adventures of Huckleberry Finn* One Hundred Years Later," guest edited by Thadious M. Davis, and the book into which these and other essays were collected, *Satire or Evasion? Black Perspectives on "Huckleberry Finn"*, edited by James S. Leonard, Thomas A. Tenney, and Thadious M. Davis. Some of the key essays on this subject included in this volume are: Rhett S. Jones, "Nigger and Knowledge: White Double-Consciousness in *Adventures of Huckleberry Finn*"; David Smith, "Huck, Jim, and American Racial Discourse"; Bernard W. Bell, "Twain's 'Nigger' Jim: The Tragic Face behind the Minstrel Mask"; Fredrick Woodard and Donnarae MacCann, "Minstrel Shackles and Nineteenth-Century 'Liberality' in *Huckleberry Finn*"; Charles H. Nichols, "'A True Book—With Some Stretchers': *Huck Finn* Today"; and Betty H. Jones, "Huck and Jim: A Reconsideration." See also Thadious Davis's "Foreword" to the special issue of the *Mark Twain Journal*. Only rarely have critics recognized in print some of the larger connections between Mark Twain's work and African-American culture. See Arnold Rampersad, "*Adventures of Huckleberry Finn* and Afro-American Literature," and Stewart Rodnon, "*The Adventures of Huckleberry Finn* and *Invisible Man*: Thematic and Structural Comparisons."

5. Richard Wright, "Memories of My Grandmother," quoted in Michel Fabre, *Richard Wright: Books & Writers,* 161; Langston Hughes, "Introduction" to Mark Twain, *Pudd'nhead Wilson,* vii–xiii; Ralph Ellison, interview with the author, 16 July 1991; David Bradley, "The First 'Nigger' Novel," speech to Annual Meeting of the Mark Twain Memorial and the New England American Studies Association, Hartford, Connecticut, May 1985.

6. Twain's linguistic virtuosity is apparent from such pieces as "Italian Without a Master," "Italian with Grammar," "The Awful German Language," "Concerning the American Language," "Introduction to 'The New Guide of the Conversation in Portuguese and English,'" "'The Jumping Frog' in English. Then in French. Then Clawed Back into a Civilized Language Once More by Patient, Unremunerated Toil."

The most recent and sophisticated discussion of Twain's sensitivity to and interest in diverse linguistic systems is David Sewell's stimulating book, *Mark Twain's Languages.* Sewell argues that "Mark Twain's understanding of language, as evidenced primarily in his fiction, transcended its origin in public-school grammar instruction and moved toward an intuition of principles just beginning to appear in his day and fully enunciated only in our own" (1–2). In addition to being adept at evoking a wide range of languages and dialects, Twain demonstrated a "facile, natural control" over what psycholinguist George F. Mahl refers to as "one of the extralinguistic dimensions of speech, the 'roughness' or 'influency' or 'normal disturbances' in word-progression" ("Everyday Speech Disturbances in *Tom Sawyer,*" 295–96; "Everyday Disturbances of Speech," 213).

In "Mark Twain and the Oral Economy: Digression in the Age of Print," David Barrow suggests that "over the course of his career" Twain was "opposed to the notion that the spoken can be translated satisfactorily into print" (10). Although he may have suspected that ultimate success in this matter was beyond his reach, Twain nonetheless labored mightily in the effort.

7. Richard Bridgman describes the phenomenon in this way:

> If one accepts provisionally the existence of a change in American prose style, then the next pertinent question is, when did it begin? Recently the date 1884 has been advanced from several quarters, most succinctly by Ernest Hemingway: "All modern American literature comes from one book by Mark Twain called *Huckleberry Finn*. . . ." As early as 1913 H. L. Mencken was championing Mark Twain: "I believe that he was the true father of our national literature, the first genuinely American artist of the blood royal." Later William Faulkner agreed, saying: "In my opinion, Mark Twain was the first truly American writer, and all of us since are his heirs, we are descended from him."
>
> This critical admiration has not extended to Mark Twain's work as a whole nor to his literary theories (such as they were), nor to his practical criticisms. One book alone has drawn the praise. Whatever the merits of Mark Twain's other writing, and whatever the weaknesses of *Huckleberry Finn*, everyone—literary hacks, artists, and critics—agrees that the style of this book has had a major effect on the development of American prose. (5–6)

8. It is not within the scope of this work to explore the ways in which African-American voices shaped other works by Twain besides *Huckleberry Finn*, but clearly such investigations have the potential to be rich and fruitful. For example, Twain's responses to slave narratives in a range of contexts warrant further examination in this light. Werner Sollors has explored some connections between slave narratives and *A Connecticut Yankee in King Arthur's Court* ("Ethnicity"). Lawrence Howe has noted the analogies to slave narrative themes in *Life on the Mississippi* in "Transcending the Limits of Experience: Mark Twain's *Life on the Mississippi*."

9. Twain preceded this comment with the following description of the Jubilee Singers' visit:

> The other night we had a detachment of the Jubilee Singers—6 I had known in London 24 years ago. Three of the 6 were born in slavery, the others were children of slaves. How charming they were—in spirit, manner,

> language, pronunciation, enunciation, grammar, phrasing, matter, carriage, clothes—in every detail that goes to make the real lady and gentleman, and welcome guest. We went down to the village hotel and bought our tickets and entered the beer-hall, where a crowd of German and Swiss men and women sat grouped at round tables with their beer mugs in front of them—self-contained and unimpressionable looking people, an indifferent and unposted and disheartened audience—and up at the far end of the room sat the Jubilees in a row. The Singers got up and stood—the talking and glass jingling went on. Then rose and swelled out above those common earthly sounds one of those rich chords the secret of whose make only the Jubilees possess, and a spell fell upon that house. It was fine to see the faces light up with the pleased wonder and surprise of it. No one was indifferent any more; and when the singers finished, the camp was theirs. It was a triumph. It reminded me of Launcelot riding in Sir Kay's armor and astonishing complacent Knights who thought they had struck a soft thing. The Jubilees sang a lot of pieces. Arduous and painstaking cultivation has not diminished or artificialized their music, but on the contrary—to my surprise—has mightily reinforced its eloquence and beauty. (SLC to Joe Twitchell, 22 August 1897, in *Mark Twain's Letters*, ed. Albert Bigelow Paine, 2:645–46)

Twain's awareness of his countrymen's failure to appreciate the value of the spirituals is echoed by Alain Locke, who noted in 1925 in "The Negro Spirituals," that "only recently have they come to be recognized as artistically precious things. It still requires vision and courage to proclaim their ultimate value and possibilities" (199–200).

10. Gustavus D. Pike, *The Singing Campaign for Ten Thousand Pounds; or, The Jubilee Singers in Great Britain*, 14; Anon., "Coming Events," *Fun* (London), 172. The text of Twain's publicity letter for the Jubilee Singers reads as follows:

> Gentlemen. The Jubilee Singers are to appear in London, and I am requested to say in their behalf what I know of them—and I most cheerfully do it. I heard

them sing once, and I would walk seven miles to hear them sing again. You will recognize that this is strong language for me to use, when you remember that I never was fond of pedestrianism, and got tired of walking that Sunday afternoon, in twenty minutes, after making up my mind to see for myself and at my own leisure how much ground his grace the Duke of Bedford's property, covered.

I think these gentlemen and ladies make eloquent music—and what is as much to the point, they reproduce the true melody of the plantations, and are the only persons I ever heard accomplish this on the public platform. The so-called "negro minstrels" simply mis-represent the thing; I do not think they ever saw a plantation or heard a slave sing.

I was reared in the South, and my father owned slaves, and I do not know when anything has so moved me as did the plaintive melodies of the Jubilee Singers. It was the first time for twenty-five or thirty years that I had heard such songs, or heard them sung in the genuine old way—and it is a way, I think, that white people cannot imitate—and never can, for that matter, for one must have been a slave himself in order to feel what that life was and so convey the pathos of it in the music. Do not fail to hear the Jubilee Singers. I am very well satisfied that you will not regret it. Yours faithfully, Saml. L. Clemens. Mark Twain. (SLC to Tom Hood and George Routledge and Sons, 10 March 1873, Hartford, reprinted in Pike, 14–15)

11. As a number of critics have noted, there are important links between speaking and singing voices in African-American culture. Henry Louis Gates Jr., for example, explains the decision to include a cassette tape with the *Norton Anthology of Afro-American Literature* as follows:

> Because of the strong oral and vernacular base of so very much of our literature, we included a cassette tape along with our anthology. . . . This means that each period section includes both the printed and spoken text of oral and musical selections of black vernacular culture: sermons, blues, spirituals, rhythm and blues,

> poets reading their own "dialect" poems, speeches—whatever! Imagine an anthology that includes Bessie Smith and Billie Holiday singing the blues, Langston Hughes reading "[I've] Known Rivers," Sterling Brown reading "Ma Rainey," James Weldon Johnson, "The Creation". . . . We will change fundamentally not only the way our literature is taught, but the way in which any literary tradition is even conceived. . . . In our anthology we wanted to incorporate performance and the black and human voice. ("The Master's Pieces" 30)

As Gates notes elsewhere, "the nature of black music is the nature of black speech, and vice versa" ("Dis and Dat" 176).

12. *Mark Twain's Autobiography,* ed. Albert Bigelow Paine, 1:112–13. Twain often told a story he had heard at that hearth, "The Golden Arm," when he gave lectures and readings. As his cousin Tabitha Quarles recalled, every night at the Quarles farm, where Twain spent his summer, the children would gather "around the fire place and [hear] the darkies tell their ghost stories. Sam just repeated those tales Uncle Dan'l and Uncle Ned told and folks said he was smart" (Anon., "Mark Twain's Cousin," 2). Twain's older brother Orion thought Twain may have confused Uncle Dan'l with Ned, one of the Clemenses' own slaves from Hannibal *(Mark Twain's Letters,* ed. Paine, 2:403 n.1). Tabitha Quarles's comment suggests that both men were important storytellers in Twain's youth.

13. SLC to Olivia L. Langdon, 15 and 16 December 1869, *Letters, vol. 3: 1869*, ed. Victor Fischer and Michael Frank, 426.

14. Photocopy of manuscript of Mark Twain, "A Family Sketch," 59, 61. Mark Twain Papers. Original in Mark Twain Collection, James S. Copley Library, La Jolla, Ca. Mark Twain's words that have been previously published only in Shelley Fisher Fishkin's *Was Huck Black? Mark Twain and African-American Voices* are quoted here and in the following two notes with the permission of Robert H. Hirst, General Editor of the Mark Twain Papers.

15. Typescript of Mark Twain's notebook 35, May–Oct. 1895, 8. Mark Twain Papers. Emphasis added.

16. The night Mary Ann Cord told her story on the porch steps at Quarry Farm made a deep impression on Olivia Clemens, as well, who referred to it in a letter to her husband which was acquired in March 1992 from the Chester Davis

estate by the Mark Twain Memorial, Hartford, Connecticut. I am grateful to Marianne Curling, Curator of the Mark Twain Memorial, for making the text of this letter available to me. Twain's full comment, with crossouts, in the 1895 journal, reads as follows: "but this is <direct> clear, compact & <vivid> coherent—yes, & vivid also, perfectly simple & unconscious." (Typescript of Mark Twain's notebook 35, May–Oct. 1895, 8. Mark Twain Papers.)

Mark Twain was exposed to African-American voices during his years as a steamboat pilot and journalist, as well as during his childhood. In *Life on the Mississippi,* for example, Twain recalled that "Negro firemen, deck-hands, and barbers" who worked on such "stately craft as the Alec Scott or the Grand Turk" were "distinguished personages in their grade of life, and they were well aware of that fact, too" (124). And as a journalist in San Francisco, Twain was friends with Phillip A. Bell, outspoken editor of the African-American newspaper, the San Francisco *Elevator* (Twain, *Early Tales and Sketches,* 2:247). (Bell's newspaper was committed to advocating "the largest political and civil liberty to all American citizens, irrespective of creed or color" (Phillip Bell, "Prospectus," 1). Upon his election to the post of Assistant Sergeant-at-Arms to the State of California in 1879, Bell was described by the *Alta California* as "a political, literary and social instructor of his race" (Anon., "Assistant," 1).

17. Sometime in 1892, Mark Twain found himself flummoxed about what to do with his current writing project. Then suddenly it became clear to him: the book he was writing "was not one story, but two stories tangled together." He wrote, "I pulled one of the stories out by the roots, and left the other one—a kind of literary Caesarean operation" *(Those Extraordinary Twins,* 119). Two books—*Pudd'nhead Wilson* and *Those Extraordinary Twins*—were the result.

Was Huck Black? Mark Twain and African-American Voices is also the result of "a kind of literary Caesarean operation." For several years I had been working on a book called *The Stories He Couldn't Tell: Mark Twain and Race* (forthcoming from Oxford), which explores Twain's attitudes toward race in the context of the racial discourse of his time. But in the spring of 1992, arguments that were forming in my mind about the genesis of *Huckleberry Finn* and about Mark Twain's response to African-American voices began to push themselves forward with unrelenting urgency. These ideas would wake me up at three in the morning. They would barge unannounced into my consciousness—at breakfast, in the library, in class. Despite my efforts to keep them "in perspective" (after all, my book was about Twain's entire career as a writer, and not just about *Huckleberry Finn*) they wouldn't subside. I began to write an essay on the subject, hoping to appease whatever force in my subconscious was responsible for those pesky three A.M. wake-up calls. It didn't work. The essay was soon well over a hundred pages long. Late one night a phrase came into my head uninvited, and refused to leave: "two stories in one" (*Those Extraordinary Twins,* 119). I decided that any solution good enough for Mark Twain was good enough for me.

The book with which I began, *The Stories He Couldn't Tell: Mark Twain and Race,* will address more ambitiously the cultural conversation that shaped Twain's writing on race and that his writing, in turn, helped shape. It will examine the controversies surrounding Twain's use of the word "nigger," and will chart the social history of efforts to ban *Huckleberry Finn* from secondary school classrooms in the 1950s and 1980s as "racist." It will explore Twain's attitudes toward various racial and ethnic "others" including African-Americans, Native Americans, Jews, and the Chinese. That study will have, I hope, time and space to examine the ways in which the ambiguities and ambivalences in Twain's work throughout his life reflect tensions inherent in his culture, and in our own, as well. By way of contrast, *Was Huck Black? Mark Twain and African-American Voices* explores in only very preliminary ways a context for understanding the attitudes toward race embodied in Twain's responses to African-American voices. However, because my argument here is so focused, specific, and coherent, I felt it could stand alone.

18. Thomas Jefferson, *Notes on Virginia,* 195. Houston Baker has observed,

> If blacks "entered" the English language with values and concepts antithetical to those of the white externality, surrounding them, then their vocabulary is less important than the underlying codes, or semantic fields, that governed meaning. What I am suggesting is the possibility that whites—moving exclusively within the boundaries of their own semantic categories—have taken the words of the black work of verbal art at face

> value, or worse, at a value assigned by their own limiting attitudes and patterns of judgment. (*The Journey Back*, 157)

Clearly, Jefferson's appraisal of African-American language use was the product of his "own limiting attitudes and patterns of judgment," and of his inability to grasp the "underlying codes, or semantic fields, that governed meaning" in the speech of African Americans.

19. George Philip Krapp, "The English of the Negro," 190. Eight years after Krapp issued this judgment George Pullen Jackson argued that African-American spirituals similarly had purely Anglo-American origins. In *White Spirituals in the Southern Uplands*, Jackson claimed that African Americans borrowed "both texts and tunes" from early white "revival hymns and other religious folksongs" (Richard Dorson, *American Folklore*, 179). As Dorson notes, throughout the 1930s, '40s, and '50s, "Southern white scholars maintained white cultural supremacy against the new generation of college-educated Negroes, who found support in the Africanist anthropologists of Northwestern University led by Melville J. Herskovits (*American Folklore*, 178–79). "The most sweeping turn of the argument," Dorson writes,

> appeared in 1953 under the imprint of the American Historical Association. *Negro Slave Songs in the United States*, by the Negro theological scholar, Miles Mark Fisher, relied on the 1867 volume of *Slave Songs* for its basic text, but bolstered its position with ample documentation from ante-bellum writings and post-bellum collections. Fisher contended that African slaves carried to the United States their cultural trait of using songs for historical records and for satirical purposes. (*American Folklore*, 179–80)

(For a useful summary of the debate over the origins and nature of African-American spirituals, see D. K. Wilgus, "The Negro-White Spiritual," 67–80.)

20. Dillard, *Black English*, 187. Dillard notes, "Payne, let it be pointed out, suggests several areas of influence which were not dealt with by Brooks, who limited himself to a highly

unsystematic approach to pronunciation matters" (*Black English,* 187). Dillard adds that

> The decisions that the Blacks were imitators of European immigrants and that the Europeans themselves brought "regional" varieties to the New World were made in dialectology before any appreciable part of the Black evidence was in. From these hastily formulated theories, it was deduced that investigation of Black populations would turn up no evidence contrary to the Eurocentric picture. Studies of Black language varieties were, therefore, not undertaken, except as Eurocentric or "white-washing" operations. ("General Introduction: Perspectives on Black English," 26)

See also Cleanth Brooks, "The English Language of the South." While claiming that he did not wish "to deny that the blacks influenced the language—through their intonation, through their own rhythms, through the development of striking metaphors, new word coinages and fresh idioms," Brooks reiterated a largely Anglicist position as late as 1985 in his book, *The Language of the American South* (12; 1–17).

21. For a useful summary of the Anglicist position, see Holton, *Down Home and Uptown,* 19–23. One of the key problems, as Lorenzo Turner noted, stemmed from the unfamiliarity of white dialect researchers with either African languages or Gullah. Given their ignorance, it is not surprising that "white American linguists refused to consider the possibility that blacks used African words in their vocabularies." The researchers would not have recognized them if they had encountered them (Asante 30).

22. *London Magazine,* 1746, quoted in A. W. Reed, "British Recognition of American Speech in the Eighteenth Century," *Dialect Notes* 6 (1933): 329, cited in John F. Szwed, "Race and the Embodiment of Culture," 26.

23. John Bennett, "Gullah: A Negro Patois," *South Atlantic Quarterly* 7 (October 1908): 339. Cited in Stewart, "Continuity and Change in American Negro Dialects," 237–38.

24. William Cabell Greet, "Southern Speech," 614. Ironically, black writers and critics coming from vastly different points on the political spectrum from Greet often expressed similar skepticism that anything of value was to be found in

Southern black vernacular culture. Wahneema Lubiano notes, for example, that Zora Neale Hurston was marginalized by black writers and critics

> because of her insistence on recreating and representing black southern dialect and folklore within her work. Hurston's focus on that language and folklore flew in the face of the prevailing wisdom. By the time she published *Their Eyes Were Watching God,* James Weldon Johnson had already delimited the use of dialect; at the same time, both politically conservative and Marxist critics were condemning the use of folklore materials as opportunistic and regressive—politically incorrect. For those critics the representation of folklore was a recourse to exploitation of the most oppressed segment of the black American group. Implicit and often explicit in their condemnation was an admission that there was nothing in black southern culture worth representing and that the people of that group existed only as objects of the most abject oppression. (444)

25. Dunn, "The Black-Southern White Dialect Controversy," 117. Not until work in the 1960s and 1970s by "Black Aestheticians," including Addison Gayle Jr., Stephen Henderson, Larry Neal, and Houston Baker, did the vernacular begin to come into its own among the critics. As Houston Baker has observed, "a Black Aesthetic generation was the first paradigmatic community to demonstrate the efficacy of the vernacular" ("Discovering America" 112). A "vernacular model," Baker notes, is "the analytical project that may serve as a paradigm for the future study of Afro-American literature and expressive culture" ("Discovering America," 112). Baker has continued to foreground the importance of African-American vernacular traditions (see *Blues, Ideology and Afro-American Literature: A Vernacular Theory*), as has Henry Louis Gates Jr., whose most recent statement on this point may be found in *Loose Canons: Notes on the Culture Wars,* 83.

26. Dunn, "The Black-Southern White Dialect Controversy," 117. This idea is echoed in an anecdote related by R. MacKaye Atwood, who reports a conversation that he had with a woman from Lynchburg, Virginia, about an incident during her childhood in the 1870s or 1880s:

> She had a younger brother, perhaps ten or so, who had as his chief playmate a black boy of his own age. One day the parents of the white lad called him in for a serious talk. They knew that soon he would have to end having him as his best friend, but more to the point was his speech. It was explained that he spoke just like his black friend, and they could not be told apart. He would have to find a more suitable companion. The boy objected, asserting, "It don't matter how I talks, everybody knows who ah is." The parents remained unmoved. (R. MacKaye Atwood, personal communication)

Ernest F. Dunn observes that whites' desire to be rid of the stigma of black speech "was intensified following the so-called Emancipation."

> Scholars like Dillard (1972) rightly pointed out that the movement of the Black into a freer environment placed him in competition with the working-class White who was forced to fall back upon his "Whiteness" as his only claim to superiority. To such people the tracing of any of their language or behavior patterns to the Negro was the bitterest of insults. (Dunn 116–17)

Former aristocrats whose positions were similarly reduced after the war also shunned the idea that anything in their own speech could have black roots. Their position was supported by the work of scholars like Krapp (1924) and Kurath (1928), who mounted Herculean efforts to deny any evidence of black influence on Southern white speech (Dunn, "The Black-Southern White Dialect Controversy," 117).

27. David E. E. Sloane, "*Adventures of Huckleberry Finn*": *American Comic Vision*, 5. See Jonathan Arac's "Nationalism, Hypercanonization, and *Huckleberry Finn*," for some interesting reflections on what Arac calls the "hypercanonicity" of this novel.

28. Robert M. Rodney, ed., *Mark Twain International: A Bibliography and Interpretation of His Worldwide Popularity*, 264. *Huckleberry Finn* has been translated into German, Dutch, French, Danish, Italian, Portuguese, Spanish, Swedish,

Albanian, Bulgarian, Czech, Bohemian, Slovak, Greek, Hungarian, Polish, Rumanian, Serbian, Serbo-Croatian, Slovenian, Macedonian, Russian, Ukrainian, Lettish, Tatar, Moldavian, Georgian, Lithuanian, Azerbaidjan, Turkmen, Uzbek, Kazakh, Kirgiz, Karelo-Finnish, Farsi, Hebrew, Turkish, Arabic, Afrikaans, Singhalese, Bengali, Gujarati, Telugu, Marathi, Tamil, Malayalam, Hindi, Assamese, Indonesian, Thai, Chinese, and Japanese. See Rodney, ed., *Mark Twain International: A Bibliography and Interpretation of His Worldwide Popularity*, 45–462, for the most complete listing of foreign editions.

29. Part of this neglect may have been related to the widespread assumption, as Walter J. Ong has put it in *Orality and Literacy*, that "oral art forms were essentially unskillful and not worth serious study" (10). Interestingly, in his effort to devise an alternative for the oxymoronic term "oral literature," Ong suggests that "we might refer to all purely oral art as 'epos,' which has the same Proto-Indian European root, *wekw-*, as the Latin word *vox* and its English equivalent 'voice,' and thus is grounded firmly in the vocal, the oral. Oral performances would thus be felt as 'voicings,' which is what they are" (13–14). My emphasis on voices that shaped Twain's imagination, and on the voice of Huck Finn, stems from a similar desire to explore, in complex, nuanced ways, some of the links between oral and literate experiences.

30. In fact, I did not begin to conceptualize the argument I lay out here until some four months after our interview.

31. A plaster bust of Twain was given to every guest at his seventieth birthday party at Delmonico's in New York City on 5 December 1905. Chesnutt was a guest at that dinner. Chesnutt's daughter notes that "the bust of Mark Twain was put in the library [in Chesnutt's home] in a place of honor" (Helen M. Chesnutt, 214).

32. Ellison drew my attention to the picture, which was displayed on the bookshelf next to his desk, during our interview. The photo, which was a gift to Ellison from a student, showed Twain at Oxford in the gown in which he received an honorary degree.

33. Ralph Ellison, *Invisible Man*, 55. I read this passage from *Invisible Man* out loud during the interview. Ellison immediately responded by acknowledging the likelihood that he had been unconsciously influenced by Twain.

34. See also Stewart Rodnon's "*The Adventures of Huckleberry Finn* and *Invisible Man:* Thematic and Structural Comparisons," for an interesting consideration of similarities between the two novels' use of language, folklore, humor, and point-of-view.

Houston Baker's controversial discussion of Trueblood as a paradigmatic figure of the African-American artist lends added significance to the potential links between Trueblood and Huck. See Baker, "To Move Without Moving: Creativity and Commerce in Ralph Ellison's Trueblood Episode," 221–48.

35. I am grateful to James A. Miller for raising this interesting point (personal communication).

36. The essay first appeared in the *Mark Twain Journal* in 1984 and is included in *Satire or Evasion? Black Perspectives on "Huckleberry Finn"* (1991).

37. Rampersad, "*Adventures of Huckleberry Finn* and Afro-American Literature," 218.

Richard Yarborough suggests that Albert Murray's *Train Whistle Guitar,* which is narrated in the first person from the point of view of a boy, may also have been influenced by *Huckleberry Finn* (personal communication).

38. Interestingly, the trope of the "talking book" had a central role in African-American culture long before Twain wrote (Gates Jr., *Signifying Monkey,* 127–216).

39. Richard Wright, quoted in Michel Fabre, *Richard Wright: Books and Writers,* 161. I am indebted to Werner Sollors for having brought his comment to my attention.

40. It is a subject I will explore in *The Stories He Couldn't Tell: Mark Twain and Race.*

41. Langston Hughes, "The Negro Speaks of Rivers," 1488. Arnold Rampersad's description of the occasion when Hughes wrote this poem lends support to the idea that it was the Mississippi above all other rivers that inspired "The Negro Speaks of Rivers":

> The sun was setting as the train reached St. Louis and began the long passage from Illinois across the Mississippi and into Missouri, where Hughes had been born. The beauty of the hour and the setting—the great muddy river glinting in the sun, the banked and tinted summer clouds, the rush of the train toward the dark, all touched an adolescent sensibility tender after the gloomy day. The sense of beauty and death, of hope

> and despair, fused in his imagination. A phrase came to him, then a sentence. Drawing an envelope from his pocket, he began to scribble. In a few minutes Langston had finished a poem: "I've known rivers" (*Life, Volume I*, 39)

Intriguing in this context, as well, is a poem Daniel Hoffman published in 1984 in the *New Yorker* entitled "Mark Twain, 1909," which reads, in part, as follows: ". . . Behind him, / in the bookcase, only one / title in focus, thick book: / "THE NILE" Always rivers, / rivers, the mind afloat on / currents, eddies . . . Memory / the raft that bears us onward. . ." (48).

42. Charles T. Davis, "Black Literature and the Critics," 51. In a similar vein, Henry Louis Gates Jr. has noted,

> In the case of the writer of African descent, his or her texts occupy spaces in at least two traditions: a European or American literary tradition, and one of the several but related distinct black traditions. The "heritage" of each black text written in a Western language is, then, a double heritage, two-toned, as it were. Its visual tones are white and black, and its aural tones are standard and vernacular. (Gates Jr., "Criticism in the Jungle," 4)

43. Eric Sundquist observes

> Neither the tradition of classic American literature nor that of Afro-American literature adequately defines the problem of race; like the larger social history that they reflect, the two traditions must be read together for their interactions and conflicts, their revisions of one another. Most of all, they must be read with careful attention to the historical contexts whose pressures have in every case formed them, with or against their will, and often by placing them in a web of reference that simple attention to the text will not uncover. ("Faulkner" 3)

44. The principal exceptions are William Andrews, David Bradley, Charles T. Davis, Henry Louis Gates Jr., Ralph Ellison, Lucinda MacKethan, Arnold Rampersad, Werner Sollors, and Eric Sundquist.

45. Werner Sollors, "A Critique of Pure Pluralism," 257. Sollors continues,

> Can Gertrude Stein be discussed with Richard Wright or only with white women expatriate German-Jewish writers? . . . In general, is the question of influence, or who came first, more interesting than investigation of the constellation in which ideas, styles, themes and forms travel? (257)

46. David Bradley, personal communication, 29 May 1992. Bradley bemoaned the fact that the critics "won't let me have my models." Presumably, he was referring to comments such as that of Charles Johnson: "Bradley has said, in his 1984 interview in *Callaloo,* that *The Chaneysville Incident,* winner of the 1982 *PEN/Faulkner Award,* is largely influenced by the writing of Robert Penn Warren, a statement that reveals more of his tendency toward self-mockery than this fascinating book, a historical novel about the historical imagination itself" (79).

47. Tillie Olsen confirmed her debt to Du Bois in December 1987, after hearing an MLA paper on "Creative Experimentation in American Nonfiction Narrative," in which I hypothesized the connection (personal communication). She reiterated the importance of this connection in a conversation on 28 December 1991. See also Shelley Fisher Fishkin, "The Borderlands of Culture: Writing by W. E. B. Du Bois, James Agee, Tillie Olsen and Gloria Anzaldúa."

As Henry Louis Gates Jr. has observed,

> [T]he most formally complex and compelling black writers—such as Jean Toomer, Sterling Brown, Langston Hughes, Zora Hurston, Richard Wright, Ralph Ellison, James Baldwin, Toni Morrison and Gwendolyn Brooks—have always blended forms of Western literature with African-American vernacular and written traditions. Then again, even a vernacular form like the spirituals took as its texts the King James version of the Old and New Testaments. . . . African-American culture, then, has been a model of multiculturalism and plurality. (*Loose Canons,* xvii)

See also Phillip M. Richards, "Phillis Wheatley and Literary Americanization."

48. *Chicago Tribune* columnist Clarence Page, for example, is a writer for whom Twain's craftsmanship (in *Huckleberry Finn*) served as a compelling example: "it was inspiring for me as a future wordsmith to see how effectively the power of words could be used to grab and persuade a reader to see a powerful point. It was inspiring enough for me to read other great American authors who were inspired by Twain. They include such great African-American authors as James Baldwin and Ralph Ellison" (7B).

49. In 1956 William Faulkner claimed Twain as a literary grandfather. What he actually said was: "[Sherwood Anderson] was the father of my generation of American writers and the tradition which our successors will carry on. . . . Dreiser is his older brother and Mark Twain the father of them both" (Faulkner, Stein interview, 46–47). Elsewhere he said, "In my opinion Mark Twain was the first truly American writer, and all of us since are his heirs, we descended from him" (quoted in Jelliffe 88).

50. Zoe Ingalls wrote in the *Chronicle of Higher Education*,

> Stephen Foster might seem out of place at the prestigious St. Petersburg International Choir Festival, which acts as host to Europe's finest professional choirs. You'd expect Handel, perhaps, or Bach. But for William A. Wyman, director of the Nebraska Wesleyan University choir, the choice of "Camptown Races" for his group's concert is a canny assessment of what Europeans like to hear when Americans perform. "A foreign audience wants to hear the things that are uniquely American," he says. It's an assessment based on experience: During his 18-year stint as director, Mr. Wyman has led the choir on concert tours of Europe and the Orient. (B6)

51. June Jordan, "For the Sake of a People's Poetry: Walt Whitman and the Rest of Us." Other examples within and outside the borders of the United States abound. For instance, African-American poet Robert Hayden was heavily influenced by Stephen Benet's poem, "John Brown's Body" (Charles T.

Davis 521). And an entire tradition of Czech poetry was inspired by African-American jazz (Josef Jarab).

52. Henry Louis Gates Jr., "'Authenticity,' or the Lesson of Little Tree." Eric Sundquist's erudite and impressive book, *To Wake the Nations: Race in American Literature and Culture, 1830–1930,* will be published this year by Harvard University Press. Werner Sollors has been working for some time on a massive study of miscegenation in Western literature; Carla Peterson is completing a book on nineteenth-century African-American women writers; Arnold Rampersad is writing a book on race and American authors. Books by David Smith on "Racial Writing, Black and White," and by Michael North on "Race, Dialect, and the Emergence of Modernism," promise to be of great interest as well. Also useful for reframing our understanding of issues of race and American culture are Aldon Lynn Nielson's 1988 study of twentieth-century white American poets and racial discourse, and Dana Nelson's 1992 book on race in early American literature. Our understanding of "cultural syncretism" is also furthered by such works as Gloria Anzaldúa's landmark book *Borderlands/La Frontera,* with its eloquent exploration of "mestiza consciousness" and "cultural mestisaje." [Ed. note: This essay was initially published in 1993 during an explosion of intercultural studies which continues today.]

American Studies Association President Cathy Davidson's comment in a recent ASA newsletter reflects the change in paradigm that is increasingly shaping the discipline:

> Multicultural representation? Gender equity? Diversity? Forget it! Just give me *good* history (whether social or literary history), a far more dangerous proposition. The investment in some kind of sanitizing, homogenizing, consensual "we" . . . may be tenable as a politician's polemic but it has weakened American Studies as a field and shut off important and fascinating areas of discussion. The Norse, probably the Chinese, and even an Italian sent by Spain to India all "discovered" a continent inhabited by various American cultures long before the Puritans made their way to these shores. Slaves and immigrants built much of the country, a country that extends far beyond New England. Roughly half of the population has always

> been female, not all of it was ever heterosexual, and relatively little of it (any gender, racial or immigrant group) has been rich. With a history like this, who needs affirmative action? (2)

53. The notion that white writers are the descendants of other white writers is a familiar theme, one which is central to what Henry Louis Gates Jr. has called "'the antebellum aesthetic position,' when men were men, and men were white, when scholar-critics were white men, and when women and persons of color were voiceless, faceless servants and laborers, pouring tea and filling brandy snifters in the boardrooms of old boys' clubs" (*Loose Canons,* 17). As Paul Lauter put it in *Canons and Contexts,*

> Consider, as an example of faulty literary history, what was until the mid-1970s the usual portrait of the evolution of fiction in North America (a portrait that still shapes curricular choices). Writers such as Charles Brockden Brown, Washington Irving, and James Fenimore Cooper, it was said, were forerunners who cleared and plowed the colonial cultural wilderness so that, in the "American Renaissance," the first generation of major writers—Poe, Hawthorne, Melville—could flourish. These were succeeded by three generations of fiction writers: Twain and James, who elaborated alternative westward-looking and eastward-looking subjects and styles; realists and naturalists like Howells, Crane, and Dreiser; and finally, in the 1920s, a new, modernist renaissance exemplified by the work of Hemingway, Fitzgerald, Dos Passos, Faulkner, and a host of others. (54)

These "older accounts of American fictional history," Lauter continued, "left us asking 'where were the blacks?'" (55).

By the same token, standard accounts of African-American literary history emphasize the all-black literary genealogies of African-American writers, often to the frustration of those writers themselves. Ralph Ellison notes, for example, that the role of James Weldon Johnson (author of *Autobiography of an Ex-Colored Man*) as one of Ellison's literary forebears was much less important than critics seem willing to accept (Fishkin interview). And David Bradley complains that critics refuse to accept the idea that white writers played a key role in shaping his art (personal communication, 29 May 1992).

54. David Bradley, "Foreword," vii. "Literary segregation," like all American segregation,

> was originally supported by perfectly legitimate nineteenth-century beliefs. . . . Indeed, one must insist that early literary segregation came about quite naturally, as an expression of what was then the American reality. One can hardly condemn the New Critics for not mingling colored and white poets in the same essay in 1941 when President Roosevelt would not "mingle colored and white enlisted personnel in the same regiment" in 1944. . . . Beginning in 1948, when President Truman issued Executive Orders 9980 and 9981, ending segregation in the federal service and the armed forces, the segregation of literature began to lose the support of the social context. By 1953, when the Supreme Court struck down the separate-but-equal doctrine in *Brown v. Board of Education*, the legal basis was lost. Soon the scientific basis too was gone; in 1958 Ralph Ellison could write sarcastically, "I know of no valid demonstration that culture is transmitted through the genes." ("Foreword," xviii)

Elsewhere Bradley has noted the impact of this segregation in American college classrooms, observing that in 1980–81, the *Bulletin* of the University of Pennsylvania advertised

> a course in "American" fiction that explicitly includes "Hawthorne, Clemens, James, Wharton, Hemingway, Fitzgerald, and Faulkner," and implicitly excludes Chesnutt, Hurston, Richard Wright and Ralph Ellison; a course in "American" poetry including "Whitman, Dickinson, Frost, Pound, Eliot, Stevens, Williams, Moore, Lowell, Roethke, and Plath," and apparently not including Dunbar, Hughes, Toomer, Gwendolyn Brooks or Sterling Brown. ("Black and American, 1982" 408)
>
> An elaborate survey of forty college and university literature departments conducted by Alan Wald

between 1986 and 1988 suggests that the pattern Bradley noted in the *Bulletin* of the University of Pennsylvania persists in American college classrooms. Wald found that "students across the country who enroll in courses called "The Modern Novel" or "Modern Poetry" will read and discuss works almost exclusively by elite white men that are interpreted through the prism of the British tradition" (Katterman 14) "The result," Wald said, "is an approach to literature that fails to indicate, and actually distorts, the rich cultural activity that has existed and still exists in the United States" (14).

William Andrews clearly summarizes the segregated nature of one branch of critical writing in his excellent 1990 essay, "Mark Twain, William Wells Brown, and the Problem of Authority in New South Writing": "Until the late 1960s," Andrews notes,

> the history and criticism of southern literature in America proceeded from the unwritten assumption that the literature of the South was the product of white, predominantly male southerners. Black writers from the South belonged to a separate province of letters that was reconstructed into Negro American literature mainly by the literary historians and critics who taught in black colleges of the South. Owing to the enormous influence of his myth and his message on both sides of the color line, Booker T. Washington was one of the few black writers who held a secure niche in both southern and Negro literature before the onset of the civil rights movement in the late 1950s. Charles W. Chesnutt, a figure of the first importance to students of Negro literature, footnoted Joel Chandler Harris in standard accounts of southern literature. In Faulkner's shadow lurked Richard Wright, but Wright's perspective on the South was judged parochial next to Faulkner's much-vaunted universality. White southern criticism chose Faulkner more than any other single writer to explain southern race relations to the world. Black critics accepted Richard Wright as a brave new spokesman for their side of the controversial issue. But until very

> recently virtually no published discourse ensued between the two literary camps. (1)

Andrews adds, in a footnote, that "A sign of a much-welcome change is Craig Werner's 'Tell Old Pharaoh: The Afro-American Response to Faulkner,' *Southern Review* 19 (Autumn 1983): 711–35" (18). For a useful overview of white critics' dismissive attitudes toward African-American writers, see Houston Baker's "Black Creativity and American Attitudes" in *The Journey Back* (144–54).

55. There is neither time nor space to give these important questions their due here, in part because of the complexity of Mark Twain's attitudes toward race, and in part because the jury is still out on the subject of Americans' reactions to the research at hand. I will explore these issues more fully in my next book. See note 17.

56. Henry Louis Gates Jr., "Introduction: Writing 'Race' and the Difference It Makes," 5. "Race," as Gates has observed,

> is the ultimate trope of difference because it is so very arbitrary in its application. The biological criteria used to determine "difference" in sex simply do not hold when applied to "race." Yet we carelessly use language in such a way as to *will* this sense *of natural* difference into our formulations. To do so is to engage in a pernicious act of language, one which exacerbates the complex problem of cultural or ethnic difference, rather than to assuage or redress it. This is especially the case at a time when, once again, racism has become fashionable. ("Writing 'Race,'" 5)

Works Cited

Abrahams, Roger D., and John Szwed. "Introduction." *After Africa: Extracts from British Travel Accounts and Journals of the Seventeenth, Eighteenth, and Nineteenth Centuries Concerning the Slaves, Their Manners, and Customs in the British West Indies.* New Haven: Yale University Press, 1983.

Alter, Robert. *Rogue's Progress: Study in the Picaresque Novel.* Cambridge: Harvard University Press, 1964.

Andrews, William L. "Mark Twain and James W. C. Pennington: Huckleberry Finn's Smallpox Lie." *Studies in American Fiction* 9 (Spring 1981): 103–12.

———. "Mark Twain, William Wells Brown, and the Problem of Authority in New South Writing." *Southern Literature and Literary Theory.* Ed. Jefferson Humphries. Athens: University of Georgia Press, 1990.

Anon. "Assistant Sergeant-at-Arms to the State of California." *Alta California,* 4 December 1879, 1.

Anon. "Coming Events." *Fun* (London), 26 April 1873, 172.

Anzaldúa, Gloria. *Borderlands/La Frontera: The New Mestiza.* San Francisco: Spinsters/Aunt Lute, 1987.

Arac, Jonathan. "Nationalism, Hypercanonization, and *Huckleberry Finn.*" "New Americanists 2." Ed. Donald Pease. *boundary 2* (19:1) (Special issue, Spring 1992): 14–33.

Armon, Dahlia, and Walter Blair. "Biographical Directory." *Huck Finn and Tom Sawyer Among the Indians and Other Unfinished Stories,* by Mark Twain. Foreword and Notes by Dahlia Armon and Walter Blair. The Mark Twain Library. Berkeley: University of California Press, 1989.

Asante, Molefi Kete. "African Elements in African-American English." *Africanisms in American Culture.* Ed. Joseph E. Holloway. Bloomington: Indiana University Press, 1990.

Atwood, R. Mackaye. Personal communication, 17 July 1992.

Baker, Houston A., Jr. *Blues, Ideology, and Afro-American Literature: A Vernacular Theory.* 1984. Chicago: University of Chicago Press, 1987.

———. "Discovering America: Generational Shifts, Afro-American Literary Criticism, and the Study of Expressive Culture." *Blues, Ideology and Afro-American Literature,* by Houston A. Baker Jr. 1984. Chicago: University of Chicago Press, 1987.

———. *The Journey Back: Issues in Black Literature and Criticism.* Chicago: University of Chicago Press, 1980.
———. "To Move Without Moving: Creativity and Commerce in Ralph Ellison's Trueblood Episode." *Black Literature and Literary Theory.* Ed. Henry Louis Gates Jr. New York: Methuen, 1984.
Barrow, David. "Mark Twain and the Oral Economy: Digression in the Age of Print." Ph.D. diss. Duke University, 1991.
Bell, Bernard W. "Twain's 'Nigger' Jim: The Tragic Face Behind the Minstrel Mask." *Satire or Evasion? Black Perspectives on "Huckleberry Finn,"* Ed. James S. Leonard, Thomas A. Tenney, and Thadious M. Davis. Durham, N.C.: Duke University Press, 1992.
Bell, P[hillip]. A "Prospectus: *The Elevator,* a Weekly Journal." San Francisco *Elevator,* 5 May 1865, 1.
Bennett, John. "Gullah: A Negro Patois." *The South Atlantic Quarterly* 7 (1908): 332–47.
Blackburn, Alexander. *The Myth of the Picaro: Continuity and Transformation of the Picaresque Novel, 1554–1954.* Chapel Hill: University of North Carolina Press, 1979.
Blair, Walter. *Mark Twain & "Huck Finn."* Berkeley: University of California Press, 1960.
Boland, Sally. "The Seven Dialects in *Huckleberry Finn." North Dakota Quarterly* 36 (Summer 1968): 30–40.
Bradley, David. "Black and American, 1982." *Esquire,* May 1982. Reprinted in Vesterman, William, ed., *Essays for the '80s.* New York: Random House, 1987.
———. *The Chaneysville Incident.* 1981. New York: Harper and Row. Perennial Library Edition, 1990.
———. "The First 'Nigger' Novel." Speech to Annual Meeting of the Mark Twain Memorial and the New England American Studies Association, Hartford, Connecticut, 1985.
———. "Foreword." *A Different Drummer,* by William Melvin Kelley. New York: Anchor-Doubleday, 1989.
———. Personal communication, 29 May 1992.
Branch, Edgar Marquess. *The Literary Apprenticeship of Mark Twain.* Urbana: University of Illinois Press, 1950.
———. "Mark Twain: Newspaper Reading and the Writer's Creativity." *Nineteenth-Century Fiction* 37:3 (1983): 576–603.
Bridgman, Richard. *The Colloquial Style in America.* New York: Oxford University Press, 1966.

Brooks, Cleanth. "The English Language of the South." *A Various Language: Perspectives on American Dialects.* Ed. Juanita V. Williamson and Virginia M. Burke. New York: Holt, Rinehart and Winston, 1971.

———. *The Language of the American South.* Mercer University Lamar Memorial Lectures, No. 28. Athens: University of Georgia Press, 1985.

Brown, Sterling A. *The Negro in American Fiction.* 1935. Port Washington, N.Y.: Kennikat Press, Inc., 1937.

Budd, Louis J. *Mark Twain: Social Philosopher.* Bloomington: Indiana University Press, 1962.

———. "The Recomposition of *Adventures of Huckleberry Finn.*" *Missouri Review* 10 (1987): 113–29. Reprinted in Laurie Champion, ed., *The Critical Response to Mark Twain's "Huckleberry Finn."* Westport, Conn.: Greenwood Press, 1991.

Cable, George Washington. *The Silent South; Together with The Freedman's Case in Equity and The Convict Lease System.* New ed. New York: Charles Scribner's Sons, 1907.

Cardwell, Guy. *The Man Who Was Mark Twain: Images and Ideologies.* New Haven: Yale University Press, 1991.

Carkeet, David. "The Dialects in *Huckleberry Finn.*" *American Literature* 51 (November 1979): 315–32.

Cash, W. J. *The Mind of the South.* New York: Alfred A. Knopf, 1941.

Chesnutt, Helen M. *Charles Waddell Chesnutt: Pioneer of the Color Line.* Chapel Hill: University of North Carolina Press, 1952.

Covici, Pascal, Jr. *Mark Twain's Humor: The Image of a World.* Dallas: Southern Methodist University Press, 1962.

Cox, James M. *Mark Twain: The Fate of Humor.* Princeton: Princeton University Press, 1966.

Cummings, Sherwood. "Mark Twain's Moveable Farm and the Evasion." *American Literature* 63:3 (1991): 440–58.

Davidson, Cathy. "Statement." *American Studies Association Newsletter* 15:1 (February 1992): 2.

Davis, Charles T. "Black Literature and the Critic." 1973. *Black Is the Color of the Cosmos: Essays on Afro-American Literature and Culture, 1942–1981,* by Charles T. Davis. Ed. Henry Louis Gates Jr. Foreword by A. Bartlett Giamatti. New York: Garland, 1982.

Davis, John A. "The Influence of Africans on American Culture." *Annals of the American Academy of Political Science* 354 (July 1964): 75–83.

Davis, Thadious M. "Foreword." "Black Writers on *Adventures of Huckleberry Finn* One Hundred Years Later." *Mark Twain Journal* 22:2 (1984): 2–3.

Dillard, J. L. *Black English: Its History and Usage in the United States.* 1972. New York: Vintage-Random, 1973.

Dorson, Richard M. *American Folklore.* Chicago: University of Chicago Press, 1959.

Dunn, Ernest F. "The Black-Southern White Dialect Controversy: Who Did What to Whom?" *Black English: A Seminar.* Ed. Deborah Sears Harrison and Tom Trabasso. Hillsdale, N.J.: Lawrence Erlbaum Associates, 1976.

Ellison, Ralph. "Change the Joke and Slip the Yoke." *Partisan Review* 25 (Spring 1958): 212–22. Reprinted in Ralph Ellison, *Shadow and Act.* New York: Random House, 1953.

———. "Going to the Territory." *Going to the Territory,* by Ralph Ellison. New York: Random House, 1987.

———. Interview with Shelley Fisher Fishkin, 16 July 1991, New York City.

———. *Invisible Man.* 1952. New York: Random-Vintage 1989.

———. "On Initiation Rites and Power: Ralph Ellison Speaks at West Point." *Contemporary Literature,* Spring 1974. Reprinted in Ralph Ellison, *Going to the Territory.* New York: Random House, 1987.

———. "Twentieth-Century Fiction and the Black Mask of Humanity." *Shadow and Act,* by Ralph Ellison. New York: Random House, 1953.

———. "What America Would Be Like Without Blacks." *Time,* 6 April 1970. Reprinted in Ralph Ellison, *Going to the Territory.* New York: Random House, 1987.

Fabre, Michel. *Richard Wright: Books and Writers.* Jackson: University Press of Mississippi, 1990.

Fiedler, Leslie A. "Come Back to the Raft Ag'in, Huck Honey." *Partisan Review* 15 (June 1948): 664–71. Reprinted in M. Thomas Inge, ed., *Huck Finn Among the Critics.* Frederick, Md.: University Publications of America, 1985.

Fisher, Miles Mark. *Negro Slave Songs in the United States.* Ithaca, N.Y.: Cornell University Press, 1953.

Fishkin, Shelley Fisher. "The Borderlands of Culture: Writing by W. E. B. Du Bois, James Agee, Tillie Olsen and Gloria

Anzaldúa." *Literary Journalism in the Twentieth Century*. Ed. Norman Sims. New York: Oxford University Press, 1990.
———. "Interview with Maxine Hong Kingston." *American Literary History* (Winter 1991): 782–91.
———. Interview with Ralph Ellison, 16 July 1991 (unpublished).
———. "Mark Twain." *From Fact to Fiction: Journalism and Imaginative Writing in America*, by Shelley Fisher Fishkin. 1985. New York: Oxford University Press, 1988.
———. "Racial Attitudes." *The Mark Twain Encyclopedia.* Ed. J. R. LeMaster and James D. Wilson. New York: Garland, 1993.
Foner, Philip. *Mark Twain: Social Critic.* 1958. Reprint. New York: International Publishers, 1969.
Gates, Henry Louis, Jr. "'Authenticity,' or the Lesson of Little Tree." *New York Times Book Review*, 24 November 1991, section 7, 1 (lexus).
———. "Criticism in the Jungle." *Black Literature and Literary Theory*. Ed. Henry Louis Gates Jr. New York: Methuen, 1984.
———. "Dis and Dat: Dialect and Descent." *Figures in Black: Words, Signs, and the "Racial" Self*, by Henry Louis Gates Jr. New York: Oxford University Press, 1987.
———. "Introduction: Writing 'Race' and the Difference It Makes." 1985. *'Race,' Writing, and Difference.* Ed. Henry Louis Gates Jr. Chicago: University of Chicago Press, 1986.
———. *Loose Canons: Notes on the Culture War.* New York: Oxford University Press, 1992.
———. "The Master's Pieces: On Canon Formation and Afro-American Tradition." *The Bounds of Race: Perspectives on Hegemony and Resistance*. Ed. Dominick LaCapra. Ithaca, N.Y.: Cornell University Press, 1991.
———. *The Signifying Monkey: A Theory of Afro-American Literary Criticism.* New York: Oxford University Press, 1988.
Greet, W. Cabell. "Southern Speech." *Culture in the South.* Ed. W. T. Couch. Chapel Hill: University of North Carolina Press, 1935.
Gribben, Alan. "'I Did Wish Tom Sawyer Was There': Boy-Book Elements in *Tom Sawyer* and *Huckleberry Finn*." *One Hundred Years of "Huckleberry Finn."* Ed. Robert Sattelmeyer and J. Donald Crowley. Columbia: University of Missouri Press, 1985.

Harris, Trudier. *Fiction and Folklore: The Novels of Toni Morrison.* Knoxville: University of Tennessee Press, 1991.

Harter, Hugh A. "Mark Twain y la tradicion picaresca." *La Picaresca: origenes, textos y estructuras.* Ed. Manuel Criade de Val. Madrid: Fundacion Universitaria Española, 1979.

Hemingway, Ernest. *Green Hills of Africa.* New York: Charles Scribner's Sons, 1935.

Herskovits, Melville J. "What Has Africa Given America?" *The New Republic* 74:1083 (4 September 1935): 92–94.

Hoffman, Daniel G. "Black Magic—and White—in *Huckleberry Finn.*" *Form and Fable in American Fiction,* by Daniel G. Hoffman. New York: Oxford University Press, 1961.

Holton, Sylvia Wallace. *Down Home and Uptown: The Representation of Black Speech in American Fiction.* Rutherford, N.J.: Fairleigh Dickinson University Press, 1984.

Howe, Lawrence. "Transcending the Limits of Experience: Mark Twain's *Life on the Mississippi.*" *American Literature* 63:3 (September 1991): 420–39.

Howells, William Dean. *My Mark Twain.* New York: Harper and Brothers, 1910.

Hughes, John B. "*Lazarillo de Tormes* y *Huckleberry Finn.*" *La Picaresca: origenes, textas y estructuras.* Ed. Manuel Criade de Val. Madrid: Fundacion Universitaria Española, 1979.

Hughes, Langston. "Introduction." *Pudd'nhead Wilson,* by Mark Twain. New York: Bantam Books, 1959.

———. "The Negro Speaks of Rivers." 1921. *The Heath Anthology of American Literature.* Vol. 2. Ed. Paul Lauter. Lexington, Mass.: D.C. Heath and Co., 1990.

Ingalls, Zoe. "A Choir Festival in St. Petersburg." *Chronicle of Higher Education* 38:37 (20 May 1992): B6.

Inge, M. Thomas, ed. *The Frontier Humorists: Critical Views.* Hamden, Conn.: Archon Books-The Shoestring Press, 1975.

Jackson, George Pullen. *White Spirituals in the Southern Uplands: The Story of the Fasola Folk, Their Songs, Singings, and "Buckwheat Notes."* Chapel Hill: University of North Carolina Press, 1933.

Jarab, Josef. "Black Stars, Red Star, and the Blues." Paper presented at the European Association for American Studies Conference, Seville, Spain, 6 April 1992. *Defining Moments in African-American Literature and History.* Ed. Werner Sollors and Maria Diedrich, forthcoming.

Jefferson, Thomas. *Notes on Virginia.* The Writings of Thomas Jefferson. Definitive ed. Vol. 1. Ed. Albert Ellery Bergh. Washington: Thomas Jefferson Memorial Association, 1907.

Jelliffe, Robert A., ed. *Faulkner at Nagano.* Tokyo: Kenkyusha Ltd., 1956.

Johnson, Charles. *Being and Race: Black Writing Since 1970.* Bloomington: Indiana University Press, 1988.

Johnson, H. P. "Who Lost the Southern R?" *American Speech* 3:4 (April 1928): 377–83.

Jones, Betty H. "Huck and Jim: A Reconsideration." *Satire or Evasion? Black Perspectives on "Huckleberry Finn."* Ed. James S. Leonard, Thomas A. Tenney, and Thadious M. Davis. Durham, N.C.: Duke University Press, 1992.

Jones, Rhett S. "Nigger and Knowledge: White Double-Consciousness in *Adventures of Huckleberry Finn.*" *Satire or Evasion? Black Perspectives on "Huckleberry Finn."* Ed. James S. Leonard, Thomas A. Tenney, and Thadious M. Davis. Durham, N.C.: Duke University Press, 1992.

Jordan, June. "For the Sake of a People's Poetry: Walt Whitman and the Rest of Us." *Walt Whitman: The Measure of His Song.* Ed. Jim Perlman, Ed Folsom, and Dam Campion. Minneapolis: Holy Cow! Press, 1981.

Kaplan, Justin. *Mr. Clemens and Mark Twain.* New York: Simon and Schuster, 1966.

Katterman, Lee. "In Search of an 'American' Literature: UM [University of Michigan] Scholar Argues That Emphasis on the British Tradition Creates Damaging Myths." *Research News* (University of Michigan) 41:1–2 (January-February 1990), 14–15.

Kingston, Maxine Hong. *The Woman Warrior: Memoirs of a Girlhood Among Ghosts.* New York: Alfred A. Knopf, 1976.

Krapp, George Philip. "The English of the Negro." *American Mercury* 2:5 (June 1924): 190–95.

Lauter, Paul. *Canons and Contexts.* New York: Oxford University Press, 1991.

Lawton, Mary. *A Lifetime with Mark Twain: The Memories of Katy Leary, for Thirty Years His Faithful and Devoted Servant.* New York: Harcourt, Brace and Co., 1925.

Leon, Eli. *Models in the Mind: African Prototypes in American Patchwork* (Exhibition Catalog). Winston-Salem, N.C.: The Diggs Gallery and Winston-Salem State University, 1992.

Leonard, James S., Thomas A. Tenney, and Thadious M. Davis, *Satire or Evasion? Black Perspectives on "Huckleberry Finn."* Durham, N.C.: Duke University Press, 1992.

Locke, Alain. "The Negro Spirituals." *The New Negro*. Ed. Alain Locke. 1925. Introduction by Arnold Rampersad. New York: Atheneum, 1992.

Logan, Rayford W. *The Betrayal of the Negro from Rutherford B. Hayes to Woodrow Wilson* [originally published as *The Negro in American Life and Thought: The Nadir, 1877–1907*]. London: Collier-Macmillan, 1965.

Lubiano, Wahneema. "Constructing and Reconstructing Afro-American Texts: The Critic as Ambassador and Referee." *American Literary History* 1:2 (Summer 1989): 432–47.

Lynn, Kenneth S. *Mark Twain and Southwestern Humor.* Boston: Little, Brown, 1959.

MacKethan, Lucinda. "*Huck Finn* and the Slave Narratives: Lighting Out as Design." *Southern Review* 20 (1984): 247–64.

McPherson, James Alan. "Indivisible Man." *Ralph Ellison: A Collection of Critical Essays*. Ed. John Hersey. Englewood Cliffs, N.J.: Prentice-Hall, Inc., 1974.

Mahl, George F. "Everyday Disturbances of Speech." *Language in Psychotherapy: Strategies of Discovery*. Ed. Robert L. Russell. New York: Plenum Press, 1987.

———. "Everyday Speech Disturbances in *Tom Sawyer*." *Explorations in Nonverbal and Vocal Behavior,* by George F. Mahl. Hillsdale, N.J.: Lawrence Erlbaum, 1987.

Marx, Leo. "The Vernacular Tradition in American Literature." *The Pilot and the Passenger: Essays in Literature, Technology and Culture in the United States,* by Leo Marx. New York: Oxford University Press, 1988.

Mencken, H. L. "The Burden of Humor." *The Smart Set* (February 1913): 151–54. Reprinted in M. Thomas Inge, ed., *Huck Finn Among the Critics.* Frederick, Md.: University Publications of America, 1985.

Miller, James A. Personal communication, 10 October 1992 and July 1990.

Morrison, Toni. Personal communication, 4 December 1991.

———. *Playing in the Dark: Whiteness and the Literary Imagination.* Cambridge: Harvard University Press, 1992.

———. "Unspeakable Things Unspoken: The Afro-American Presence in American Literature." *Michigan Quarterly Review* 28:1 (Winter 1989): 1–34.

Murray, Albert. *Train Whistle Guitar.* 1974. Foreword by Robert O'Meally. Northeastern Library of Black Literature, Richard Yarborough, Series Editor. Boston: Northeastern University Press, 1989.

Nelson, Dana D. *The Word in Black and White: Reading "Race" in American Literature 1638–1897.* New York: Oxford University Press, 1992.

Nichols, Charles H. "'A True Book—With Some Stretchers': *Huck Finn* Today." *Satire or Evasion? Black Perspectives on "Huckleberry Finn."* Ed. James S. Leonard, Thomas A. Tenney, and Thadious M. Davis. Durham, N.C.: Duke University Press, 1992.

Nichols, Thomas L. *Forty Years of American Life.* Vols. 1 and 2. London: John Maxwell and Company, 1864.

Nielson, Aldon Lynn. *Reading Race: White American Poets and Racial Discourse in the Twentieth Century.* Athens: University of Georgia Press, 1988.

Olsen, Tillie. Personal communication, 28 December 1991 and December 1987.

Ong, Walter J. *Orality and Literacy: The Technologizing of the Word.* London and New York: Methuen, 1982.

Page, Clarence. "Black Voice Enriches Maligned Masterpiece" (syndicated column from Chicago *Tribune*). San Jose *Mercury News,* 9 July 1992, 7B.

Payne, L. W. "A Word List from East Alabama." *Dialect Notes* 3 (1905): 279–328, 343–91.

Pederson, Lee A. "Negro Speech in *The Adventures of Huckleberry Finn.*" *Mark Twain Journal* 13 (Winter 1965–1966): 1–4.

Pettit, Arthur G. *Mark Twain and the South.* Lexington: University of Kentucky Press, 1974.

Pike, Gustavus D. *The Singing Campaign for Ten Thousand Pounds; or, The Jubilee Singers in Great Britain.* Rev. ed. New York: American Missionary Association, 1875.

Rampersad, Arnold. "*Adventures of Huckleberry Finn* and Afro-American Literature." *Satire or Evasion? Black Perspectives on "Huckleberry Finn."* Ed. James S. Leonard, Thomas A. Tenney, and Thadious M. Davis. Durham, N.C.: Duke University Press, 1992.

———. *The Life of Langston Hughes. Volume I: 1902–1941. I, Too, Sing America.* New York: Oxford University Press, 1986.

———. *The Life of Langston Hughes. Volume II: 1941–1967. I Dream a World.* New York: Oxford University Press, 1988.

Reed, A. W. "British Recognition of American Speech in the Eighteenth Century." *Dialect Notes* 6 (1933).

Richards, Phillip M. "Phillis Wheatley and Literary Americanization." *American Quarterly* 44:2 (June 1992): 163–91.

Robinson, Forrest G. "The Characterization of Jim in *Huckleberry Finn*." *Nineteenth-Century Literature* 43:3 (December 1988): 361–91. Reprinted in Laurie Champion, ed., *The Critical Response to Mark Twain's "Huckleberry Finn."* Westport, Conn.: Greenwood Press, 1991.

Rodney, Robert M., ed. and comp. *Mark Twain International: A Bibliography and Interpretation of His Worldwide Popularity.* Westport, Conn.: Greenwood Press, 1982.

Rodnon, Stewart. "*The Adventures of Huckleberry Finn* and *Invisible Man:* Thematic and Structural Comparisons." *Negro American Literature Forum* 4 (July 1970): 45–51.

Rubin, Louis, Jr. "Southern Local Color and the Black Man." *Southern Review* 6 (October 1970): 1026–30.

Rulon, Curt Morris. "The Dialects in *Huckleberry Finn*." Ph.D. diss. University of Iowa, 1967.

Sage, Howard. "An Interview with Ralph Ellison: Visible Man." *Pulp* 2:2 (Summer 1976): 10–12.

Sewell, David R. *Mark Twain's Languages: Discourse, Dialogue and Linguistic Variety.* Berkeley: University of California Press, 1987.

Sloane, David E. E. "*Adventures of Huckleberry Finn*": *American Comic Vision.* Boston: Twayne, 1988.

———. *Mark Twain as a Literary Comedian.* Baton Rouge: Louisiana State University Press, 1979.

Smith, David L. "Huck, Jim, and American Racial Discourse." *Satire or Evasion? Black Perspectives on "Huckleberry Finn."* Ed. James S. Leonard, Thomas A. Tenney, and Thadious M. Davis. Durham, N.C.: Duke University Press, 1992.

Smith, Henry Nash. *Mark Twain: The Development of a Writer.* Cambridge: Belknap-Harvard University Press, 1962.

Sollors, Werner. "A Critique of Pure Pluralism." *Reconstructing American Literary History.* Ed. Sacvan Bercovitch. Cambridge: Harvard University Press, 1986.

———. "Ethnicity." *Critical Terms for Literary Study*. Ed. Frank Lentricchia and Thomas McLaughlin. Chicago: University of Chicago Press, 1990.

Starke, Catherine Juanita. *Black Portraiture in American Fiction: Stock Characters, Archetypes, and Individuals.* New York: Basic Books, 1971.

Stein, Jean. "The Art of Fiction XIII: William Faulkner." *The Paris Review* 12 (Spring 1956): 28–52.

Stepto, Robert B. "Sharing the Thunder: The Literary Exchanges of Harriet Beecher Stowe, Henry Bibb, and Frederick Douglass." *New Essays on "Uncle Tom's Cabin."* Ed. Eric J. Sundquist. Cambridge and New York: Cambridge University Press, 1986.

Stewart, William A. "Continuity and Change in American Negro Dialects." *Florida FL Reporter* 6:1 (Spring 1968): 3–4, 14–16, 18. Reprinted in J. L. Dillard, ed., *Perspectives on Black English.* The Hague: Mouton, 1975.

Stuckey, Sterling. "True Huck." *The Nation,* 14 December 1985, 2.

Sundquist, Eric J. "Faulkner, Race, and the Forms of American Fiction." *Faulkner and Race: Faulkner and Yoknapatawpha, 1986*. Ed. Doreen Fowler and Ann J. Abadie. Jackson: University Press of Mississippi, 1987.

———. *To Wake the Nations: Race in the Making of American Literature*. Cambridge: Belknap-Harvard University Press, 1993.

Szwed, John F. "Race and the Embodiment of Culture." *Ethnicity* 2:1 (1975): 19–33.

Tenney, Thomas A. "For Further Reading." *Satire or Evasion? Black Perspectives on "Huckleberry Finn."* Ed. James S. Leonard, Thomas A. Tenney, and Thadious M. Davis. Durham, N.C.: Duke University Press, 1992.

Thompson, Robert Farris. "The Kongo Atlantic Tradition." Lecture presented at the University of Texas, Austin, 28 February 1992.

Tidwell, James Nathan. "Mark Twain's Representation of Negro Speech." *American Speech* 17 (October 1942): 174–76.

Twain, Mark [Samuel Clemens]. *Adventures of Huckleberry Finn.* Ed. Walter Blair and Victor Fischer, with the assistance of Dahlia Armon and Harriet Elinor Smith. *The Works of Mark Twain*. Berkeley: University of California Press, 1988. All citations of *Huckleberry Finn* refer to this edition.

———. *The Autobiography of Mark Twain.* Ed. Charles Neider. New York: Harper and Row, Perennial Library, 1966. When the *Autobiography* is cited without a volume number, the reference is to this edition.

———. "The Awful German Language" [in *A Tramp Abroad,* 2]. *The Favorite Works of Mark Twain.* Deluxe ed. Garden City, N.Y.: Garden City Publishing Co., Inc., 1939.

———. "Concerning the American Language" [in *The Stolen White Elephant,* etc.]. Reprinted in *Tom Sawyer Abroad, Tom Sawyer, Detective, and Other Stories, Etc., Etc.* Hillcrest edition. New York: Harper and Brothers, 1906.

———. *Early Tales and Sketches.* Vol. 2 (1864–1865). Ed. Edgar Marquess Branch and Robert H. Hirst, with the assistance of Harriet Elinor Smith. The Works of Mark Twain. Berkeley: University of California Press, 1981.

———. "A Family Sketch," no. 1, 1906, photocopy of manuscript and typescript of manuscript in the Mark Twain Papers, Bancroft Library, University of California, Berkeley. Original in Mark Twain Collection, James S. Copley Library, La Jolla, California.

———. "Introduction to 'The New Guide of the Conversation in Portuguese and English.'" *The $30,000 Bequest.* New York: Harper and Brothers, American Artists Edition, 1917.

———. "Italian with Grammar." *The $30,000 Bequest.* New York: Harper and Brothers, American Artists Edition, 1917.

———. "Italian without a Master." *The $30,000 Bequest.* New York: Harper and Brothers, American Artists Edition, 1917.

———. "The Jumping Frog in English. Then in French. Then Clawed Back into a Civilized Language Once More by Patient, Unremunerated Toil." *Mark Twain's Sketches, New and Old.* Hartford: American Publishing Co., 1875.

———. *Life on the Mississippi.* New York: Penguin, 1984.

———. Mark Twain Papers. Bancroft Library. University of California, Berkeley. Under the curatorship of Robert H. Hirst.

———. *Mark Twain's Autobiography.* 2 vols. Ed. Albert Bigelow Paine. New York: Harper and Brothers, 1924.

———. *Mark Twain's Letters.* 2 vols. Ed. Albert Bigelow Paine. New York: Harper and Brothers, 1917.

———. *Mark Twain's Letters, Vol. 3: 1869.* Ed. Victor Fischer, Michael B. Frank, and Dahlia Armon. The Mark Twain

Papers, under the General Editorship of Robert H. Hirst. Berkeley: University of California Press, 1992.
———. Notebooks and typescripts of notebooks. Mark Twain Papers. Bancroft Library. University of California, Berkeley.
———. *Pudd'nhead Wilson.* 1894. Reprint. New York: Bantam, 1959.
———. *Those Extraordinary Twins.* 1894. Reprint. Ed. Sidney E. Berger. New York: W.W. Norton and Co., 1980.
———. "A True Story, Repeated Word for Word as I Heard It." *Mark Twain's Sketches, New and Old,* by Mark Twain. Hartford: American Publishing Co., 1875.
Weaver, Thomas, and Merline A. Williams. "Mark Twain's Jim: Identity as an Index to Cultural Attitudes." *American Literary Realism* 13 (Spring 1980): 19–29.
Werner, Craig. "'Tell Old Pharaoh': The Afro-American Response to Faulkner." *Southern Review* 19 (Autumn 1983): 711–35.
Wilgus, D. K. "The Negro-White Spiritual." *Anglo-American Folksong Scholarship Since 1898.* New Brunswick: n.p., 1959. Reprinted in Alan Dundes, ed., *Mother Wit from the Laughing Barrel.* Jackson: University Press of Mississippi, 1990.
Woodard, Fredrick, and Donnarae MacCann. "Minstrel Shackles and Nineteenth-Century 'Liberality' in *Huckleberry Finn.*" *Satire or Evasion? Black Perspectives on "Huckleberry Finn."* Ed. James S. Leonard, Thomas A. Tenney, and Thadious M. Davis. Durham, N.C.: Duke University Press, 1992.
Woodward, C. Vann. "Clio with Soul." *Journal of American History* 1:56 (June 1969): 5–20.
Yarborough, Richard. Personal communication, 18 July 1992.
———. "Strategies of Characterization in *Uncle Tom's Cabin* and the Early Afro-American Novel." *New Essays on "Uncle Tom's Cabin."* Ed. Eric Sundquist. Cambridge and New York: Cambridge University Press, 1986.

A Trick of Mediation: Charles Chesnutt's Conflicted Literary Relationship with Albion Tourgée

Peter Caccavari

In a major study of Charles Chesnutt, Eric Sundquist recently wrote that Chesnutt is as important a literary figure as Herman Melville and Mark Twain (14). In fact, he goes so far as to assert that Chesnutt and W. E. B. Du Bois "are the equals of most any writers in the history of American literature" (7). In the same year, Duke University published in separate volumes Chesnutt's conjure stories and his journals under the editorship of Richard Brodhead. This flurry of critical activity focused on Chesnutt is a welcomed and necessary one. However, an aspect that gets little more than superficial treatment is the writers who influenced Chesnutt. One of his most important early influences was a now little-known white novelist, Albion Tourgée. Tourgée was born in northeastern Ohio, fought in the Civil War for the Union, and afterwards moved to North Carolina, where he spent Reconstruction as a Republican activist for civil rights and superior court judge. He wrote of his experience in fiction, and his Reconstruction novel, *A Fool's Errand* (1879), was a best-seller. This book helped inspire Chesnutt to take up fiction and began his relationship, initially indirect but later quite direct, with Tourgée. Chesnutt wrote in his journal of March 16, 1880:

> And if Judge Tourgee, with his necessarily limited intercourse with colored people, and with his limited stay in the South, can write such interesting descriptions, such vivid pictures of Southern life and character as to make himself rich and famous, why could not a colored man, who has lived among colored people all his life; who is familiar with their habits, their ruling passions, their prejudices; their whole

> moral and social condition; their public and private ambitions; their religious tendencies and habits;—why could not a colored man who knew all this, and who, besides, had possessed such opportunities for observation and conversation with the better class of white men in the south as to understand their modes of thinking; who was familiar with the political history of the country, and especially with all the phases of the slavery question;—why could not such a man, if he possessed the same ability, write a far better book about the South than Judge Tourgee or Mrs. Stowe has written? Answer who can! But the man is yet to make his appearance; and if I can't be the man I shall be the first to rejoice at his *dèbut,* and give God speed! to his work. (125–26)[1]

Tourgée's race, in Chesnutt's view, is not a hindrance to writing good fiction about African Americans in the South. Earlier in the entry, Chesnutt says that Tourgée is "a close observer of men and things" and that the north, because of its distance, "sees the south as it is . . ." (125). However, Chesnutt does assert that Tourgée's race is necessarily limiting in the kind of portrayals he creates. Chesnutt feels that his own experience as a black man among blacks is a key difference between himself and Tourgée, and that his knowledge of both whites and blacks gives him the potential to surpass Tourgée, but Chesnutt does not assume that either biological race or racial cultural experience alone is sufficient. He would need to possess "the same ability." Tourgée made a similar point in his essay, "The South as a Field for Fiction": "The mere fact of having suffered or enjoyed does not imply the power to portray. . . ."

However, the remainder of that passage points out some of the limitations which Chesnutt indicated. Tourgée goes on to say that

> the Negro race in America has other attributes besides mere imagination. It has absorbed the best blood of the South, and it is quite within the possibilities that it may itself become a power in literature, of which even the descendants of the old regime shall be as proud as they

> now are of the dwellers in "Broomsedge Cove" and on the "Great Smoky." (411)

Although Tourgée is acknowledging the interrelatedness of the races due to miscegenation in such a way as to undermine white Southern myths of racial purity and superiority (something Chesnutt also did in his work), he is also making a left-handed compliment to African Americans as deriving their literary power from their "white blood."

It was Chesnutt's belief that he could provide a truer picture of African-American life and culture than Tourgée could that helped him see a way to proceed in his writing distinct from Tourgée's. Richard Brodhead remarks that in this journal entry "[i]t is notable that Chesnutt moves straight from his meditation of Tourgée's success to a literary foraging plan of his own . . ." (22). In that passage, Chesnutt wants to make fiction less fictive and more factual, becoming an even closer observer of men and things than Tourgée:

> I intend to record my impressions of men and things, and such incidents or conversations which take place within my knowledge, with a view to future use in literary work. I shall not record stale negro minstrel jokes, or worn out newspaper squibs on the "man and brother." I shall leave the realm of fiction, where most of this stuff is manufactured, and come down to hard facts. (126)

Besides Tourgée's "necessarily limited intercourse with colored people," Chesnutt criticized Tourgée's "limited stay in the South," but by 1880 Chesnutt had lived in North Carolina as long as Tourgée had, fourteen years. Chesnutt also does not seem concerned with the fact that he, like Tourgée, was born in northeastern Ohio, not the South. It is true that Chesnutt spent more of his formative years in the South (Chesnutt moved there at age 8, Tourgée at age 27), and it is also true that his parents were originally from North Carolina, but his beliefs here raise important issues about how one comes to know a community into which one was not born. It also brings into question whether or not birth alone is sufficient to belong to a community, not to mention if there is any such thing as a singular, stable, coherent entity as "a" community. In this respect Tourgée's efforts to examine not only the coherence—or lack of it—of local communities but by extension the unity or disunity of the nation following civil war greatly influenced Chesnutt's writing, even while he himself questioned Tourgée in those terms. The idea of "carpetbaggers"—those who moved from the North to the South after the Civil War for political, economic, or ideological reasons—brings this difficult question into focus in Chesnutt's writing, linking together issues of race and regionalism in terms of community identification. Just as Tourgée and Chesnutt, in different ways, call into question the idea of biological racialism and racial essentialism, so too they interrogate the idea of regional coherence and organicism.[2]

Ten years after Chesnutt's journal entry, he was more critical of Tourgée. In a letter from June 5, 1890 to the white Southern novelist, essayist, and lecturer, George Washington Cable, Chesnutt complained about Tourgée's black characters: "Judge Tourgée's cultivated white Negroes are always bewailing their fate and cursing the drop of black blood which 'taints'—I hate the word, it implies corruption—their otherwise pure race." Contrasting Tourgée to any English writer, Chesnutt wrote in the same letter: "He would not be obliged to kill off his characters or immerse them in convents, as Tourgée does his latest heroine [in *Pactolus Prime*], to save them from a fate worse than death, i.e., the confession of inferiority by reason of color" (H. Chesnutt 58–59). As with Tourgée's comment in "The South as a Field for Fiction," to Chesnutt *Pactolus Prime* is another troubling treatment of miscegenation. By this time Chesnutt had had some fiction and essays published in such important magazines as the *Atlantic Monthly* and the *Independent*, and it appears that Chesnutt had become more confident with his own ability than he had been ten years earlier, knowing that he could now be that man who could write a far better book than Tourgée.

I want to concentrate my discussion of Chesnutt's literary relationship with Tourgée on Chesnutt's *Conjure Woman* (1899) and Tourgée's *A Fool's Errand*. I see *The Conjure Woman* as a rewriting of Tourgée's influence on both Chesnutt and the white readership of *A Fool's Errand*, as well as a contending interpretation of Reconstruction. *The Conjure Woman* is an example of "signifying"—a complicated nexus of rhetorical strategies within African and African-American oral traditions that use, among other methods, indirection and irony for expression.[3] The signifying that occurs in the book is not only that of black culture on white culture, but of Chesnutt on Tourgée. This relationship is not one of antagonism, although it is a conflicted one. Chesnutt corresponded with Tourgée for some fifteen years until the end of Tourgée's life. Chesnutt, with nine other African Americans, signed a resolution which was read at Tourgée's funeral in 1905. This resolution, "in the name of the colored people of the United States," praised Tourgée as "ever the consistent advocate of equal rights and equal justice for the Negro" and one "who placed humanity above race, color, and artificial social distinctions" (Tourgée Papers, item #9874). But this respect does not preclude criticism or revision, and Chesnutt uses the method of signifying to do this. In fact, Chesnutt's relationship with Tourgée modelled what he hoped the larger relationship between blacks and whites in the United States in the aftermath of slavery and civil war could be like: a relationship characterized by room for disagreement and the acknowledgment of the differing goals and needs of various communities, while still maintaining respect and cordiality for each other.[4]

Henry Louis Gates Jr. says that the Monkey in African and African-American folklore, interacting with the Lion and the Elephant, uses "a trick of mediation. Indeed, the Monkey is a term of (anti)mediation, as are all trickster figures, between two forces he seeks to oppose for his own contentious purposes, and then to reconcile" (56). It would be possible, to an extent, to draw parallels to the Monkey/Lion/Elephant triad using Julius, John and Annie in *The Conjure Woman*. It would also be possible to draw parallels to Chesnutt, Tourgée, and the writers of the Plantation Tradition of Southern writing in a similar manner. Finally, a third parallel triad would be that of emancipated blacks and free people of color, Northern whites, and Southern whites. However, I wish instead to use this image of mediator more broadly with less of a one-to-one correspondence. It is through indirection and irony, through acknowledgement and revision, that Chesnutt searches for a way to find a place for himself as a writer distinguished but within a tradition, as well as envisioning a nation diverse but not divided. He hopes to use certain forms of mediation to reconcile forces that in the 1880s and 1890s often seemed hopelessly irreconcilable.

In *To Wake the Nations: Race in the Making of American Literature*, Eric Sundquist has written arguably the most important long work on Chesnutt in recent years, and there he notes some important relationships between *The Conjure Woman* and *A Fool's Errand*:

> Because the general premise of the narrator's move to North Carolina [in *The Conjure Woman*] deliberately echoes that of Albion Tourgée in *A Fool's Errand* (Chesnutt's fixation on the success of Tourgée's novel, which he noted on at least two occasions, supports the likelihood that the trope of settling in the South combined Tourgée's experience with Chesnutt's own life as a displaced southerner), the tale also looks backward in its literary genealogy. Like Tourgée's autobiographical narrator [Colonel Comfort Servosse in *A Fool's Errand*], John [the narrator of *The Conjure Woman*] from the beginning is locked into the mode of foolish naiveté that characterizes his perspective in many instances throughout the tales; and his position as an outsider to the South, even when it is treated sympathetically, is the means for Chesnutt to scrutinize both his moral pretensions and his cultural, racial blindness. (361)

Thus, Sundquist sets up some of the basic elements in the literary genealogy which encompasses both Tourgée and Chesnutt: regionalism as a literary form, outsider/insider status as a position of observation, and naiveté/irony as a mode of observation. Both books deal with the sectional disputes of the day, and through those issues explore the idea of carpetbagging not only in its historical manifestations but also in its literary and epistemological implications. Both Tourgée and Chesnutt explored such quandaries as how one decides what community one belongs to and if one does belong to a certain community, how one can understand someone from a different community. Both authors used ironic naiveté, in different ways, to reveal moral pretensions and cultural/racial blindness. Whereas Tourgée uses Servosse as one who self-consciously "plays the fool" to show the foolishness of conventional wisdom, Chesnutt uses a naive narrator to demonstrate the limits of such liberal Northern white advocates of civil rights as Tourgée. John, like Tourgée whose "tainted" mixed-race characters angered Chesnutt, believes in the equality of the races, but he understands neither Julius, the freedman who works for him, nor his culture, despite John's good intentions and educational qualifications. In this way, Chesnutt uses irony as a way of showing boundaries between communities that are highly defined—John and Julius represent clear "outsides" and "insides"—but he also uses irony as a way of eventually mediating between those communities and making those boundaries more permeable. To do so, Chesnutt combines both the literary technique of situational irony and the oral technique of signifying.

Tourgée's *A Fool's Errand* was published anonymously in 1879, said to be "By One of the Fools." It achieved commercial success, becoming a best seller. The titular fool is Colonel Comfort Servosse, who was born and raised in Michigan and fought in the Civil War on the side of the Union. At the end of the war, Servosse is contemplating moving to the South. In a letter his former college president, Dr. Enos Martin, encourages such a move, writing: "I look and hope for considerable movements of population, both from the North to the South, and *vice versa*; because I think it is only by such intermingling of the people of the two sections that they can ever become one, and the danger of future evil be averted" (27). With this advice Tourgée decides to move to Verdenton, North Carolina and buy a plantation there called Warrington. Servosse is soon branded a "carpetbagger" and ostracized by most of the surrounding white community, eventually having a run-in with the Ku Klux Klan. Ultimately, Reconstruction as a political program fails, but Servosse's daughter is set to marry a Southern man when the novel ends, the typical trope of the day for sectional reunification. But Tourgée has no illusions about the actual success of Reconstruction; it has been a failure and the marriage is more of a hope than a promise.

In fact, Servosse and his wife leave the South, as Tourgée himself had done after Reconstruction. Servosse leaves North Carolina to go even further south, to Central America:

> He had been engaged by a company of capitalists to take charge of their interests in one of the republics of Central America. The work was of the most important character, not only to the parties having a pecuniary interest therein, but also as having a weighty bearing upon that strange contest between civilization and semi-

> barbarism which is constantly being waged in that wonderfully strange region, where Nature seems to have set her subtlest forces in battle-array against what, in these modern times is denominated "progress." While the earth produces in an abundance unknown to other regions, the mind seems stricken with irresistible lassitude, and only the monitions of sense seem able to awaken the body from lethargic slumber. (390)

Servosse leaves one plantation for another, carrying on in intrahemispheric terms the kind of intermingling that Dr. Martin had seen as the hope for the United States, uniting diverse peoples under the aegis of capitalism and progress. Tourgée shows the relationship between nature and human enterprise, how civilization contends with barbarism, and how capitalism contends with the environment.

But the mode of expression of the fool is irony, and Tourgée's admiration of "that wonderfully strange region" acts as a counterpoint to his ironic view of "progress." In fact, the irony is especially dense here, because the fool is usually idealistic and impractical but ethically correct, whereas in this instance his adventurism seems to be criticized by the narrator. The battle between civilization and barbarism was often the language used by racist whites in denunciation of blacks, and Tourgée is using it here to suggest another misguided battle, this one against Nature in the name of an illusory "progress." It is "only the monitions of sense" which seem able to make people active enough to subdue the land, but we get the feeling that such sense may in fact be nonsense, just as wisdom may actually be foolishness and what is deemed foolish may in reality be wisdom. Servosse returns to his plantation in North Carolina to find an epidemic of yellow fever "which mocks at human skill. . . . He had wondered at the mystery before which science is as powerless as superstition . . ." (391). In these circumstances sense and nonsense, science and superstition, wisdom and folly do not look so very different. Servosse contracts the disease, dies, and is buried at Warrington. Although he had gained a grudging respect from the native white Southerners, the book ends with a sense of failure that parallels the failure of Reconstruction. The last image in the first edition of the novel was that of Servosse's gravestone. Although it does not appear in the illustration, the epitaph on the gravestone reads: "He followed the counsel of the Wise, / And became a Fool thereby" (403). The hope of intersectional marriage is warily balanced by the despair of the father's grave.

Chesnutt's *Conjure Woman* appeared in 1899 as a collection of some of his stories involving a character named Uncle Julius which appeared in magazines in the 1880s and 1890s. In the first story, "The Goophered Grapevine," the narrator, John, is a white man who, like Servosse, comes from the Great Lakes region, this time from Tourgée's and Chesnutt's birthplace of northern Ohio. After the war, John and his wife, Annie, look to move to warmer climes because of Annie's poor health. After considering places such as France, Spain, and southern California, the couple decide on Patesville, North Carolina. Having raised grapes in Ohio, John had heard about comparable business opportunities in North Carolina. While examining an abandoned plantation, John and Annie come across a freedman, Uncle Julius. Upon their initial meeting, John makes an egalitarian gesture; as Julius begins to move away from the white couple, John says, "'Don't let us disturb you . . . . There is plenty of room for us all'" (9). Like *A Fool's Errand*, *The Conjure Woman* is about Reconstruction, and clearly John's remark is meant to imply the white Northern liberal gesture of political and economic inclusion towards blacks in the post-war era. But John's egalitarianism is immediately shown to be severely limited. John notices that Julius

> was not entirely black, and this fact, together with the quality of his hair, which was about six inches long and very bushy, except on the top of his head, where he was quite bald, suggested a slight strain of other than negro blood. There was a shrewdness in his eyes, too, which was not altogether African, and which, as we afterwards learned from experience, was indicative of a corresponding shrewdness in his character. (9–10)

John's comment sounds very much like Tourgée's in "The South as a Field for Fiction," attributing literary power to white lineage. Like Chesnutt himself, Julius is of mixed-race heritage. Many years later, Chesnutt reflected on his writing career in his 1931 essay, "Post-Bellum—Pre-Harlem," and noted the prominence of mixed-race characters in his fiction, but he did not see Julius as a part of that project:

> As a matter of fact, substantially all of my writings, with the exception of *The Conjure Woman*, have dealt with the problems of people of mixed blood, which, while in the main the same as those of the true Negro, are in some instances and in some respects much more complex and difficult of treatment, in fiction as in life (54).

Chesnutt has often been criticized for his focus on mixed-race characters, appearing to valorize them over full-blooded African Americans.[5] While there may be those who contend that Chesnutt is wrong in saying that some of the problems of people of mixed blood are "much more complex and difficult of treatment" than some of those of "the true Negro," despite his qualification of this statement, what is important here for my purposes is his concern with racial mixture. In a sense, the same sort of "intermingling" which Dr. Martin had advocated to Servosse as a solution to sectional divisiveness is precisely the same sort of solution which Chesnutt contemplates. Just as a Northerner and Southerner will intermarry after the end of *A Fool's Errand* to provide hope of national unity, so too the intermingling of the races becomes a trope for racial as well as national unity.

In his series of three essays entitled "The Future American" which appeared in the Boston *Evening Transcript* in 1900, Chesnutt wrote about the inevitability of racial amalgamation which would bring the nation together in a way which the Civil War, Emancipation, and Reconstruction had been unable to do. There he notes that "The conception of a pure Aryan, Indo-European race has been abandoned in scientific circles, and the secret of the progress of Europe has been found in racial heterogeneity, rather than in racial purity" (96). As Servosse had seen science and superstition put on the same level, so Chesnutt saw the science of race as a kind of white superstition. In contradiction to this superstition, Chesnutt argues that from racial heterogeneity a kind of homogeneity could result. "From a negroid nation, which ours is already, we would have become a composite and homogenous people, and the elements of racial discord which have troubled our civil life so gravely and still threaten our free institutions, would have been entirely eliminated" (99). Chesnutt saw equality as ultimately coming from biology rather than law (despite the fact that he himself had passed the bar and made his living from a court reporting business). Or more precisely, he saw equality as coming from the *perception* of biology rather than law. In fact, the future American would only be a more thoroughly amalgamated version of the present American. "It is only a social fiction, indeed, which makes a person seven-eighths white a Negro; he is really more a white man" (106). This social fiction was upheld four years earlier in *Plessy v. Ferguson* when the U.S. Supreme Court maintained that a man who was not visibly identifiable as a black man could be put off a train car because he was, in a racialist perspective, "really" black. Chesnutt's own social fiction aimed at illustrating how race was a socially constructed means of creating group identity for the purpose of excluding others.

Chesnutt is right in saying that Julius is not a character in which his racial mixture is a central issue in the story. This is the only mention of it in *The Conjure Woman*. However, it is an important, if brief, episode. John's conclusion that Julius's shrewdness must come from his Anglo-Saxon heritage demonstrates that he is not as open-minded as he first appears. John sees Julius as the opposite of the "tainted" white negro which Chesnutt complained about—not as a largely white person with a small portion of black blood (as in Chesnutt's case), but as a largely black man with only enough white blood to account for any cleverness he might have. Julius is the example of slavery's biological intermingling of the races which mirrors Reconstruction's cultural intermingling of the races.

As such, Chesnutt uses the site of the Southern plantation as the setting for his collection of short stories to illustrate the turning point between slavery and Reconstruction. *A Fool's Errand* also takes place on a plantation, but it is consciously set against the Plantation Tradition in fiction by not invoking either African-American servants or much agricultural activity. In fact, African Americans serve largely as a backdrop for the story which is primarily about how whites attempt to solve the political, cultural, and racial divisions of the nation.

Chesnutt, in contrast, takes a trickier (in a variety of senses) path. The post-Reconstruction version of the ante-bellum Plantation Tradition as developed by Joel Chandler Harris and Thomas Nelson Page came after *A Fool's Errand* and during

Chesnutt's writing of the conjure stories. Chesnutt chose to use the trappings of the Plantation Tradition, writing especially in response to Harris's Uncle Remus stories.[6] Although he was signifying on this white literary tradition from within and without it, such irony involved potential dangers. John M. Reilly has noted about Chesnutt's 1901 novel, *The Marrow of Tradition*, that a problem of irony as a rhetorical device of the oppressed writer is that "it may cut both ways, aggravating the writer's feelings of impotence while identifying the villainy of his oppressors" (31–32).

Just as troublesome, such irony may be lost on a white audience which might only see what it wants to see, what it has been conditioned to see, like the narrator John. White readers may only see Julius in terms of Plantation Tradition slaves and freed people or minstrel-show African Americans rather than the three-dimensional human being Chesnutt was trying to flesh out. Chesnutt worried about this in a letter to Tourgée on September 26, 1889. At that time Chesnutt sent Tourgée one of the Julius stories that did not appear in *The Conjure Woman*, "Dave's Neckliss," and wrote: "I think I have about used up the old Negro who serves as mouthpiece, and I shall drop him in future stories, as well as much of the dialect" (Tourgée Papers, item #4026, pp. 1–2). William Andrews says of this passage that "Chesnutt could have sailed his three initial conjure stories toward greater fame as a dialectician and southern regionalist. But, in fact, his better judgment warned against charting such a literary course." Andrews refers to "the limitations of the conjure materials and plot devices which had already begun to confine him . . . ." He goes on to say that Chesnutt decided not "to exploit the old ex-slave character type" or the "quaint features of slave culture . . . . He had started to demonstrate a more searching and critical interest in racial affairs through printed and private essays written during 1889" (21–22).

I agree with Andrews that these were Chesnutt's feelings at the time, but I disagree with his assessment of the conjure stories. The stories are not limited, exploitative, or quaint, and Chesnutt's essays did not "demonstrate a more searching and critical interest in racial affairs." Chesnutt's concerns over the effects of irony in the plantation setting were valid ones, but his work in overturning and refuting that tradition is both searching and critical. Sundquist writes: "Plantation literature and culture did not simply demand a febrile return to the past;

it was the deceptive screen for keeping contemporary African Americans in bondage to the whole white race . . ." (287). Like the post-war plantation literature Sundquist describes, *The Conjure Woman* is not a febrile return to the past but a transplanted description of the present and a blueprint for the future. Unlike plantation literature, *The Conjure Woman* is not a deceptive screen for keeping contemporary blacks in bondage to whites, but a trick of mediation which could show how blacks and whites might be brought together on mutually affirming (if not ideal) terms. Although the stories Julius tells all took place during slavery, they do not glamorize it or make the reader nostalgic for a more orderly and peaceful world. All the stories are in some sense tragic. In a move that demonstrates the North's implication in the popularity of plantation literature, Chesnutt has John narrating the beginning of "Mars Jeems's Nightmare" in which he attributes Julius's knowledge of the land to being "doubtless due to the simplicity of a life that had kept him close to nature" (64). One of the important messages of Julius's stories is that life under slavery was anything but simple. Furthermore, Chesnutt is transforming the Plantation Tradition from a social fiction of bondage (previously a physical bondage, later a legal one) to a social fiction of cultural intermingling (which falls short of forming a new and unified community, as such intermingling had in *A Fool's Errand*). At the time of the publication of *The Conjure Woman*, segregation had replaced the stratified intermingling of the races under slavery. Chesnutt's version of plantation literature both denounces slavery's stratified intermingling and post-Reconstruction's segregation by imagining another stratified intermingling (employer and employee rather than master and slave) that at least at the time had the potential for a more egalitarian arrangement of community based on mutual understanding. Nonetheless, Chesnutt had no illusions about the power relationships involved in the new economics of Emancipation.

Andrews's comments about Chesnutt being restricted to a "southern regionalist," while probably an accurate reflection of Chesnutt's concerns, miss a crucial aspect of Chesnutt's fiction and an important connection to Tourgée. Sundquist notes, "Also, even though Chesnutt no more identified with John's obtuse morality than did Melville with Delano's [in *Benito Cereno*], John also stands to a degree for Chesnutt's own entry into the South as a northern author, though in his case one with distinctly southern roots" (362). Racially, Chesnutt's conception of the future American was a justification of himself as a man of mixed race. He wrote in his journal on January 3, 1881 "I occupy here a position similar to that of Mahomet's Coffin. I am neither fish[,] flesh, nor fowl—neither 'nigger,' poor white, nor 'buckrah.' Too 'stuck-up' for the colored folks, and, of course, not recognized by the whites" (157–58). Regionally, Chesnutt's portrayal of the carpetbagger John was a justification of his geographical and cultural fluidity. By virtue of being of different races and regions, Chesnutt is both inside and outside a variety of communities. In *The Conjure Woman*, he fashions a fiction which attempts to show the positive aspects of such multiplicity. In fact, Julius's "lies" in the folk tradition of the trickster and the unconscious irony of which John is the object are examples of a kind of *duplicity* which represents the permeable borders of communities in what Mary Louise Pratt has called "contact zones," which are cultural, racial, and geographical. Pratt defines contact zones as "social spaces where cultures meet, clash, and grapple with each other, often in contexts of highly asymmetrical relations of power, such as colonialism, slavery, or their aftermaths . . ." ("Arts" 34). The intermingling of regions and cultures in the wake of conquest was a fundamental goal of Reconstruction and it was a fundamental goal of Tourgée's fiction. But Chesnutt takes that goal further than Tourgée did. Whereas Servosse is Tourgée's unified and relatively uncomplicated fictional alter ego, Chesnutt splits himself into both John and Julius (their first names beginning with "J" perhaps indicates that they are in some ways two aspects of the same person), portraying his white and black, Northern and Southern sides. Tourgée treats the division of the nation as an intellectual problem that to some extent can be solved by rational observation and explanation, whereas Chesnutt feels a much more intimate affinity with the problem of national divisiveness, for he feels divided within himself. In *The Conjure Woman*, however, this divisiveness does not take the form of the tragic mulatto, in part because the divisiveness is made regional and national in addition to racial.[7]

In Pratt's terminology, *The Conjure Woman* represents an act of "transculturation," a process "whereby members of subordinated or marginal groups select and invent from materials transmitted by a dominant or metropolitan culture .... While subordinate peoples do not usually control what emanates from the dominate culture, they do determine to varying extents what gets absorbed into their own and what it gets used for" ("Arts" 36). Chesnutt's reworking not only of racist plantation literature but of sympathetic Northern liberals such as Tourgée is his version of transculturation, appropriating white literary forms and creating a melange with African-American folklore to produce a viable composite guide to living in the volatile contact zone of the late nineteenth century United States. As a text engaging in transculturation, *The Conjure Woman* is an "autoethnographic text," as Pratt puts it, "in which people undertake to describe themselves in ways that engage with representations others have made of them" ("Arts" 35). As such, autoethnographic texts "are not, then, what are usually thought of as 'authentic' or autochthonous forms of self-representation .... Rather autoethnography involves partial collaboration with and appropriation of the idioms of the conqueror" (*Imperial Eyes* 7). Chesnutt is indeed a collaborator, but not in the way that he is sometimes chastised for being. In the sense that Julius is "duplicitous," that is both deceptive and moving between communities, so Chesnutt is a collaborator in that he is working with the occupation forces (racially, regionally, and culturally, as Julius does) and in that he is trying to create some common ground among heterogenous communities, not by fiat but by negotiation and consensus-building using a variety of materials at hand from these communities.

In the 1889 letter to Tourgée, Chesnutt wrote of "Dave's Neckliss": "I tried in this story to get out of the realm of superstition into the region of feeling and passion—with what degree of success the story itself can testify" (2). It is noteworthy that Chesnutt uses metaphors of place—"realm" and "region"—regarding superstition, for Andrews comments on the use of superstition as a limitation and marker of regionalist writing. Again, Andrews is right about Chesnutt's uneasiness concerning his use of superstition, both in terms of its effects on his literary career and on white (and black) perceptions of blacks and their "social uplift." But Chesnutt's attitudes towards superstition and their relationship to his portrayal of superstition are extremely complex. In his 1901 essay, "Superstitions and Folklore of the South," Chesnutt is fairly condescending towards superstition, referring to "[t]he credulity of ignorance" and being "tricked" (372), "lying," being "self-deluded," and "palpable fraud" (373), giving rational explanations for magical events (374), and equating conjure stories to "fairy tales" (376). These are much the same sort of terms which John uses to characterize Julius's stories. Of Julius's stories John says some were "palpable inventions" which demonstrated "the shadow . . . of slavery and ignorance" (168). In "Sis' Becky's Pickaninny" John, after hearing the story of a slave woman, Becky, who is conjured into various birds so she can fly to her son who has been sold away from her, remarks: "That is a very ingenious fairy tale, Julius . . ." (159). In fact, John sees the conjure stories and superstition as one of the chief obstacles to the equality of the races. He tells Julius that "your people will never rise in the world until they throw off these childish superstitions and learn to live by the light of reason and common sense" (135).

It is the issue of superstition which helps ironize John and which represents the interaction of two cultures attempting to understand each other. John poses an opposition of sense and nonsense, like Servosse's civilization and barbarism, which is used to explore differing cultural assumptions. John is always skeptical of Julius's stories, looking on them as benign entertainment at best, as self-defeating superstition at worst. Even his wife Annie at times takes on this attitude, calling Julius's stories "nonsense" (107, 127). But when Annie expresses this view, Julius ultimately shows her that the stories are not to be taken literally but metaphorically. She comes to understand, in a way that John never quite does, that the stories portray the slave past and the narrative present of Reconstruction (and the reader is meant to see the implication of Chesnutt's present of segregation), not in the way that John is used to in expository histories, but in stories that portray the inner life of African Americans during those periods. Chesnutt was wrong when he thought that "Dave's Neckliss" could "get out of the realm of superstition into the region of feeling and passion"; in fact, it was *through* superstition that he so successfully represented the feeling and passion of African Americans.

In "The Gray Wolf's Ha'nt" John reads Annie a passage from a book of philosophy. The passage is complex jargon which in reality says very little and nothing profound, but he still regards it as the kind of sense in which he has so much faith. Annie responds, "I wish you would stop reading that nonsense . . . ." John replies narratively to the reader, "I had never been able to interest my wife in the study of philosophy, even when presented in the simplest and most lucid form" (164). In this, the penultimate story of the book, Annie discovers what the real nonsense in the book is, although John's faith in its truthfulness goes unshaken. Just as in *A Fool's Errand* the "wise men" are really fools, so in *The Conjure Woman* John's sense is shown to be nonsense. Ultimately, science and superstition are put on the same level in *The Conjure Woman* in a manner similar to that in which the narrator of *A Fool's Errand* does when speaking of yellow fever, saying that Servosse "had wondered at the mystery before which science is as powerless as superstition . . . ." That is not to say that Chesnutt considers them to be equal; he clearly does not. But he does see them as differing interpretations of the world which reflect certain cultural values and which both have stories that need to be told.

John does not see that the conjure stories represent a different cultural outlook which he does not understand. Tourgée's Dr. Martin thought that an intermingling of Northerners and Southerners would result in national unity, and although Chesnutt's John comes south for more personal reasons—economic and marital—he becomes part of the larger Reconstruction project which tried to heal the war's wounds by cultural exchange. The problem is that John's exchange is rather one-sided, or at least limited (in a way that the stories, Andrews's criticism to the contrary, are not). His sense of "progress" is much like that of the capitalists in Central America which the narrator of *A Fool's Errand* describes, erecting a "battle-array" in a system of conquest, rather than dialogue.

Despite John's monologic world-view, however, dialogue is fundamental to the structure of *The Conjure Woman*. John's language is everywhere contrasted to Julius's.[8] John's language is highly literate in diction, the result obviously of extensive reading and education. Julius's language is that of slave dialect. In a similar vein, John represents the written word, while Julius represents oral tradition. In fact, the relationship of standard English to dialect and written language to an oral tradition parallels the relationships of employer to employee, Northerner to Southerner, white to black, master to slave which appear in various facets of the stories throughout the book. Because both John and Julius tell stories, they both vie for narrative power

(John narrates the book while Julius narrates the conjure stories within the book), and through their stories vie for economic power (John as a writer profits from Julius's stories which sell the book while Julius by telling his stories to John and Annie gains such things as a new building for his church, a job for his grandson, and a new suit of clothes for himself). Although John ostensibly has the most power as the book's narrator, in a sense encompassing Julius's stories in his outer narrative, Julius uses the conjure stories to undermine John's narrative authority. One of the primary aims of *The Conjure Woman* is to give voice to African-American experience. Although Chesnutt admired *A Fool's Errand*, blacks do not have much voice there; it is primarily about whites hashing out sectional and racial problems. (Tourgée would do a much better job in giving voice to African-American characters in his next Reconstruction novel, *Bricks Without Straw*.)

Chesnutt ended his essay on superstition with a touching expression of making a people's voice heard which could sum up his vision of the dialogic structure of *The Conjure Woman*. He tells of a conjure story in which a jealous woman steals the beautiful voice of another woman. When the guilty woman is caught, she is penitent but cannot restore the voice. "The case is still pending, I understand; I shall sometime take steps to find out how it terminates." Chesnutt would have to wait to see how successful his stories were at restoring the stolen voice (as Emancipation had restored the stolen body). Chesnutt concludes the essay with another "lie" or tall tale "of the words which were frozen silent during the extreme cold of an Arctic winter, and became audible again the following summer when they had thawed out" (375–76). In a sense Chesnutt's stories were an attempt to thaw the ice of the winter of racial discontent at the turn of the century when segregation had been firmly fixed in the South and lynching continued to plague the region.

The Conjure Woman concludes with "Hot-Foot Hannibal," a story which, like *A Fool's Errand*, involves the marriage of a Southern man to a Northern woman (in this case, Annie's sister). The intermingling of sections which has been shown in the communal life of John, Annie, and Julius on the plantation grows, extending like concentric ripples in a pond. Sundquist has written, "In an age dominated by literary accounts of sectional reunion, symbolized by North-South romantic alliances, Chesnutt's stories of reunion were typically dedicated to the postbellum reunification of scattered or racially divided black families" (300). Chesnutt is also concerned with divided black families in *The Conjure Woman*, and he uses this theme toward a specific end. He does include a typical sectional romantic alliance among whites, but it is in conjunction with folklore about the division of African-American families under slavery. Except for "The Goophered Grapevine" and "The Conjurer's Revenge," the stories in the book all deal with the separation of couples or, in the case of "Sis' Becky's Pickaninny," a mother and child. Only in "Sis' Becky" is there a successful reunion. All the other tales end tragically. In "Hot-Foot Hannibal," Chloe, a jealous slave woman, is tricked into causing Jeff, her lover, to be sold away because she believes him to be unfaithful. When she finds out the deceit, she discovers that Jeff has since drowned.

Julius tells this tale because the horse which is pulling the coach containing John, Annie, and her sister, Mabel, who has had a terrible argument with Murchison, her lover, has stopped. Julius says the horse sees the ghost of the disconsolate Chloe. He has apparently caused the horse to balk so that the party would take a different path. They take the different path, meet up with Murchison, who, about to leave town, reconciles with Mabel. Thus, Chesnutt takes the rather pedestrian literary trope of the North-South marriage and makes it something different by having it mirror the love of an African-American couple. Considering that slaves were not allowed to be married, in part because they were not considered human or capable of the kind of romanticized love of which whites, especially Southern whites under the Cult of True Womanhood, were capable, Chesnutt's stories, and this one in particular, show that part of the cultural education of whites was to see that whites and blacks are linked by their common human feelings. In this way superstition and passion were not mutually exclusive. Moreover, Julius's ability to sympathize with a white Southerner and to see the love of white couples to be the same as that of black couples holds out a more thorough picture of Reconstruction (if not a less idealistic one) than the usual image of a strictly white marriage. After Mabel and Murchison get married, they offer Julius a position in their household. John notes, "For some reason or other, however, he preferred to remain with us" (229). Julius's reasons remain unstated, but they seem to include both self-interest and the hope of further intercultural understanding, as well as bonds, not of steel, but of affection. Superstition has become the medium of feeling and passion across racial and regional barriers.

In her essay, "'The Future American Race': Charles W. Chesnutt's Utopian Illusion," Arlene Elder has evaluated Chesnutt's career using an image which ties him directly to Tourgée:

> Chesnutt's progress toward assimilation and away from the common black experience can be traced easily in his business and social careers and, most tellingly, in his art. Uncle Julius, the narrator of the stories in *The Conjure Woman* (1899), stands at the opposite end of the racial spectrum from Colonel French, the protagonist of Chesnutt's last published work, *The Colonel's Dream* (1905). It is, perhaps, not completely coincidental that the author's gradual movement from identification with the perspective of Julius, the black trickster artist, grounded in folklore and methods of subversion, to that of the naive, liberal, northern white businessman coincides with Chesnutt's deepening pessimism about America's racism. Julius assures himself a place in the post-war South through the magic of black orature; French returns to the North, carrying his dead past and dead future with him, his "fool's errand" emblematic of Chesnutt's own disappointment with a society where "[W]hite men go their way, and black men theirs, and those ways grow wider apart, and no one knows the outcome" (*The Colonel's Dream*, 194). (127)

Elder is correct to see Chesnutt's despair at the end of his literary career (some twenty-seven years before the end of his life) as being similar to Servosse's (and Tourgée's) pessimism about the intransigence of racism in the United States. It is also true that the dialogic and communal quality of *The Conjure Woman* was too optimistic for Chesnutt by 1905; no longer could he hope that Julius and John and Annie could live together striving for mutual understanding. Instead, the rigid and violent segregation of the period compelled each race by law and mob rule to "go their way."

But what I take issue with in Elder's analysis is the idea that Julius as a character and folklore as a genre are expressive of an authentic black experience (which she contrasts to what she sees as Chesnutt's assimilationist tendencies). In this way, Elder is looking for an autochthonous text, as Pratt would say, rather than an autoethnographic text. Julius is indeed the "black trickster artist," but he is also of mixed race, an inhabitant of the contact zone. He is using tricks of mediation to make the contact zone a livable place for all involved without resorting to either violence or self-effacement. From the beginning, Chesnutt was concerned with the interaction of a variety of communities, how they could live together and understand each other. Chesnutt knew that the intermingling of the races under slavery meant that there could never be any such thing as *the* common black experience, any more than there could be *the* common white experience, and there certainly could not be *the* common American experience.[9] Tourgée's fiction had shown Chesnutt how varied white experience was, depicting Northerners, carpetbaggers, scalawags, Southern white supremacists, etc. It was also in part Tourgée's fiction which showed Chesnutt the value of irony, which showed the permeability of cultures and perspectives and revealed how the idolization of any one cultural aspect—even the folk—petrified culture and eliminated that permeability, only contributing further to the social polarization which both men hoped to eliminate.

Notes

1. Helen Chesnutt provides a very different version of this journal entry, one with very different implications: "why could not such a man, if he possessed the same ability, write *as good a book* [italics mine] about the South as Judge Tourgée has written?" (20).

2. Richard O. Lewis discusses Tourgée's possible influence on Chesnutt regarding carpetbagging as a romantic means of economic self-improvement in *The Conjure Woman* (163–64). Lewis asserts that Chesnutt may be drawing from "Tourgée's romantic idea that a man might change his fortunes by removing from one location and reestablishing himself in a more advantageous setting . . ." (163). Self-improvement is undoubtedly a recurrent theme in much of Chesnutt's work, and Chesnutt definitely saw his move from the South back to the North as allowing him greater freedom, but what I think Lewis misses here is that in neither Tourgée, and certainly not in Chesnutt, does this self-improvement take on the unbridled optimism of the American myth of rugged individualism. These writers use carpetbagging and "racial uplift" not so much as an individualist's *Bildungsroman* as a tale of interaction between and within communities.

3. For a detailed discussion of what he terms Signifyin(g), see Gates, Chapters 2–3.

4. Chesnutt attempted a similar understanding of unity and conflict within the African-American community in his relationship with Booker T. Washington. See Elder, "Chesnutt on Washington."

5. For two recent examples, see Ferguson, "Chesnutt's Genuine Blacks" and Elder, "'The Future American Race.'" For two earlier examples, see Baraka and Gayle.

6. For an extended discussion of the relationship between Chesnutt and Harris, see Sundquist, pp. 323–59.

7. Richard Brodhead notes that Chesnutt's conjure tales "follow a single formula, which might be labeled the plot of cultural tourism" (*Conjure Woman* 2). This formula did not originate with Chesnutt, but as Brodhead shows, Chesnutt transformed it. As I have discussed it, Chesnutt alters the cultural tourism of what Lewis characterizes as the romantic element of carpetbagging into what Pratt describes as a contact zone. As such, Brodhead is right to conclude that the

relationship between Julius and John "is one of conflict, not the cross-cultural harmony the genre typically evokes" (6). It is in fact by revealing the conflict—albeit through the indirection of irony and signifying—rather than repressing it, that Chesnutt hopes to achieve, if not actual harmony, at least greater cross-cultural understanding and tolerance.

8. Brodhead refers to this as "the plot of bilingualism" in the conjure tales (*Conjure Woman* 2).

9. Brodhead notes: "One of the more curious ironies of *The Conjure Woman* is that in social and cultural terms Chesnutt himself was considerably closer to John's position than to Julius's. To identify Chesnutt with Julius's black vernacular, as is commonly done, is to fall into this genre's trap of identifying all blacks with a single image of black culture" (*Conjure Woman* 14).

Works Cited

Andrews, William L. *The Literary Career of Charles W. Chesnutt*. Baton Rouge: Louisiana State University Press, 1980.

Baraka, Amiri (Leroi Jones). "The Myth of a 'Negro Literature.'" *Home: Social Essays*. New York: William Morrow, 1966.

Chesnutt, Charles W. *The Colonel's Dream*. New York, 1905.

———. *The Conjure Woman*. 1899; rpt. Ann Arbor: University of Michigan, 1969. All references to *The Conjure Woman* are to this text.

———. *The Conjure Woman and Other Conjure Tales*. Ed. Richard Brodhead. Durham and London: Duke University Press, 1993.

———. "The Future American." *MELUS* 15 (1988): 96–107.

———. *The Journals of Charles W. Chesnutt*. Ed. Richard Brodhead. Durham and London: Duke University Press, 1993.

———. "Post-Bellum—Pre-Harlem." Ed. Elmer Adler. *Breaking into Print: Being a Compilation of Papers wherein Each of a Select Group of Authors Tells of the Difficulties of Authorship and How Such Trials Are Met*. New York: Simon and Schuster, 1937. 47–56. Originally published in *The Colophon*, February 1931.

———. "Superstitions and Folklore of the South." Ed. Alan Dundes. *Mother Wit from the Laughing Barrel: Readings in the Interpretation of Afro-American Folklore*. Englewood Cliffs, N.J.: Prentice-Hall, 1973. 369–76. Originally published in *Modern Culture* 13 (1901): 231–35.

Chesnutt, Helen M. *Charles Waddell Chesnutt: Pioneer of the Color Line*. Chapel Hill: University of North Carolina Press, 1952.

Elder, Arlene A. "Chesnutt on Washington: An Essential Ambivalence." *Phylon* 38 (1977): 1–8.

———. "'The Future American Race': Charles W. Chesnutt's Utopian Illusion." *MELUS* 15 (1988): 121–29.

Ferguson, Sally Ann H. "Chesnutt's Genuine Blacks and Future Americans." *MELUS* 15 (1988): 109–19.

Gates, Henry Louis, Jr. *The Signifying Monkey: A Theory of African-American Literary Criticism*. New York and Oxford: Oxford University Press, 1988.

Gayle, Addison, Jr. *The Way of the New World: The Black Novel in America*. Garden City, N.Y.: Anchor Doubleday, 1975.

Lewis, Richard O. "Romanticism in the Fiction of Charles W. Chesnutt: The Influence of Dickens, Scott, Tourgée, and Douglass." *CLA Journal* 26 (1982): 145–71.

Pratt, Mary Louise. "Arts of the Contact Zone." *Profession 91*. The Modern Language Association of America. 33–40.

———. *Imperial Eyes: Travel Writing and Transculturation*. London and New York: Routledge, 1992.

Reilly, John M. "The Dilemma in Chesnutt's *The Marrow of Tradition*." *Phylon* 32 (1971): 31–38.

Sundquist, Eric. *To Wake the Nations: Race in the Making of American Literature*. Cambridge: Belknap-Harvard University Press, 1993.

Tourgée, Albion W. *A Fool's Errand*. 1879; rpt. Cambridge: Belknap-Harvard University Press, 1961.

———. Papers. Chautauqua County Historical Society, Westfield, N.Y.

———. "The South as a Field for Fiction." *Forum* 6 (1888): 403–13.

African-American and Irish Literature

"About Us, For Us, Near Us": The Irish and Harlem Renaissances

Brian Gallagher

The Harlem Renaissance of the 1920s, which lasted through the 1930s in a much diminished form, constituted the first widespread movement in African-American literary history. For the first time, Black writers, as well as painters, sculptors and musicians, had direct contact with dozens of their fellow artists. Harlem had become the acknowledged "cultural capital" of Black America, for, fed by ever-increasing numbers from the "Great Migration" of Blacks from rural South to urban North, New York City by 1920 had replaced Washington, D.C., as the largest Black urban center in the nation.

In their attempt to comprehend and expand the role Harlem had in this cultural revolution, Black writers often looked beyond national boundaries for models, and one of the most commonly evoked was the Irish Renaissance.[1] "Harlem has the same rôle to play for the New Negro as Dublin has had for the New Ireland. . ." wrote Alain Locke in the introduction to his landmark 1925 interpretative anthology, *The New Negro* (7). While it would be too much to claim that modern Irish writers had a strong influence on the writers of the Harlem Renaissance, it can be said that the paradigm of an oppressed people rising to literary greatness in one short generation did serve as a continuing inspiration and occasional guide for African-American writers in the 1920s. Moreover, the situation of the Irish writer around the turn of the century—with respect to *language, heritage,* and *cultural institutions*—is remarkably similar to that of the African-American writer in the 1920s, a fact which suggests the two literatures, Anglo-Irish and African-American, may profitably be looked at in a comparative framework.

The first issue writers in both Renaissances had to face was whether they represented a genuine, and at least partly autonomous, cultural unit within the dominant culture, be it English or white American. "Like Irish writers," says Nathan Huggins in his thoroughgoing study, *Harlem Renaissance,* "the Negro artists had to resolve the question of whether there was a special Negro voice and art" (203). The facts of linguistic history would seem to indicate the basis for a distinct, discernible "voice" in both instances: "Irish English," circa 1900, reflected the phrasings, locutions, idioms and vocabulary survivals of a nation that had been, until but fifty years before, half Gaelic-speaking. "Black English," circa 1920, although it contained certain survivals from various West African languages, derived its special character more from the process of linguistic adaptation and differentiation forced on Blacks in a racist society, that is, as a means of cultural preservation and survival. The strict concept of "Black English" is one that has evolved only over the last thirty years, although African-American writers in the Renaissance and earlier periods were well aware of the numerous ways in which English as used by most Black Americans differed from English as used by most white Americans. Both dialects—and here I would state my disagreement with those who see either as separate languages—are characterized by one major verb construction missing in standard English: the Irish tendency, because of its absence in the Irish language, to eschew the perfect tense ("have gone") in favor of a combination of a preposition with the present progressive ("after going"); the Black employment of the "be-durative" to distinguish habitual actions ("He be late") from singular occurrences ("He is late"). Both dialects reflect, perhaps because oppressed groups often have to direct anger inward, stylized patterns of belittlement: from the addition of the diminutive "-een" to names to the ironic use of the most elaborate hyperbole in Irish English; and from derogatory terms like "dicty," for pretentious persons or acts, to the elaborate insult system of "the dozens" in Black English. And both dialects encourage, almost demand, eloquence, particularly of the oratorical variety.

Of course, neither group of Renaissance writers was interested primarily in the literal transcription of speech patterns, however distinctive. Even John Synge, a thoroughly mimetic writer linguistically, saw his artistic task as a distillation, and not a direct representation, of the "fiery and magnificent, and tender" imagination of "the Irish peasantry"—to create "poetic" works very much in opposition to those by writers like "Ibsen and Zola dealing with reality in joyless and pallid words" (7). When, at the beginning of the Harlem Renaissance, James Weldon Johnson tried to chart a course for African-American literature to steer between the "absolutely dead" stereotype of "Negro dialect" and the tepid, acultural use of conventional English, he tellingly invoked the example of what Synge had been able to create through the fresh use of language:

> What the colored poet in the United States needs to do is something like what Synge did for the Irish: he needs to find a form that will express the racial spirit by symbols from within rather than by symbols from without, such as the mere mutilation of English spelling and pronunciation. He needs a form that is freer and larger than dialect, but which will still hold the racial flavor; a form expressing the imagery, the idioms, the peculiar turns of thought, and the distinctive humor and pathos, too, of the Negro, but which will also be capable of voicing the deepest and highest emotions and aspirations, and allow of the widest range of subjects and the widest scope of treatment. ("Preface," *Book* 41–42)

In the preface to his major creative contribution to the Harlem Renaissance, *God's Trombones: Seven Negro Sermons in Verse* (1927), Johnson quoted this passage verbatim as an explanation of what he was trying to achieve in his suite of poems. His verse sermons are meant to represent the particular combination of linguistic, religious, and cultural elements that characterize the noble "old-time preaching" of the ministers Johnson types as "God's trombones": their chromatic cadences:

> Weep not, weep not,
> She is not dead;
> She's resting in the bosom of Jesus. (27)

their recalls of Biblical phraseology:

> But the boy was stubborn in his head,
> And haughty in his heart,
> And he took his share of his father's goods,
> And went into a far-off country. (22)

their vivid imagery:

> And the sun will go out like a candle in the wind,
> The moon will turn to dripping blood,
> The stars will fall like cinders,
> And the sea will burn like tar. (56)

and their reliance on dramatic repetitions:

> Sinners came a-running down to the ark
> Sinners came a-swimming all round the ark
> Sinners pleaded and sinners prayed—
> Sinners wept and sinners wailed—
> But Noah'd done barred the door. (36)

Similar reflections of the spoken language and oral tradition abound in the literature of the Irish Renaissance. For instance, the Blind Man in Yeats's *On Baile's Strand* (1903, 1906) speaks in cadenced repetitions: "There had been a fight, a great fight, a tremendous great fight" (*Plays* 21). When Lady Gregory announced her intention to set her cycle of Cuchulain tales in the Kiltartan idiom of her native Galway, she did so in locutions that very much reflected the Irish language from which the tales had passed into English: "I have told the whole story in plain and simple words, in the same way my old nurse Mary Sheridan used to be telling stories from the Irish long ago, and I a child at Roxborough" ("Dedication" 5). Naturally, Synge's combination of linguistic and cultural elements most closely parallels that in *God's Trombones*. Maurya's lament after Bartley's departure in *Riders to the Sea* comes from much the same kind of vivid, simple folk imagination found in Johnson's "sermons": "He's gone now, God spare us, and we'll not see him again. He's gone now, and when the black night is falling I'll have no son left me in the world" (*Plays* 87).

In *The Weary Blues* (1927), Langston Hughes, the most important young writer to emerge from the Harlem Renaissance, sought a more "secular" solution than Johnson to the problem of inventing a language fully adequate to the nuances of the African-American experience. Often he looked to the short lines and repetition patterns that characterize blues and jazz lyrics:

> Weary,
> Weary,
> Trouble, pain.
> Sun's gonna shine
> Somewhere
> Again.
>
> I got a railroad ticket,
> Pack my trunk and ride.
>
> Sing 'em, sister!
>
> Got a railroad ticket,
> Pack my trunk and ride.
> And when I get on the train
> I'll cast my blues aside. (37)

In other poems, Hughes sought to capture the ungrammatical eloquence of the long-suffering: "Well, son, I'll tell you: / Life for me ain't been no crystal stair" (107). Jimmy Farrell, in Synge's *Playboy,* expresses an equally ungrammatical, if somewhat more surreal, vision of life's trials and tribulations: "It's a fright surely. I knew a party was kicked in the head by a red mare, and he went killing horses a great while, till he eat the insides of a clock and died after" (57).

Conversely, writers in both Renaissances would sometimes resort to the extremes of lyricism in an attempt to break down traditional genre boundaries and thereby suggest the poetic quality of their "racial" stories. Jean Toomer's *Cane* (1923) mingles poetry and prose, lyrical flight and scrupulous description, in its evocation of Black Southern life. The heroic plays of Yeats's early theater period, too, mix high rhetoric with high emotion, as in Deirdre's insistence on seeing the body of her beloved, murdered Naoise: "For I will see him / All blood-bedabbled and his beauty gone" (*Plays* 70). Later, writers in both groups would reintroduce dialect in their attempt to explore the symbiotic relationship between imposed and evolved identity, between the comic stereotype and achieved individuation. Zora Neale Hurston's *Mules and Men* (1936), a depiction of Black Southern folkways, and *Their Eyes Were Watching God* (1937), a novel, in this regard much resemble Sean O'Casey's dissection of Dublin tenement life in plays like *Juno and the Paycock* (1924) and *The Plough and the Stars* (1926).

With regard to the cultural heritage out of which they approached the reality of the present, Irish writers and Black writers faced a similar dilemma, namely, that the dominant culture in large measure refused to recognize that heritage, or at least its validity. Irish writers, starting with Standish O'Grady in the late 1870s, as a consequence began to revive, and update, the body of heroic legend and lore—specifically the cycle of Red Branch tales, centering on Cuchulain and Conchubar, and the later cycle of Fenian tales—which made Ireland the cultural equal, at least in terms of cultural continuity, of any European nation. The image of a lost golden past permeates Yeats's very early narrative poem, "The wanderings of Oisin" (1889):

> 'Men's hearts of old were drops of flame
> That from the saffron morning came,
> Or drops of silver joy that fell
> Out of the moon's pale twisted shell.'
> (Yeats, *Poems* 358)

Yeats's youthful desire to "Sing of old Eire and the ancient ways"—which meant to hymn "A Druid land, a Druid tune!" (*Poems* 31, 50)—eventually gave way to the more valid and viable task of using the ancient legends as frames for the depiction of present historical and personal concerns with abiding human ones—a process exemplified by the cycle of Cuchulain plays Yeats produced over a thirty-five year span, the last, "The Death of Cuchulain," being, fittingly, written in his final years. The African-American writer in the 1920s, unfortunately, did not have so definite a body of heroic lore on which to draw. There were, it is true, scores of heroic tales from the period of slavery, particularly the large number centering around the legendary figure of "High John the Conqueror," as well as the African-based tales of that archetypal trickster figure "Brer Rabbit," but such legend was highly compromised both by its origin in slavery, where heroism was strictly of the resistive kind, and, more significantly, by the white co-optation and sanitization of it in works like Joel Chandler Harris's "Uncle Remus" tales.

What many Black writers opted for instead in the romanticizing 1920s was a vision of the land of origin, Africa, the land from which the original slaves were so rudely torn, as an ancient, fully developed civilization. Claude McKay's "Africa" is typical:

> The sun sought thy dim bed and brought forth light,
> The sciences were sucklings at thy breast;
> When all the world was young in pregnant night
> Thy slaves toiled at thy monumental best.
> Thou ancient treasure-land, thou modern prize,
> New peoples marvel at thy pyramids! (40)

Often the image of mythical land is combined with that of present reality in a way which suggests a significant degree of primal racial experience survives in modern African-American life, as in the opening lines of Hughes's "Nude Young Dancer": "What jungle tree have you slept under, / Midnight dancer of the jazzy hour?" (33). Sometimes the invocation of the African past is informed more by wish fulfillment than by historical understanding, in a manner resembling Padriac Pearse's somewhat strained attempt to make Cuchulain a living part of modern Irish culture. The opening stanza of the "Proem" in *The Weary Blues* is just such an instance: "I am a Negro: / Black as the night is black, / Black like the depths of my Africa" (19).

If African-American writers could grow nostalgic over a land from which they were geographically separated, Irish writers could grow equally nostalgic over a land from which they were historically separated. The literal statement of Synge's Deirdre, "it's a lonesome to be away from Ireland always" (248), might also be heard as the symbolic lament of the early Irish Renaissance writers, who saw themselves historically stranded in a tawdry and unheroic present. Kathleen ni Houlihan, that symbol of tragic and suffering Ireland employed by Yeats and others, derives from the same backward-looking impulse to turn a history of oppression into a fount of racial wisdom that informs Hughes's "The Negro Speaks of Rivers"—"My soul has grown deep like the rivers" (51)—and Arna Bontemps "A Black Man Talks of Reaping"—"I have sown beside all the waters in my days" (Johnson, *Book* 262).

More than occasionally the very writers who celebrated the mythic past would despair over its seeming irrelevance for the present. Yeats's poetic sneer in "September 1913" is well known: "Romantic Ireland's dead and gone, / It's with O'Leary in the grave" (*Poems* 106). In "Heritage," Countee Cullen expresses a decided ambivalence towards the "homeland" he readily evoked in a number of other poems:

> Africa? A book one thumbs
> Listlessly, till slumber comes.
>
> One three centuries removed
> From the scenes his father loved,
> Spicy grove, cinnamon tree,
> What is Africa to me? (Johnson, *Book* 222–23)

Obviously, both groups of writers saw a mythical "national" past as something of a fiction, but a necessary fiction, if a literary and cultural renaissance were not to be stillborn.

The very need to reaffirm a significant racial past, even at the cost of some conscious myth making, derived in part from the ongoing fight against racial stereotypes propagated by the cultural institutions controlled by the dominant culture: universities, newspapers, publishing companies, and, most particularly, the stage. "At first," notes Sterling Brown in *Negro Poetry and Drama,* "like the Irish in English drama, because of a roughly similar social position, the Negro seemed doomed to be the comic relief in plays"(103). Of course, the remarkable success of Yeats, Lady Gregory, and others in founding a national theater for Ireland epitomized the early achievement of the Irish Renaissance. Not only did they kill off the "stage Irishman," that happy-go-lucky roarer, they also, in conjunction with the Fay brothers and other Abbey players, fostered a new acting style noteworthy for its combination of poetic intensity and physical quietude. In 1926, W. E. B. Du Bois, writing in *The Crisis,* would outline four principles for a Negro theater movement, principles virtually identical in spirit to those on which the Irish theater movement was based:

> Negro theater must be: I. *About us.* That is, they must have plots which reveal Negro life as it is. II. *By us.* That is, they must be written by Negro authors who understand from birth and continual association just what it means to be a Negro today. III. *For us.* That is, the theatre must cater primarily to Negro audiences and be supported and sustained by their entertainment and approval. IV. *Near us.* The theatre must be in a Negro neighborhood near the mass of ordinary Negro people. (qtd. Huggins 292)

Although it would be three decades before Du Bois's plan was realized on any significant scale, the theater it encouraged had much the same counteractive intent Yeats and Lady Gregory expressed in founding a national theater that would "show that Ireland is not the home of buffoonery and of easy sentiment, as it has been represented, but the home of ancient idealism" (Gregory, *Theatre* 9).

Other cultural institutions, most particularly publishing, also remained largely beyond the control of both Irish and African-American writers, often to their great disadvantage. Without the help of the dilettante author Carl Van Vechten, who dabbled in Negro culture, many authors of the Harlem Renaissance would not have gotten a hearing from publishers. Nor was there always a public ready or willing to understand what the "new" Irish or Black author was trying to say about them: the controversy over *Playboy* in the United States was even worse than in Dublin.

To control cultural institutions ultimately means to control the vision of one's past, to control one's history. In this respect, Du Bois's long editorship (1910–34) of the NAACP periodical *The Crisis* was especially significant, for he not only set social and racial situations in their national and international contexts, but he also published much of the important African-American literature growing out of, and reflecting, those contexts. The continuing value of such a symbiotic relationship between cultural awareness and the literature it fosters is attested to by Lady Gregory's assessment of the significance of the Gaelic League:

> It was a movement for keeping the Irish language a spoken one, with, as a chief end, the preserving of our

> own nationality. That does not sound like the beginning of a revolution, yet it was one. It was the discovery, the disclosure of the folk-learning, the folk-poetry, the folk-tradition. Our Theatre was caught into that current, and it is that current, as I believe, that has brought it on its triumphant way. It is chiefly known now as a folk-theatre. It has not only the great mass of primitive material and legend to draw on, but it has been made a living thing by the excitement of that discovery. (*Theatre* 76)

The literature of both Renaissances is characterized by another, rather more negative, desire for social control—namely, the desire to forge some sort of memorial dignity out of the losing, often fatal, confrontations with the dominant culture. Yeats's grudging paean to the "heroes" in "Easter 1916" reflects this impulse:

> We know their dream; enough
> To know they dreamed and are dead;
> And what if excess of love
> Bewildered them till they died?
>
> I write it out in a verse—
> MacDonagh and MacBride
> And Connolly and Pearse
> Now and in time to be,
> Wherever green is worn,
> Are changed, changed utterly:
> A terrible beauty is born. (*Poems* 179–80)

The rallying tone of McKay's anti-lynching sonnet, "If We Must Die," bespeaks a similar impulse:

> If we must die, let it not be like hogs
> Hunted and penned in an inglorious spot,
> While round us bark the mad and hungry dogs,
> Making their mock of our accursed lot.
> If we must die, O let us nobly die. . . . (36)

The intent here, as in Yeats, is to control, if not the event, at least its tenor and meaning.

The parallel between these two developing literatures holds for works and writers after each Renaissance. For instance, towards the end of *A Portrait of the Artist as a Young Man,* Stephen Dedalus has, when speaking to an English Jesuit at the university, this revelation of cultural dissociation:

> The language in which we are speaking is his before it is mine. How different are the words *home, Christ, ale, master,* on his lips and on mine! I cannot speak or write these words without unrest of spirit. His language, so familiar and so foreign, will always be for me an acquired speech. I have not made or accepted its words. My voice holds them at bay. My soul frets in the shadow of his language. (189)

James Baldwin undergoes a parallel revelation in a remote Swiss village:

> For this village, even were it incomparably more remote and incredibly more primitive, is the West, the West onto which I have been so strangely grafted. These people cannot be, from the point of view of power, strangers anywhere in the world; they have made the modern world, in effect, even if they do not know it. The most illiterate among them is related, in a way that I am not, to Dante, Shakespeare, Michael-angelo, Aeschylus, Da Vinci, Rembrandt, and Racine. (140)

More recently, writers in both groups have dealt significantly with the issue of how to survive, personally and artistically, in a hybrid culture. John Montague's "A Grafted Tongue" typifies a certain bitter fatality about the Irish linguistic, and hence cultural, situation: "To grow / a second tongue, as / harsh a humiliation / as twice to be born" (111). African-American writers have tended, though, to be more hopeful, opting either for a vision of the African-American experience as a microcosm of the American experience, represented by Ralph Ellison's *Invisible Man,* or for a vision of the Black American experience in a Pan-African nexus, represented by the writers and theorists of the "Black Aesthetic."[2]

One could draw other valid parallels between the Irish Renaissance and the Harlem Renaissance—for instance, that the essentially celebratory spirit of each soon provoked major naturalistic works as counterforces, namely Joyce's *Dubliners* (1914) and Richard Wright's *Native Son* (1940). However, to avoid overemphasizing the congruities of the two literary periods, and the two literatures, both incongruities and outright dissimilarities should be borne in mind. Whereas the Irish Renaissance had from the beginning, in the works of Synge and especially of Yeats, a literature of genius, the Harlem Renaissance reached its apotheosis long after its closure, with *Invisible Man* (1952). And, since 1922, Irish literature has been a national literature in the literal sense, whereas African-American literature has, at most, aspired to a cultural nationalism, which some modern Black writers would reject. Still, the valid parallels between modern Irish literature and modern African-American literature—parallels which grow out of much the same kind of experience of cultural imperialism—suggest the grouping of the two literatures in at least one alternate theoretical *and* pedagogical framework. Having taught courses in both African-American literature and Irish literature, as well as having used Black and Irish writers in close conjunction in courses like "Art, Politics and Protest," I can attest to the pedagogical efficacy of viewing the two literatures in conjunction and using one to illuminate the other.

At present, African-American literature is often placed alongside Irish-American literature in the burgeoning, and necessary, field of "Ethnic Studies." Yet, the African-American experience, and the literature reflecting it, is really much closer to the Irish national experience, and the literature reflecting it. Similarly, much Irish literature—especially by writers like O'Casey, Frank O'Connor and Brendan Behan—describes an experience, and a world, more like that found in African-American literature than in English literature, under which Irish literature is still so regularly subsumed. Since categorizations imply, if not determine, interpretations and valuations, we might do well to keep the parallels between modern Irish literature and modern African-American literature in mind, if only as a check against the too-rigid schematization of either literature.

Notes

This essay first appeared in *Éire-Ireland: A Journal of Irish Studies*, 16:4 (Winter 1981). *Éire-Ireland* is a publication of the Irish American Cultural Institute in St. Paul, Minnesota.

1. "Irish Renaissance" is used here in its narrower sense—chiefly the decade 1900–1910 and most significantly the work of Lady Gregory, Synge and Yeats. A much broader delineation of the period—spanning the more than half-century from 1885–1940—appears in Richard Fallis's *Irish Renaissance*.

2. The most important statements, definitions, and examples of this aesthetic are contained in Addison Gayle's 1971 anthology, *The Black Aesthetic*.

Works Cited

Baldwin, James. "Stranger in the Village." *Notes of a Native Son.* 1955. New York: Bantam Books, 1968. 135–49.

Brown, Sterling. *Negro Poetry and Drama.* 1937. New York: Atheneum, 1969.

Fallis, Richard. *Irish Renaissance.* Syracuse: Syracuse University Press, 1977.

Gayle, Addison, ed. *The Black Aesthetic.* Garden City, N.Y.: Doubleday Anchor, 1971.

Gregory, Augusta. "Dedication of the Irish Edition to the People of Kiltartan." *Cuchulain of Muirthemne.* 1902. Gerrards Cross, Buckinghamshire: Colin Smythe, 1973. 5–6.

———. *Our Irish Theatre.* 1913. New York: Capricorn Books, 1965.

Huggins, Nathan. *Harlem Renaissance.* 1971. New York: Oxford University Press, 1973.

Hughes, Langston. *The Weary Blues.* 1927. New York: Alfred A. Knopf, 1931.

Johnson, James Weldon. *God's Trombones: Seven Negro Sermons in Verse.* 1927. New York: Penguin Books, 1976.

———. ed. *The Book of American Negro Poetry,* rev. ed. New York: Harcourt, Brace and World, 1931.

Joyce, James. *A Portrait of the Artist as a Young Man.* 1916. New York: Viking Press, 1964.

Locke, Alain, ed. *The New Negro.* 1925. New York: Atheneum, 1970.

McKay, Claude. *Selected Poems of Claude McKay.* New York: Harcourt, Brace and World, 1953.

Montague, John. *Selected Poems.* Winston-Salem, N.C.: Wake Forest University Press, 1982.

Synge, John Millington. *The Complete Plays of John M. Synge.* New York: Vintage Books, 1960.

Yeats, William Butler. *The Collected Poems of W. B. Yeats.* New York: Macmillan, 1956.

———. *Eleven Plays.* Ed. A. Norman Jeffares. New York: Collier Books, 1964.

Afro-Celtic Connections: From Frederick Douglass to *The Commitments*

George Bornstein

In Roddy Doyle's raucous novel *The Commitments*, recently made into a successful film, the irrepressible Irish impresario Jimmy Rabbitte shocks his new band (and us) with the following dialogue, in which Dublin Irish and black American speech rhythms flow back and forth:

> Your music should be abou' where you're from an' the sort o' people yeh come from.——Say it once, say it loud, I'm black and I'm proud.
>
> They looked at him . . . .
>
> They were stunned by what came next.
>
> —The Irish are the niggers of Europe, lads.
>
> They nearly gasped: it was so true.
>
> —An' Dubliners are the niggers of Ireland. The culchies have fuckin' everythin'. An' the northside Dubliners are the niggers o' Dublin.——Say it loud, I'm black and I'm proud. (9)

As the novel progresses, the euphoric efforts of the newly formed Irish rock group The Commitments to bring black American soul music to Dublin collapse on the very brink of success, with the band disintegrating just at the time that it is offered a record contract. Most of The Commitments lack the commitment to effect such intercultural exchange, and only the fantasy-struck Joey the Lips keeps the faith by leaving Ireland to return yet again to America. But if most of the band turns away from what we now call multiculturalism, the novel itself does not. Indeed, not just in its semantic content but in its speech rhythms, the novel exists in a liminal zone between two races, two ethnicities, two linguistic communities. This means that the novel (like the film) is not simply *about* the encounter of two cultures but in a literal sense *is* that encounter, an encounter which calls into question the adequacy both of any alleged single culture and of a binary model that produces both that monoculture and its inevitable Other. Instead, such mixture or hybridity may be the normal condition of culture and the precondition of its creation, particularly in the modern world.

The Afro-Celticism of *The Commitments* reflects a long history of cross-constructions between those two cultures, usually driven by a common experience of oppression and hope of emancipation. An early exemplar is the nineteenth-century American figure of Frederick Douglass, who himself rose from slavery to become one of the great authors and abolitionists of his time and, at the end of a later career of government service, minister to Haiti. Few Americans now remember or are taught that in 1845, the year of first publication of his celebrated *Life of Frederick Douglass*, he made an invited lecture tour of Ireland. From the last week of August 1845 through the first week of the following January, Douglass gave a series of fiery anti-slavery lectures in Dublin, Wexford, Waterford, Cork, Limerick, and Belfast, sometimes drawing parallels between Irish and American slave experiences and more often distinguishing between them as forms of oppression. While he found American slavery worse in that in his view it deprived people of *all* of their rights rather than some of their rights and property, he drew no such distinction between comparative misery of what he had seen in the American South and what he saw in early famine Ireland. A letter back home to the abolitionist William Lloyd Garrison published in *The Liberator* begins by declaring that "it is the glory of the *Liberator*, that in it the oppressed of every class, color and clime, may have their wrongs fully set forth, and their rights boldly vindicated." Douglass then reports:

> I had heard much of the misery and wretchedness of the Irish people. . . . But I must confess, my experience has convinced me that the half has not been told. . . . During my stay in Dublin, I took occasion to visit the huts of the poor in its vicinity—and of all places to witness human misery, ignorance, degradation, filth and wretchedness, an Irish hut is pre-eminent. . . . Four mud walls about six feet high,

> occupying a space of ground about ten feet square, covered or thatched with straw . . . without floor, without windows, and sometimes without a chimney . . . a piece of pine board . . . a pile of straw . . . a picture representing the crucifixion of Christ . . . a little peat in the fire place . . . a man and his wife and five children, and a pig. In front of the doorway, and within a step of it, is a hole . . . into [which] all the filth and dirt of the hut are put . . . frequently covered with a green scum, which at times stands in bubbles, as decomposition goes on. Here you have an Irish hut or cabin, such as millions of the people of Ireland live in . . . in much the same degradation as the American slaves. I see much here to remind me of my former condition, and I confess I should be ashamed to lift my voice against American slavery, but that I know the cause of humanity is one the world over. He who really and truly feels for the American slave, cannot steel his heart to the woes of others. (*Life* 1:140–41)

Douglass's powerful rhetoric first creates a detailed visual picture of Irish poverty for his reader before moving on to the broader analogy between Irish and American conditions. His own status as an emancipated slave adds authority to his account, which must have struck his nineteenth-century readers with exceptional force. For us at the end of the twentieth century, the greatest shock of recognition may be at the spectacle of Frederick Douglass himself writing that the misery in Famine Ireland was so great that he would be ashamed to lift his voice against American slavery were it not that he saw the cause of humanity as one the world over.

The comparisons and alliances did not all flow one way. No less a figure than Daniel O'Connell may stand for reciprocal interest on the Irish side. Converted to the antislavery cause by the English abolitionist James Cropper, O'Connell noted that the Catholic Emancipation bill had passed with strong support from antislavery MPs, and he reciprocated by marshalling Irish votes for the 1833 Emancipation Act that began abolition of slavery in the British West Indies. Sometimes negotiation between the antislavery and the Irish causes was difficult, as when patriots called for attention to Ireland's wrongs first. But O'Connell never slackened in the sentiments he ringingly announced in his "Speech Delivered at the Great Anti-Colonization Meeting in London, 1833," where he intoned: "I would adopt the language of the poet, but reverse the imagery, and say 'In the deepest hell, there is a depth still more profound,' and that is to be found in the conduct of the American slave-owners. (Cheers). They are the basest of the base—the most execrable of the execrable" (9). Douglass paraphrased that remark in his own address on slavery in Cork on 14 October 1845, where he announced that "I am determined wherever I go, and whatever position I may fill, to speak with grateful emotions of Mr. O'Connell's labours" (*Papers* 1:44). Six weeks earlier, Douglass had taken care to give his first speech in Dublin in the very jail where O'Connell had been confined, and he had been delighted subsequently to be asked to deliver a few remarks at a Repeal meeting at which O'Connell was the featured speaker. For both liberators, the cause of humanity was indeed one.

Conditions were so bad for both the Irish and enslaved African Americans in the nineteenth century that commentators regularly compared them, as we have already seen with both Douglass and O'Connell. A French traveller to both America and Ireland reported that "I have seen the Indian in his forests and the Negro in his chains, and thought, as I contemplated their pitiable condition, that I saw the very extreme of human wretchedness; but I did not then know the condition of unfortunate Ireland" (quoted in Greeley 34–35). As the African-American economic historian Thomas Sowell has noted, slaves in the United States had longer life expectancy, better diets, and superior living conditions to those of Irish peasants (18, 22). American slaves had a life expectancy of thirty-six years compared to the nineteen-year expectancy of Irish peasants, and the death rate on the coffin ships of the Famine year 1847 was 20%, more than double the death rate of slaves transported on British vessels in the nineteenth century. There is no need to set up a competition in relative rates of such horrendous suffering, and the aspects in which blacks were better treated presumably derive from their involuntary status as valuable property rather than from any supposed humanitarianism of their owners. The point is rather the extraordinary oppression of both groups. Irish immigrants to America were even referred to as "White Negroes," or more offensively as "White Niggers."

One response to such suffering was to sentimentalize it, as in the plays of Dion Boucicault, the Irish playwright, actor, and theater manager who did so much to create the stage Irishman. Before that, he helped to create the stage Negro as well, in his famous melodrama *The Octoroon*, first performed in New York a few days after the execution of the abolitionist leader John Brown. There Boucicault constructed a simplistic image of the freed slave as the innocent, virtuous, and persecuted octoroon Zoe, who finally kills herself rather than give pain to her protector. The next year Boucicault finished the first of his three outstanding Irish melodramas—*The Colleen Bawn, or the Brides of Garryowen; Arrah-na-Pogue, or the Wicklow Wedding*, and finally *The Shaughraun*. In those plays Boucicault more than any other writer helped create the image of the stage Irishman, giving a positive spin to the negative representations of the Irish on the earlier English stage and presenting Irish people as quaint, sentimental, humorous, and witty.

Boucicault's sentimental constructions formed one pole of a binary opposition, whose necessary counter was a view of Irish people as animalistic rather than sentimental, subhuman rather than unworldly, and repulsive rather than charming. These racist stereotypes usually drew on a debased Darwinism, in which both blacks and Irish were somehow nearer to apes, and hence less human, than purer Anglo-Saxon types. Two illustrations from the influential American magazine *Harper's Weekly* (whose subtitle "A Journal of Civilization" sounds ironic a century later) make the point.[1] The first (see Figure 1) shows an alleged similarity between "Irish Iberian" and "Negro" features in contrast to the higher "Anglo-Teutonic." The accompanying caption indicates that the Iberians were somehow an originally African race who invaded first Spain and then, apparently, Ireland, where they intermarried with native savages and "thus made way . . . for superior races" (like the English) to rule over them. In the second (Figure 2), the cartoonist Nast offers a political caricature entitled "The Ignorant Vote." There the new black vote in the South for Republicans balances the new white (Irish) vote in the North for Democrats. The African American appears a sort of Sambo-like caricature, and the simian Irishman's boots and clay pipe in hatband indicate his ethnicity clearly. Such prejudice was worse against blacks in the South and against Irish in the North. No less an authority on discrimination than W. E. B. Du Bois recalled that

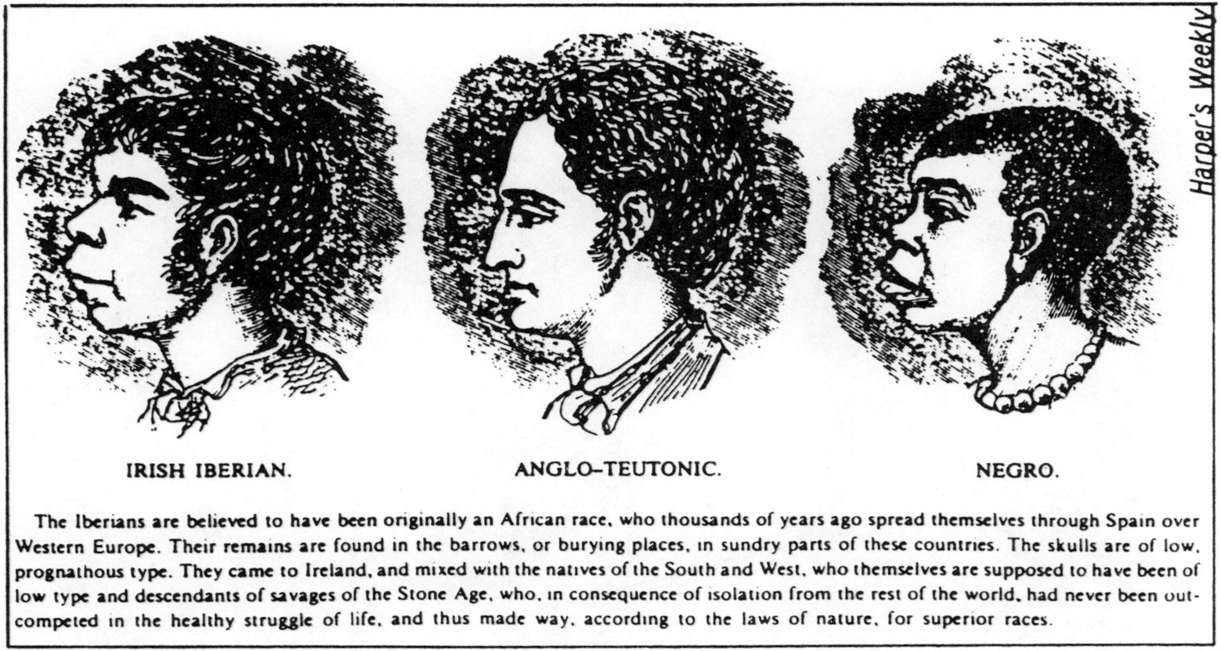
Harper's Weekly
IRISH IBERIAN.
ANGLO–TEUTONIC.
NEGRO.
The Iberians are believed to have been originally an African race, who thousands of years ago spread themselves through Spain over Western Europe. Their remains are found in the barrows, or burying places, in sundry parts of these countries. The skulls are of low, prognathous type. They came to Ireland, and mixed with the natives of the South and West, who themselves are supposed to have been of low type and descendants of savages of the Stone Age, who, in consequence of isolation from the rest of the world, had never been out-competed in the healthy struggle of life, and thus made way, according to the laws of nature, for superior races.

Figure 1: "Irish Iberians" and "Negroes" contrasted to "Anglo-Teutonics"

Figure 2: "The Ignorant Vote"

in growing up in Great Barrington, Massachusetts, in the 1870s, "the racial angle was more clearly defined against the Irish than against me" (*Dusk* 563).

Reactions against such stereotyped constructions helped to drive first the Irish and then the Harlem Renaissances.[2] Both the one created in the Ireland of the late nineteenth and early twentieth century by W. B. Yeats, John Synge, Lady Gregory, Douglas Hyde, and others, and the slightly later one created in the Harlem of the 1920s and 1930s by Langston Hughes, Zora Neale Hurston, James Weldon Johnson and their cohorts, in some ways shared similar goals. Those included reclaiming (or perhaps inventing) a cultural legacy for an oppressed group, using that recuperated heritage to instill ethnic pride and current achievement, and so to enable a future renegotiation of power culturally and politically. Both efforts ran into similar problems, including the contested representation of the folk, the painful ambiguity of using a language associated with the oppressor (perhaps redeemed by inflecting that language with one's own parole), and the struggle to create new cultural institutions.

Writers of the Harlem Renaissance invoked their Irish forerunners as models publicly and explicitly. For example, in his landmark anthology *The Book of American Negro Poetry* (1922), the poet and critic James Weldon Johnson interrupted a discussion of the problems of dialect literature to proclaim:

> What the colored poet in the United States needs to do is something like what Synge did for the Irish; he needs to find a form that will express the racial spirit by symbols from within rather than by symbols from without, such as mere mutilation of English spelling and pronunciation. (41)

Johnson thought the point so important that he reprinted that passage verbatim in the "Preface" to his book of his own verse *God's Trombones* a few years later. That view of "what Synge did for the Irish" involves the substitution of authentic folk image and speech for imposed stereotypes and caricatured dialect. As Synge expressed it in his famous *Preface to the Playboy of the Western World*, "all art is a collaboration" between the artist and the folk-imagination of the people (3). But we may pause over Johnson's call for the artist to "express" the racial spirit. For what

Synge and his cohorts did involved creation as much as expression of such a spirit, and others would arise to contest those representations.

Johnson's contemporary Alain Locke saw the political implication of such constructions and also their potential for divisiveness clearly in his own seminal anthology, *The New Negro: Voices of the Harlem Renaissance* (1925). There he again invoked the Afro-Celtic analogy in linking "folk-expression" explicitly to "self-determination" in declaring that "Harlem has the same role to play for the New Negro as Dublin has had for the New Ireland or Prague for the New Czechoslovakia" (7). The political and social encodings of such artworks inevitably made them sites of contestation, and Locke saw clearly the need for artists and audiences alike to resist both the idealization and the puritanism of those who valued art only for its capacity to "fight social battles and compensate social wrongs." "Just as with the Irish Renaissance, there were the riots and controversies over Synge's folk plays and other frank realisms of the younger school, so we are having and will have turbulent discussion and dissatisfaction with the stories, plays and poems of the younger Negro group," wrote Locke in a passage that current advocates of political purity might well ponder. "But writers like Rudolph Fisher, Zora Hurston, Jean Toomer, Eric Walrond, Willis Richardson, and Langston Hughes take their material objectively with detached artistic vision; they have no thought of their racy folk types as typical of anything but themselves or of their being taken or mistaken as racially representative" (50). Usually African-American writers exploited the Celtic analogy explicitly in critical prose and implicitly in their fiction or poetry, though the Harlem Renaissance did produce poems like Countee Cullen's lyric entitled "After a Visit (At Padraic Colum's where there were Irish poets)." That poem grew out of an invitation to a gathering at Colum's rooms in Paris, where according to his biographer Cullen found "a basis of comparison between the Irish writer's relationship to British letters and the Negro writer's place in American literature" (119). And somewhat earlier Paul Laurence Dunbar himself produced "Circumstances Alter Cases," where a poet best-known for his black vernacular verse makes an astonishing effort to capture Irish dialect, replete with Gaelic interpolation. Here is the first stanza:

> Tim Murphy's gon' walkin' wid Maggie O'Neill,
> O chone!
> If I was her muther, I'd frown on sich foolin',
> O chone!
> I'm sure it's unmutherlike, darin' an' wrong
> To let a gyrul hear tell the sass an' the song
> Of every young felly that happens along,
> O chone! (431–32)

The link between Irish and African-American liberation regularly appeared in more purely political contexts as well, as the spectrum spanned by the black nationalist Marcus Garvey and the Marxist apologist Claude McKay illustrates. Garvey regularly cited the Irish national struggle as a paradigm for liberation movements, emphasizing particularly its seven-hundred-year duration, its blood sacrifice, and its devotion to freedom. He even named his headquarters in New York Liberty Hall in direct emulation of James Connolly's headquarters at Liberty Hall in Dublin, and he justified the inclusion of green along with black and red in the familiar international African flag of the Universal Negro Improvement Association because green symbolized the Irish struggle for freedom. Indeed, at the long-awaited first convention of his Association in Madison Square Garden in 1920, Garvey began his rousing speech first by reading to loud applause a telegram of support for the twin causes of Negro emancipation and Jewish Zionism and then by announcing:

> I hold also in my hand a telegram to be sent to the Hon. Edmund De Valera, President [sic] of the Irish Republic: "25,000 Negro delegates assembled in Madison Square Garden in mass convention, representing 400,000,000 Negroes of the world, send you greetings as President of the Irish Republic. Please accept sympathy of Negroes of the world for your cause. We believe Ireland should be free even as Africa shall be free for the Negroes of the world. [loud applause] Keep up the fight for a free Ireland." (Hill 499)

Interested in solving racial problems more through class than national solidarity, Claude McKay brought a different perspective to the Irish-black connection, yet he too saw and felt the affinities. In his article "How Black Sees Green and Red" McKay told of attending a Sinn Fein demonstration in Trafalgar Square, during which he was greeted as "Black Murphy" and "Black Irish." Although the leaders and participants were too bourgeois for McKay's taste, he still felt sympathy with them. "For that day at least I was filled with the spirit of Irish nationalism—although I am black!" he wrote. "I suffer with the Irish. I think I understand the Irish. My belonging to a subject race entitles me to some understanding of them" (58–59). Indeed, a literal look at their ancestry might indicate another reason why black American leaders might feel sympathy for Irish troubles. Ishmael Reed has pointed out that if Alex Haley had set off the "roots" craze by tracing his ancestry back through his father's side rather than his mother's, he would have ended up in Ireland rather than in Gambia (227). The recent CBS miniseries *Queen*, controversially portraying a romance between the parents of Haley's half-Irish slave grandmother, made that heritage well known; at the time of his death, Haley planned to use the story as the basis of a book to be titled significantly *The Merging*. And the historian Clayborne Carson's research for the *Martin Luther King Jr. Papers* project has led to the discovery that one of King's grandfathers was probably half-Irish (1:19). Appropriately enough, then, songs of the non-violent Civil Rights Movement in America of the 1960s became anthems of the movement for Catholic Civil Rights in Northern Ireland of the 1970s onward, whose Irish adherents particularly favored "We Shall Overcome." The very terms "black" and "white" apparently display a simplistic binary opposition badly in need of questioning.

The literary genre that in some ways seemed to exemplify the emerging political and cultural impulses was drama, with its public audiences, its need of institutions like official theaters, and its seeming capacity to represent ethnic life directly. The Irish National Theatre, that still-surviving institution of the modern Irish Renaissance, seemed an ideal model to many Harlem cultural figures. W. E. B. Du Bois's famous call for a Negro theater in his magazine *The Crisis* for July, 1926—that it be "I. About us. . . . II. By us. . . . III. For us. . . . IV. Near us"—echoed cries by Yeats and others in works like *The Irish Dramatic Movement* that Irish theater needed Irish subjects, Irish authors, Irish audiences, and Irish institutions. The black playwright Willis Richardson, whose drama *Compromise (A Folk*

Play) Alain Locke had included in *The New Negro* anthology, caught the Irish analogy even earlier than Du Bois. In his article "The Hope of a Negro Drama" published in *The Crisis* for November 1919, Richardson wrote:

> An excellent model, and one by which we ought to profit, is the case of the Irish National Theater . . . with no richer material, and among a population of less than five millions, the Irish have built a national drama, encouraged and sustained playwrights, who are respected the same as are the other members of their profession in other countries, and trained a company of actors who have made a decent living by their work on the stage. Had it not been for the Irish Theater, perhaps such names as Synge, Yeats and Lady Gregory, Ervine, Colum and Murray would never have been known among the world dramatists. As it is, they stand high and are honored. This being the case, what ought the Negro Drama in the United States be capable of among a population of fundamentally artistic people which twice outnumbers the population of Ireland? (338)

As with poetry, the impact of Irish drama on the black stage was more implicit than explicit, with few achieving the direct transference of a contemporary work like Mustapha Matura's *Playboy of the West Indies* (1988). That play was first performed in England on the BBC and then revived for a successful run at Lincoln Center in New York in 1993. Matura successfully adapts the plot and dialogue of Synge's Mayo to his own Trinidad, metamorphosing Pegeen Mike into a character named Peggy whose famous closing exclamation comes out in these Caribbean cadences: "Oh Lord, oh Lord, oh Lord. A lose im, a lose im, a lose de only playboy a de West Indies" (73).

A comparison of Synge's *Playboy of the Western World* (1907) and the Zora Neale Hurston-Langston Hughes collaboration *Mule Bone* (1930) exemplifies the parallelism in both dramatic accomplishment and controversial reception of the two Renaissances. Just as Synge set his play in the west of Ireland, the Celtic heartland so to speak, did Hurston and Hughes set theirs in the American South, the most "authentic" region of black folk life. Each play features a common gathering spot in a somewhat isolated rural community, with Michael James's pub finding its analogue in Joe Clarke's store. Both dramas intertwine a plot of violence by a homely implement (Christy's alleged murder of his father with a loy, Jim's attempt to kill Dave with a mule bone) with a romantic one (Pegeen Mike's broken romance with Christy, Daisy's unsuccessful flirtation with both Jim and Dave). In both cases violence between males leads primarily to reconciliation and bonding, with the two male leads going off together at the end of each play rather than one of them marrying the willing but demanding heroine. Both plays foreground vibrant, comic use of non-standard English in their construction of an ethnic community previously presented on the stage primarily in caricature.

And both plays triggered angry responses by members of their own ethnic communities. As is well known, the *Playboy* provoked riots and denunciations on its first performances both in Ireland in 1907 and on its American tour in 1911. Irish nationalists on both sides of the water denounced the play as what we would now call politically incorrect, condemning particularly its representations of race (the Irish), class (the peasantry), and gender (Irish womanhood). As Lady Gregory recalled of the protests in Providence, Rhode Island, during the 1911 tour, "the police people said they had had the same trouble about a negro play said to misrepresent people of colour" (185). It is less well-known that the trouble about alleged misrepresentation did not even wait for the first performance of *Mule Bone*, which took place only in 1991 in New York because of the falling out of its two authors. For several years before 1991, the merits of staging the play at all had been vigorously debated, as at a special forum held after a reading at Lincoln Center in 1988. Hughes's longtime secretary George Bass took a leading role in arranging the 1991 premiere. In his posthumous introduction to the printed version, Bass criticized the play's deviance from political pieties for a 1990s audience in somewhat euphemistic fashion before stating the case bluntly:

> On close reading of the script, it became very clear that a production of the 1930 draft of the text could become quite problematic in terms of the current cultural, social, and political sensibilities of the American public. Rites and Reason Theatre became a collaborator in the task of developing the playscript left by Hurston and Hughes into a viable performance work for a popular theatre

> audience sixty years after the script was created. . . . Many of the comic characters, comic devices, and forms of laughter that were sources of renewal and release within the black community before 1960 are now inhibited by the politics of race and gender. (2–3)

In short, before its initial performance *Mule Bone* was censored and partially rewritten to make it conform as far as possible to currently acceptable modes of representation of African-American character and speech. At the same time, the account conceals personal agency behind impersonal formulations ("It was thought," "Rites and Reason Theatre became") while creating dubiously homogenous social groups ("*the* American public" and "*the* black community") to validate its contentions.

Like other Afro-Celtic connections, the controversies over both *Playboy* and *Mule Bone* do more than remind us that such ethnic constructions inevitably become contested sites of cultural and political power. They suggest too that much art is socially liminal, created often at the intersection of two or more different cultures, and that the purity and separatism of ethnic identity is even more a fabrication than is cultural interaction. It would be easy enough to compile a list of great African-American writers of the past century who have movingly described such interactions. The list might include, for example, W. E. B. Du Bois in the famous passage of *The Souls of Black Folk* where he invokes sitting with Shakespeare and meeting Balzac, Dumas, Aristotle and Aurelius; Paul Robeson in his autobiography when he identifies the key influence on his education being his father taking him through Homer and Virgil in the original Greek and Latin; Zora Neale Hurston recounting in *Dust Tracks on a Road* her desire to be an English teacher to impart to others her fervor for English Romantic poets, especially Coleridge; or Ralph Ellison in his great essay "Hidden Name and Complex Fate" identifying his passion for T. S. Eliot's *Waste Land* as a poem that "seized my mind" and prompted "my conscious education in literature" (159–60). And yet to stop with such attestations might provide too easy a picture of the real stress involved in multicultural creation and response. Perhaps nearer to the mark are two avowals, each well known in its own tradition but whose congruence with the other tradition I emphasize here. The first is Du Bois's famous passage on "double consciousness," itself a term continuing the Wordsworthian echo of the opening section of *Souls of Black Folk*:

> One ever feels his twoness,—an American, a Negro; two souls, two thoughts, two unreconciled strivings; two warring ideals in one dark body, whose dogged strength alone keeps it from being torn asunder. The history of the American Negro is the history of this strife. . . . In this merging he wishes neither of the older selves to be lost . . . to be both a Negro and an American . . . to be a co-worker in the kingdom of culture. (*Souls* 3)

Correspondingly, the great Irish writer W. B. Yeats described his own double consciousness of both Irish and English elements this way in his late essay "A General Introduction for my Work":

> The "Irishry" have preserved their ancient "deposit" through wars which, during the sixteenth and seventeenth centuries, became wars of extermination. No people, Lecky said at the opening of his *Ireland in the Eighteenth Century*, have undergone greater persecution, nor did that persecution altogether cease up to our own day. No people hate as we do in whom that past is always alive, there are moments when hatred poisons my life. . . . Then I remind myself that though mine is the first English marriage I know of in the direct line, all my family names are English, and that I owe my soul to Shakespeare, to Spenser, and to Blake, perhaps also to William Morris, and to the English language in which I think, speak, and write, that everything I love has come to me through English; my hatred tortures me with love, my love with hate. (518–19)

Far from unusual, such avowals of multiple allegiance seem the normal condition of writers, and of ourselves. We write as and are members of various groups—whether defined by "race," ethnicity, class, gender, family, religion, or nationality—and yet of a broader community as well. In that sense, Du Bois's noble aspiration is our own: "to be a co-worker in the kingdom of culture."

Our present criticism has sought relentlessly to demystify claims of art to "universality," unmasking instead the social contingency of its production and reception. Perhaps the tracing of Afro-Celtic connections here suggests that ethnic interaction is the normal state of cultural production, and that fantasies of separatist purity and tradition are themselves urgently in need of demystification. In recent books two leading African-American critics have urged just those contentions. In his *Prophetic Thought in Modern Times* (1993) Cornel West writes that

> from the very beginning we must call into question any notions of pure traditions or pristine heritages, or any civilization or culture having a monopoly on virtue or insight. Ambiguous legacies, hybrid cultures. By hybrid, of course, we mean cross-cultural fertilization. Every culture that we know is a result of the weaving of antecedent cultures.[3] (4)

In a similar vein, Henry Louis Gates Jr. also uses the metaphor of hybridity in *Loose Canons: Notes on the Culture Wars* (1992): "Pluralism sees culture as porous, dynamic, and interactive, rather than as the fixed property of particular ethnic groups . . . the world we live in is multicultural already. Mixing and hybridity are the rule, not the exception" (xvi). All culture may be multiculture already, and the task of education may be to reveal the multiculturalism that is already there rather than to imagine a separatism that never was on land or sea. Thinking of the relation of narrative to reality, Synge's Pegeen Mike exclaims, "There's a great gap between a gallous story and a dirty deed" (77). There may be less of a gap between an American mule bone and the clout of an Irish loy than we sometimes think.

Notes

This essay was originally published in the *Sewanee Review.*

1. For further comparisons see L. Perry Curtis Jr., *Apes and Angels: The Irishman in Victorian Caricature* (Washington, D.C.: Smithsonian Institution Press, 1971). Curtis's seminal monograph has engendered a lively debate; for a recent discussion citing earlier positions, see the title essay of R. F. Foster's *Paddy and Mr. Punch: Connections in Irish and English History* (London: Allen Lane–The Penguin Press, 1993).

2. The best and fullest study of the relation between the two renaissances is Tracy Mishkin, *Black/Irish: Comparing the Harlem and Irish Renaissances*, forthcoming from University Press of Florida. See, too, Brian Gallagher's helpful precursor article, "About Us, For Us, Near Us: The Irish and Harlem Renaissances," *Éire-Ireland* 16:4 (1981): 14–26. [*Ed.* A selection from the former and the latter in its entirety are included in this volume.] I am grateful for many helpful discussions with Professor Mishkin about the interaction of Irish and African-American literature during the time that she was writing her doctoral thesis at the University of Michigan.

3. In the related area of contemporary postcolonial discourse, the term "hybridity" is particularly associated with the work of Homi Bhabha; see his *The Location of Culture* (London and New York: Routledge, 1994), *passim*, especially the essay "Signs Taken for Wonders: Questions of Ambivalence and Authority under a Tree outside Delhi, May 1817," pp. 102–122.

Works Cited

Bass, George Houston. "Another Bone of Contention." *Mule Bone: A Comedy of Negro Life*. By Langston Hughes and Zora Neale Hurston. Ed. George Houston Bass and Henry Louis Gates. New York: Harper, 1991.

Bhabha, Homi. *The Location of Culture*. London and New York: Routledge, 1994.

Carson, Clayborne et al., eds. *The Papers of Martin Luther King, Jr.* Berkeley: University of California Press, 1992–.

Curtis, L. Perry, Jr. *Apes and Angels: The Irishman in Victorian Caricature*. Washington, D.C.: Smithsonian Institution Press, 1971.

Douglass, Frederick. *The Frederick Douglass Papers*. Ed. John W. Blassingame. New Haven: Yale University Press, 1979.

———. *The Life and Writings of Frederick Douglass*. Ed. Philip S. Foner. New York: International Publishers, 1950.

Doyle, Roddy. *The Commitments*. New York: Vintage Books, 1989.

Du Bois, W. E. B. *Dusk of Dawn*. In *Writings*. New York: Library of America, 1986.

———. *The Souls of Black Folk*. Ed. Henry Louis Gates Jr. New York: Bantam, 1989.

Dunbar, Paul Laurence. *Complete Poems*. New York: Dodd, Mead, 1968.

Ellison, Ralph. *Shadow and Act*. New York: Vintage, 1972.

Ferguson, Blanche E. *Countee Cullen and the Negro Renaissance*. New York: Dodd, Mead, 1966.

Foster, R. F. *Paddy and Mr. Punch: Connections in Irish and English History*. London: Allen Lane–The Penguin Press, 1993.

Gallagher, Brian. "About Us, For Us, Near Us: The Irish and Harlem Renaissances." *Éire-Ireland* 16:4 (1981): 14–26.

Gates, Henry Louis, Jr. *Loose Canons: Notes on the Culture Wars*. New York: Oxford University Press, 1992.

Greeley, Andrew M. *That Distressful Nation*. New York: Quadrangle Books, 1972.

Gregory, Lady Augusta. *Our Irish Theatre*. New York: Capricorn, 1965.

Hill, Robert A., ed. *The Marcus Garvey and Universal Negro Improvement Association Papers*. Berkeley: University of California Press, 1983–.

Johnson, James Weldon, ed. *The Book of American Negro Poetry.* 1922. New York: Harcourt, Brace, 1969.

Locke, Alain, ed. *The New Negro: Voices of the Harlem Renaissance.* 1925. New York: Atheneum, 1992.

Matura, Mustapha. *Playboy of the West Indies.* New York: Broadway Play Publishing, 1988.

McKay, Claude. "How Black Sees Green and Red." *The Passion of Claude McKay: Selected Poetry and Prose.* Ed. Wayne Cooper. New York: Schocken Books, 1973.

Mishkin, Tracy. *Black/Irish: Comparing the Harlem and Irish Renaissances.* Gainesville: University Press of Florida, forthcoming.

O'Connell, Daniel. *Daniel O'Connell upon American Slavery.* New York: American Anti-Slavery Society, 1860.

Reed, Ishmael et al. "Is Ethnicity Obsolete?" *The Invention of Ethnicity.* Ed. Werner Sollors. New York: Oxford University Press, 1991.

Richardson, Willis. "The Hope of a Negro Drama." *Crisis* 19 (1919): 338–39.

Sowell, Thomas. *Ethnic America: A History.* New York: Basic Books, 1981.

Synge, John. *The Complete Plays.* New York: Vintage Books, 1960.

West, Cornel. *Prophetic Thought in Modern Times.* Monroe, Maine: Common Courage Press, 1993.

Yeats, W. B. *Essays and Introductions.* New York: Macmillan, 1961.

"How Black Sees Green and Red": African-American and Irish Interaction in the Early Twentieth Century

Tracy Mishkin

Tim Murphy's gon' walkin' wid Maggie O'Neill, / O chone!

Paul Laurence Dunbar, African-American poet

O! George, you may, without a blush, confess your love for the Octoroon.

Dion Boucicault, Irish playwright

The Abbey Theatre's 1911 tour of the United States caused unrest in several cities over John Synge's *Playboy of the Western World:* many theater-goers felt that the play inaccurately represented rural Irish people, especially women. Their counterparts in Ireland had already condemned Synge's work and others of the Irish Renaissance: in 1907 the *Freeman's Journal* described it as "unmitigated, protracted libel on Irish peasant men and, worse still upon Irish peasant girlhood" (quoted in Greene and Stephens 257). However, even as eggs and potatoes were hurled at the actors (Dalsimer 77), the Abbey's representations of Irish life caught the imagination of those Americans interested in exploring the various facets of their own national identity, including several people, black and white, who went on to participate in the Harlem Renaissance of the 1920s. They noted the many similarities between Irish culture and history and that of African Americans, and they advocated following the Irish model for literary renaissance and social change.

Although their depictions of Irish life had come under fire at home as well as abroad, the Abbey's use of folk culture and of Irish dialects was intended to create more accurate portrayals of Irish people than those found on the British stage. As the theater's co-founders W. B. Yeats and Augusta Gregory wrote in an 1898 manifesto, "[w]e will show that Ireland is not the home of buffoonery and of easy sentiment, as it has been represented. . ." (Gregory 9). The Irish Renaissance inspired Americans to attempt a similar type of literature using black culture as a base. In 1926, W. E. B. Du Bois marked the founding of the Krigwa Players Little Negro Theatre by publishing an essay which put forth a definition of a black theater movement. It stated, in part, that "[t]he plays of a real Negro theatre must be [about us]. That is, they must have plots which reveal Negro life as it is" (134). Du Bois did not mention the Abbey Theatre in his article, but the Krigwa Players were part of the Little Theatre movement that was engendered by the Abbey's American tours.

Unfortunately for both the Harlem and Irish Renaissances, many community leaders were interested not in realistic representations but in idealized portraits because they wanted to enlist literature to fight prejudice. This clashed with the writers' desire for artistic freedom, which did not necessarily favor realism either. For these reasons, the dreams of Yeats, Gregory, and Du Bois were not easily fulfilled. The Harlem Renaissance's depictions of the folk proved to be as controversial as those of the Irish movement.

In 1911, borrowing ideas from and comparing one's movement to other ethnic groups struggling for political freedom and cultural identity had been common in Europe and in the Americas for over one hundred years, indeed since the origins of nationalism itself in the late eighteenth century. As Benedict Anderson writes in *Imagined Communities,*

> when history made it possible, in 1811, for Venezuelan revolutionaries to draw up a constitution for the First Venezuelan Republic, they saw nothing slavish in borrowing verbatim from the Constitution of the United States of America. For what the men in Philadelphia had written was in the Venezuelans' eyes not something North American, but rather something of universal truth and value. (192)

Thus, the influence of the Irish Renaissance on African-American writers and intellectuals is not unusual, despite the fact that black people and Irish-Americans were not on the best of terms in America's cities, nor does it imply black cultural dependence on the "white" Irish culture. Indeed, as I will discuss later, Irish people also compared themselves to African Americans and often sympathized with them politically.

Although comparisons of Irish people and African Americans date back to at least the late eighteenth century, before the twentieth century the two peoples were rarely discussed together in positive terms by members of either group: both high- and popular-culture depictions posited inferiority or at best pitiability as the terms of comparison. For example, the English ethnologist John Beddoe claimed that his Index of Nigrescence showed that as one moved from east to west in the British Isles, the people became more and more Africanoid, sporting dark complexions, large jaws, and long nostrils. Although his Index was scientifically specious, Beddoe's mass of data, the result of over thirty years of fieldwork, was highly convincing to his late nineteenth-century audience (Curtis 19-20). On the other hand, Gustave de Beaumont, a French traveller, wrote in 1839:

> I have seen the Indian in his forests, and the negro in his chains, and thought, as I contemplated their pitiable condition, that I saw the very extreme of human wretchedness; but I did not then know the condition of unfortunate Ireland.[1] (268)

In the early twentieth century, American representations began to change as black people began writing in increasing numbers and as news of the Irish Renaissance spread. In addition to derogatory or pitying comparisons, artistic and political ones emerged, with both white and black Americans noting the potential usefulness of the Irish Renaissance for those interested in portraying African-American lives. Ridgely Torrence, a versatile white author not well known today, provides an early example of a writer being inspired by the Irish Renaissance to produce literature on African-American subjects. Torrence had seen the Abbey Theatre's 1911 productions in New York City, and, as he explained in 1917, "[t]he parallel . . . with the Irish race and its national drama, made a deep impression on me. I wanted to make the experiment, and try to contribute something, if I could, to a possible Negro drama, as vital and as charming as the Irish" ("The New Negro Theatre" 80). His play *Granny Maumee* was written and first produced in 1914, and, in 1917, two of Torrence's other "Negro plays," *The Rider of Dreams* and *Simon the Cyrenian*, joined it on the New York stage at the Garden Theatre. The latter production was notable for its use of African-American actors, at that time still a rarity outside of amateur black theater. Despite his reference to Irish drama as "charming," Torrence's plays were often anything but. In *Granny Maumee*, for example, he explored the issue of racial purity from a black perspective, an unusual approach for a white author and one which made his audiences uncomfortable (Gale 140).

Torrence's works were well received by both white and black audiences. Several white critics called them significant and compared them to the plays of the Irish Renaissance. After the 1914 production, Carl Van Vechten, future Harlem Renaissance promoter, wrote that he hoped *Granny Maumee* would not be "a flash in the pan," calling it "as important an event in our [American] theater as the production of the first play of Synge was to the Irish movement" ("Beginnings of a Negro Drama" 1114). In 1917 Zona Gale, a novelist and journalist, stated in a review in *Theatre Arts Magazine* of Torrence's plays that

> [t]o do for the negro theatrically what has been done for the Irish by the Irish Theatre movement is magnificently worthwhile. This is to interpret to the public—and perhaps to itself—a race never yet understood, in a land which is not of its own choosing. (139)

Journalist Heywood Broun echoed Gale's comments in a *New York Tribune* article, stating that until the production of Torrence's work, "negro life ha[d] meant little to the stage but burnt cork, lumbago, and the word 'massa'" (11).

White reviewers like Van Vechten, Gale, and Broun hoped that Torrence's plays would usher in a new and important form of American drama and improve the extant dramatic representations of African Americans, and they often drew explicit connections to the Irish theater movement to make their points. African Americans also reviewed Torrence's plays, but the Irish theater connection received less attention than Torrence's respectful presentation of black lives. For example, James Weldon Johnson wrote in the *New York Age*, an African-American newspaper, that "[i]t is almost amazing to think how Mr. Torrence . . . could write plays of Negro life with such intimate knowledge, with such deep insight and sympathy" ("The Negro and the Drama"). On the other hand, Lester Walton, the *Age*'s drama critic, took Torrence to task for using dialect for all of his characters, because he felt that it was "hardly probable that *Dr. Williams*, with a college education, would employ Negro dialect in conversation" ("Negro Actors Make Debut in Drama at Garden Theatre; Given Most Cordial Welcome").

Reviewers of the 1910s, black and white alike, generally found Torrence's work realistic and sincere. Few expressed a concern that he might have experienced difficulty depicting African-American lives. One anonymous essayist did say that because he or she had only seen reviews by white people, "it was too early to conclude whether, like Synge, Torrence [had] penetrated the real psychology of a race. . ." ("Beginnings of a Negro Drama" 1114). As time passed, more African Americans preferred black depictions of black characters—Du Bois's 1926 article says a Negro theater must have Negro authors—but in 1917, serious dramatic representation of African Americans was so new that merely using a black cast met most critics' desires for realistic representation.[2]

Although by the 1920s black representations of black lives were more in demand, African-American intellectuals were still comfortable with borrowing ideas from other cultures. In the decade after Torrence's second production of "Negro plays," they not only took up the comparison to the Irish dramatic movement but also expanded it to include other genres and extra-literary phenomena. In 1925, Alain Locke wrote in the introduction to the *New Negro* anthology that "[w]ithout pretense to [its] political significance, Harlem has the same rôle to play for the New Negro as Dublin has had for the New Ireland. . ." (7). Locke suggested a largely cultural connection, but both political and cultural comparisons were made by other African-American writers, intellectuals, and politicians.

Dramatist Willis Richardson initiated the literary comparisons in his 1919 article "The Hope of a Negro Drama." After explaining his definition of "Negro plays," that is, those which surpass mere "plays with Negro characters" and propaganda plays and, instead, show "the soul of the people," he called the Irish theater movement "an excellent model, and one by which we ought to profit" (338). Richardson exhorted African Americans to build a "Negro Drama," stating that Ireland had built a respected national drama with a much smaller population as a resource. He looked forward to the day when "a company of Negro Players with Negro Plays" would tour America and Europe, much as the Abbey Theatre had toured Ireland and the United States (339). However, Richardson does not discuss the controversies over the Abbey Theatre's representations of Irish people. He was either not aware of them, which seems unlikely, given the reception of the Abbey tours, or the company's accomplishments were more important to him than the fact that "the soul of the people" was highly contested.

In the early 1920s, James Weldon Johnson began to apply Irish ideas to black poetry. In the preface to his 1922 anthology, *The Book of American Negro Poetry*, he wrote of his desire for African-American poets to set aside dialect poetry in favor of less restrictive forms:

> [w]hat the colored poet in the United States needs to do is something like what Synge did for the Irish; he needs to find a form that will express the racial spirit by symbols from within rather than by symbols from without, such as the mere mutilation of English spelling and pronunciation. He needs a form that is freer and larger than dialect, but which will still hold the racial flavor; a form expressing the imagery, the idioms, the peculiar turns of thought, and the distinctive humor and pathos, too, of the Negro, but which will also be capable of voicing the deepest and highest emotions and aspirations, and allow of the widest range of subjects and the widest scope of treatment. (xl-xli)

Johnson found dialect poetry a limited form, allowing only the expression of "humor and pathos." He was not opposed to the use of African-American dialects *per se*, but to the "limitations on Negro dialect [poetry] imposed by the fixing effects of long convention," that is, the association with "'possums . . . [and] watermelons" (xxxix-xl). Johnson felt that the problems with dialect could be resolved by an approach similar to Synge's which would accent Standard English with the idioms of African-American speech. In 1927 he published *God's Trombones,* a collection of African-American sermons rendered as poetry, in which he attempted to follow his own advice to black writers. In the introduction to this volume, Johnson went so far as to reprint his comments about Synge from his earlier book, declaring, "because I cannot say it better, I quote. . ." (8). Like Richardson, Johnson focussed on accomplishments rather than controversies. Synge was, however, often at the center of the storms surrounding the Abbey, as his dialect and characters were literary inventions in a country hungry for and expecting realistic representations of speech and person.

Alain Locke was among the most frequent commentators on the Harlem and Irish Renaissances, discussing such similarities between the two movements as their urban bases, their use of folk cultures, and the responses of their audiences. Although in the introduction to *The New Negro* Locke discounted any political comparison between the two movements, his dismissal of politics did not extend to a dismissal of controversy. In fact, he seems more aware than Johnson or Richardson of the problems the Irish Renaissance had faced. Later in the same work, in an essay entitled "Negro Youth Speaks," he explained why the fledgling Harlem Renaissance was garnering mixed reviews in African-American communities:

> [j]ust as with the Irish Renaissance, there were the riots and controversies over Synge's folk plays and other frank realisms of the younger school, so we are having and will have turbulent discussions and dissatisfaction with the stories, plays and poems of the younger Negro group. (50)

Locke noted that, just as in Ireland, those who wanted literature primarily to fight prejudice were uncomfortable with the "frank realisms" of writers such as Jean Toomer, Zora Neale Hurston, Willis Richardson, and Langston Hughes because they feared their work would cast all African Americans in a negative light.

Writers in both movements wanted the freedom to choose their own subject matter, but whether that meant Synge's peasants or Hurston's, many Irish people and African Americans were angered by them.

The Irish Renaissance served as both exhortation and explanation for African-American writers and intellectuals: the Abbey Theatre's work suggested the use of folk plays and mediated dialect to Richardson and Johnson, and the Irish movement's negative experiences helped Locke explain similar occurrences to African Americans. The examples given here seem to suggest that their knowledge of Irish literature was limited to drama, and their knowledge of drama to John Synge's work. Synge was certainly well known, but other less famous Irish writers inspired black authors as well: Countee Cullen, for example, felt poetically revitalized after attending a Parisian party at which he met several Irish poets (Ferguson 119–20).

While Locke had spoken "[w]ithout pretense to [its] political significance," others such as Marcus Garvey, A. Philip Randolph, and Claude McKay found a great deal of "political significance" in a comparison of African-American and Irish people. Before twenty-five thousand delegates at the 1920 Universal Negro Improvement Association (UNIA) convention in Madison Square Garden, Marcus Garvey began his keynote address by reading a telegram he was sending—not to a famous person of African descent, but to Eamon de Valera, president of the year-old Dáil Éireann, the Irish Parliament. Referring to the ongoing Irish war for independence from England, Garvey read, "We believe Ireland should be free even as Africa shall be free for the Negroes of the world. Keep up the fight for a free Ireland" (Hill 499).[3] The Irish struggle for cultural and political autonomy had inspired the leader of the Back to Africa movement, and Garvey, who had built his movement largely on pageantry, knew a good symbol when he saw one.

Garvey's sometime ally A. Philip Randolph, editor of the radical black journal *The Messenger*, also compared the Irish political situation to that of his own people, though his goal was to convert African Americans to socialism. In the summer of 1919, as racial violence flared in America and many blacks took up the banner of the New Negro, Randolph exhorted them to follow the revolutionary activities occurring world-wide. In an article entitled "A New Crowd—A New Negro," he stated, with more enthusiasm than orthographic accuracy, "The Seine Feiners are the New Crowd in Ireland fighting for self-determination" (Huggins 19).[4] Old Crowds around the world he likened to appendixes, useless and potentially harmful. Randolph and Garvey both made use of the Irish struggle for independence, but though it succeeded where they did not, its outcome was not entirely positive. The Irish Free State had a repressive and isolationist government which practiced extreme forms of censorship and chose not to side with the Allies in World War II because it did not wish to help England. Though inspirational, Ireland for the Irish became as problematic as Africa for the Africans.

The Jamaican-born writer Claude McKay seems to have had a special affinity for the Irish Renaissance and Irish politics, although he knew of and was sympathetic to many cultural and political movements. During the summer of 1920, he wore a green necktie to a Sinn Fein demonstration in London and was addressed with camaraderie as "Black Murphy" and "Black Irish." Back in America a year later, McKay wrote an article entitled "How Black Sees Green and Red" for the radical journal *Liberator*. In this piece he described the demonstration in London and stated that "[f]or that day at least I was filled with the spirit of Irish nationalism—although I am black!" (58). McKay felt that his position as a colonial subject and his peasant roots helped him understand Irish people better than the English government, the English socialists, or what he termed the "anglicized Irish" like George Bernard Shaw (60). He described his empathy for the Irish people as one based in their common "peasant's passion for the soil" (59).[5]

McKay's relation to Irish people and the cause of Irish independence illustrates not only the possibilities but also the dangers of this type of ethnic comparison. His reference to the "peasant's passion for the soil" is a vague and troublesome notion of similarity. The primitivist mindset of the times, which affected both whites and blacks, played a role in making ethnic comparisons available, often creating spurious similarities between disempowered groups. Many believed, for example, that non-white peoples and certain white ethnic groups like the Irish were emotional, sensual, and child-like. One might think of Torrence's reference to Irish drama as "vital . . . and charming" ("The New Negro Theatre" 80).

I am often asked whether Irish people were influenced by African Americans; that is, whether the connection worked both ways. In fact, Irish self-comparisons to black people date back to the late eighteenth and early nineteenth centuries when political leaders such as John Philpot Curran and Daniel O'Connell compared their struggle for Catholic Emancipation and repeal of the Act of Union between England and Ireland to the abolitionists' fight against the slave trade. O'Connell spoke out so strongly against slavery that he drew criticism in Ireland and America for not making the repeal movement his paramount concern, and he lost much of his American support when he would not compromise his humanitarian principles. In a March 1845 speech to the Repeal Association, O'Connell thundered, "I want no American aid if it comes across the Atlantic stained in Negro blood" (O'Ferrall 44–45). However, not all Irish politicians were comfortable with even occasional comparisons between their people and African-descended slaves: Arthur Griffith spent more than a quarter of his 1913 preface to John Mitchel's 1854 *Jail Journal* defending Mitchel's pro-slavery views and indignantly added, "as if excuse were needed for an Irish Nationalist declining to hold the negro his peer in right" (xiv). Although Irish people did not always agree about the similarity of their situation to that of American slaves, it was part of a hot debate for decades.

Early comparisons also occurred in the arts. Four days after the hanging of John Brown in 1859, a play by the prolific and popular Irish playwright Dion Boucicault entitled *The Octoroon; Or, Life in Louisiana* opened in New York. *The Octoroon* was a melodrama which aimed to please pro- and anti-slavery factions: the author presented both bucolic plantation scenes and the horrors of slavery. Although Boucicault straddled the fence on the slavery question, the play differed enough from standard nineteenth-century depictions of African Americans for Montgomery Gregory to praise it in the 1927 anthology he co-edited with Alain Locke, *Plays of Negro Life*. Gregory wrote that *The Octoroon* represented a welcome respite from the flood of minstrel shows popular in the second half of the nineteenth century, as it "accustomed the theatre-going public to the experience of seeing a number of Negro characters in other than the conventional 'darkey' rôles" (409–10). Gregory exaggerated: the title character, Zoe, is the only non-"darkey" character, although one was enough to infuriate a New York theater critic who pronounced the play abolitionist propaganda and Zoe an impossible creation ("'The Octoroon'. A Disgrace to the North, a Libel on the South" 1).[6]

Since Gregory's comments in 1927, other critics have also distorted Boucicault's attitudes and accomplishments, overstating the degree to which he perceived a connection between Irish and African-American oppressions. For example, biographer Richard Fawkes stated that "[a]s an Irishman, a member of a subjugated nation, Boucicault felt keenly the indignity of slavery, of one race being beholden to another" (109). Fawkes does not successfully substantiate this claim with Boucicault's writings. In fact, in an 1861 letter to the *London Times,* Boucicault claimed that his years of residence in Louisiana had shown him that slavery was not as terrible as the abolitionists asserted: "I found the slaves, as a race, a happy, gentle, kindly-treated population, and the restraints upon their liberty so slight as to be rarely perceptible" (5). It may not be a coincidence that Boucicault's plays written in the decade or so after the production of *The Octoroon* included his most famous Irish comic political melodramas, *The Colleen Bawn, Arrah-na-Pogue,* and *The Shaughraun*; however, the assertion that Boucicault explicitly connected African-American and Irish oppressions remains conjectural.

References to African Americans also appear in the writings of W. B. Yeats and Lady Gregory. In the 1905 edition of the Abbey publication *Samhain,* Yeats complained about the harsh reception of the company's plays in Ireland. Searching for a way to explain this phenomenon, he suggested that the Irish people's loss of self-confidence, which he connected to the decline of the Irish language, caused their reluctance to accept humorous, imaginative, or critical presentations of Irish life. "If Ireland had not lost the Gaelic," he wrote, "she never would have had this sensitiveness as of a *parvenu* when presented at Court for the first time, or of a negro newspaper" (192). Yeats's correlation of the "sensitiveness" of Irish nationalists and African-American journalists was accurate: apparently the latter's outspoken condemnation of negative coverage in the mainstream press was known across the Atlantic as well as in America.

Lady Gregory experienced several connections between black and Irish culture while touring America with the Abbey Theatre in 1911. For instance, when the company arrived in

Providence, Rhode Island, in October of that year, they found a petition against *The Playboy of the Western World* waiting for them at the Police Commissioners' office. Lady Gregory recorded in *Our Irish Theatre* that after she had successfully responded to accusations of obscenity and misrepresentation and ensured that the play would be produced, "[t]he police people said that they had had the same trouble about a negro play said to misrepresent people of colour" (185). The officers may have been thinking of *The Clansman,* an adaptation of Thomas Dixon's popular 1905 novel which asserted white superiority. *New York Age* drama critic Lester Walton noted that the play was protested by African Americans in Camden, New Jersey, late in 1909, and since black characters figured in so few plays at the time, *The Clansman* may well have been the one protested in Providence two years later ("Theatrical Comment").

Lady Gregory continued her train of thought from Lowell, Massachusetts, remarking the "sensitiveness" of the various ethnic groups who had managed to require police reports not to disclose the nationality of those charged with crimes (186). Her attitude parallels Yeats's on "negro newspapers"—interested, but not altogether sympathetic since she felt excess "sensitiveness" produced the mobs who disrupted plays at the Abbey. Because they encountered African Americans reacting to prejudice rather than as fellow artists, Yeats and Lady Gregory understandably associated them with the overzealous nationalists of their own country.

When black writers came in contact with people of Irish descent, the results were quite different. Claude McKay appears to have been quite successful at gaining Irish and Irish-American sympathy. In addition to the warm reception at the 1920 Sinn Fein rally described in his essay "How Black Sees Green and Red," he recorded two incidents in his autobiography, *A Long Way from Home,* in which Irish-Americans made a connection between his racial situation and Ireland's (post)colonial status. In the winter of 1921, shortly after returning from London, he visited his old mentor Frank Harris, editor of *Pearson's Magazine.* McKay brought along a copy of his first publication outside Jamaica, *Spring in New Hampshire.* Harris congratulated him on publishing in London but then grew angry when he realized that McKay had left his militant poem "If We Must Die" out of the book on the advice of his publishers. McKay described Harris's reaction as follows:

> "You are a bloody traitor to your race, sir!" Frank Harris shouted. "A damned traitor to your own integrity. That's what the English and civilization have done to your people. . . . The English make obscene sycophants of their subject peoples. I am Irish and I know. But we Irish have guts the English cannot rip out of us. I'm ashamed of you, sir." (98)

Harris's harsh words sparked a change of mind about omitting "If We Must Die" and several other powerful poems, and McKay resolved to include them in his forthcoming American publication, *Harlem Shadows.* Harris had been able to give him this advice, McKay believed, because he was also a member of one of England's "subject peoples" and therefore understood McKay's situation.

Several years later, McKay was once again helped by an Irish American who he felt made a connection between racial and colonial oppression. During the spring and summer of 1926, McKay worked for the Irish-American movie director Rex Ingram in France. Ingram wrote poetry, shared many of McKay's radical opinions, and was an informed conversationalist on "the life and thought and achievements of minority groups" (274). His friendliness with McKay, which extended to inviting him to dine at his private table, incurred the wrath of many of the American film crew and of one Italian who had lived in America and acquired its prejudices. The Italian man goaded McKay until he pulled a knife and chased him around a bus. When his anger faded, McKay realized that he had just enacted the stereotype of the knife-wielding Negro, and he was certain that he had lost his job. Although another employee played up the stereotype to Ingram in an attempt to get McKay fired, Ingram refused even to chastise McKay, and, when the movie season was over, he gave him a train ticket and six hundred francs. McKay did not record Ingram's explanation for his open-minded and generous actions, writing simply, "Rex Ingram's face revealed that he possessed an intuitive understanding of poets. He is Irish" (276). For the primitivist McKay, who believed in the poetic nature of Irish people, that was all that needed to be said. However, Ingram's motivation is, at bottom, unknown, despite McKay's assertions.

McKay recorded more black/Irish connections than anyone, but we don't know how many of them were all in his head.

Because Yeats and Lady Gregory did not meet African-American writers like McKay and they knew little of American racial politics, they were less sympathetic to black people than the Irish Americans McKay encountered. Indeed, it would have been difficult for Irish people to have made black/Irish comparisons equally often, for while America enjoyed the Abbey Theatre's tours, the corresponding black entertainment in Ireland consisted of "funny nigger comics" in the 1880s and "nine real American negroes" a generation later—that is, minstrel shows (O'Brien 47). However, despite the frequent lack of information and interaction, Irish and Irish-American people in the early twentieth century often made explicit connections to their own experiences when assessing African-American actions. Although these comparisons were sometimes rooted in stereotypes, the inspiration they gave to the writers suggests the usefulness of cross-cultural study and the limitations of investigating only intraracial literary interaction.

While earlier in this century more African Americans drew connections between themselves and Irish people than vice versa, the opposite is true today. With world communications simplified and a larger body of black literature extant, Irish people often compare themselves to black Americans or South Africans, despite the fact that racism is a problem in Ireland. In an interview with Richard Kearney, the Irish musician Bono of the group U2 listed the blues and gospel music among his band's influences and compared the Irish and black quests for identity (189–90). According to Bill Rolston, wall murals in Belfast have compared black South African and Irish struggles against colonialism (23). The film and novel *The Commitments* explored the influence of soul music on an Irish band of the same name. Although ill-conceived comparisons still occur, connections between ethnic groups are explored more fully today than in the past century. The inability of "The Commitments" to finally commit to soul music is a poignantly ironic example.

Although black/Irish comparisons are popular in Ireland, they are less so among African Americanists, many of whom are more interested in building a canon of black literature, which often means restricting oneself to the study of internal influences. Comments like Maya Angelou's, who said in 1992 that she would like to see her play *And Still I Rise* performed with an Irish cast, are rare. As Aijaz Ahmad writes in *In Theory: Classes, Nations, Literatures*:

> The axiomatic fact about *any* canon formation, even when it initially takes shape as a counter-canon, is that when a period is defined and homogenized, or the desired literary typology is constructed, the canonizing agency selects certain kinds of authors, texts, styles, and criteria of classification and judgement, privileging them over others which may also belong in the same period, arising out of the same space of production, but which manifestly fall outside the principles of inclusion enunciated by that self-same agency. . . . (123)

With the canon now largely built, I hope African Americanists will feel more comfortable exploring cross-cultural influences, for despite their somewhat compromised origins, the connections between black and Irish culture continue to inspire today.

Notes

1. Cited in Sowell, p. 18. Luke Gibbons notes that comparisons of Irish people and Native Americans date back to 1562.

2. See, for example, Walton, "Using the Real Thing." He argues that the new trend of using African-American actors to play black roles should continue.

3. A glance at Hill's index reveals numerous references to Ireland and Irish politics in Garvey's speeches.

4. The correct spelling is "Sinn Fein."

5. See Cooper, pp. 12, 18 for a description of McKay's complex class status.

6. Although Zoe does not fit the "darkey" stereotype, she is one of the first stage incarnations of the "tragic mulatto."

Works Cited

Ahmad, Aijaz. *In Theory: Classes, Nations, Literatures.* London: Verso, 1992.

Anderson, Benedict. *Imagined Communities: Reflections on the Origin and Spread of Nationalism.* Rev. ed. London: Verso, 1991.

Angelou, Maya. Interview with Paul Brown. *Morning Edition.* National Public Radio. 11 September 1992.

Beaumont, Gustave de. *Ireland: Social, Political, and Religious.* Vol. 1. London, 1839.

"Beginnings of a Negro Drama." *Literary Digest* 9 May 1914: 1114.

Boucicault, Dion. Letter. *London Times* 20 November 1861: 5.

Broun, Heywood. "Negro Players Score Success in Interesting Bill of Short Plays." *New York Tribune* 6 April 1917: 11.

Cooper, Wayne F. *Claude McKay: Rebel Sojourner in the Harlem Renaissance.* Baton Rouge: Louisiana State University Press, 1987.

Curtis, L. Perry, Jr. *Apes and Angels: The Irishman in Victorian Caricature.* Washington: Smithsonian, 1971.

Dalsimer, Adele M. "Players in the Western World: The Abbey Theatre's American Tours." *Éire-Ireland* 16 (1981): 75–93.

Doyle, Roddy. *The Commitments.* 1987. New York: Vintage-Random, 1989; *The Commitments.* Dir. Alan Parker. 20th Century Fox, 1991.

Du Bois, W. E. B. "Krigwa Players Little Negro Theatre." *Crisis* 32 (1926): 134.

Fawkes, Richard. *Dion Boucicault: A Biography.* London: Quartet, 1979.

Ferguson, Blanche. *Countee Cullen and the Negro Renaissance.* New York: Dodd, Mead, 1966.

Gale, Zona. "The Colored Players and Their Plays." *Theatre Arts Magazine* 1 (1917): 139–40.

Gibbons, Luke. "Race Against Time: Racial Discourse and Irish History." *Oxford Literary Review* 13 (1991): 95–117.

Greene, David H., and Edward M. Stephens. *J. M. Synge 1871–1909.* Rev. ed. New York: New York University Press, 1989.

Gregory, Augusta. *Our Irish Theatre.* New York: Putnam, 1913.

Gregory, Montgomery, and Alain Locke, eds. *Plays of Negro Life.* New York: Harper, 1927.

Griffith, Arthur. Preface. *Jail Journal*. By John Mitchel. Dublin: Gill, 1913.

Hill, Robert A., ed. *The Marcus Garvey and Universal Negro Improvement Association Papers*. Vol. 2. Berkeley: University of California Press, 1983.

Huggins, Nathan Irvin, ed. *Voices from the Harlem Renaissance*. New York: Oxford University Press, 1976.

Johnson, James Weldon, ed. *The Book of American Negro Poetry*. New York: Harcourt, 1922.

———. *God's Trombones: Seven Negro Sermons in Verse*. 1927. New York: Viking-Penguin, 1990.

———. "The Negro and the Drama." *New York Age* 19 April 1917. N. pag.

Kearney, Richard. *Across the Frontiers: Ireland in the 1990s*. Dublin: Wolfhound, 1988.

Locke, Alain, ed. *The New Negro: An Interpretation*. 1925. New York: Arno, 1968.

McKay, Claude. "How Black Sees Green and Red." *The Passion of Claude McKay*. Ed. Wayne Cooper. New York: Schocken, 1973.

———. *A Long Way From Home*. New York: Furman, 1937.

"The New Negro Theatre." *Crisis* 14 (1917): 80–81.

O' Brien, Joseph V. *"Dear, Dirty Dublin": A City in Distress, 1899–1916*. Berkeley: University of California Press, 1982.

"'The Octoroon'. A Disgrace to the North, a Libel on the South." Rev. of *The Octoroon*. *Spirit of the Times* 17 December 1859: 1.

O'Ferrall, Fergus. "Liberty and Catholic Politics 1790–1990." *Daniel O'Connell: Political Pioneer*. Ed. Maurice O'Connell. Dublin: Institute of Public Administration, 1991.

Richardson, Willis. "The Hope of a Negro Drama." *Crisis* 19 (1919): 338–39.

Rolston, Bill. "Politics, Painting and Popular Culture: The Political Wall Murals of Northern Ireland." *Media, Culture and Society* 9 (1987): 5–28.

Sowell, Thomas. *Ethnic America*. New York: Basic, 1981.

Walton, Lester A. "Negro Actors Make Debut in Drama at Garden Theatre; Given Most Cordial Welcome." *New York Age* 12 April 1917. N. pag.

———. "Theatrical Comment." *New York Age* 25 November 1909. N. pag.

———. "Using the Real Thing." *New York Age* 5 October 1911. N. pag.

Yeats, W. B. *Explorations*. London: Macmillan, 1962.

Early to Mid-Twentieth Century

Irony without Condescension: Sterling A. Brown's Nod to Robert Frost

Mark Jeffreys

Unlike many more anxious poets, Sterling Allen Brown did not shy away from discussing his literary influences, African American or otherwise.[1] He freely acknowledged his indebtedness, not only to predecessors such as Paul Lawrence Dunbar but also to contemporaries and near-contemporaries such as Claude McKay, Jean Toomer, Langston Hughes, Richard Wright, and Ralph Ellison ("A Son's Return" 24, 28; Rowell 812–13). He just as freely acknowledged several white writers who influenced his development as a poet, including Yeats, Whitman, and Wordsworth. In particular, he credited Robert Burns, Edwin Arlington Robinson, Carl Sandburg, and Robert Frost as poets whose work helped prepare him for writing his new kind of dialect poetry that was technically dazzling in its innovative mixture of blues, ballads, and free-verse forms and that did not mock or sentimentalize the people whose lives and voices it portrayed:

> I went over to Boston one day [while a graduate student at Harvard in 1922] and bought a copy of Untermeyer's *Modern American Poetry*. . . . I read Edwin Arlington Robinson, particularly the poems about Tilbury Town, where he takes the poor, the undistinguished, and the ordinary; he gets at the extraordinary in their lives. . . . I had Robinson and [Robert] Frost. Frost was a great influence—and Sandburg. I always loved language, I loved slang, and I loved the folk stuff I knew. . . . So I always had an ear for the spoken word. I always had an ear for the ballad. I go to college, and I get this book. I read Frost and I read Sandburg and I read Edgar Lee Masters. I saw what could happen with the American

> idiom. But I hadn't seen it done with the Negro folk idiom much. (Rowell 812)

In the final analysis, it was "the Negro folk idiom" itself, far more than any white literary figure, that most influenced Brown's work. But he remained generous in his criticism of those writers whom he saw as enablers of his poetry, even when they soiled their populist efforts with blatant racism. Of an Edgar Lee Masters poem that contains the ugly couplet, "Just think for a minute, how the Negroes excell / Can you beat them with a banjo or a broiling pan?" Brown sternly observes that "Although sharply critical of typical American attitudes, Edgar Lee Masters himself furthers one"—and yet the rebuke is tempered with appreciation for past achievement: "This is hardly worthy of the poet of Spoon River" (*Negro Poetry and Drama* 95–96).

Brown's acknowledgments of influence are woven into his story of his emergence as the poet of *Southern Road*, a narrative sequence that begins with Dunbar and ends with Big Boy Davis, an itinerant guitarist and singer whom he met and befriended while teaching at the Virginia Seminary in the 1920s and who is the hero of the eponymous "Odyssey of Big Boy" and "When de Saints Go Ma'ching Home"—the first and fourth poems of *Southern Road*, respectively. Indeed, it is to explain to his interviewer just how he was able to recognize the importance of Davis's songs that Brown detours through the account of his reading of Robinson, et al. while at Harvard, saying apologetically at one point, "This is a long way to Big Boy" (Rowell 812). So the importance of these white poets to Brown must be understood not merely in terms of how they directly influenced the form and content of Brown's poetry but in how they helped him to recognize the potential materials for his own writing in the oral poetry of Big Boy Davis and other Southern "Negro folk." Davis is Brown's model poet, not Robinson or Sandburg or Frost. Brown was not interested in imitation—he was fed up with black poets who wrote "more from the library than from life," who "turned away from their people and from their own interesting personalities" (*Negro Poetry and Drama* 55, 59)—but he was interested in parallel opportunities: "I saw what could be done with the American idiom; I hadn't seen it done with the Negro folk idiom much."

Still, the kinship of Brown's poetry with that of some of the white poets whom he cites as strong influences is fairly obvious. In Robert Burns's Scots poems we find honest dialect similar to Brown's, graceful as Dunbar's but without the shackles of minstrel stereotypes and sentimentality. Edwin Arlington Robinson's ironic character sketches are direct antecedents for Brown poems such as "Sam Smiley," "Funeral," and "Sporting Beasley"—poems that observe oppressed and ordinary people and get at "the extraordinary in their lives," often with a bitter twist at the finish. Sandburg's free-verse lines and rhythms also show up frequently, and Brown turns Sandburg's phrase "The strong men keep coming on" directly into a dialect chant of hope and resistance, "The strong men keep a-comin' on / The strong men git stronger."

Such obvious connections are not visible, however, between Brown's poems and the poems of Robert Frost. In the *Collected Poems of Sterling A. Brown,* one has to strain to see any bridge to Frost's largely ahistorical, gnomic, and metronomic lyrics, and no particular technique of dialect or versification in Brown's poetry seems traceable to him. So it seems curious that it is Frost, not Robinson or Sandburg, whom Brown praises most warmly and with whom Brown explicitly identifies himself ("A Son's Return" 28–30).

What was it, exactly, that Brown saw in Frost? Among the pieces that Brown contributed to *The Reader's Companion to World Literature* in 1956 was a two-page entry on Frost. In that entry, he praises Frost's regionalism and depth of respect for his New England characters. Frost, he writes, "is a regionalist in the best sense: his loving care for the local leads to the universal" ("Frost" 175). Brown means by "the local" a specific people, in Frost's case rural, white New Englanders. "Here are living people, rooted in New England, but realized so deeply that their lives have meaning for the world" ("Frost" 175). His admiration implies an important point. For Brown, Frost's poetry demonstrates that it is not necessary to write only of "universal" or "timeless" subjects for one's poetry to "have meaning for the world." On the contrary, the best route to the universal is in "loving care for the local." Frost's characters are "living people, rooted in New England," just as Brown's characters are living people, rooted in African-American experience, and both poets have the right to claim "meaning for the world."

Brown's acknowledgment of Frost is one of kindred spirit more than kindred technique. He goes out of his way to make clear that the language of Frost's personae "is not dialect," relying as it does on what Frost called "tones of voice" to achieve "the translation of living speech into poetry" ("Frost" 175). It is Frost's attitude, both toward his sources of inspiration and toward life more generally, that Brown admires. "The personality that he reveals opposes romantic self-pity, scoffs at 'literary tears,' is that of a ruminative, quizzical stoic. . . . Aware of the evil of the world, he still will take his chance" ("Frost" 175–76). That Frost was "[a]ware of the evil of the world" seems certain enough, but it is peculiarly Brown's take on Frost to add that "he still will take his chance."

As evidence of this willingness to "take his chance," Brown then quotes a couplet from Frost's "In Dives' Dive"—"As long as the Declaration guards / My right to be equal in number of cards." The whole poem is quite brief, and quoting it in full reveals the gambling trope to which Brown alludes:

> It is late at night and still I am losing,
> But still I am steady and unaccusing.
>
> As long as the Declaration guards
> My right to be equal in number of cards,
>
> It is nothing to me who runs the Dive.
> Let's have a look at another five. (*Collected Poems* 310)

Two implications of the poem now stand out. The first is that whoever is dealing the cards in "Dives' Dive" may well be cheating, a possibility suggested by the persona's pointed boast in the opening couplet, "still I am steady and unaccusing." The second implication is that the owner or manager of the place is disreputable, as the third couplet jeers "It is nothing to me who runs the Dive." The poem's tone of bravado, the desperation and perhaps danger of its situation, the implications that the game may be fixed, and the mildly satirical thrust of its political allusion ("As long as the Declaration guards / My right to be equal in number of cards") were all important to Brown.

Eighteen years after his entry on Frost was published in *The Reader's Companion to World Literature*, Brown reiterated and clarified his admiration for what he saw as Frost's willingness to "take his chance" in a speech at Williams College, his alma mater. In doing so, he once again chose as his exemplary text "In Dives' Dive." This time, however, the poem not only represents Frost, it represents Brown himself. Introducing the poem defensively, Brown uses it to conclude a ruminative address that looks back at his life at Williams fifty years earlier and that attempts to sum up what his life and career since then have been all about:

> Now I'm going to close with a poem from a man who taught at Dartmouth. . . . a man who has meant a great deal to me. . . . And this is the end of my 72nd year to you. I swear I'm not going to say one word after I explain this poem. I must explain it. Because you will say, "Why does a man who studied T. S. Eliot and Ezra Pound give us this doggerel?" It is not doggerel. This, to me, says more than a whole lot of the *Cantos*. . . ("A Son's Return" 28).

That Brown is so defensive about Frost's poem hints at the extent to which he identifies himself with Frost, a hint which is borne out by the explication that follows, beginning with an anecdote about meeting Frost and discussing this very poem:

> This poem is called "In Dives' Dive." I met Robert Frost once and quoted this to him and he said that I was the only person he knew that knew this poem and respected it. I loved it. He asked me did I play poker and I told him no and he said that he didn't play good poker either. We talked about poker and there were a whole slough [sic] of new poets there. He and I were the old poets talking about "Dives' Dive." ("A Son's Return" 28)

Actually, Frost and Brown were separated in age by about thirty-two years, a full generation, but Brown's opposing the two of them to the younger poets is as much a statement about poetic understanding as about age. He moves easily from "old poets" to "an Old Book" to explain the allusion in Frost's title and, more significantly, to link Frost's poem to the old spirituals that for him embodied "the speech of the people [that] is capable of expressing whatever the people are" (Strong 25):

> Ladies and gentlemen, from an Old Book known as the *Bible*, there was a character named Dives. And in the spiritual it is:
>
> Rich man Dives he lived so well, don't you see
> Rich man Dives lived so well, don't you see
> Rich man Dives lived so well,
> When he died he found a home in hell
> He had a home in that Rock, don't you see.
>
> Po' boy Lazarus, po' as I, don't you see
> Po' boy Lazarus, po' as I, don't you see
> Po' boy Lazarus, po' as I,
> When he died he found a home on high
> I got a home in that Rock, don't you see.
>
> So Frost takes Brother Dives. ("A Son's Return" 28–29)

Here Brown pauses to explain what a "dive" is to his audience of "privileged children" and to give vent to a passionate, sarcastic outburst about the New Critical method of separating the "speaker" from any biographical connection to the writer of the poem:

> I am trying to give you now an exegesis in the manner of the New Critics. I want you to understand the language and then you get the meaning. And of course the structure of the poem is the important thing. The biography of the author has nothing to do with it. So you get your meaning [from the New Critics], but I want you to know *what in the hell I'm talking about*. They're talking about a game named "poker." I've got to explain it afterwards, because if you don't like this poem my evening is ruined. And don't throw "Ash Wednesday" at me either. This is a poem for me. This is an autobiographic "sounding off." ("A Son's Return" 29)

Since Brown's entire speech, to this point, has been "an autobiographic 'sounding off,'" his defense of Frost's poem is rapidly becoming indistinguishable from his defense of himself. This conflation of Brown's version of Frost and of Frost's persona in "In Dives' Dive" with Brown's version of himself is then carried out through his line-by-line explication of the poem. Brown wishes his audience to read the poem as Brown's own statement:

> Frost is gambling, and he has been a loser all of his life. As far as I am concerned, I have been a loser most of my life. But in the seventies, I've been a winner; you know, like coming back to Williams, etc. "It is late at night": Frost was in his seventies or later, that's what "late at night" means. It is late at night and still I'm losing. But *still* I am steady and unaccusing. He is not laying any blame on anybody. If I lose I am not singing blues about anybody else causing it. I am steady and unaccusing. ("A Son's Return" 29)

At this point Brown reaches what is, for him, the heart of the matter, the part of the poem that obliquely places the individual loser in a sociopolitical context, a context that for Brown includes race. He separates himself from Frost only enough to suggest that at some level it always *does* matter "who runs the dive," while he embraces the bravado of the persona that pretends not to care, that refuses to acknowledge being beaten by whoever has rigged the game, that juts a jaw and demands "a look at another five." His explication continues:

> As long as the Declaration—*the Declaration of Independence* as long as the Declaration guards—g-u-a-r-d-s. "As long as the Declaration *guards* my right to be *equal* in number of cards." You don't have any more cards than I have. We got the same number of cards. As long as the Declaration guards my right to be equal in number of cards, it does not matter to me who runs the dive. Now that's where a lot of my liberal friends would disagree, and I too would agree with them somewhat. It matters who runs it. But he is saying that it does not matter who runs the dive. . . . Let's have a look at another five. That means he wants five more cards, his right in the game. I'm going to play my hand out with the cards that come. . . ("A Son's Return" 29–30)

Brown concludes his speech with the upbeat observation that Frost's poem, to him, "is a strong statement of a man's belief in America and himself" ("A Son's Return" 30). At the last moment, he swerves from his "autobiographic 'sounding off'" to finish on a note that his audience of "privileged children" can happily applaud. But the full value of the poem to Brown lies beyond any simplistic expression of patriotic individualism. It lies in the desperation of the scene set in "a haunt of iniquity" and in the tough-guy attitude of the poet's persona, who lets us know that he knows he is being cheated but warns us that he is not conceding and might yet win anyway.

In his defiant, knowing attitude, the persona of "In Dives' Dive" is close kin to Brown's own "badmen" personae. Robert O'Meally has noted that "Brown drew upon the rich and ironic and badman patrolled lore of the people themselves," not only to recreate in his poetry the legendary John Henry and historical Jack Johnson but also to create badmen characters of his own such as Big Boy, Wild Bill, Big Jess, Slim, and Ole Lem (45). Although O'Meally does not address Brown's fondness for Frost, he does employ the terminology of fighting and gaming to describe the folk tradition of the badman:

> Like his counterpart and sometimes his adversary, the trickster, the badman violates social conventions and spaces, virtually at will, and thereby represents not just black disdain for American oppression (and, by extension, trouble of all sorts), but the ability to face hardship and to win. . . . When he does not win, the badman nonetheless goes down swinging or shooting, not sorry for his deeds, requesting no mercy at all; if anything, just "a cool drink of water before I die." (44)

It is the attitude of the badman that Frost, at least momentarily, takes on in "Dives' Dive." He knows that he is losing and most likely will go on losing. He suspects that the deck is stacked against him. He knows that the proprietor is the heartless rich man Dives, that he, by implication, is "po' Lazarus," and he lets us know that he knows. But he is not sorry—he asks "no mercy at all," just his fair number of cards when each hand is dealt, and he reminds us ironically that this is a right that "the Declaration guards."

This wry attitude and its considerably more badass variants are common among Brown's characters. In "Memphis Blues," the gambling man's defiant answer to the threat of doom is a dialect version of Frost's refusal to fold:

> Watcha gonna do when de flood roll fas',
> Flood roll fas', Mistah Gamblin' Man?
> Gonna pick up my dice fo' one las' pass—
> Gonna fade my way to de lucky lan',
> Gonna throw my las' seven—oh, my Lawd!
> (*Collected Poems* 61)

Indeed, the gambling man's response is but one of several like it expressing the badman ethic:

> Watcha gonna do when de tall flames roar,
> Tall flames roar, Mistah Lovin' Man?
> Gonna love my brownskin better'n before—
> Gonna love my baby lak a do right man,
> Gonna love my brown baby, oh, my Lawd!
>
> Watcha gonna do when Memphis falls down,
> Memphis falls down, Mistah Music Man?
> Gonna plunk on dat box as long as it soun',
> Gonna plunk dat box fo' to beat de ban',
> Gonna tickle dem ivories, oh, my Lawd!
> (*Collected Poems* 60–61)

Taken together with the similarly resilient responses of the preaching man ("Gonna pray to Jesus and nebber tire") and the working man ("Gonna put dem buildings up again"), the badmen's responses to disaster reflect the knowledge that Memphis belongs to rich men like the biblical Dives, and its survival or loss is the owners' affair:

> All dese cities
> Ashes, rust. . . .
> De win' sing sperrichals
> Through deir dus'. (*Collected Poems* 61)

The black gambler who refuses to quit, even in the face of the white man's rigged odds and, hence, inevitable doom, remained a favorite type of the badman for Brown. His masterful, rollicking, satiric narrative poem *The Last Ride of Wild Bill* opens with an impossible challenge gamely accepted:

> The new Chief of police
> Banged his desk
> Called in the force, and swore
> That the number-running game was done
> And Wild Bill
> Would ride no more.
>
> The rumor
> Spread quickly
> Caught up with Wild Bill,
> In Darktown
> At his rendezvous.
> It left him untouched
> Left him cool,
> He went on shooting
> His game of pool.
> He ran up fifteen
> And then he spat.
> "Rack 'em up," he said.
> His voice was flat.
> He put a lead slug
> In the telephone
> He spoke to the Chief
> In a tone
> Colorless, sad,
> As if what he had
> To say was hurting him
> Pretty bad.
> "I just heard the news
> You spread over town.
> I raise you one,
> I call your bluff.
> Your cops are not quite tough
> Enough.
> And you ain't so smart,
> I will be bound,
> To run the
> Great Wild Bill

To ground.
I'd like you to know,
What I thought you knew,
You have bit off more
Than you'll ever chew.
As long as loose change
Is in this town
Wild Bill
Will still
Run the numbers down. (*Collected Poems* 132)

Of course, the police chief is unable to capture Wild Bill legally and only ends up defeating him by leaving a money drop rigged with explosives for him to pick up and be killed by. As an added irony, in Wild Bill's race to evade the police and still pick up his drops, we learn that many of his best customers in the illicit numbers game are among Atlanta's white elite, gamblers all who are only too happy to bet on the outcome of the race. Truly, Wild Bill is playing in "Dives' Dive." Finally, transcending even death, he arrives in hell a hero, as the demons themselves rush up to find out the "numbers."

However, there is more to Frost's influence on Brown than a single, somewhat atypical scrap of Frost's verse figuring life in America as a game of poker. Brown refers to Frost's influence as something he felt when he was a graduate student at Harvard in the early 1920s. "In Dives' Dive" was first published in *Poetry* in 1936, years after Brown had left Harvard and after many of his poems most like it had already been written (Frost 563n). Given that Brown's affection for "In Dives' Dive" was a matter of his delighted recognition of a kindred spirit rather than a tribute to a text of seminal influence on his career, what was the nature of the earlier impact of Frost's poetry? Brown does not answer this directly, but in the same essay for the 1956 *Reader's Companion to World Literature* in which he first quotes from "In Dives' Dive," he lists as exemplary several early Frost poems, most of which are from a single volume, *North of Boston* (American publication date 1915). These poems are all "dramatic monologues and dialogues" that he cites as illustrative of Frost's "loving care for the local" that keeps honest his "picture of the barren farms and tough-grained people North of Boston."

In particular, Brown emphasizes the diversity of character in Frost's portrayals: "the loneliness in *Home Burial;* the bleakness in *The Housekeeper* and *Snow;* the eccentricity in *The Witch of Coos,* the neighborliness in *The Death of the Hired Man;* the self-respect in *The Code;* the pawky humor and grit in *Brown's Descent*" ("Frost" 175). He then follows this list with the striking accolade, quoted earlier: "Here are living people, rooted in New England, but realized so deeply that their lives have meaning for the world." This praise for the range and depth of Frost's characterizations has since been echoed in critical praise for Brown himself, as in the observation that "Brown treated the products of folk-imagination as self-conscious wisdom—tragic, comic, ironic, shrewd, emotionally elastic and attitudinally complex, capable of supporting a variety of stances toward life" (Wright 340).

It is the complexity of attitude among the ordinary, often downtrodden folk of Frost's early monologues and dialogues that seems to be the source of Brown's admiration. Unlike Eliot, Pound, or the New Critics, Frost did not arrogate the privilege of self-conscious irony to an intellectual elite but discovered it in the rural and the little educated as well. This discovery Brown admired and sought to rediscover in Negro dialect. Again and again in his critical prose he reiterates his thesis that folk speech and folk song are *intrinsically* complex, self-aware, and demanding of respect. He writes of "the sly and sardonic folk-rhymes and the profoundly revealing spirituals," of "irony and satire," "terse and tonic shrewdness," "double-meanings either lost upon or concealed from collectors," "hard irony," "quiet despair," "the melancholy and irony of the folk blues" (*Negro Poetry and Drama* 13, 27, 28, 40, 62, 72).

It was Brown's contention that the fault of dialect poetry did not inhere in dialect itself, but in the assumption by dialect poets, "in a period of conciliation and middle-class striving for recognition and respectability," that nonstandard English went hand-in-hand with a lack of self-awareness and sophistication:

> Many of the authors [of dialect poetry] were preachers and teachers, consciously literary, who looked down with good humored condescension upon a ridiculous way of life, or were shocked by the departures of the folk from gentility. A few pat phrases, a few stock situations and characteristics, some misspelling: these

> were the chief things necessary. The wit and beauty possible to folkspeech, the folk-shrewdness, the humanity, the stoicism of these people they seldom saw. (*Negro Poetry and Drama* 42)

Brown's terms of praise here, "shrewdness," "humanity," "stoicism," are of a piece with the qualities he attributed to Frost's characters—"tough-grained," "self-respect," "pawky humor and grit"—and once again serve to illustrate how ordinary, difficult lives can "have meaning for the world." As the son of a renowned minister and teacher, educated at Williams and Harvard, friendly with the sophisticated leaders of the New Negro Movement, Brown could have easily chosen to "look down with condescension upon a ridiculous way of life," or to turn his back on folk traditions entirely. That he did not, and that, at the age of seventy-three, he took an interviewer down a long detour through his first experiences with Frost and Robinson and Sandburg in order to help explain how the singer Big Boy Davis came to mean so much to him, suggests that the direction in which his appreciation for Frost's early monologues and dialogues nudged him was toward an attempt at a new, honest, respectful presentation of the *character* of black dialect in poetry. "We must accept the responsibility of being ultimate interpreters of our own," he said in a much earlier interview, "without condescension and without idealization—a just and realistic portrayal. For such a portrayal we shall have to go to the sources, the people themselves, for the authentic folk-stuff of poetry" (Strong 25).

Brown was able to accomplish this portrayal in part because, as Gary Smith has observed, his poetry "first assumes that Black Americans are as inherently complex and diverse as white Americans" (394). Brown did not simply admire Frost—he drew a necessary parallel where others had seen none. Perhaps nowhere is that parallel clearer than between Frost's "The Code" (36–39), which for Brown exemplified "self-respect," and Brown's own "Uncle Joe" (*Collected Poems* 229–30). Both poems contain a dialogue between an outsider to folkways and a local farm laborer, and in both poems the outsider appears to be an autobiographical character—a "town-bred farmer" in Frost's poem, a "teacher" with "store-bought tobacco" in Brown's. Each poem contains a hyperbolic narrative told by the local to the outsider that ends with a defiant boast mixing ironic self-awareness with meaningful challenge.

Most importantly, both poems are about the protection of the poor man's self-respect by his own resourcefulness when his right to go about his business as a free and dignified adult is threatened. There is no redress of injustice by appeal to the laws of the land, only the solitary enforcement of an unwritten code and the stoic refusal to be scared into making oppression easy. The great difference between the two poems, aside from Frost's eschewing of a dialect rendering of his farmhand's speech, is that "The Code" allows its "town-bred" outsider less understanding than "Uncle Joe" allows its teacher. This is only appropriate, since the teacher of "Uncle Joe" is himself a black man, although neither a farmer nor a Creole, and, as Uncle Joe observes "ain't got, nohow, de teacher's talk."

Frost's farmer is nonplused when one of his field hands, "thrusting pitchfork in the ground, / Marched himself off the field and home." The remaining field hand patiently explains to him that "He thought you meant to find fault with his work" by commenting that they needed to take pains cocking the hay: "That's what the average farmer would have meant." The town-bred farmer finds this ridiculous, especially since the field hand, James, took nearly a half-hour to decide that he had indeed been insulted. At this point, the remaining field hand chides the farmer and launches into a story of his own to illustrate his point:

> "Don't let it bother you. You've found out something.
> The hand that knows his business won't be told
> To do work better or faster—those two things.
> . . . .
> Tell you a story of what happened once:
> I was up here in Salem, at a man's
> Named Sanders, with a gang of four or five
> Doing the haying. No one like the boss.
> . . . .
> But what he like was someone to encourage.
> Them that he couldn't lead he'd get behind
> And drive, the way you can, you know, in mowing—
> Keep at their heels and threaten to mow their legs off.
> . . . .
> So when he paired off with me in the hayfield

To load the load, thinks I, Look out for trouble.
. . . .
Everything went well till we reached the barn
With a big jag to empty in a bay.
You understand that mean the easy job
For the man up on top, of throwing *down*
The hay and rolling it off wholesale,
Where on a mow it would have been slow lifting.
You wouldn't think a fellow'd need much urging
Under those circumstances, would you now?
But the old fool seizes his fork in both hands,
And looking up bewhiskered out of the pit,
Shouts like an army captain, 'Let her come!'
Thinks I, D'ye mean it? 'What was that you said?'
I asked out loud, so's there be no mistake,
'Did you say, "Let her come"?' 'Yes, let her come.'
He said it over, but he said it softer.
Never you say a thing like that to a man,
Not if he values what he is. God, I'd as soon
Murdered him as left out his middle name.
I'd built the load and knew right where to find it.
Two or three forkfuls I picked lightly round for
Like meditating, and then I just dug in
And dumped the rackful on him in ten lots.
I looked over the side once in the dust
And caught sight of him treading-water-like,
Keeping his head above. 'Damn ye,' I says,
'That gets ye!' He squeaked like a squeezed rat.
That was the last I saw or heard of him.
I cleaned the rack and drove out to cool off." (36–38)

As it turned out, Sanders was not dead, but he never returned to harassing his hired help; in fact, he never returned to the fields at all that day, "He kept away from us all afternoon." The story itself is not vouched for by any other source within the poem—it may or may not be true, but it gives the farmer something to think about before he ever again exhorts his help with the assumption that a farmhand could not do his job without being patronizingly goaded. When he asks of the field hand if he had not been "relieved to find [Sanders] wasn't dead," the field hand replies that "it's hard to say. / I went about to kill him fair enough." And when he asks if he lost his job, the field hand answers, pointedly, "Discharge me? No! He knew I did just right."

As Brown points out, "The Code" is a poem about self-respect, and it is to underscore and protect his self-respect that the field hand tells his cautionary tale. Brown's Creole character, Uncle Joe, has faced considerably more terrifying situations than an abusive, condescending employer, yet he also spins a narrative that *simultaneously* boasts of past insults defiantly answered and is itself a kind of defiant answer. The act of telling a hyperbolic story about how one refused to be broken is one of the finest ways of refusing to be broken:

> So one Sunday on de way home dey [Cajun whites]
> surround us
> In our buggy, and throw up dey big hats
> To scare our mule, but our mule don't scare good.
> And at Papa Lastrape's gate dey put up a rail.
> And gimme de dare to take it down.
> Dey had dey shotguns across dey saddles,
> But dey had to have some good reason to mob us up,
> Cause dey hadn't so long left Father Antoine.
> Well, I ain't scared, an' my ma she don't scare.
> I didn't say nottin'. She didn't say nottin'!
> But I had heart enough to take de rail down.
> So dey talked aroun', den dey galloped off whoopin'
> Into de woods, an' a shootin' dey guns.
> Den, dey luh us alone. But me I'm Baptist now.
> (*Collected Poems* 229–30)

At this point Brown allows his autobiographical outsider to be an insider, to get in on Uncle Joe's joke. In so doing, he also takes his poem's recognition of Uncle Joe's dignity one step further by revealing what Frost only implies—the character's keen and ironic self-awareness. Uncle Joe pauses to stare at the teacher a moment, then grins. When the teacher grins back, Uncle Joe knows that he understands: "He looked at me, and grinned, then I grinned. / 'You know, I gret big liar, me,' he said." Behind the story, now, we see the teller, proud of telling it well. Finally, Uncle Joe lets the teacher, and thus the reader, glimpse what lies deeper even than his awareness of his role as storyteller, the fiery core of his pride: "'But still I kin do what I gots to do. / And dats no lie.'" To this, Brown's autobiographical persona adds, "And me, I knew it wasn't."

Brown's ability to incise remarkably layered portraits in just a few blues quatrains or brief fragments of dialogue was by no means entirely inspired by the early poetry of Robert Frost. But Frost, more than any other poet, seems to have encouraged him in his project to present the "true dialect" of the folk as being just as filled with stoicism, pride, and the capacity for ironic self-awareness as it is with verbal music and striking tropes.

Notes

All lines from "The Last Ride of Wild Bill" are from *The Collected Poems of Sterling A. Brown,* ed. Michael S. Harper. Copyright © 1980 by Sterling A. Brown. Reprinted by permission of HarperCollins Publishers, Inc.

1. My colleague Virginia Whatley Smith has suggested that much of this essay's commentary on the relationship of Sterling A. Brown's poetry to that of Robert Frost could be profitably framed in terms of Henry Louis Gates's theory of "signifyin'." However, I have chosen to avoid Gates's terminology in order to present Brown's connection to Frost in terms as similar as possible to Brown's own.

Works Cited

Brown, Sterling A. *The Collected Poems of Sterling A. Brown*. Ed. Michael S. Harper. The National Poetry Series. New York: Harper & Row, 1980.

———. *Negro Poetry and Drama and The Negro in American Fiction*. Studies in American Negro Life. New York: Athenaeum, 1969.

———. "Frost, Robert." *A Reader's Companion to World Literature*. Ed. Lillian H. Hornstein and G. D. Percy. New York: New American Library, 1956. 174–76.

———. "A Son's Return: 'Oh Didn't He Ramble.'" *Berkshire Review* 10 (Summer 1974): 9–30.

Frost, Robert. *The Poetry of Robert Frost: The Collected Poems, Complete and Unabridged*. Ed. Edward Connery Lathem. New York: Henry Holt, 1969.

O'Meally, Robert G. "'Game to the Heart': Sterling Brown and the Badman." *Callaloo* 5 (1982): 43–54.

Rowell, Charles H. "'Let Me Be with Ole Jazzbo': An Interview with Sterling A. Brown." *Callaloo* 14.4 (1991): 795–815.

Smith, Gary. 'The Literary Ballads of Sterling A. Brown." *CLA Journal* 23.4 (1989): 393–409.

Strong, Mary Louise. "Poetry Corner: Sterling Brown." (Interview) *Scholastic* 36 (April 29, 1940): 25, 27.

Wright, John S. "Sterling Brown's Folk Odyssey." *American Literature, Culture, and Ideology: Essays in Memory of Henry Nash Smith*. Ed. Beverly R. Voloshin. American University Studies, Series 24, American Literature, vol. 8. New York: Peter Lang, 1990. 331–43.

Carlos Bulosan's Literary Debt to Richard Wright

Helen Jaskoski

> I was fortunate to find work in a library and to be close to books. In later years I remembered this opportunity when I read that the American Negro writer, Richard Wright, had not been allowed to borrow books from his local library because of his color.
>
> Carlos Bulosan, *America Is in the Heart* (71)

Richard Wright's account, in *Black Boy*, of his difficulty in obtaining books made a deep impression on Filipino immigrant Carlos Bulosan. Indeed, in his own autobiography, *America Is in the Heart*, Bulosan echoes the theme and language of Wright's story in relating an episode from his life in 1930s California. Bulosan describes working as a dishwasher in the Opal cafe in Lompoc, California:

> Once a local businessman came into the back room with a bottle of whisky. He sarcastically said to me:
>
> "Mr. Opal says that you are reading books. Is it true?"
>
> "Yes, sir." But realizing that my tone had a challenging note in it, I said immediately: "Well, sir, there is nothing else to do after working hours. I hate to go to the Mexican quarters because, as you know, gambling and prostitution are going on there all the time. And I'm a little tired of the phonograph in my room, playing the same records over and over. I find escape in books, and also discovery of a world I had not known before. . . ."

The incident recapitulates the experience Wright recounts in *Black Boy* of being suspect because of his reading. When Wright checks out library books on a card belonging to a white co-worker the librarian voices her suspicions:

> "You're not using these books, are you?" she asked pointedly.
> "Oh, no, ma'am. I can't read." (262)

Wright's other co-workers are similarly suspicious:

> Whenever I brought a book to the job, I wrapped it in newspaper—a habit that was to persist for years in other cities and under other circumstances. But some of the white men pried into my packages when I was absent and they questioned me.
> "Boy, what are you reading those books for?"
> "Oh, I don't know, sir."
> "You'll addle your brains if you don't watch out." (295)

In the paragraphs preceding this conversation, Wright describes the value of reading as an escape, as well as the capacity of books to open up a world heretofore unknown:

> Who were these men about whom Mencken was talking so passionately? Who was Anatole France? Joseph Conrad? . . . Sinclair Lewis, Sherwood Anderson, Dostoevski, George Moore, Gustave Flaubert, Maupassant, Tolstoy, Frank Harris, Mark Twain . . . and scores of others? Were these men real? Did they exist, or had they existed? . . . Reading was like a drug, a dope. The novels created moods in which I lived for days. (293–95)

Black Boy may well have been one of the books that Carlos Bulosan read during the two years he spent in Los Angeles County Hospital convalescing from tuberculosis, when, he says, he read a book a day; however, it does not appear on the list of books he offers as the foundation for his self-education. Although Wright is not mentioned, Bulosan's approach to the books he read and to his experience as an autodidact strongly echoes Wright's account in *Black Boy*. Half a dozen authors, mainly the heroic Russian novelists, show up on both men's reading lists: Pushkin, Gorky, Turgenev, Dostoyevsky, Gogol, Tolstoy. One American appears on both: Mark Twain. However, whereas Wright says that Sinclair Lewis, Dreiser, and literary realism inspired him most, Bulosan reports being first drawn by the expansive romanticism of Hart Crane and Walt Whitman.

Wright and Bulosan both found in fiction a method to analyze their relationship to the world around them. Wright mentions how his reading of *Babbitt*[1] gave him an insight into his boss:

> I would smile when I saw him lugging his golf bags into the office. . . . I could feel the very limits of his narrow life. And this had happened because I had read a novel about a mythical man called George F. Babbitt. (284)

Bulosan found a literary example for his own loneliness in the story of Robinson Crusoe, which he refers to three times in his book (22; 254; 323). His aspirations to write were kindled first by reading American poets—Hart Crane, John Gould Fletcher, Vachel Lindsay, Carl Sandburg (228)—but major inspiration came from European poets—Rilke, Lorca, Heine (237)—and from his identification of himself with Maxim Gorki:

> But it was Gorki, the vagabond and tramp, the tubercular outcast, who most attracted me. Perhaps it was because I identified myself with him in his lowly birth, his wanderings in the vast Russian land, his sufferings and the nameless people who had suffered with him. (246)

Besides solace and self-knowledge, fiction provided both men with a fundamental analytical tool. According to Wright,

> [i]t would have been impossible for me to have told anyone what I derived from these novels, for it was nothing less than a sense of life itself. All my life had shaped me for the realism, the naturalism of the

> modern novel, and I could not read enough of them. (295)

Bulosan acknowledged the guidance of mentors like Elizabeth O'Dell, who introduced him to Marxist analysis, but also traced his sense of understanding to his encounters with books:

> From day to day I read, and reading widened my mental horizon, creating a spiritual kinship with other men who had pondered over the miseries of their countries. Then it came to me that the place did not matter: these sensitive writers reacted to the social dynamics of their time. I, too, reacted to my time. . . . I plunged into books, boring through the earth's core, leveling all seas and oceans, swimming in the constellations. (246)

It is not surprising that the Filipino immigrant Carlos Bulosan found more in common with African-American Richard Wright than access to a library. The situation of Filipino farm workers on the West Coast had many parallels with the conditions of African Americans in the rural South during the same decades of the 1920s and 30s. Racism was not only legal but actually prescribed by law. Jim Crow segregation laws were most extreme in the South. Throughout the country federal immigration law denied naturalized citizenship to Asian immigrants, and in the West Coast states restrictive covenants and anti-miscegenation laws underlay the same discriminatory practices that Southern segregation laws supported. African Americans and Asians suffered from discrimination in employment and housing, police and vigilante brutality, and unfair labor practices.[2]

Carlos Bulosan, Filipino peasant with three years of formal education, became widely recognized for his poetry and fiction as well as for documenting the plight of Filipino laborers in California and the Western states generally. In California, according to Bulosan's indictment, Filipinos were prohibited from buying or leasing real estate, holding civil service jobs, practicing law, marrying, becoming naturalized citizens, or using the same recreational facilities as other residents (268). Ill treatment by police was rampant, as was labor exploitation and violence; *America Is in the Heart* abounds with illustrative episodes.

All Asians, and migrant workers generally, suffered the kinds of outrages Bulosan describes, but Filipinos endured an especially painful predicament. The Philippines were a colony of the United States. After the United States army had suppressed the Philippine independence movement at the turn of the century, an army of teachers followed the army of occupation and established a school system intended to instill American-style values and aspirations in a citizenry being "prepared" for independence as a republic. However, the same government that supported this remarkable educational enterprise also maintained the Spanish colonial system of land distribution and economic structures and kept in place a political infrastructure susceptible to infinite corruption.

It is possible to find many parallels between the Philippines under United States occupation during the twenties and thirties and the American South of the same era. The first section of Bulosan's book, dealing with his life until he immigrated to the United States, depicts the effects of the system on the poorest of the rural poor, represented by his own family. However, Bulosan then goes on in the remaining three sections of the book to portray the existence of those same colonial structures inside the "promised land" to which he immigrates. California was part of that "north" in which southern Black Boys like Richard Wright might hope to find a better life, but for Pinoys (Filipino peasants) it was clear that the America of equality and democracy that had been promoted in the Philippine education system had to exist mainly in the heart, since it did not exist in the United States, certainly not in the Western states.

Some episodes in *America Is in the Heart* are striking in their resemblance to similar events related in *Black Boy*. One example is the depiction of infant drunkenness. Wright describes a period of debauchery around the age of six, when saloon patrons plied him with liquor. Bulosan relates an incident in which a group of Filipinos sharing a house in Los Angeles give wine to a five-year-old Mexican boy. Elements of the episodes are very similar, as is the descriptive language in each:

> Wright: To beg drinks in the saloon became an obsession. Many evenings my mother would find me wandering in a daze and take me home and beat me; but the next morning, no sooner had she gone to her job than I would run to the saloon and wait for someone

> to take me in and buy me a drink. My mother protested tearfully to the proprietor of the saloon, who ordered me to keep out of his place. But the men—reluctant to surrender their sport—would buy me drinks anyway, letting me drink out of their flasks on the streets, urging me to repeat obscenities. (24–25)
>
> Bulosan: I was ashamed of his [the child's] debauchery. . . . But I knew that he had to drink, that he would drink. . . . Mary [a young woman sharing the house with Carlos and Jose] came home one afternoon and saw the Mexican boy with the bottle of wine. She took it away and slapped him sharply. Then she pushed him outside the house. He did not resist. He waited patiently in the backyard. When he was sure that Mary had gone, he threw pebbles at the window. Jose went out with the bottle. They drank the wine standing, passing the bottle back and forth. When it was empty they started cursing each other; then Jose smashed the bottle against the wall of the house. (302)

It is apparent that some passages are imported in detail from *Black Boy* into *America Is in the Heart*; the account of suspect reading practices noted above would be one of these, and Bulosan's mention of this particular episode in Wright's book calls attention to the parallel. Another such importation seems to be the description of encounters with nude white women. These parallel passages are of interest for the way in which Bulosan reconceives and rewrites the episode.

Wright tells an anecdote about his brief career as a bellboy in a Southern hotel. A white prostitute and her customer, both nude, send for Wright to bring liquor to their room. Wright describes how the woman "slid out of bed and waddled across the floor to get her money from the dresser drawer. Without realizing it, I watched her." Wright shows how, when threatened by the woman's client, he had to depend for survival on a posture of shame and appeasement: "'Nigger, what in hell are you looking at?' the white man asked. . . . 'Nothing, sir,' I answered, looking suddenly miles deep into the blank wall of the room" (238).

Bulosan describes a similar episode which he says took place when he was helping his older brother Macario, who had a position as cook/housekeeper for a wealthy household in Hollywood. Carlos, deputed to carry a breakfast tray, finds that

> [t]he lady of the house was still in bed. She got up and went to the bathroom when she heard me knock on the door. She came back to the room without clothes, the red hair on her body gleaming with tiny drops of water. It was the first time I had seen the onionlike whiteness of a white woman's body. I stared at her, naturally, but looked away as fast as I could when she turned in my direction. She had caught a glimpse of my ecstasy in the tall mirror, where she was nakedly admiring herself.
>
> "What are you staring at?" she said.
>
> "Your body, madam," I said, and immediately regretted it. (141)

The way in which Bulosan recasts the episode offers a protagonist who is bolder and more at ease with his own sensuality, even as he shares with the reader his consciousness of the impossible predicament the prevailing mores set for him. Further, Bulosan's narrator refuses to deny the woman's exhibitionism or her complicity in this sexual charade that has as its purpose the enactment of racialist power relationships. Conversing directly with the woman, he establishes them both as pawns set out on opposite sides in the same game. Although he says that at the time he "immediately regretted" his remark, as Wright had "gazed at the wall," Bulosan's regret at the moment is later displaced by the defiant inscription of his "ecstasy."

In *America Is in the Heart*, however, Bulosan does not draw explicit parallels between the lives of African Americans in the South and Asians in the West. It is, rather, both narrators' sense of their development as writers that offers the most resonant parallels between *America Is in the Heart* and *Black Boy*. Born November 24, 1913, in the rural Philippines, Carlos Bulosan was a close contemporary of Richard Wright. At thirteen he left home to try to find a living away from the desperate poverty of his landless peasant family, finding work eventually with the American woman who introduced him to libraries. At seventeen he left the Philippines, arriving in Seattle on July 22,

1930 (McWilliams xv). His farewell to the Philippines echoes Richard Wright's elegiac recollection of leaving the South:

> Bulosan: I was determined to leave that environment and all its crushing forces, and if I were successful in escaping unscathed, I would go back someday to understand what it meant to be born of the peasantry. I would go back because I was a part of it, because I could not really escape from it no matter what became of me. I would go back to give significance to all that was starved and thwarted in my life. (62)
>
> Wright: I was leaving the South to fling myself into the unknown, to meet other situations that would perhaps elicit from me other responses. . . . I was not leaving the South to forget the South, but so that some day I might understand it, might come to know what its rigors had done to me, to its children. I fled so that the numbness of my defensive living might thaw out and let me feel the pain—years later and far away—of what living in the South had meant.
>
> Yet, deep down, I knew that I could never really leave the South, for my feelings had already been formed by the South. (495–96)

The similarities are striking, yet one difference stands out. In this passage, as elsewhere throughout his book, Bulosan reiterates his desire to carry back to the Philippines the knowledge and understanding he has gained from his triumphs and ordeals. Wright, in the parallel passage, anticipates no such return. Unlike Carlos Bulosan, Richard Wright, for all the desperate conditions of his life in the South, could claim United States citizenship and whatever moral or legal leverage it might imply. While the North had problems of segregation and discrimination, it was not a place of exile, as America was for Filipino men.

America Is in the Heart most resembles *Black Boy* in its conceptualization and rhetorical strategies. Both Bulosan and Wright create works that blur the distinction between autobiography and fiction in ways that critics have found at once challenging and troubling. Narrators of both works bear the same name as the authors: Wright's narrator is "Richard" or

"Dick" and Bulosan identifies his persona first as "Allos" and then as "Carlos," the name he wrote under. The story line in each follows the conventions of autobiography, tracing the development of an autonomous self. However, it has been argued that Wright intended *American Hunger* (the first title of *Black Boy*) as fiction, and inclusion of material either invented or drawn from other people's experience has rendered his text problematic for genre critics. Adams, reviewing these issues, resolves the question by claiming that "what makes *Black Boy* so compelling is its ability to remain autobiography despite its obvious subordination of historicity" (80).

Similarly, Bulosan's friend and mentor Carey McWilliams, in his Introduction to the 1973 edition of *America Is in the Heart*, feels that the factuality of Bulosan's account is its most important quality but is also problematic:

> One may doubt that Bulosan personally experienced each and every one of the manifold brutalities and indecencies so vividly described in this book, but it can fairly be said—making allowances for occasional minor histrionics—that some Filipino was indeed the victim of each of these or similar incidents. (vii)

Critics engaged with Bulosan's texts have attempted compromise formulations similar to those put forward for Wright's. Orendain calls *America Is in the Heart* "fictionalized autobiography," a form characterized by "realism" (369), and to account for "discrepancies between his documented biography and his life as recounted in the book" (370) cites Daroy: "Although Bulosan's works are autobiographical, they are a reconstruction not of his personal life, but of the general condition of the working class" (370).

Clearly Bulosan was influenced by Wright, but the aptness of the influence stemmed from genuine parallels in the lives and conditions of the men and their communities. Some of the episodes in *America Is in the Heart* are clearly shaped or even imported wholesale from *Black Boy*; examples would be the stories of suspect reading habits and naked women discussed above. On the other hand, in some instances the parallel between the two stories arises from similar exigencies in the narrators' actual lives. For instance, both Wright and Bulosan relate episodes of theft. Wright steals from a theater owner, a neighbor, and eventually a Negro school. Bulosan burglarizes a neighbor and grabs a diamond ring. Both men feel severely pressed by demands they perceive as urgent and for which they have no resources: Wright must leave the South or be driven to violence; Bulosan must find medical help for his severely ill brother. Both men also express a fear of what they themselves can be driven to do in the face of such trials. These episodes and others like them are similar because the lives of the men and of the many they speak for are similar.

Still other episodes in both books reflect issues of poverty and discrimination that have almost the character of universal folklore. Wright tells the story familiar in African-American folklore of the preacher who comes to dinner and, after blessing the food for so long that everything gets cold, takes all the tastiest morsels for himself. Bulosan tells a similar story of food scarcity, of the village woman so poor that to get a taste of fish she was compelled to dip her hands into the salted fish brine and then drink the water she rinsed them off with. I heard a similar story once from a woman in Tuscany, who related that her family hung a salt fish over the kitchen table and then rubbed their pieces of polenta against it to flavor the porridge. These are not cases of direct literary influence, but of the authors' re-presentation of age-old expressions of the meaning of poverty.

Nevertheless, the problem of the "autobiographical contract" remains. The solutions offered by Adams, McWilliams, Orendain, and others—"remain autobiography despite . . . suppression of historicity," "fictionalized autobiography," and "reconstruction . . . of the general condition of the working class"—are not satisfactory. Such formulations attempt to resolve what may be an unresolvable conflict between what Adams distinguishes as "historical truth" versus "narrative truth" (82–83). Adams appears to be restating Aristotle's categories of the "possible implausible" (history) and the "plausible impossible" (tragedy, fiction). Persuasiveness, in the rhetorical sense, belongs with the plausible impossible, so that the writer who hopes to move his audience to belief and action will understandably be drawn to offer that audience compelling fiction rather than difficult-to-swallow history. The designation "realism" or "naturalism" begs the question, since what is real*istic* is by definition not real, what is natural*istic* is not natural.

If persuasiveness alone were the issue a depiction that would move the audience to assent would be sufficient, and the question of fact or history would be irrelevant. But Richard Wright and Carlos Bulosan were, as Bulosan says of Mikhail Sholokov, writing "with a *purpose*" (246). *Black Boy* and *America Is in the Heart* belong to the literature of witness, in which the uncovering of social or moral evil is of itself an action taken against that evil. Wright and Bulosan wrote to inform as well as to persuade, to enlighten their readers about what life was like, in fact, for African Americans and Asians in the United States. Fictionalizing tends to vitiate the claims of such works to a moral imperative based on the documentation of actual evil.[3] This conflict between the requirements for validity of documentation and the necessity for persuasiveness merits further exploration. The relationship of *America Is in the Heart* and *Black Boy* offers a unique opportunity for further inquiry.

Notes

1. Wright says the book was *Main Street*; considering the number of books he read in such a short time, it is no surprise that titles and characters became tangled in his memory.

2. Young offers a concise overview of the parallel evolution of racist legislation and practice directed towards African Americans and emigrants from Asia.

3. The same problem may be seen in a later text clearly marked as fiction, Lawrence Thornton's *Imagining Argentina*, which raises the question of the relationship of fictional characters and imaginary solutions to repression and torture in Argentina set against the real horrors of the "dirty war" as documented by Amnesty International and other human rights groups. It is precisely the referentiality of the documentation produced by organizations like Amnesty International which gives their claims weight, validity—and effectiveness. While it is possible to make a purely structural analysis of a deposition on torture, to limit critical consideration to that dimension misses the fundamental rhetorical and moral grounding of the document.

Works Cited

Adams, Timothy Dow. *Telling Lies in Modern American Autobiography*. Chapel Hill: University of North Carolina Press, 1990.

Bulosan, Carlos. *America Is in the Heart.* Introduction. Carey McWilliams. Seattle: University of Washington Press, 1988.

Daroy, Petronilo B. "Carlos Bulosan: The Politics of Literature," *Saint Louis Quarterly* 6 (June 1968): 197.

McWilliams, Carey. Introduction. *America Is in the Heart.* i–xxiv.

Orendain, Margarita R. "Understanding the Dynamics of Third World Writing in Bulosan's *America Is in the Heart.*" *Saint Louis University Research Journal* 19.2 (1988): 365–75.

Thornton, Lawrence. *Imagining Argentina.* New York: Bantam, 1987.

Wright, Richard. *Black Boy*. 1937. New York: Harper, 1993.

Young, Mary E. *Mules and Dragons: Popular Culture Images in the Selected Writings of African-American and Chinese-American Women Writers.* Westport, Conn.: Greenwood Press, 1993.

Theoretical Dimensions of *Invisible Man*

Pierre A. Walker

Barbara Herrnstein Smith would argue that one sign of the potential value of Ralph Ellison's *Invisible Man* is the extent to which it lends itself to a variety of literary critical interests. In her influential and frequently cited essay on canon formation, Smith states that literary texts are deemed valuable because they satisfy certain needs:

> An object or artifact that performs certain desired/able functions particularly well . . . will have an immediate survival advantage; for, relative to . . . other comparable objects or artifacts . . . it will not only be better protected from physical deterioration but will also be more frequently . . . read or recited, copied or reprinted, translated, imitated, cited, and commented upon. . . . (31)

In practice, Smith's theory means that teachers include particular texts in their reading lists and scholars research and publish about particular texts as a result of the extent to which these texts illustrate, exemplify, and fulfill teachers' and scholars' perceived needs and interests. Furthermore, these perceived needs are constituted by the theories of literature which predominate and to which the teachers and scholars subscribe.

According to Smith's model, *Invisible Man* would be especially apt to be valued: under a predominantly formalist critical paradigm, Ellison's novel appeals to readers who delight in its complex narrative structure and web of intertextual references, and at a time when historically-, politically-, and ideologically-based types of literary criticism prevail, *Invisible Man*'s treatment of ethnic marginalization and American social history ought to attract serious attention.[1] Because of its high degree of suitability as a model for a range of critical and theoretical interests, *Invisible Man* is likely to become all the more firmly entrenched in the canon of twentieth-century literature. To demonstrate this high degree of suitability—and therefore to further this entrenchment and to suggest the extent of this novel's influence—I have chosen to focus on three theoretical "dimensions" of Ellison's novel, three theories or theorists that seem especially pertinent to important aspects of *Invisible Man*: Harold Bloom's theory of literary influence, Michel Foucault's theory of history, and the view of culture central to cultural studies.[2]

Invisible Man tells the story of the growth of its protagonist's self-awareness. This growth is most clearly shown through the relationship of the title character to black oral and folk culture, which he at first rejects as beneath him but later comes to see as an eloquent and meaningful vehicle of expression. "*Invisible Man*," as Joseph Skerrett Jr. points out, "asserts again and again the crucial role of both folk personalities . . . and folk culture . . . in the development of a spiritually acute black leader" (225). As a result, *Invisible Man* is a highly referential work, and the interpretation of the role of folk culture in the novel fills a considerable portion of the commentary on this novel.[3] *Invisible Man* also refers often to canonical literature, both African American and Euro-American, and this receives some, though perhaps not as much, attention from the novel's critics. Invisibility is the central metaphor in *Invisible Man*, and its treatment in Ellison's novel contrasts with the treatment it receives in *Native Son*, where it also plays an important role. Because in 1952, Wright's novel was the most famous African-American novel and its author the most famous African-American writer in the world, it is Ellison's primary predecessor in the literary treatment of the metaphor of invisibility. This is one reason why it is appropriate to see Ellison's version of the metaphor of invisibility as an example of the kind of misprision or rewriting of the predecessor so central to Bloom's theory of the anxiety of influence. Ellison's novel celebrates the African-American literary tradition by rewriting—in the Bloomian sense—*Native Son*'s metaphor of invisibility. Furthermore, *Invisible Man*'s treatment of the metaphor of invisibility is related to the novel's proto-Foucauldian philosophy of history, which itself is related to the view of American identity expressed in the epilogue. As a result, *Invisible Man* presents a view of historical marginalization and the diversity of American culture which has only much more recently become attractive to American academic intellectuals.

The metaphor of invisibility is a recurrent theme in African-American literature; Todd Lieber explores this metaphor (and the related metaphor of the mask) in *Invisible Man* (at some length) and in the context of some of its other African-American literary manifestations, including *Native Son* (which receives a summary treatment [89–91]), Claude McKay's "The Outcast" (87–88, 96, 98), Paul Laurence Dunbar's "We Wear the Mask" (92–94), James Weldon Johnson's *The Autobiography of an Ex-Colored Man* (93), and Charles Chesnutt's Conjure stories (94).[4] Invisibility, says Lieber, "evokes much that has been of crucial import in the black man's American experience . . . it reflects the conditions of a group whose basic plight was long overlooked or pushed into obscure shadows" (86). Invisibility, along with its correlatives, blindness and vision, is central in both *Native Son* and *Invisible Man*; in spite of the different ways invisibility is manifested in the two novels, in both texts it is emblematic of the indifference or the refusal of white-dominated America to let itself be aware of—to see—the adversity in the African-American situation.

Harold Bloom's theory of influence relies on the idea that writers rewrite their predecessors. To a certain extent, writers are inspired by their admiration of their precursors' accomplishments and seek to emulate and surpass them; at the same time, writers fear or envy those same accomplishments and thus "misread" them so as to create the need to improve or correct their faults. As Terry Eagleton paraphrases Bloom:

> The poet, locked in Oedipal rivalry with his castrating "precursor," will seek to disarm that strength by entering it from within, writing in a way which revises, displaces and recasts the precursor poem; in this sense all poems can be read as rewritings of other poems, and as "misreadings" or "misprisions" of them. . . . (183)

This sort of rereading or rewriting is very much what Ellison in *Invisible Man* did to Richard Wright's *Native Son* and its central metaphor of invisibility.

Critics have documented and commented extensively on Ellison's relationship with Wright,[5] and Ellison himself has left a significant autobiographical record and commentary in "The World and the Jug" (*Shadow* 115–47) and "Remembering Richard Wright" (*Territory* 198–216) and in his published interviews. In spite of this, commentators on Ellison's novel tend to focus on *Black Boy*, rather than *Native Son*, when they discuss Wright in relation to *Invisible Man*.[6] It matters little that in "The World and the Jug" Ellison himself denied the importance of Wright's work to his own artistic creation; as Robert O'Meally says, "There has been much ado about Ralph Ellison's complex debt to Richard Wright. Ellison himself shifts back and forth uncomfortably" ("Rules of Magic" 245). In keeping with Bloom's position, I am not arguing for what the author may have been consciously thinking as he wrote but for the kind of interpretation and understanding that follows from reading a text, like *Invisible Man*, in relation to an earlier one, like *Native Son*.[7]

Readers today who try to keep *Native Son* in their minds when reading *Invisible Man* in the way it might have been to a reader in 1952 can see that Ellison's novel explicitly presents the less explicit version of invisibility that pervades Wright's novel and which is best articulated by Wright's mouthpiece in *Native Son*, the lawyer, Max, when he urges the court not to condemn Bigger Thomas to the electric chair:

> In [Bigger] and men like him is what was in our forefathers when they first came to these strange shores hundreds of years ago. . . . We found a land whose tasks called forth the deepest and best we had; and we built a nation, mighty and feared. We poured and are still pouring our soul into it. But we have told them: "This is a white man's country!" (814)

Max argues here, and throughout his speech to the court, the parallel between the oppression which was the catalyst to much of the European settling of North America, the American Revolution, and the ideals upon which the United States was founded and the modern oppression of African Americans. It is the same point that Wright himself makes a year later in *Twelve Million Black Voices*:

> We black folk, our history and our present being, are a mirror of all the manifold experiences of America. What

> we want, what we represent, what we endure is what America *is*. If we black folk perish, America will perish.... The differences between black folk and white folk are not blood or color, and the ties that bind us are deeper than those that separate us.... Look at us and know us and you will know yourselves, for *we* are *you*, looking back at you from the dark mirror of our lives! (146)

It is the same point that Ellison's narrator makes in the epilogue to *Invisible Man* when he once again thinks over his grandfather's dying injunction to "overcome 'em with yesses, undermine 'em with grins, agree 'em to death and destruction" (16):

> Could he have meant—hell, he *must* have meant the principle, that we were to affirm the principle on which the country was built ... [—] the principle [which] was greater than the men, greater than the numbers and the vicious power and all the methods used to corrupt its name? Did he mean to affirm the principle, which they themselves had dreamed into being out of the chaos and darkness of the feudal past ... ?[8] (574)

All these passages make the same argument: the history of African Americans *is* a microcosm of American history; the idealized view of American history which most Americans learn in grade school emphasizes the various ideals and myths—the Founding Fathers, the land of opportunity, the melting pot, etc.—behind the Revolutionary War and the establishment and prosperity of the country, and yet the very presence and oppression of black Americans is to Wright, to Max, to Ellison's narrator a living reminder of the very same conditions of adversity which led to the need for those ideals, to the colonies' revolt, and to the establishing of the country upon principles of democratic equality. Therefore to ignore the particular circumstances in which black Americans find themselves is to ignore the very essence of the American character.

However the irony and the hypocrisy, as both Wright's Max and Ellison's narrator imply, is that while white America has fashioned an image of itself as a nation born out of oppression and based on ideals that were the antithesis of that oppression, it has been reluctant to acknowledge the claim of black Americans to an identical image. This reluctance is represented in both novels as a refusal or inability to see; this is the metaphor of invisibility. In *Native Son,* it is explicitly stated by Max during his courtroom speech. Condemning Bigger would just continue the willful refusal to see or acknowledge the plight of African Americans, but sparing him would amount to white America's at least confronting and acknowledging the situation: "But our decision as to whether this black boy is to live or die can be made in accordance with what actually exists. It will at least indicate that we *see* and *know*" (825).

There are several differences in the ways the two novels treat invisibility, differences which reveal Ellison's misprision of *Native Son,* his sense that Wright did not get things quite right. A most significant difference is that Wright has a white character articulate the notion of invisibility while Ellison's narrative voice—which is associated with a black man—expresses it in *Invisible Man.* Another difference is that Wright's novel makes it clear what invisibility means yet never uses the word invisible; however, in Ellison's novel the trope is apparent—so visible as it were—because of the title, the novel's first sentence—"I am an invisible man" (3)—and the surrealistic way in which Ellison's character is invisible (he is no H. G. Wells character), but it is never explicitly explained. Ellison did not need to spell out an explanation of what invisibility means in a novel about a young black man in a big northern city, because the best known novel of the time about a young black man in a big northern city—one of whose existence no habitual reader of African-American novels in 1952 would be ignorant—has already defined it clearly enough.

Ellison's transformation of Wright's treatment of invisibility also differs in its ideological resolution to white America's neglect of the black American. The solution *Native Son* most overtly espouses is found in Max's Marxist call in his last conversation with Bigger to a brotherhood of workers and the dispossessed (846–48). *Invisible Man,* of course, rejects such a solution by ultimately condemning the quasi-Stalinist Brotherhood as just another way for white America to "Keep This Nigger-Boy Running" (33)[9] and offers instead an appeal for a redefined sense of American identity:

> America is woven of many strands; I would recognize them and let it so remain. . . . Our fate is to become one, and yet many—This is not prophecy, but description. Thus one of the greatest jokes in the world is the spectacle of the whites busy escaping blackness and becoming blacker every day, and the blacks striving toward whiteness, becoming quite dull and gray. None of us seems to know who he is or where he's going. (577)

In this passage Ellison's narrator is arguing a view of African-American identity as American identity (and the reverse, too, American identity as African-American identity) which at first glance seems essentially the same as Wright's own point in the passage quoted earlier from *Twelve Million Black Voices*: black America is America; the meaning of America is found in the meaning of black America. But in an attempt to preserve diversity within similarity, Ellison adds a caveat which is a significant distinction from Wright: "Our fate is to become one, and yet many" (577). While America may be "woven of many strands," it is in part the individuality of the various strands that makes American identity what it is. Wright's novel serves as an appeal to a Marxist solution that would unify all economically disadvantaged people and relies upon its own shock value to remove the blinders that keep the rest of America from seeing beyond African Americans' invisibility. Max's Chicago skyline-inspired Marxist speech to Bigger in the closing pages of *Native Son* (846–48) is really an appeal to homogeneity, to something fundamental that would or could unite people across ethnic or racial boundaries. In a sense, this appeal is the American melting pot in another form, one that implies, "We're all in this together." Ellison's solution is quite different; as a student of mine once pointed out, Wright's/Max's vision is a stew (the melting pot) while Ellison's "one, and yet many," strands is a chef's salad. Ellison's novel suggests as a solution that not only should its readers, black or white, try to see beyond the same invisibility but also to see their own selves better. This is one of the major differences in Ellison's rewriting of Wright, and it means that while Wright could only lodge a protest, Ellison could not only lodge a protest but also validate and glorify the richness of African-American culture and posit that validation as a resolution to American racial problems.

Ellison is also arguing a view of social history which predates, but is similar to, the view Michel Foucault articulates fifteen years later in *The Archaeology of Knowledge*. Central to Foucault's study of history throughout his career was a concern with the marginal and the local. Rather than focusing on how power emanated from a central authority, a national ruler, or a central government, Foucault studied how in the modern age power operated and identity and history were created at the local level and in loci of marginalization, like prisons and mental hospitals. With only a few exceptions, *Invisible Man*'s critics have not cited Foucault in discussing Ellison's novel; nonetheless, writing two decades before Foucault's major work, Ellison had his narrator present a view of the significance of the marginalized in history that is very much related to Foucault's.[10]

In his self-deceived modes, when he subscribes to the quasi-Emersonian self-reliant ideology of the Booker T. Washington inspired college and when he believes in the Brotherhood, Ellison's invisible man believes in a linear, progressive notion of history: in "a reliable relation between cause and effect ... the existence of causal connections ... and that material awards await the virtuous" (V. Smith, "Meaning of Narration" 30). The college represents a belief that working hard will lead to middle-class success and power: "a progressive or linear vision of time is fundamental to both the American dream and the myth of racial uplift; moreover, it is the cornerstone upon which the college was founded" (V. Smith, "Meaning of Narration" 32). The Brotherhood espouses a view of history as "a force in a laboratory experiment" (*Invisible Man* 441). These linear notions are precisely the notions of history which Foucault argues in *The Archaeology of Knowledge* "we must rid ourselves of": "the notion of tradition ... the notion of influence ... the notions of development and evolution," causality, etc. (21-22). Having discovered "that history moves not like an arrow or an objective, scientific argument, but like a boomerang: swiftly, cyclically, and dangerously" (O'Meally, *Craft* 103), Ellison's narrator ultimately rejects such traditional notions, substituting for the ideas of linear history or of history as a spiral the conceit of history as a boomerang: "And that spiral business, that progress goo! ... Beware of those who speak of the *spiral* of history; they are preparing a boomerang" (*Invisible Man* 509, 6). Thus, as John F. Callahan points out, Ellison "spoofs the progressive spiral conception of history, conjures up 'grooves' of history, and suggests that any number of people may pass their lives outside history" (139). The shooting of Tod Clifton leads the invisible man to the realization that history is written by the victors, that it is a story (i.e. a lie, to use the common African-American vernacular term for story) imposed upon the chaos of events:[11]

> history records the patterns of men's lives, they say.... All things, it is said, are duly recorded—all things of importance, that is. But not quite, for actually it is only the known, the seen, the heard and only those events that the recorder regards as important that are put down, those lies his keepers keep their power by. (439)

There is no place in this battles-and-kings view of history for the "transitory ones," for those "natures too ambiguous for the most ambiguous words, and too distant from the centers of historical decision to sign or even to applaud the signers of historical documents" (*Invisible Man* 439). This traditional view of history has the same homogenizing tendency which the narrator condemns in the passage on identity from the epilogue quoted above: the destiny of American identity "is to become one, and yet many" (577). America contains many more strands than just baseball and apple pie, and to celebrate American diversity within unity is one of Ellison's own reasons for optimism; as he said when he accepted the National Book Award: "We are fortunate as American writers in that with our variety of racial and national traditions, idioms and manners, we are yet one. On its profoundest level American experience is of a whole. Its truth lies in its diversity and swiftness of change" (*Shadow* 114).

Foucault argues much the same ideas when he contrasts traditional history with his view of what history should be:

> The old questions ... (What link should be made between disparate events? How can a causal succession be established between them? What continuity or overall significance do they possess? Is it possible to define a totality ... ?) are now being replaced.... There are the *epistemological acts and thresholds* described by Bachelard: they suspend the continuous

> accumulation of knowledge . . . and force it to enter a new time [we recall that for *Invisible Man*'s narrator, falling outside of history is falling outside of time (439–41)]. . . . There are the *displacements* and *transformations* of concepts . . . they show that the history of a concept is not wholly and entirely that of its progressive refinement, its continuously increasing rationality. . . . There is the distinction . . . between the *microscopic* and *macroscopic scales* of the history of the sciences, in which events and their consequences are not arranged in the same way. . . . (3–4)

This passage reads like a prescription for the view of history expressed in *Invisible Man*. The view of linear time and history in the ideologies of the college and the Brotherhood is just like Foucault's description of the questions asked in traditional historical analysis; for both Foucault and Ellison's narrator, causality, evolution, and progress are rejected.[12] What arises instead is also similar; for Foucault we have "the possibility of a *total history* . . . one that seeks to reconstitute the overall form of a civilization" (9), and in Ellison we have the attempt to grasp the paradox of diversity within unity at the same time.

This new view of history brings invisibility, identity, and history together in Ellison's novel, for it includes the marginalized, those to whom Ellison's novel refers as "outside of history" (438), and thus reflects the diversity within unity of American identity. This creates the possibility for "an invisible man [to have] a socially responsible role to play" (581), for once the invisible man comes out of "hibernation" (580) and writes, telling about "what was really happening when your eyes were looking through" him (581), the marginalized "who write no novels, histories or other books" (439) have in fact begun the celebration of the diversity of American identity.

Thus Ellison offers a very different resolution of the metaphor of invisibility from Wright's. *Native Son* tries to shock its readers out of their blindness; we still have causality, since shock therapy relies on a belief in the efficacy of a brute form of cause and effect, and thus still a linear sense of history. *Invisible Man* offers on the other hand a sense of history and of storytelling that makes use of invisibility both as a good in itself and as a way of transcending the constraints imposed by being invisible. Once again, Wright's and Ellison's views of the

African-American part in American history are different: while African-American history is a microcosm of all American history for Wright, it is something more paradoxical for Ellison; it both reflects the fundamental principles of America in general at the same time that it offers a distinction.

True to Bloom's theory of the anxiety of influence, *Invisible Man* lies in a relationship of similarity and difference to its precursor, *Native Son*. If *Native Son* is a protest novel, so too is *Invisible Man*. However, Wright's novel expresses its protest in terms of the mainstream American ideology of the struggle against oppression and for freedom, while Ellison's takes a playful and paradoxical stance towards the quintessential American value of self-reliance and the myth of racial uplift, one that seems much more akin to, say, Zora Neale Hurston's *Dust Tracks on a Road*. If Wright represented both the protest tradition in African-American literature and the adoption of mainstream European and American fictional form (naturalism), and Hurston exemplified a populist tradition and the derivation of a literary form from the aesthetic of oral culture, *Invisible Man* contains aspects of both and is the conjunction of the two. All at the same time, *Invisible Man* is a work of protest and a valorization of folk culture while it also takes a form influenced by both high modernism and the same kind of oral aesthetic that shapes Hurston's work. This is because part of the story of both the text and the character of *Invisible Man* is its valorization of folk or "low" culture in relation to "high," and it is because of this that *Invisible Man* can be seen to anticipate one of the latest trends in academic literary criticism, cultural studies.

One of the key points repeatedly emphasized in cultural studies is that the distinction between "high" and "low" culture is, if not false, at least inoperative. Cultural critics, as Ross Murfin has pointed out, are just as interested in relations between a text and an artifact of "high" culture and one of "low" culture, since "culture" includes both the high and the low.

> [O]ne of the goals of cultural criticism is to oppose Culture with a capital C, in other words, that *view* of culture which always and only equates it with what we sometimes call "high culture." Cultural critics want to make the term *culture* refer to *popular* culture as well as to . . . the so-called classics. Cultural critics . . . want to break down the boundary between high and low, and

> to dismantle the hierarchy that the distinction implies. (326)

Central to cultural studies, writes Gerald Graff, is the attempt at "putting highbrow and lowbrow traditions back into the dialogical relation in which they have actually existed in our cultural history" (60). *Invisible Man* not only anticipated so catholic a view of culture but made the realization of the value of "low" culture an integral part of its protagonist's story.[13]

Part of the agenda of cultural studies is to valorize artifacts along the full spectrum that constitutes "culture," and the suspicion of a hierarchical view of culture recurs again and again in discussions of cultural studies. This suspicion is certainly to some extent a reaction against the conservative defenses of the literary canon and of traditional schools of literary interpretation that appeared in the mid-1980s (which were themselves reactions to challenges of the late 1970s and early 1980s against received ideas of literary value) (Brantlinger 3–11; Balsamo 145).

Perceived in the light of the cultural critics' view of culture, *Invisible Man* appears an allegory of the culture wars.[14] At first its hero is certain of his Emersonian destiny (he promises Mr. Norton he will read Emerson [108])—a destiny characterized by his belief in the related ideals of racial uplift, self-reliance, and the myth of American success—and he has only contempt for folk culture, as when he scorns the incestuous squatter, Jim Trueblood (46–47, 68), the jive-talking Peter Wheatstraw (172–77), and the offer of a Southern breakfast of "'Pork chops, grits, one egg, hot biscuits and coffee!'" (178). However, when the invisible man learns the content of President Bledsoe's letter about him to the college trustees and realizes that he has been the brunt of a joke, he suddenly finds himself unable to forget the song, "They Picked Poor Robin" (193–94). This is an important moment in the novel because here the protagonist realizes that folk culture can be a legitimate source of solace and a suitable vehicle for his feelings; an analogous moment comes when the invisible man relishes eating a hot yam and fantasizes about calling Bledsoe "'a shameless chitterling eater!'" (263–66). Thus Ellison's narrator learns to disregard the cultural values implicit in his schooling and in the ideology of assimilation and expands his definition of and consideration for culture.

Invisible Man underlines its protagonist's appreciation of an expanded notion of what constitutes culture by itself referring to, modeling itself upon, or acknowledging intertexts from all across the cultural spectrum. Folk culture makes a major appearance, of course, in the novel, manifesting itself, for example, in instances of signifying and playing the dozens, in the quoting of songs such as "They Picked Poor Robin"[15] and Louis Armstrong's "(What Did I Do To Be So) Black and Blue," and in the black church sermon, call and response technique of most of the narrator's public speeches. *Invisible Man* emphasizes its relationship to monuments of the African-American literary tradition, and not just in its anxiety of influence relationship to Wright's *Native Son* (or his "The Man Who Lived Underground"): it directly quotes Booker T. Washington's Atlanta convention speech, it uses James Weldon Johnson's *The Autobiography of an Ex-Colored Man* as a "prototype,"[16] and "By linking the narrative act to the achievement of identity, Ellison['s text] places his protagonist in a tradition of Afro-American letters that originated with the slave narratives of the late-eighteenth and nineteenth centuries" (V. Smith, "Meaning of Narration" 27).[17] Finally, *Invisible Man* emphasizes its relationship to the monuments of European and Euro-American literature: Emerson's essays, through the name given one of the trustees; Dostoyevsky, through its connection and the connection of Wright's "The Man Who Lived Underground" to *Notes from Underground*; Melville and T. S. Eliot, whom it quotes directly in the epigraph;[18] and high modernist fiction, like Joyce's *Ulysses*, through its formal and narrative techniques.[19]

Invisible Man can be read as a novel *about* the range of culture and the dangers its protagonist encounters when he denies culture its full range, a danger which the novel equates to a lack of self-knowledge. When he is relishing the hot yam, in a rare moment of accurate introspection, the invisible man asks himself: "What and how much had I lost by trying to do only what was expected of me instead of what I myself had wished to do?" (266). The novel offers formal parallels to the protagonist's own struggle over dominant ideology versus folk culture through its use of modernist literary technique and attributes of African-American oral culture like signifying and call and response speeches and through the range of evoked intertexts. The novel uses techniques found in (though not necessarily unique to) much Modernist literature and many European and European-American novels, like an unreliable narrator, intertextual citation, and symbolism; it also evokes mainstream American values, like Horatio Alger and Emersonian self-reliance. Ultimately, however, it concludes like Frederick Douglass's *Narrative*, with the anticipation of the writing of the story just told. Just as the novel urges readers to value diversity in American history and life, to preserve difference within similarity, these formal parallels to the protagonist's dilemma over "high" versus "low" culture ask us to value the variety of culture, not to limit our attention and appreciation to one strand only, as Ellison's protagonist did in his college-going phase. Just as American history has several strands, so too does American culture; in both cases, they are not strands of a homogeneous unity but, paradoxically, of a heterogeneous unit. This is the lesson of cultural studies, but one which *Invisible Man* anticipated by several decades.

Of the three theoretical dimensions of *Invisible Man* which I have explored, only the first—the novel's "anxiety of influence" relationship to *Native Son*—is about influence in the traditional sense of an earlier literary text influencing the writing or reading and interpreting of a later one. My argument is really for the influence of *Invisible Man* on our acceptance of contemporary literary theory. We can value *Invisible Man* all the more because of the extent to which it can serve as a model for Bloom's theory—and conversely, we can value Bloom's theory all the more because of the extent to which it helps us value *Invisible Man* and its relationship to prior novels by African-American authors.[20] As long as we value Bloom as a theorist, we are more likely to pay attention to Ellison's novel (and its relation to Wright's), and vice versa. The same goes for the relationship between *Invisible Man* and both Foucault and cultural studies. Influence in the usual sense does not seem to be the issue here; Foucault could have read Ellison's novel (it was first translated into French in 1954), and so too could have Stuart Hall or Raymond Williams, but *Invisible Man* receives no explicit acknowledgment in their work. Nevertheless, all three—Ellison, Foucault, and cultural studies—have emerged in a world that has given an audience to the issue of marginalization as never before; to use an old-fashioned view of literary history of which Foucault would disapprove heartily,

Invisible Man, Foucauldian history, and cultural studies all seem to be part of the same *zeitgeist*.

This constitutes a claim for two things: the relationship of works of literature to theory and the influence of *Invisible Man* (as opposed to the influence upon it). The relationship between literary theory and the literature it theorizes should be perceived as organic: they both influence each other. Hypotheses require substantiating data, which in literary theory means that theoretical critics need texts which lend themselves to an adequate demonstration of the theory, and *Invisible Man* is exemplary in this respect to a number of theoretical approaches. We return to Barbara Herrnstein Smith and her model of value as contingent on needs and interests. The suitability of a text to demonstrate a theory, for Smith, is likely to ensure a text's survival, and at a certain point, survival itself tends to become self-perpetuating ("a work . . . will . . . begin to perform certain characteristic cultural functions by virtue of the very fact that it *has* endured" [32]).

The relationship of dependency that Smith describes—the text relies on the prevailing critical theoretical paradigm for its survival—works in the reverse sense, too. The survival of theories can depend on the extent to which the texts that are valued are suitable to those theories. According to Smith, "the canonical work begins increasingly not merely to survive within but to shape and create the culture in which its value is produced and transmitted and, for that very reason, to perpetuate the conditions of its own flourishing" (32–33). This is the case with *Invisible Man*, at least within the sub-culture of academic literary criticism. Although Ellison's stature and influence may have waned in the sixties, when he "fell out of step with the advocates of black power and the black aesthetic" (O'Meally, *Craft* 180) and with liberals like Irving Howe, the powerful influence of his novel endures today and is most apparent in the resemblances of contemporary literary theories—like those based on Foucault's work and cultural studies—to aspects of *Invisible Man*.

Notes

1. It is, of course, possible for a text to receive negative attention, as *Invisible Man* did in the 1960s, when Irving Howe excoriated Ellison and James Baldwin in "Black Boys and Native Sons." In Smith's model, though, this kind of negative attention is more likely than no attention to lead to canonical status. Furthermore, once a text achieves a certain degree of canonicity, this position in itself tends to guarantee both that the text will continue to attract attention and that the attention will be positive. Today, *Invisible Man* is more securely in such a position than it was in the 1960s and is less likely to be the target of challenges such as Howe's; in part, this is because of the way Ellison and others met Howe's challenge.

2. Ellison's one critic to see the post-structuralist theoretical dimensions of *Invisible Man* to an extent that I share is Alan Nadel, who argues that "Ellison's narrator, at the end of *Invisible Man*, is in a role analogous to that of a postmodern critic" (18) and who calls *Invisible Man*'s narrator "a semiotician" (23), which he describes as "the narrator's assuming a postmodern stance, as interpreter of signs, outside of time, framing experience with a new set of questions" (26).

3. "One of the outstanding characteristics of *Invisible Man*," according to Joseph Frank, "is its use of Negro folk culture, not as a source of quaint exoticism and 'folksy' local color, but as a symbol of a realm of values set off against the various ideologies with which the narrator becomes engaged" (234). For the connection between *Invisible Man* and the oral tradition, see Robert O'Meally (*Craft* 78-104). O'Meally also provides a summary of some of the many critics who have discussed folklore and *Invisible Man* (*Craft* 79).

4. In relation to Ellison's novel, Lieber focuses especially on the metaphor of invisibility and the related metaphor of the mask in "We Wear the Mask," *The Autobiography of an Ex-Colored Man*, and Chesnutt's Conjure stories. He does not explore the relationship of invisibility in *Native Son* and *Invisible Man* as I do.

5. See, for example, Robert Stepto (162, 176–77), Michel Fabre (208–9), and Joseph Skerrett Jr. (224–29); see also Gates (*Figures* 236–46, 253; *Signifying Monkey* 104–12), who points out that "Ellison's definition of the relation his works bear to those of Richard Wright constitutes our definition of narrative

signification, pastiche, or critical parody" (*Figures* 245). For an extended discussion of Ellison's ostensible view of Wright's work, see O'Meally (*Craft* 44–49), who nonetheless concludes that for all Ellison's nods to "Hemingway . . . and Malraux and Dostoievsky and Faulkner" in "The World and the Jug" (Ellison, *Shadow* 145), "*Native Son*, 'The Man Who Lived Underground,' and *Black Boy* (that first-person 'blues' narrative about a bright boy who endures everything, including a battle royal) seem to have been at Ellison's elbow as he was creating *Invisible Man*" (O'Meally, *Craft* 49).

6. One of the rare exceptions to the general preference of *Black Boy* over *Native Son* in relation to *Invisible Man* is Stepto's brief remark that, in the implied parallel between the relationship between Mr. Norton and his daughter and Jim Trueblood's incestuous relationship with his daughter,

> Ellison is up to some devilish tricks regarding what is unstated about Mr. Dalton and his virginal Mary in *Native Son*. Surely it is not stretching things to draw a parallel between Norton giving money for toys to the Truebloods and Dalton giving pingpong paddles to the "bloods" at the South Side Boys Club. (182)

Gates discusses the way Ellison's title, *Invisible Man*, tropes on Wright's titles, *Black Boy* and *Native Son* (*Figures* 245–46; *Signifying* 106). Charles T. Davis discusses Ellison's novel in relation to Wright's *The Outsider* (278–79) and in contrast to *Native Son* (281).

7. For discussions specifically of Harold Bloom in relation to *Invisible Man*, see Nadel (38–41) and Skerrett, who, to put it as Bloom would, "encourage us . . . to read *Invisible Man* as an impassioned domestic romance about literary sons (and grandsons) who struggle with their various inheritances to learn the complexity of their names as Afro-Americans" (Blount 676).

8. Stepto cites this passage as a restating of W. E. B. Du Bois (169–70).

9. In his 1955 *Paris Review* interview, Ellison explicitly rejected identifying his fictional Brotherhood with the American Communist Party (*Shadow* 179). Nevertheless, the irony and perhaps an additional Wrightian influence on *Invisible Man* is found in the fact that Wright's own disillusionment with the Communist Party so closely parallels Ellison's invisible man's

with the Brotherhood. Ellison, of course, knew Wright best at the time the celebrated novelist was experiencing difficulties with the Party, which may explain why the narration of the invisible man's experience with the Brotherhood reads so much like Wright's *American Hunger*. For a biographical elaboration on Wright's and Ellison's relationship during this period, see Fabre.

10. The one critic to comment on *The Archaeology of Knowledge* in relation to Ellison's novel—and only very briefly—is Houston Baker (*Blues* 61–62). Nadel, the only critic to apply post-structuralist theory extensively to Ellison's work, discusses Foucault specifically (14–15) and points out that in *Invisible Man*, "Ellison . . . does not create a deconstruction but rather reconstructs a coherent alternative to the 'accepted' ways of reading American history and literature in 1952" (26). Marcellus Blount reads "the 'insane' black men who hang out at the Golden Day" as Foucault might: "As Foucault predicts, these black men have refused to suppress their true identities, and their defiance must be socially contained" (679).

11. O'Meally uses Kenneth Burke to read this episode ("Rules of Magic" 264–68). John F. Callahan's "Chaos, Complexity, and Possibility: The Historical Frequencies of Ralph Waldo Ellison" discusses in depth Ellison's uncollected essay, "The Uses of History in Fiction," and its relevance to reading *Invisible Man*. In a position similar to my own, Callahan writes that in the epilogue to *Invisible Man*,

> [T]here emerges a notion of history as a name for the process by which man shapes his destiny out of the chaos of circumstances. Everywhere in Ellison's work chaos appears as the front man for possibility. It is, Ellison believes, man's fate to defy the formlessness of chaos and the abyss, and at the same time to recognize that possibility flows from chaos. (128)

Valerie Smith demonstrates the connection between the invisible man's identity and his traditional and misguided views of history and causality in her very insightful reading, "The Meaning of Narration in *Invisible Man*," which is slightly revised from the fourth chapter of her *Self-Discovery and Authority in Afro-American Narrative*.

12. Although he makes no mention of Foucault, Stepto is one of the few critics of *Invisible Man* to perceive the significance of the novel's critique of history or, as he puts it, "its brave assertion that there is a self and form to be discovered beyond the lockstep of linear movement within imposed definitions of reality." For this reason, *Invisible Man* has to be framed as it is with its prologue and epilogue, otherwise its "narrator's steady progression to voice and selfhood" would appear to "stand alone as the *narrative* of Ellison's hero. The tale must be framed, and in that sense controlled, because progression as a protean literary form and progress as a protean cultural myth must be contextualized" (168). Although by no means influenced by Foucault, Russell G. Fischer reads *Invisible Man* as an allegory of "three major epochs of Negro American history from Reconstruction to the Second World War" (367).

13. A theoretical dimension to *Invisible Man* which I do not explore here but which is inextricably related to cultural studies and which certainly merits examination is reading the novel for its multiple voices, as Bakhtin would have, and as Henry Louis Gates Jr. (*Figures* 247–49; *Signifying Monkey* 111–13), Thomas R. Whitaker (395), Berndt Ostendorf (101), and William Henry Lyne suggest.

14. In a related view, Baker suggests that "The experience of *Invisible Man*'s protagonist is" not unlike that of "'minority' ... literary scholars in recent years [who, as they have] ... pursued ... the archaeology of knowledge ... have revealed the limiting boundaries of traditional American discourse" (*Blues* 62).

15. This song is itself an object of parody and signifying for jazz musicians (Gates, *Figures* 244 and *Signifying Monkey* 105; Ellison, *Shadow* 226–27).

16. For Johnson and *Invisible Man*, see Baker's "A Forgotten Prototype: *The Autobiography of an Ex-Colored Man* and *Invisible Man*" in his *Singers of Daybreak* (17–31) and Stepto (176–77). For Frederick Douglass and W. E. B. Du Bois and *Invisible Man*, see Stepto (162–94).

17. In her other version of this same essay, "Ellison's Invisible Autobiographer," from her *Self-Discovery and Authority in Afro-American Narrative*, Valerie Smith also specifically mentions here "the structures of ... Johnson's *Autobiography*, and of Wright's *Native Son*" (91).

18. For Dostoyevsky and *Invisible Man*, see Joseph Frank's "Ralph Ellison and a Literary 'Ancestor': Dostoevski." Kimberly W. Benston suggests that *Invisible Man* can be viewed as an extended trope on *Moby Dick*: "The blackness of blackness is, of course, Ralph Ellison's antic-deconstructive riff off Melville's meditation on whiteness. . ." (159). For the relationship between Homer Barbee's description of the black college's Founder's death and Whitman's "When Lilacs Last in the Dooryard Bloom'd" see Marvin Mengeling and Stepto (180); see also Nadel, who "demonstrates convincingly the extent to which Ellison inserts himself consciously into the texts of Melville, Whitman, Emerson, Twain, and . . . Lewis Mumford" (Blount 678). For Thomas Schaub, the opening words of *Invisible Man* "are an act of self-definition meant to evoke the beginnings of *Walden*, *Moby-Dick*, and *Huckleberry Finn*" (130) in contrast to Poe, with whom, of course, *Invisible Man*'s second sentence explicitly denies any grounds for comparison (*Invisible Man* 3). For an interesting reading of *Invisible Man* in its relation to Poe, see Mary F. Sisney (87–90).

19. For Joyce and *Invisible Man*, see Robert List's *Dedalus in Harlem: The Joyce-Ellison Connection.*

20. Not all scholars of African-American literature care for Bloom's theory of influence in respect to *Invisible Man* and its antecedents; see, for example, Gates: "My work with signification has now led me to undertake the analysis of the principles of interpretation . . . in a manner only roughly related to Harold Bloom's use of Kabbalah" (*Figures* 236). Nevertheless, Gates provides a way of seeing an analogy between Bloom's theory of influence and his own Afrocentric theory of the African-American literary tradition by offering a chart of traditional rhetorical figures, Bloom's revisionary ratios, African-American "signifyin(g) tropes," and their Yoruba correlates (*Signifying Monkey* 87). A frequent criticism of Bloom's theory is that it focuses almost exclusively on canonical authors, making no mention of the dynamics of influence in marginalized traditions, like the African-American novel or literature by women (see, for example, Annette Kolodny's "A Map for Rereading" [453, 465]). This is a valid criticism, but it does not mean that Bloom's theory cannot be modified or revised to accommodate or apply to alternative traditions, as, indeed, Kolodny, Sandra Gilbert and Susan Gubar (46–53), and others (Renza 198) have shown.

Works Cited

Baker, Houston A., Jr. *Blues, Ideology, and Afro-American Literature: A Vernacular Theory*. Chicago: University of Chicago Press, 1984.

———. *Singers of Daybreak: Studies in Black American Literature*. 1974; rpt. Washington: Howard University Press, 1983.

Balsamo, Anne. "Cultural Studies and the Undergraduate Literature Curriculum." *Cultural Studies in the English Classroom*. Eds. James A. Berlin and Michael J. Vivion. Portsmouth N.H.: Boynton, 1992. 145–64.

Benston, Kimberly W. "I Yam What I Am: The Topos of Un(naming) in Afro-American Literature." *Black Literature and Literary Theory*. Ed. Henry Louis Gates Jr. New York: Methuen, 1984. 151–72.

Blount, Marcellus. "'A Certain Eloquence': Ralph Ellison and the Afro-American Artist." *American Literary History* 1 (1989): 675–88.

Brantlinger, Patrick. *Crusoe's Footprints: Cultural Studies in Britain and America*. New York: Routledge, 1990.

Callahan, John F. "Chaos, Complexity, and Possibility: The Historical Frequencies of Ralph Waldo Ellison." *Speaking for You: The Vision of Ralph Ellison*. Ed. Kimberly W. Benston. Washington: Howard University Press, 1987. 125–43.

Davis, Charles T. 'The Mixed Heritage of the Modern Black Novel: Ralph Ellison and Friends." *Speaking for You: The Vision of Ralph Ellison*. Ed. Kimberly W. Benston. Washington: Howard University Press, 1987. 272–282.

Eagleton, Terry. *Literary Theory: An Introduction*. Minneapolis: University of Minnesota Press, 1983.

Ellison, Ralph. *Going to the Territory*. New York: Vintage-Random, 1987.

———. *Invisible Man*. 1952; rpt. New York: Vintage-Random, 1989.

———. *Shadow and Act*. 1964; rpt. New York: Signet-NAL, 1966.

———. "The Uses of History in Fiction." *Southern Literary Journal* 1 (Spring 1969): 57–90.

Fabre, Michel. "From *Native Son* to *Invisible Man*: Some Notes on Ralph Ellison's Evolution in the 1950s." *Speaking for You: The Vision of Ralph Ellison*. Ed. Kimberly W. Benston. Washington: Howard University Press, 1987. 199–216.

Fischer, Russell G. "*Invisible Man* as History." *College Language Association Journal* 17 (1974): 338–67.

Foucault, Michel. *The Archaeology of Knowledge*. 1969; trans. A. M. Sheridan Smith. New York: Pantheon, 1972.

Frank, Joseph. "Ralph Ellison and a Literary 'Ancestor': Dostoevski." *Speaking for You: The Vision of Ralph Ellison*. Ed. Kimberly W. Benston. Washington: Howard University Press, 1987. 231–44.

Gates, Henry Louis, Jr. *Figures in Black: Words, Signs, and the "Racial" Self*. New York: Oxford University Press, 1987.

———. *The Signifying Monkey: A Theory of African-American Literary Criticism*. New York: Oxford University Press, 1988.

Gilbert, Sandra M., and Susan Gubar. *The Madwoman in the Attic: The Woman Writer and the Nineteenth-Century Literary Imagination*. New Haven: Yale University Press, 1979.

Graff, Gerald. "Teach the Conflicts." *The Politics of Liberal Education*. Eds. Darryl J. Gless and Barbara Herrnstein Smith. Durham N.C.: Duke University Press, 1992. 57–73.

Howe, Irving. "Black Boys and Native Sons." *Dissent* 10 (1963): 353–68. Rpt. in *A World More Attractive: A View of Modern Literature and Politics*. New York: Horizon Press, 1963. 98–122.

Kolodny, Annette. "A Map for Rereading: or, Gender and the Interpretation of Literary Texts." *New Literary History* 11 (1980): 451–67.

Lieber, Todd M. "Ralph Ellison and the Metaphor of Invisibility in Black Literary Tradition." *American Quarterly* 24 (1972): 86–100.

List, Robert N. *Dedalus in Harlem: The Joyce-Ellison Connection*. Washington: University Press of America, 1982.

Lyne, William Henry. "An Invisible Dialogue: James, Ellison, Bakhtin and the Middle Ground of the Modern Novel." *DAI* 53 (1992): 151. University of Virginia.

Mengeling, Marvin E. "Whitman and Ellison: Older Symbols in a Modern Mainstream." *Walt Whitman Review* 12 (Sept. 1966): 67–70.

Murfin, Ross C. "What Is Cultural Criticism?" *Edith Wharton:* The House of Mirth*: Complete, Authoritative Text with Biographical and Historical Contexts, Critical History, and Essays from Five Contemporary Critical Perspectives*. Ed. Shari Benstock. Case Studies in Contemporary Criticism. Boston: Bedford-St. Martin's, 1994. 326–39.

Nadel, Alan. *Invisible Criticism: Ralph Ellison and the American Canon*. Iowa City: University of Iowa Press, 1988.

O'Meally, Robert G. *The Craft of Ralph Ellison*. Cambridge: Harvard University Press, 1980.

———. "The Rules of Magic: Hemingway as Ellison's 'Ancestor.'" *Speaking for You: The Vision of Ralph Ellison*. Ed. Kimberly W. Benston. Washington: Howard University Press, 1987. 245–71.

Ostendorf, Berndt. "Ralph Waldo Ellison: Anthropology, Modernism, and Jazz." *New Essays on* Invisible Man. Ed. Robert O'Meally. Cambridge: Cambridge University Press, 1988. 95–121.

Renza, Louis A. "Influence." *Critical Terms for Literary Study*. Eds. Frank Lentricchia and Thomas McLaughlin. Chicago: University of Chicago Press, 1990. 186–202.

Schaub, Thomas. "Ellison's Masks and the Novel of Reality." *New Essays on* Invisible Man. Ed. Robert O'Meally. Cambridge: Cambridge University Press, 1988. 123–56.

Sisney, Mary F. "The Power and Horror of Whiteness: Wright and Ellison respond to Poe." *College Language Association Journal* 29 (1985): 82–90.

Skerrett, Joseph T., Jr. "The Wright Interpretation: Ralph Ellison and the Anxiety of Influence." *Speaking for You: The Vision of Ralph Ellison*. Ed. Kimberly W. Benston. Washington: Howard University Press, 1987. 217–30.

Smith, Barbara Herrnstein. "Contingencies of Value." *Canons*. Ed. Robert von Hallberg. Chicago: University of Chicago Press, 1984. 5–39.

Smith, Valerie. "The Meaning of Narration in *Invisible Man*." *New Essays on* Invisible Man. Ed. Robert O'Meally. Cambridge: Cambridge University Press, 1988. 25–53.

———. *Self-Discovery and Authority in Afro-American Narrative*. Cambridge: Harvard University Press, 1987.

Stepto, Robert B. *From Behind the Veil: A Study of Afro-American Narrative*. Urbana: University of Illinois Press, 1979.

Whitaker, Thomas R. "Spokesman for Invisibility." *Speaking for You: The Vision of Ralph Ellison*. Ed. Kimberly W. Benston. Washington: Howard University Press, 1987. 386–403.

Wright, Richard. *Black Boy (American Hunger). Later Works: Black Boy (American Hunger); The Outsider*. New York: Library of America, 1991.

———. *Native Son. Early Works: Lawd Today!; Uncle Tom's Children; Native Son*. New York: Library of America, 1991.

———. *Twelve Million Black Voices*. 1941; rpt. New York: Harper, 1969.

Contemporary

Swing to the White, Back to the Black: Writing and "Sourcery" in Ishmael Reed's *Mumbo Jumbo*

Richard Hardack

The mythology cleaves close to Nature; and what else was it they represented in Pan. . . . Such homage did the Greek pay to the unscrutable force we call Instinct, or Nature . . . [Pan] could intoxicate by the strain of his shepherds' pipe. . . . aboriginal, old as Nature, and saying, like poor Topsy, "Never was born; growed."

Ralph Waldo Emerson

The earliest Ragtime songs, like Topsy, "jes' grew" . . . the tune was irresistible, and belonged to nobody.

James Weldon Johnson

I mean when the parody is better than the original a mutation occurs which renders the original obsolete. Reed's law.

Ishmael Reed

The last section of Robert Scholes's *Fabulations and Metafiction* is devoted to Ishmael Reed, the writer of science fiction. In various contexts, Reed has been treated as science-fiction writer, allegorist, satirist, black aesthetician, revisionist, radical chauvinist, and traitor. But Reed is more of a trader, a hybrid stylist not likely to be considered a traditional writer in any genre. This proliferation of personas leaves *Mumbo Jumbo* a disturbing text, whose aims and methodologies are hard to pinpoint. This book about constructing a future black aesthetic winds up using nineteenth-century American pantheism—

Emerson's own and Stowe's projected versions of Topsy, black nature, or a self-growing Pan—as its most immediate epistemological source. Reed seems unable to decide whether to be Pan-African or Pan-American, an opposition he creates for himself at all turns. Trying to be a self-created writer, in imitation of his "self-propagating" Jes Grew, while simultaneously trying to acknowledge at least his black sources, Reed by necessity winds up better at satirizing than at creating. In order to accommodate his vision of Jes Grew, Reed is forced to prophesy on the basis of his own prefabricated history, while simultaneously pledging allegiance to an alleged history; for Reed, all history is not simply retrospective, but retroactive. It is not just that Reed's cyclic chronology dooms us to forget the past, but that according to his elaborations the art which we create in the future must still stem from that past. In the end, Reed appropriates American Renaissance tropes to critique the modernist co-optation of the Harlem Renaissance. As a result, Reed often seems unable to determine whether the Harlem Renaissance is a parody of the American Renaissance or vice-versa, and to which he should pledge his artistic birthright. Though comic, Reed's myth of origins has tragic implications.

The question is then how to situate Reed in relation to black literature, and to his black and white sources. For Reed winds up, at least in *Mumbo Jumbo*, attributing his voice not to black culture, but to an American version of universal nature; Jes Grew ultimately seeks its text of blackness in the way Emerson's nature seeks the voice of a representative American man. I argue that for Reed, the identity of nature in the American Renaissance comes to determine the nature of identity during the Harlem Renaissance. Jes Grew is ineluctably a form of American transcendentalism: nature's Oversoul, Pan, possessing and dispossessing individual wills. The crux of my argument is that Reed fences a white transcendental version of nature or Pan, which he claims is stolen property to begin with, as a version of blackness. Many of Reed's rhetorical moves parallel Emerson's, whom I here use in shorthand as representative of transcendental American Renaissance writers. As Edward Said would phrase it, Reed gives Jes Grew an origin, a pre-cultural, pre-intentional, source, yet must also argue that it has a specifically black, culturally intended beginning. Toward the end of this essay, I trace Reed's reclamation of Pan, a "Jes Grew" aspect of Western culture, as Egyptian/black, with an unannounced pit-stop at the Masonic pyramids of mid-nineteenth-century America.

Mumbo Jumbo ostensibly reconfigures all Western history, including the birth of the West, as a perpetual restaging of the conflict between "primitive," pre-Western, black, or "Jes Grew" beliefs—currently represented both by PaPa LaBas, the hoodoo detective, and the Mu'takifah, who liberate art from Western museums or art detention centers—and repressed, Western, white, or "Atonist" creeds—currently represented by the Wallflower Order, inheritors of the religious and political traditions of Teutonic Knights and Masons. The "plague" of Jes Grew periodically erupts from beneath the surface of Western culture and tries to reclaim its denied heritage; the particular manifestation Reed focuses on concerns attempts during the Harlem Renaissance to reconstruct a text of blackness. This text of blackness or Jes Grew has repeatedly been fragmented like the body of the pantheistic Egyptian god Osiris, a dismemberment which also represents the appropriation and dispersion—in effect the white-washing—of numerous pre-Western cultures. Against his twentieth-century American backdrop, Reed presents a parallel narrative which recounts how Osiris's jealous brother Set—and then Moses, Freud, and most Western writers in his wake—first tried to suppress the artistic and spiritual "epidemic" of Jes Grew in ancient Egypt, ultimately discrediting all worship of nature from Osirian pantheism to Haitian voodoo. They all hear the Knocking, but they won't let the "it" of nature in.

In this elaborate parable of Western history, Reed attributes a fundamental pantheism to his Egyptian/black heritage, and he proposes not just a recuperation of Pan in America, but of "Egypt of America."[1] Through his essentially Bacchic pantheism, Reed ascribes divinity to a universal, non-anthropomorphic, and non-hierarchic nature, which leads him to intimate that Western culture in its entirety is exploitative and repressive. Reed's problem is that he can't consistently own only what he desires from the West as Jes Grew, while simultaneously rejecting the exigent underside of the West or pantheism as somehow extrinsic to blackness. Pan is in a unique position because he represents a kind of fissure within Western culture. Not simply a pagan element persisting within the Christianized West, Pan far more dramatically denotes the very "disease" within the West that Reed has been looking for all along. Pan then serves as a locus for reassessing the ways in which Reed manages in the same book to argue that there are no fundamental differences between cultures; that black culture outperforms white culture even on its own terms; and that black culture can't be judged by the same standards as white culture—sometimes inferior, sometimes not, sometimes incommensurate. Before getting to my final discussion of Reed's status in American literature and his remarkable and essentially unacknowledged use of Stowe's and Emerson's versions of black nature, I wish in the first half of this essay to assess Reed's aesthetic in designing *Mumbo Jumbo* as a text about constructing texts. Reed fabricates a myth of origins, which comes complete with an aesthetic that itself "jes grew."

Like Baraka, Reed questions what he wants to create from within his structures, critiquing the medium he adapts. But Reed would parody or subvert his medium and yet have it taken seriously and have his work accepted within the literary community and without. Given its frontal attack on Western art, should *Mumbo Jumbo* itself be dismissed as a kind of art detention? If for Reed all art is propaganda, *Mumbo Jumbo* is only the propaganda of the disenfranchised. If Reed has qualms about being in some respects an anti-intellectual, he overcomes them with "intellectual" ploys, proceeding by invoking the rules he has proscribed. (Even a prescription for less proscription is a prescription.) Reed wants to produce a manifesto for a universal, non-hierarchic art, but he is also simultaneously trying to formulate a specifically black aesthetic which can both accommodate a heterogeneous literary history and offer a model for future unity in variety. Put simply, is Reed's neo-hoodoo aesthetic compatible with black aesthetics, and, if not, who gets to ostracize whom? If perceived as traditional literature—which it is seeking to supplant—*Mumbo Jumbo* appears to be a comedic polemic, but its black humor does not seem particularly black, Reed's evocation of Hurston not withstanding. It remains unclear whether Reed's parody is aimed most at Western culture, black/Western culture, or the reader, and which, if not all, it seeks to render obsolete. Like any literary work, the book seeks to justify its own aesthetic, but in this instance is particularly pressed to do so.

Mumbo Jumbo is less about Jes Grew seeking its text than this text seeking (to create) its paternity. But Reed owes more allegiance to the American Renaissance than to the Harlem

Renaissance, and to a self-generated fable of antiquity labeled black after the fact. By implication, Reed must discard the very art he wishes to advocate; the renamed black baby goes out with the white Baptist's bathwater. Yet there must be something which will make Jes Grew itself, if not its text, something more than a few purloined letters. As many of Reed's critics, including Henry Louis Gates, have noted, Jes Grew is the real person in *Mumbo Jumbo,* possesses the real hunger, leaving the other figures kinds of cotton characters. But Jes Grew must ultimately remain an empty cipher; what has been structured behind a periodic and parodic myth of black cultural genesis?

In this essay, I seek to portray Reed not as black aesthetician but as eclectic reappropriator and to suggest that ultimately his work is most comparable to that of white "transcendental" writers, though that may be as little an anomaly or anachronism as a black Mason or a PaPa LaBas. Despite his tirades, the type of criticism Reed practices is wholly Western. Only those within the system, or somehow assimilated to it, produce such an artifact: such self-correction is in fact a significant function of Western art. But by his own standards, Reed cannot avoid being co-opted. The black dissociation from the West which Reed would seem to require, even if it were possible, cannot be effected through a process which produces *Mumbo Jumbo*. And the toleration, or proliferation, Reed demands, is at odds with the secession he requires. Though he traces his parodic aesthetic to Africa, Reed knows "this kind of humor has been a feature of multi-cultural art for thousands of years" (*Shrovetide* 7). The "Trope-a-dope," as Kim Benston has called it, can help us diagnose the dualism Gates opens, but, as those in Spiraling Agony suggest, it also results in a different kind of "doubling-up": in laughter and sickness (87).[2] As exemplified by Jes Grew, Reed desires to see only the positive aspects of his polymorphous polytheism and the negative aspects of any presumably single-sided entity. If Reed is a window on the West in the tradition of its best commentators—somehow within but apart from American culture—he must also incur the brand that these other critics have always endured: made in the West. If Reed seriously sanctions a radical dissolution with the culture which forms the entire backdrop for his work, then *Mumbo Jumbo* is an absolute concession to necessity; for it is the voice of the West criticizing itself, not the voice of an identifiably black critique. Jes Grew will compose its own future text, but the very notion of that text can never be specifically black; it must admit, as Reed would probably allow, to anything, if especially to the Jes Grew he advocates. The term has become so vague and broad that it incorporates almost anything within its reach.

Though Reed clamors for a black aesthetic, he seems to have clambered away from the black community. For Reed, the satirization of the white is, despite his numerous slights of pen, more thorough than his homage to/parody of the black. Through such burlesque can one sway to the side without jazz becoming swing, blues becoming black and white, writing becoming whiting? Whose side, if any, is Reed on? Since valorized art serves to "glorif[y] Western Culture," then all "unauthorized" art can do is upstage it (64). If the realization that "serious works of art" is "a code for White" resides at the heart of *Mumbo Jumbo,* then the book is not parody at all, but takes itself, in its parody, extremely seriously. But at the limits of satire, Reed can only reject a white aesthetic, and ultimately fails to effect a workable cultural ethic of his own (129). Reed is an art critic, but an art critic seeking to write himself out of a job.[3] Though as a satirist Reed needs to distort his opponents, he cannot reduce them too much or he will make his protagonists seem feeble. Much of Reed's own construction to replace what he has relegated must emerge as insufficient and unformulated, as simply as close an antithesis as possible to what he maligns. Perhaps like any dynamic interpretation, Reed's reassessment of white mythology should reflect not simply a shift in taste but a redefinition of taste itself. Without this reevaluation of the standards of judgment, Reed would simply be expressing a preference no better or worse than those of the Atonists and artists he ridicules.

In rewriting Western history, Reed also needs to revise black history into the present. Though presenting a satirical veiled history of the Harlem Renaissance, *Mumbo Jumbo* remains more concerned with the origins of culture, with the attribution of sources, than with the contemporary black cultures it tries to encompass and valorize. Reed can jokingly rebuke charges of mystification with etymology, becoming a master of phonetics; but such diversion, such as the deliberate exploitation of mumbo jumbo, relies on the same techniques as the white code (215, 55). Reed to a degree has then been deMilled but not exHumed.

These generalizing remarks are not meant to imply that the only difference among Aristophanes, Swift, and Reed is the extent of their bitterness and their method of self-invention, but that the role of the Western satirist remains fundamentally unaltered. It is a satirist's exaggeration for Reed to claim he is somehow post-Western, or that his satire is doing, or calumniating, anything, and to a degree even anyone, different from that of his predecessors. Given the promulgation of hoodoo aesthetics, of doing one's own thing (perhaps as well as others'), a black manifesto would have to become the universal blackprint of healthy creativity. By setting his opponents up as psychopaths, Reed insists that his standards are the only ones viable. The difficulty here is not that Reed is wrong—he might not be—but that he is inconsistent. That his work is, in truth, not specifically formulated as black literature, but that that should also be irrelevant, at least by Reed's own standards, is the unnecessary dead-end into which Reed has cornered himself. The peculiar mystification of the past, the hybridization of history as either inevitable fiction or meretricious pretense to fact, even in parody, suggests that Reed's main purpose is not to laud a black messiah but rail against the order which will refuse to canonize him (e.g. 130, 215, 247). Though he clearly pokes fun at aspects of black literature—the patched eye, Marxism, the three-story structure of history at the edge of Chinatown—Reed's writing owes more to the aptly nominated Twain than to Wright.

Yet Reed persists in a kind of black chauvinism which his own writing would seem to belie. Reed the writer/critic seems to belabor under the very misapprehension he attacks, that what "real black people" think is paradigmatic simply because it's thought by "real black [people]" (117). He winds up 'Re(ed)ifying' the concept of blackness, turning it into an essential, ahistorical category. This sort of blind embrace of a culture is inappropriate for Reed, as questionable as unconditional acceptance of the disenfranchised or rejection of the margins. It is ironic, though reasonable, that Reed the individualist critic of socialist dogma himself purports that art be constrained by an historical, and hence for Reed "mythified," social reality. (Because the appeal to history is always a form of mythification for Reed, all reference to history to establish precedent or authority is a form of obfuscation. Reed, however, makes the very same move in using not history, but nature, as his universal and indisputable referent.) But the guidelines resulting from this constraint conflict directly with Reed's antirealist text as well as his treatment of black culture.

Not all intellectual theories are imperialist, yet Reed's self-professed aesthetic pantheism tends to preclude all expression which is not inclined toward aesthetic pantheism. An artistic and a social aesthetic are warring within Reed's work and certainly no community of interpretation emerges here. One can discern a kind of joyous if abstract affirmation of Ellison's individualist stance within black culture, coupled with a parodic appraisal of even black literature. Reed makes the troubled spirits of ancestors depart by writing about them but also by writing them off. Mystifying the past is a way for Reed to mythologize ancestors, yet they are not genuine black ancestors. They form part of a reclaimed, equally rewritten history which does not claim to speak for the black community, because Reed does not believe in community and might therefore, by his own rules, not be taken as black. But Reed also essentially redefines blacks who do not partake of Jes Grew as appropriated, as would-be-whites. Jes Grew, however, must represent everything, including the white underbelly of blackness. If all the gods are metaphorically traced back to black figures, then white civilization is entirely an illicit mockery. But blackness is and blackness ain't, because the gods are a rather mixed lot, and, true to its origins, the black side of Jes Grew has its ineluctable white side, the aesthetic by definition having its own flaws built in (183). Yet in *Mumbo Jumbo,* Reed systematically tries to suppress the demonology his appropriated and naturalized Jes Grew/pantheism always retains.

Reed in effect tries to take credit for what he rejects, for the West and Atonism itself: god accepts the devil as his responsibility. "Faust was an actual person. . . . a Black man," a wandering quack who begins to manipulate the Work; yet "a Yellow or Black hand will [not] push the button" of destruction, only a robot-like, white descendant of Faust (103–4). Reed reclaims Faust's magic, but not his misery. Black turns white over time, but is always present at inceptions, even demonic ones: all rivers have the Nile as their source. Reed maintains that blacks can do it all better than whites, while rejecting the very standards used to make the evaluations and eventually the process of evaluation itself. On the one hand, "Christ is so unlike African Loas and Orishas, in so many essential ways, that this alien becomes a dangerous presence in the Afro-American mind" (111). But this assertion reifies blackness, universalizes it to a single perspective. This monolithic African-American mind is then being categorized by Atonist standards. In order to be ontologically black, Africans must reject Christ, even if Reed would remind us that Christ only represents a perversion of some African deity. The West demands that art be universal, "universal being a word co-opted by the Catholic Church when the Atonists took over Rome, as a way of measuring every 1 by their ideals" (153). But this universalization is the very trap Reed falls into; while insisting that African writers should not be judged by the measure of Elizabethan poets, Reed would still insist that the former could write better sonnets.

After denying their relevance, Reed often uses white standards to validate black artists: "The dazzling parodying punning mischievous pre-Joycean style-play of your Cakewalking your Calinda your Minstrelsy give-and-take of the ultra absurd" (174). While arguing for the priority and primacy of the African-American tradition, Reed also allows Joyce to remain a universal standard of comparison.[4] For Reed, all art becomes a question of intellectual property, and of obfuscating "sourcery." (By this term, I refer to Reed's best conjuring trick; Reed simultaneously debunks the plausibility of identifying definitive sources for art, while also attributing all forms of aesthetic sorcery, from pantheism to voodoo, to black sources.) Like Faust, "the Masonic mysteries were of a Blacker origin than we thought . . . this man had in his possession a black sacred book." But if the West's Atonism and its debased Masonism are derived wholecloth from a black Egypt, no hard distinctions between the two can remain; in this sense, Reed writes the very blackness out of his own myth. Reed of course has more than just cause to complain that "They were accusing us of trespassing on our own property. . . . The White man will never admit his real references. He will steal everything you have and still call you names" (223). But as Reed twice quotes James Weldon Johnson, "It belonged to nobody" (12, 239). Jes Grew is given a specific source in Ragtime, but Reed entirely undercuts this attribution by suggesting that Jes Grew chooses its nature-friendly hosts periodically, indiscriminately, and without warning. Reed is caught between wanting to return Jes

Grew to a universally accessible abstraction and wanting to claim it solely for a mythically historicized but inevitably fictional black heritage. This "It," whether addressed by Emerson or Reed, always turns out to be some form of impersonal and emphatically pre-cultural, i.e. transcendental, nature. (And, as D. H. Lawrence suggests in his essays on the American Renaissance, this impersonal "It" which takes over our bodies and voices turns out to be a "dusky" or black nature; the epidemic, pantheistic IT within us represents a black god, a black Pan. The blackness which is the alterior to the West also turns out to be its ulterior. As Reed writes, "Strange. It seems that the most insightful pictures of America are done by Europeans or Blacks" [239]. Blacks then occupy both a position of critical distance from America yet also one of interior insight. When it is to his advantage, Reed continues to link blacks with the very European or Western tradition he otherwise claims is antithetical to blackness.) Like Emerson, Reed in *Mumbo Jumbo* is less interested in particular political reform, than in forms of abstract and universal idealism, and indeed both writers could make the tenuous argument that you can't address the former without having secured the latter.

* * *

> Escaped slaves, we might say, people the republics of Liberia or Haiti. . . . Are we to look at America the same way? A vast republic of escaped slaves. . . . We are only the actors, we are never wholly the authors of our own deeds or works. IT is the author. . . . You have got to pull the democratic and idealistic clothes off American utterance, and see what you can of the dusky body of IT underneath.
>
> D. H. Lawrence

> "Oh you mean you can take my body but not my soul?" "That's the one. Americans, both North and South, hate the slaves, and they're slaves themselves. . . ."

> **It** was sipping from a glass of wine and listening to the radio. . . . **It** is lying in the President's bed, just as in "Flight to Canada" it bragged about lying in Swille's bed. The poem had gotten **It** here. . . . What else did the poem have in mind for it. **Its** creation, but in a sense, Swille's bloodhound. . . . "Flight to Canada" was responsible for getting him to Canada. And so for

him, freedom was his writing. His writing was his HooDoo. . . . It fascinated him, it possessed him; his typewriter was his drum he danced to.

Ishmael Reed

With his hybrid-sounding name, Ishmael Reed himself conjures the sound, and the Nile banks and temples, of ancient Egypt. Like the Haitians who reconcile Catholicism with Hoodoo, Reed manages to maintain an allegiance to black American culture, invoke related but distinct African and Haitian mythologies, and still practice a Western art. Like LaBas, Reed is a self-licensed metaphysical detective, but he traces a fabricated heritage, a construct, a metaphor, and needs the reader to take it literally. *Mumbo Jumbo* becomes a kind of detective science-fiction. Perhaps guilty of the very Griffin eclecticism Abdul warns against, Reed is an extensive revisionary of black culture. Though parodic, his framework reduces all cultural forms—from blues to Phi Beta Kappa—to either Jes Grew or Jes Didn't: his is a conspiracy theory of art history. Civilization in its entirety becomes a warped record of a single complex power struggle, a neurotic sibling rivalry within and among cultures. With Jes Grew as the possible catalyst of the big bang and the central "initiating repository" of all culture, white culture, from Moses to Freud, becomes a rip off and a put on. At least metaphorically, all pragmatism is labeled as white, all emotiveness as black, with the only off-white as perhaps an aesthetic imperative: the world is still divided, only the signs have changed. White culture is the result of a great anal mindSet, and a constipated pain in the ass for the Osirians. Those hopping on that white anti-bandwagon—perhaps from Set to Booker T. to W. W. Jefferson—are not acting as blacks, or, given the roles of androids, perhaps even as human beings. Reed has, even if in parody, substituted a kind of mysticism which his own aesthetic should rebel against. And that old black magic, in allegedly seeking Reed as its text, may be trying to tell him, rather than the reader, something. Aside from inconsistencies and ambiguities in the novel—e.g., the unclarified difference between entertainment and art, or how to handle fits of intense relativism—Reed never seems to resolve his relation to his muse, his patron, his created predecessor.

True, this is not our world; not only does Reed present a jumble of history and names, but he does not, and of course cannot, address Jes Grew in realistic terms—his Work creates a parable of intolerance of intolerance, and is created by a skirting and embracing of influence. Reed is a mutation: an angry young man, indeed black, but primarily, if justifiably, angry; he is not just modernist, but by his own definition actually "classical" in refusing classification and stealing from "primitive" sources. And these sources can't be Reed's own because, as Johnson reminds him, they belong to nobody. Yet Reed remains obsessed with his "sourcery," for example, describing "Charlie Parker, [as] the houngan (a word derived from *n'gana gana*)" (17). Consistently tracing language and concepts back to African and non-Western sources, Reed tries to give credit where it has been denied. Reed complains that white Western artists—e.g. Picasso and Dreiser—steal from African sources; but Reed takes this process further, and he covers his own tracks in even more elaborate ways. For Reed has also criticized the whole process of attributing authority to any source, individual or cultural, and he has further used "non-black" aesthetics to argue for both the restitution of origins and the erasure of that category in favor of beginnings. Respectively before and after *Mumbo Jumbo*, H. D. in *Trilogy* and Thomas Pynchon in *Gravity's Rainbow* construct similar, specifically American Osiris myths—myths of fragmented divine bodies, fragmented and restored texts, and a silenced, transcendental and pantheistic nature. But where Pynchon refers to Reed himself within *Gravity's Rainbow*, Reed does not allude to any of his white sources except to point out their appropriations.[5] We can begin to perceive Reed as a transcendental American writer, one, like Emerson, who oscillates between the lure of the universal and the pull of the particular. Reed's parody does not render the original obsolete: it ties itself irrevocably to what it parodies while seeking to white it out. (The Atonism of *Mumbo Jumbo* then represents Reed's post *Yellow Back Radio* version of a "Western.") In the end, Reed co-opts American Renaissance tropes to critique the modernist co-optation of the Harlem Renaissance.

Like Freud himself, Reed tends to prefigure and assimilate all arguments against his position as further proof of his validity. He turns Freud against Freud, the West against the West—which is perhaps a trickster's trick, but is also a Western standard. Unfortunately, Reed too closely comes to resemble the monster he battles. (In fact, Reed's comprehensive theory of Western repression revises but still borrows much of its impetus from *Civilization and Its Discontents.*) Even in parody, all alienation can't be attributed to Atonism, and a specifically black redemption can't be found in Jes Grew. Jes Grew will dance with anybody. Before its opponents can "sterilize the Jes Grew forever," the Work demonstrates a healthy love for sexuality, but then its very existence is the result of a thorough cross-breeding. Jes Grew represents unrestrained fecundity, growth, and all-encompassing nature filtered through art. Yet for Reed all Western religion as a catholic generalization becomes a confining, claustrophobic suppression of the "something or Other" of Jes Grew (239). Reed rejects Abdul's pragmatism, his straightforward social realism, his empty text, in favor of a mystical but real entity, yet his fabrication of the absolute and self-willed conspiracy belittles such a conception, proposes a colossal Masonic cover-up rather than a history gone haywire. Neither Kipling, Tolstoy, Eco, nor even Pynchon could grasp Reed's Masonic handshakes. Jes Grew, as the Hegelian spirit of history seeking its historical moment, waits to erupt into the world through us. But this spirit hardly seems either black or redemptive: we can now swear on it as our text, but it still bears the same curse. Though alleged even to affect animals, Jes Grew is not simply nature, despite Reed's intimations, for like any allegedly pre- or supra-cultural discourse used to validate particular social premises, it is too ideological to remain so basic. (While the parallels between Emerson's Pan and Reed's Jes Grew are crucial, neither allegedly natural construct should be accepted in the primarily pre- or post-cultural terms proposed by their authors.) Outside of history, Jes Grew is the film's director, somehow made sympathetic to man.

Yet no Atonism is perceived behind the Atonists, no demonic cult; Jes Grew itself is dualistic, but its rites are inherently neither good nor evil, though perhaps doubly ravishing. There is only a second-rate magic and devastating science behind the opposing conspiracy, the great depression of the West, leaving Jes Grew to encompass all else, benevolent or not. To treat Jes Grew as distinctly benign to man is to anthropomorphize the anti-anthropomorphic myth. Elsewhere in African-American literature, Bacchus figures will not only be hinted to be Janus-faced but will often bite the hands that feed them. Reed then suppresses the underside of Jes Grew and offers us only white Masonry in its stead. And since Jes Grew remains inextricable from the original mysteries usurped from the sacred black books, even Masonry is made a black/Jes Grew phenomenon (222). Ultimately, Reed has not been able to use his medium to transcend his medium. Most cultures have "Atonist" and "pantheist" sides, versions of Osiris and Set; Reed tries too simply to arrogate Osiris and pantheism as his heritage and relegate all else to the West. Yet pantheism is a central component of the West, unless one adheres strictly to an "originist" view which insists that since the West derived pantheism, it cannot lay claim to it. For Reed, Set is the first Westerner, the "1st man to shut nature out of himself," and even the one who "probably invented taxes" (185). But even in this parodic myth of origin, Set is still a black man, in fact brother to Osiris. Reed may have reversed some of the polarities of fraternal biblical stories of racial origin, but he maintains their structure, contrary to his need to refute all stories which project our own natures, or our own evils, onto brothers, others, and origins.

As Theodore Mason suggests, indeterminacy is a weakness as well as a strength of *Mumbo Jumbo.* Mason claims Reed's text "breaks down because of the conflict between his interest in history and his emphasis on indeterminacy" (106, 109). In fact, Reed seems not to recognize the conflict between his insistence that Western history is indeterminate at worst, or indebted to African sources at best—a conflict in itself—and his position that history cannot be written, or that no origins can ever be accurately determined. Because Reed, like his Osiris, is a pantheist and a polymath, his inconsistency almost begins to appear consistent with the tradition he criticizes.

Though Reed would probably never trace his pantheism to the American Renaissance, Jes Grew in many respects virtually mirrors Emerson's Pan. Crucially, one common source of this formulation of Pan or nature lies in *Uncle Tom's Cabin*. Here, Miss Ophelia questions the eight- or nine-year-old black girl, Topsy, about her parentage. Topsy repeatedly avers, "Never was born, never had no father nor mother, nor nothin' . . . I spect I grow'd. Don't think nobody never made me" (242–43). Even in Stowe's version of black identity, which Reed will turn upside down, blackness jes grew. For Stowe as well as Reed, blackness represents a nature without a creator. For Emerson as well, nature/Pan, at least for a crucial elliptical moment, in turn becomes entirely associated with blackness. Pan is a shapeless giant, uncreated; in his journal, Emerson explicitly asserts that natural instinct, the behemoth of Pan himself, "like poor Topsy, never was born; growed" (*Journals*, XII, 35).[6] Reed closely mimics, yet conceals, this Emersonian approach to Pan's blackness, and he includes only James Weldon Johnson's passage at the beginning of *Mumbo Jumbo*: "The earliest Ragtime songs, like Topsy, Jes Grew" (12). Yet Reed's approach veers far closer to Emerson's than Johnson's, for *Mumbo Jumbo* is less about the achievements of black culture than about the inscription of a black American nature. Reed of course uses his version of Topsy/Jes Grew for far different purposes, to ally *nature* with his culture, rather than follow Stowe's alliance of a largely fabricated black culture with nature; yet he surprisingly leaves the makeshift scaffolding of such a move intact.

Through this complicated series of calls and responses, from Stowe's depiction of a naturalized black identity under slavery, to Emerson's telling interception of this motif for Pan, we end with Reed's reappropriation of this by-now iconic image of nature. Reed then plays a game of endless sourcery. To be godlike, self-generated, to grow without being born, is to be absolutely self-reliant, bypassing Stowe's deification of motherhood, and justifying Emerson's deification of hermaphroditic/male parthenogenesis. Topsy is not just without parents, but particularly, and to Stowe horrifyingly, without a creator, without god, without source; a being who jes grew, who has no origin, cannot be appropriated. Reed is then engaged in a project which pursues, but also renounces, a system of originations which has denied his ancestors their birthright, heritage, and polity. For Reed, Pan/Jes Grew "knows no class no race no consciousness. It is self-propagating" (8). Where Stowe and Melville typically use the blackness and whiteness of nature to address race, Emerson and to a lesser extent even Reed seem to use the blackness and whiteness of race to address nature. Though Reed perpetually contradicts himself regarding the ownership and blackness of Jes Grew—e.g. "they wanted us out of the mysteries because they were our mysteries,"—he always maintains that his version of Pan or nature "jes grew," and is, like Topsy, self-creating (222). Reed winds up proposing an origin which is precisely as much a mystification as Freud's fictions of cultural genesis in *Totem and Taboo,* one of *Mumbo Jumbo*'s many objects of ridicule. Giving a specific historical account which is overridden by the absolute and ahistorical presence of Jes Grew and by his own playful rewriting of a history always up for grabs, Reed obfuscates the origins of an aesthetic which he claims cannot be confined to race, yet which is intrinsically black; and while having this specifically black genesis, was never created, never dies, and simply grows.[7]

One could readily argue that the "Jes Grew" or race-based pantheistic aspects of the American Renaissance were derived from European Romanticism and that most such Western transcendentalisms were cloaking a veneer of what Edward Said terms Orientalism. Pan in America then represents a form of what Richard Slotkin calls regeneration through violence and locates the dispossession and ideological translation of native and non-Western animism or views of a once animate and pantheistic nature. Emerson's pantheism could itself be traced in scholarly fashion to his occasionally cited Asian influences and in some ways to African and African-American sources. In fact, almost on Emerson's behalf, Reed insists that Dionysus brought his revelry and nature worship to Greece from Egypt, an Egypt he would sharply divorce from, and yet maintain as the origin for, the West (191). But Emerson's work exists in a Western tradition of criticism emerging alongside Christianity, one that often employs pre-Christian sources to reassess Christianity. Pantheism is a Western shadow of Hellenism and Christianity, so Reed eradicates the very differences he seeks to emphasize by using pantheism to challenge Christianity. When Reed tries to define all forms of pantheism as non-Western in character as well as origin, he unravels his own argument. The singers of Jes Grew, the afflatus which repeatedly becomes "PANDEMIC," are as much Pan's devotees as Emerson's orphic poets: "They would play upon instruments, reeded stringed and percussive . . . open their valves, and allow nature to pour through its libation" (27, 120, 184). The reeded instrument of Pan, of nature, becomes a universal yet Western artifact Reed has (re)appropriated for his version of blackness, his pipeline of divinity.

While I can't launch into a full-scale comparison of Emerson and Reed in this essay nor review what I consider the astonishingly pervasive extent of Emerson's pantheism, I would suggest that Reed's language throughout *Mumbo Jumbo* affords a comprehensive and hitherto unacknowledged parody of and homage to Emerson's Works. (Those who parody Emerson most thoroughly, like Melville, typically erase their tracks.) As much as it would be for Reed, for Emerson "Man does not possess [the forces of Nature], he is a pipe through which their currents flow" (*Works*, X, 74). In "Pan," Emerson writes:

> O What are Heroes, prophets, men,
> But pipes through which the breath of Pan doth blow
> A momentary music
> . . . .
> Their dust, pervaded by the nerves of God,
> Throbs with an overmastering energy. . . .
> (*Works*, IX, 360)

In the most fundamental ways, Emerson's pantheistic nature operates like Jes Grew: "Thought is all light and publishes itself to the universe. It will speak, though you were dumb, by its own miraculous organ" (*Works*, I, 187). This divinely possessive and self-propagating "IT" of the American Renaissance, as writers as diametrically opposed as D. H. Lawrence and Toni Morrison aver, also represents the denied, but always revenant, black body of American culture. Emerson's text of a highly cultivated nature is republished as Reed's black text of Jes Grew. The dumb American man is always possessed by a nature, and finally a black nature, which speaks through him.

Reed thus directly recapitulates the Emersonian merger with the divine, purporting in *Mumbo Jumbo* that "Nature spoke through mankind. The Work" (192). As Emerson writes, "Through me, God acts; through me, speaks" (*Works*, I, 129). Throughout his essays and poems, Emerson uses the term Nature interchangeably with Pan, and both as designations for God—e.g. virtually all Emerson's references to "nature" in the essay "Nature," including its title, were before publication originally references to "Pan"; Emerson thus provides an abstract model for Reed's account of Jes Grew's lineage. Like Emerson's most representative men, Reed's sympathetic characters conflate nature with god: the Egyptians "worshipped the sun in a pantheistic manner" (198). Osiris's nature religion offers a paraphrasis of Emerson's own merger with nature: "Osiris had developed such a fondness and attachment for Nature that people couldn't tell them apart" (189). In limited contexts, one also couldn't tell Emerson's and Reed's pantheisms apart nor ultimately what either of their sources are. Both consistently depict nature as pre-Western and hence non-white. Both writers also produce essential images of a "truncated" society—Emerson for example in his depiction of the man literally amputated by society in "The American Scholar," who needs to merge with the whole or All of nature, and Reed in his descriptions of an amputated Osiris and a universal text of nature, the book of Jes Grew seeking to recover its fragments. The crucial difference is that where Emerson converts all evil to a higher good and tries to subsume even the unnatural to the natural, Reed projects all evil outside the domain of his nature.

Of course Reed's agenda in associating himself with Pan is polemical and specific, but that agenda winds up being about aesthetics and cultural genesis and not specifically about black literature. Osiris, whose body parts are dispersed and gathered like the book of Jes Grew, represents not blackness but nature seeking its text. Great Pan is dead but continues to be reborn, like Jes Grew periodically reawakening; yet in Reed's version, the Harlem Renaissance acts as midwife to a Jes Grew which was last revived during the American Renaissance. Reed tries to link Osiris/blackness ineluctably to nature: "One of the shocks for the candidates in the 'mysteries' was the revelation Osiris is a **black** god" (183). Reed further asserts that Dionysus "taught the Greek guides to identify the Osirian Art," and thus turned Osiris into Pan (192). Looking back into the future, we see that Reed's Jes Grew is only a version of Emerson's Pan, who is only a version of Osiris. Present circumstance then becomes a genealogical footnote to the primacy of this mythic black past, a past not of the Harlem but of the Egyptian nascence: PaPa LaBas is described as "a descendant from a long line of people who made their pact with nature long ago" (50). But what is truly startling here is that Reed has tried to link blackness with nature—a disturbing move which gives a pre-cultural origin to blackness—and that Emerson, at least in his crucial journal passage, links Pan, his natural divinity, with the figure of Topsy, with blackness. For while Osiris could stand in for Pan, in Western metaphysics Pan could not represent Osiris. Reed cannot make blackness as universal as nature while also claiming it as particular racial heritage. Blackness can be a part of nature, but Reed can't successfully argue that nature is a part of blackness. Where Emerson reads nature as a version of black

Jes Grew, Reed tries to reappropriate nature as a black cultural artifact.

At this juncture, I need to return briefly to my initial question of aesthetics and to Reed's condemnation and simultaneous pursuit of a universal but non-Western standard for art criticism. For Reed, Pan and Loas and nature all occupy the same structural position, form part of the same eternal story of an innate natural and cultural dialectic. History is offered as a mythic contest between the Atonists and the pantheists, where all specific variations are irrelevant in light of the immutable repetitions. Reed wants no textbook histories but needs a history to account for the Western usurpation of African culture. The history he produces is predicated on a universal model of cultural genesis, yet such a maneuver courts the very universalization he condemns in the Catholic Church. For Pan represents a universal nature, recognizing no cultural differences, only one all-encompassing unity. Reed could be trying to liberate universality from being a code for white standards, but what standards does he wind up with instead? Reed has in fact produced a theory of cyclical writing in which black literature has no place as black literature but only as a structural placeholder in a series of renaissances; next time around, black androids and Atonists could be suppressing the next wave of American pantheists. In this transcendental, Emersonian scheme of history, each generation translates an eternal conflict into its own language, but the specifics of that language are entirely secondary. Reed has failed to define a black aesthetic as either innate or as culturally variable. In Reed's hands, Emerson's Pan becomes Jes Grew, and the inspiration of Jes Grew a translation of the Oversoul. Collective, impersonal, and transcendent nature seeks its text in man as expressed through two intensely individualistic, self-creating, and self-propagating American men.

The many differences between Emerson's and Reed's uses of pantheism are here less interesting than their surprising similarities. Emerson certainly borrowed from other cultures, but he is, like Reed, first and foremost an American idealist. An ahistorical thinker, Emerson reifies consciousness, and, though a reformer, he is interested not in social reality but in abstract ideals. In this light, the present always becomes that social reality, and the past always an ideal fiction. Following this agenda, Reed doesn't render the original obsolete; he supplants it, assumes its mask. Of course Reed's version of Pan is far more overtly Dionysian than Emerson's and certainly more in keeping with the celebration, rather than universal classification, of nature. But like Emerson, Reed uncritically projects the American to be the universal; Reed naturalizes Jes Grew, for him a particularly American formulation of nature, and insists that it is in fact Pan-American and ubiquitous, producing a truly odd admixture of American transcendentalism and Haitian voodoo. (PaPa LaBas even remarks that the "ancient Vodun aesthetic [is] pantheistic," so Reed himself consistently mixes ancient, as well as North American, pantheisms with Caribbean, voodoo 'reformulations' of pantheism {39}. Though Reed wants to historicize, for example, American military and political incursions into Haiti, he persists in partially rendering Haitian voodoo as ahistorical and hence equivalent to all other forms of nature worship.)

It is all the more ironic, then, that when Reed was reviewed for tenure at Berkeley, he was accused of not writing sufficiently in the Western tradition; for Reed has vexingly used that tradition to undermine itself, while still assuming the persona of a representative man (*Shrovetide* 219–36). Where does this inclusive indeterminacy leave Reed, science-fiction writer, transcendentalist, black aesthetician, thief, and visionary? Once he has defended his lineage, which has been denigrated and usurped, Reed emerges as an appropriator himself, one who denies the validity of cultural determinism. If we can take Reed's sourcery less seriously, perhaps we can also treat the best of his writing as less exclusively parodic and recognize its theoretical implications for American Studies as a whole. In his sourcery, his version of American hieroglyphics, Reed can redress the present only by revising the past, which is perhaps the fate of all idealists who try to create themselves anew.

In the end, Reed can appear alarmingly bitter for a proponent of universal tolerance, pluralism and pantheism. Reed's difficulty, like Pynchon's, is that their paranoia, even when justified, leaves their madness infecting you, so the divisions Reed would transcend are reinforced by his "interdependence" on what he decries. Reed assumes if you can't beat them, join them, unify them, make them monolithic, and then fight freemasonry with freemasonry. No doubt, the greatest social movement is any dervish dance. But Reed's ball, despite the sometimes shaky rhythms, is still masked: he is grinning, donning "the Afro-American mask with . . . inverted U lips," steering us to ideas of "U turns" (110, 233). The act is revolving, so we can "stand it on its head. Upside-down the plantation" (119).

If he has not been whited out, Reed may turn out to be a Hegelian reverser, swinging both ways. In some ways, Reed hasn't come down off the fence, is trying to sell us some stolen, some original goods—he tries simultaneously to reverse the polarity of a white/black dialectic while eradicating the very conceptual framework of hierarchy and dialectic. Voodoo is pantheistic and pluralistic but also dialectical. Reed could then never produce a stable aesthetic, only a process in which blackness is a constantly changing element in a system whose stability lies only in structural positions. Atonism is "a single Loa," any monotheism of religion, interpretation, or personality: the ocean won't fit your head if it is too small, if the milk bottle is too narrowly shaped (26). Milking Western history, Reed must insure he doesn't turn white while Prometheus is rebound. To a pantheist, the notion of "a common thread" uniting Western dilemmas should be unwound until the cloth spins off in all directions. Not swing to the white, but if Western history is a mistake then U must turn back and correct it, critique but not discard. As long as he steers clear of the Mason's dixie lines, Reed should be able to swing the censor back and the pendulum forward.

Notes

I would like to thank Kim Benston and Joan Dayan for their generous assistance with this essay. An earlier version appeared in *The Arizona Quarterly* 49:4 (Winter 1993): 117–38.

1. Many white pantheist writers, like Melville, also attribute nature worship to Egypt as well as Greece, even if they don't always configure Egypt as black. D. H. Lawrence writes, e.g., that "In the Egyptians, the spark between man and the living universe remains alight for ever. . . ." See Lawrence, "Him with His Tail in His Mouth," *Reflections on the Death of a Porcupine, Collected Works*, Ed. Michael Herbert (Cambridge: Cambridge University Press, 1988), p. 316.

2. See Kim Benston, "I Yam What I Am; the Topos of (Un)naming in Afro-American Literature," in *Black Literature and Literary Theory*, Ed. Henry Louis Gates (New York: Methuen, 1984), pp. 151–72.

3. See Henry Louis Gates, "The 'Blackness of Blackness': A Critique of the Sign and the Signifying Monkey," in *Figures in Black: Words, Signs, and the Racial Self* (New York: Oxford University Press, 1987) pp. 235–76.

4. To accusations that he is "too ethnic" and needs to be "more universal," Quickskill in *Flight to Canada* replies, "How can I be universal with a steel collar around my neck and my hands cuffed all the time and my feet bound. I can't be universal gagged" (107). (Of course, some writers and critics precisely try to use such material to reflect on the ahistorical universality of man's existential or spiritual condition.) Rather than attempt to embrace universality, in *Flight* Reed more consistently embraces the particularity of his culture. Reed for instance here fully reclaims the cakewalk which James Weldon Johnson, who is used to begin *Mumbo Jumbo*, slightly depreciates in *The Autobiography of an Ex-Colored Man*. There Johnson writes that

> There are a great many coloured people who are ashamed of cake-walk, but I think they ought to be proud of it. . . . Rag-time music and the cake-walk [demonstrate our originality and artistic conception]. . . . These are lower forms of art, but they give evidence of

> a power that will someday be applied to the higher forms. (87)

Reed is very careful to validate what is labeled the "folk-art" or folklore of African-American culture which even many African-American writers, like Richard Wright and to this much lesser extent even Johnson, devalue or only apologetically praise.

We can find another reason Reed might cite Joyce in this context in Ralph Ellison's "Change the Joke and Slip the Yoke": Ellison mentions Ulysses as a quintessential trickster figure (though one Reed would trace back to African models rather than the reverse). After noting with regret that his middle name is Waldo, Ellison remarks that

> I knew the trickster Ulysses just as early as I knew the wily rabbit of Negro American lore, and I could easily imagine myself a pint-sized Ulysses but hardly a rabbit, no matter how human and resourceful or Negro. (72)

Reed uses such referents, I argue, to imagine himself a rabbit.

5. Reed, who certainly has no aversion to alluding to real authors throughout *Mumbo Jumbo,* makes no mention of H. D.'s *Trilogy,* which uses the same Egyptian pantheism to redefine American identity. Fairly enough, Toni Morrison can make no direct allusion to Reed, or her distaste for his work, in *Jazz,* her restaging of the Jes Grew of the Harlem Renaissance, a possessive music seeking its words or text. In Morrison's novel, for example, what Alice hates most about Jazz—Morrison's inscription of Jes Grew music—is "its appetite. Its longing for the bash, the slit; a kind of careless hunger. . ." (59). This It is reIterated throughout Morrison's text in much the way the ravenous It of nature is reiterated throughout history in Reed's. Morrison's incarnation of a sentient nature in the very narrator of her text, however, though still impersonal in its Modernist fragmentation, is also personalized in its voyeuristic interest in human affairs. Throughout *Jazz,* Morrison also reminds us that Topsy, American nature, is not just black, but, like her own character of Wild, also emphatically female, a recalibration Reed never attempts in reclaiming Jes Grew. In contrasting

Reed's and Morrison's depictions of a very possessive nature, one can also begin to develop a far-reaching overview of Pan and trickster figures in American literature. For a fuller discussion of Morrison's non-Reedian reformulation of a black American nature, see my "A Music Seeking Its Words: Double-Timing in Toni Morrison's *Jazz*," in the *Black Warrior Review* 19:2 (1993): 151–71.

6. The implications of Emerson's association of blackness with nature are beyond the scope of this article, but I would like to suggest that representations of race, nature, and identity are closely and similarly connected in Emerson's and Melville's works. Reed's projection of evil outside what he defines as blackness then echoes Emerson's projection of demonology outside what he defines as nature. It is also important to note, as Eric Sundquist has observed in "Slavery, Revolution, and the American Renaissance," that though Hawthorne imagined the "monstrous birth" of slavery, an other/It within his white America's midst, he also describes a group of runaway slaves as "akin to the fawns and rustic deities of olden times" (7). Thus, Hawthorne like Emerson applies his own rhetoric of pantheism, here echoing *The Marble Faun*, to blackness and associates Pan with the condition of slavery. Such a move corroborates not only the correlation of pantheism/nature with blackness, but the effects of slavery on the body, effects which mimic or parallel those of pantheistic dismemberment, truncation, and dispossession during the American Renaissance. The slave who does not own his body becomes a version of the white pantheist who entirely merges his body with nature or loses control of his body to Pan/the market economy. I would argue that white male pantheists sacralize the alienating effects of slavery in their deification of a dispossessive nature, one ultimately coded as black and female.

The demonology of disease projected onto blackness of course takes on a particularly disturbing relevance since the incursion of AIDS. Though *Mumbo Jumbo* was published well before AIDS became a recognized disease and any direct invocation of the treatment of Haitians in Reed's text in the context of AIDS would be anachronistic, a striking parallel does exist between Reed's chronicled response to Haitians as carriers of the Jes Grew epidemic and the media's response to Haitians as carriers of AIDS. In voodoo belief, people act as "carriers" for the god's attributes, or their fetishes; this form of "carrying" made it possible for American reporters to transfer the metaphor of carrying in voodoo to AIDS. Haitian poverty, which most Western sociologists and literary critics find inextricable from the development of voodoo beliefs, has led many outsiders to conflate voodoo not just with the possession of the carrier but the carrying of disease.

In the American imagination, Haitians remain more susceptible to AIDS than other people—though the claim has been refuted by medical evidence—and AIDS is often assumed to emerge from the "contagion," the psychic epidemic, of Haitian voodoo. In his 1987 essay, "A Mask on the Face of Death," Dr. Richard Selzer recorded the following conversation between himself and the "reigning American pastor":

> "It is voodoo that is the devil here." He warms to his subject. "It is demonic religion, a cancer on Haiti. Voodoo is worse than AIDS. And it is one of the reasons for the epidemic. Did you know that in order for a man to become a *houngan* he must perform anal sodomy on another man? . . . Fornication," he says. "It is Sodom and Gomorrah all over again, so what can you expect from these people? . . . By the way," the pastor says, "what is your religion?" . . . "While I am in Haiti," I tell him, "it will be voodoo or it will be nothing at all." Abruptly, the smile breaks. (214)

The pastor's rhetoric and his association of demonism, imagery of disease, and voodoo evokes a frighteningly familiar Atonism from Reed's text. Reed's depiction of Haitians in *Mumbo Jumbo* and his attempts to validate Haitian religious beliefs could then be read as a prophetic critique of Western attitudes toward Haitians, disease, and race. Still, as Robert Elliot Fox notes in *Conscientious Sorcerers*, Reed too indiscriminately accepted the politics of Papa Doc Duvalier along with his religious practices (91-92).

7. Such immutability marks the essence of nature—which can neither be created nor destroyed, only transformed—for American transcendentalists from Emerson to Pynchon's Wernher von Braun in *Gravity's Rainbow*.

The comparison of Reed with Pynchon seems ripe for further development. I present here a very condensed overview of the extent of their stylistic and thematic overlap, in which I mean to intimate the shape of a common post-modern and "transcendental male" thematics in operation in their works, one which began its development during the American Renaissance. By all criteria, if Reed's is a Jes Grew text then so is Pynchon's; both have cornered aspects of the "black market." From the adaptation of the California detective novel to the manipulation of codes on the page, from colored ovals to film squares, Pynchon and Reed write what is often complementary fiction. As in *V.*, Reed stages failed museum robberies in *Mumbo Jumbo.* Jes Grew's search for a text mirrors Stencil's search for his time's literal assembly. The authors' distrust of singularity, whiteness, purity, obsession, mechanization, structure and stricture are singularly parallel. Despite their abhorrence of uniformity, both tend to concentrate their multiply doubled worlds in all-encompassing symbols: the rocket, V., Tristero, Jes Grew. Both authors play untraditional music against traditional forms, even similarly valorizing kazoos; both mock yet perpetually employ initials and code (J. G. C.). Characters' names often sound interchangeable: Biff Musclewhite could be a Pynchon character, while Weissman, Bianca, and Dominus Blicero could belong to Reed. Pynchon's Orpheus and Reed's Osiris can in some ways be considered coterminous in their writings. In the works of both, the yin-yang symbol is frequently wheeled out and recast; and both feature a similar display of deliberate and sometimes tedious misspellings: Reed's Kathedral/Kongress and 1's, and Pynchon's ubiquitous Sez, among others. Pynchon would agree, in fact has virtually said, "the book of Science Fiction might be more revolutionary than any number of tracts . . . of the political realm" (20). Reed's seemingly gratuitous landing of aliens is familiar to Pynchon (189). The mock poem with "De steamship of de White whore . . . a zoot-sooted shark" is straightforwardly Pynchonesque (181). Reed's following passages read as if they were lifted directly from *V.*: "For some, it's a disease, a plague, but in fact it is an anti-plague . . . germs that avoided words" (36). As Pynchon also dramatizes, "Plastic will soon prevail over flesh and bones" (71). The skin-lightening technique reflects Pynchon's characters' whitewashing of the world and the white-house; the talking android even appears in both writers' works. Both authors espouse a kind of aesthetic and natural pantheism; Reed's knockings—"when the seasons change on Mars, I sympathize with them"—resemble Pynchon's general animism and empathy with nature (28). Both embrace the "pantheistic" animism of ancient religions (39, 183). As they delve into the interdependence of animate and inanimate life, both authors depict their characters frequently talking to animals, if not to rocks and worse than senseless things (40). Chronicling the dissolution of the natural world, whether in the genocide of races of men and birds or the "impending extinction of the elephant," both writers attempt to anthropomorphize nature while rendering man more natural; the animation of the world, from skyscrapers to locomobiles, occurs throughout their works (50). Both authors delineate versions of the Atonists' "species count; the name and number of life near extinction" (73); the "several other species" the Atonists want to rub out including man (175); and their explicit hatred of color and desire to bleach the world (160). The pet zombie, sphinx, and "Lounge Lizard," are also Pynchon refugees (61). Characters like Slothrop and Osiris blend with nature to the point of indistinguishability. Nature is repeatedly embodied and given voice (188).

Masons and codes also figure prominently in Pynchon and Reed: "hieroglyphs" appear consistently and in similar contexts in their works (41); and Egyptian cryptology, "strange symbols," double riders, and strange handshakes are intertextual motifs (81, 150). The explicit connection between the quest, the red cross, the crusades, knights templar, Masons, and the decline and fall of natural man are intertwined through their novels, perhaps culminating in Reed's image of the Mason's tower of babel (Pynchon's "gigantic Masonic hall, not a window on the whole massive monolith" [679]). Pynchon even notes that "Spectro is one of the original seven owners of The Book .... It rotates, the mysterious Book, among its co-owners. . ." (53). Both invoke and mock Freud, and his or Rolland's oceanic feeling as a diagnosis of animism (50, 238). Like Pynchon, Reed sides with King Kong, with the Other side of any quest, "the dragons of Jes Grew" foaming against the white knights (130). One can find similar subversions of Christianity, and almost identical invocations of Cecil B. De Mille in both writers (71); the dispersion of the text to vessels: and the "historical" tracing of the white sorcerer who will soon be able to annihilate millions with the push of a button (104). Both evoke a specific kind of naturalized, as opposed to technological, phallicism, typically healthier for Reed than

Pynchon. They share the supposition that the university—Harvard for both, if not also Cornell for Pynchon—is a conditioning center or Masonic breeding ground. Atonists are rendered the close kin of Pynchon's Puritans, and, to a degree, blacks the distant kin of the preterite. Such intertextuality can be traced not just to Reed's and Pynchon's similar aesthetic and political sensibilities but to a shared historical sense of the role of a transcendental nature or pantheism in American literature.

Works Cited

Benston, Kim. "I Yam What I Am; the Topos of (Un)naming in Afro-American Literature." *Black Literature and Literary Theory*. Ed. Henry Louis Gates Jr. New York: Methuen, 1984. 151–72.

Ellison, Ralph. *Shadow and Act*. New York: New American Library, 1964.

Emerson, Ralph Waldo. *Complete Works*. Boston: Houghton Mifflin, 1904.

———. *Journals and Miscellaneous Notebooks of Ralph Waldo Emerson*. Ed. William H. Gilman, et al. Cambridge: Belknap-Harvard University Press. Volumes 1–16. 1960–1982.

Fox, Robert Elliot. *Conscientious Sorcerers*. New York: Greenwood Press, 1987.

Freud, Sigmund. *Civilization and Its Discontents*. Ed and trans. James Strachey. New York: Norton, 1961.

———. *Totem and Taboo*. New York: Dodd, Mead, 1920.

Gates, Henry Louis, Jr. "The 'Blackness of Blackness': A Critique of the Sign and the Signifying Monkey." *Figures in Black: Words, Signs, and the Racial Self*. New York: Oxford University Press, 1987. 235–76.

H. D. *Trilogy*. New York: New Directions, 1973.

Hardack, Richard. "A Music Seeking Its Words: Double-Timing in Toni Morrison's *Jazz*." *Black Warrior Review* 19:2 (1993). 151–71.

Hawthorne, Nathaniel. *The Marble Faun*. New York: A. L. Burt Co., 1900.

Johnson, James Weldon. *The Autobiography of an Ex-Colored Man*. New York: Hill and Wang, 1960.

Lawrence, D. H. "Him with His Tail in His Mouth." *Reflections on the Death of a Porcupine. Collected Works*. Ed. Michael Herbert. Cambridge: Cambridge University Press, 1988.

———. *Studies in Classic American Literature*. New York: Penguin, 1977.

Mason, Theodore. "Performance, History, and Myth: The Problem of Ishmael Reed's *Mumbo Jumbo*." *Modern Fiction Studies* 34:1 (97–109).

Morrison, Toni. *Jazz*. New York: Knopf, 1992.

Pynchon, Thomas. *Gravity's Rainbow*. New York: Viking, 1973.

———. *V*. Philadelphia: Lippincott, 1963.

Reed, Ishmael. *Flight to Canada.* New York: Random House, 1976.
———. *Mumbo Jumbo.* New York: Avon, 1972.
———. *Shrovetide in Old New Orleans.* New York: Doubleday, 1978.
———. *Yellow Back Radio Broke-down.* Garden City, N.Y.: Doubleday, 1969.
Said, Edward. *Orientalism.* New York: Pantheon, 1978.
Scholes, Robert. *Fabulation and Metafiction.* Chicago: University of Illinois Press, 1979.
Selzer, Richard. "A Mask on the Face of Death." *The Best American Essays 1988.* Ed. Annie Dillard. New York: Ticknor and Fields, 1988.
Slotkin, Richard. *Regeneration through Violence: The Mythology of the American Frontier, 1600–1860.* Middletown, Conn.: Wesleyan University Press, 1973.
Stowe, Harriet Beecher. *Uncle Tom's Cabin.* New York: Harper and Row, 1965.
Sundquist, Eric. "Slavery, Revolution, and the American Renaissance." *The American Renaissance Reconsidered.* Eds. Walter Benn Michaels and Donald Pease. Baltimore: The Johns Hopkins University Press, 1985.

"Kin and Kin": The Poetry of Lucille Clifton

Alicia Ostriker

Yes, the work must be political. It must have that as its thrust. That's a pejorative term in critical circles now: if a work of art has any political influence in it, somehow it's tainted. My feeling is just the opposite. . . . It seems to me that the best art is political and you ought to make it unquestionably political and irrevocably beautiful at the same time.

Toni Morrison

O for God's sake
they are connected
underneath

Muriel Rukeyser, "Islands"

From the strong comes forth sweetness. Or perhaps it is the other way around; perhaps sweetness emanates strength. Or, as I begin to suspect in tracking Lucille Clifton's dense and vivid mythmaking, her strength and sweetness derive from a further source, of which she is an extraordinarily efficient conduit. I would like, in this essay, to show how spiritually complicated an apparently "easy" poet can be. I would like also to suggest the kind of emotional responses she provokes, at least in myself. These responses are complicated and personal; I must trust that they will speak for others besides myself.

* * *

Lucille Clifton's writing is deceptively simple. The poems are short, unrhymed, the lines typically between four and two beats. The sentences are usually declarative and direct, the punctuation light, the diction a smooth mix of standard English with varying styles and degrees of black vernacular. Almost nothing (including "i" and beginnings of sentences) is capitalized. Some poems have titles, others do not, a fact which may disconcert the reader and is probably intended to. Marilyn Hacker has written that Clifton's poems remind her, in grace and deftness, of Japanese ink drawings (24). They remind me of a drum held in a woman's lap. The woman sits on a plain wooden chair, or on the earth. A community surrounds her. She slaps the drum with her bare hands. "Oh children," this drummer says in the title poem of Clifton's first book, "think about the good times."

The work of a minimalist artist like Clifton makes empty space resonate. Silence in such art is not mere absence of noise but locates us as it were on a cosmic stage. We are meant to understand the unsaid, to take our humble places with a sense of balance and belonging instead of the anxiety and alienation promoted by more conspicuously sublime and ambitious artistries. Omissions, as Marianne Moore remarks in quite another context, are not accidents; and as William Carlos Williams observes, in this mode perfection is basic. Whatever the content of a particular piece, we should experience the craftsmanship of the minimalist as a set of unerring gestures governed by a constraining and shaping discipline, so habitual it seems effortless.

While the white space in such art stands for the largeness of space and time in which we human creatures find ourselves, the figured space stands for thick experience—experience which has been philosophically contemplated for an extended period. The artist, having patiently learned something quite exact about the dynamics of reality, offers it in concentrated form.

A byproduct of such concentration may be humor, the sacred levity associated with adepts in numerous traditions of religious art. Think of the Zen image of the laughing monk; John Cage's playfulness; the jokes of the thirteenth century Sufi poet Rumi, or those in the Chasidic stories told by Martin Buber; the trickster pranks of Coyote in Native American folktales, or Monkey King leaping to the end of the universe and peeing on the Buddha's little finger in a Chinese tale; remember the boyishly erotic mischievousness of the young Krishna in Hindu mythology. Then think of how Clifton fuses high comedy and high seriousness when she describes the poetic vocation, a topic most poets approach with a solemnity proportional to their/our insecurity. Clifton's "admonitions," the last poem in *good times,* ends:

children
when they ask you
why is your mama so funny
say
she is a poet
she don't have no sense[1]

Another early poem about her vocation is "prayer," which asks an unnamed listener to "lighten up," wonders why his hand is so heavy on "just poor / me," and receives a response which makes this poem cunningly parallel Milton's complaint of blindness:

answer

this is the stuff
i made the heroes out of
all the saints
and prophets and things
had to come by
this (70)

Has Clifton read Milton's sonnet, which questions how God can exact the "day-labor" of poetry from a blind man, and ends in the famous "They also serve who only stand and wait"? Whether she has or not, what impresses me (and makes me laugh) is the identical structure of these two poems in which the poet interrogates God's fairness and gets fairly answered—and the marvelous freshness of Clifton's version. It thrills me as an American that this sacred conversation, this *de profundis,* can occur in my American language that, as Marianne Moore says, cats and dogs can read (46). I enjoy the down-home familiarity between Clifton and her God; I applaud a woman lining herself up with the heroes and prophets; and I feel, as well, for her struggle—which is not Milton's blindness, or Gerard Manley Hopkins's conviction of sin, but an American black woman's struggle which I can guess at. In a much later piece, "the making of poems," humility and comic afflatus again meet:

the reason why i do it
though i fail and fail

in the giving of true names
is i am adam and his mother
and these failures are my job. (186)

What does it mean when a woman calls herself "adam and his mother?" The mother could be Eve, or a nameless pre-monotheistic goddess, or just any mother doing her homely work—and that conflation of myth and modernity is part of the joke. Making the poet double-gendered is another part.[2] "True names" registers the archaic notion that language is not arbitrary, that poetry names true essences of things—while the poet's failure, it seems to me, conflates individual inadequacy with the imperfect meshing of signifiers and signified in a non-mythic world. How *could* "adam and his mother" find language for the way we live in the twentieth century? Still, they have to try. As with the simple double gesture of "this" to stand for the hardship god inflicts on saints and prophets, the idea of the poet's work as an impossible yet sacred task is effectively rendered in the plainest of language—right down to calling it not a task but a job. "The making of poems" demystifies poetic labor and dignifies maternal and manly labor. What these poems tell us is that high and low things can meet, along with the union of the holy and the comic, if one knows enough about both.

* * *

Let me talk a little more about meetings and mergings in Clifton, how they belie the poetry's apparent simplicity, and how they feed its spirituality. Born in upper New York State in 1936, Lucille Clifton was the daughter of Sam Clifton, a steel worker, and Thelma Louise, who died at age forty-four. She was the great-granddaughter of Caroline Sale, a Virginia midwife who remembered Africa, the slave ship, and walking from New Orleans to Virginia at the age of eight. She attended Howard University and Fredonia State Teacher's College, met and was influenced by Leroi Jones, Ishmael Reed, Gwendolyn Brooks. Reed showed some of her poems to Langston Hughes, who published them in an anthology. Robert Hayden sent some to Carolyn Kizer, who sent them to the 1969 YM-WHA Discovery contest, which Clifton won. Her first book of poems was selected by *The New York Times* as one of the ten best books of that same year.

Clifton began writing during the explosive Black Arts movement of the late 1960s and early 1970s, and her early subjects include the memory of slavery, the facts of poverty, urban riots. She mourns assassinated black leaders and praises live ones, tells family stories, records her womanly conversion from bleaching cream and "whiteful ways" (*Good Woman* 62) to the love of blackness. Black anger and black pride stand at the core of her work. Her family memoir, *Generations,* begins with an epigraph from the Book of Job: "Lo, mine eye hath seen all this, mine ear hath heard and understood it. What ye know, the same do I know also; I am not inferior unto you" (12:3). The second epigraph, which forms a powerful refrain both in the memoir and in Clifton's poems, quotes "Mammy Ca'line:" "Get what you want, you from Dahomey women."

The black inheritance joins others. Walt Whitman's transcendental expansiveness and Emily Dickinson's verbal compression feel uniquely wedded in Clifton. Epigraphs from Whitman mark the sections of *Generations,* and the elliptical Emily might well consider the intensely playful Lucille one of her daughters. Audrey McCluskey notices her Dickinsonian "simultaneous acknowledgment of pain and possibility" (142); I notice the ghost of the Dickinson who felt the size of her small life swelling like horizons in her breast, and "sneered—softly—'small!'" (124). Technically, the contemporary poet she most resembles in cadence, quality of ellipsis, and syntactic ambiguity, is Robert Creeley, though unlike Creeley's her verse feels not ascetic or spare but fully embodied, thickly material, communal.

An early instance of her communality would be Clifton's much-anthologized "miss rosie:"

> when i watch you
> wrapped up like garbage
> sitting, surrounded by the smell
> of too old potato peels
> or
> when i watch you
> in your old man's shoes
> with the little toe cut out
> sitting, waiting for your mind
> like next week's grocery
> i say

when i watch you
you wet brown bag of a woman
who used to be the best looking gal in georgia
used to be called the Georgia Rose
i stand up
through your destruction
i stand up (19)

Structurally, this poem resembles a Shakespeare sonnet. The thrice repeated "when i watch you" works in fact like sonnet 64's triple "When I have seen . . ." to produce, section by section, a crescendo of urgency. The verb "watch," like "have seen," implies a sustained attentiveness. Unlike Shakespeare's verb, it also implies intimacy: it tells us that the speaker and the object of her gaze are neighbors. The poem's music is a matter of subtle assonances, alliterations, repetitions: notice the p's, s's and o's in "wrapped up . . . sitting, surrounded, smell . . . old potato peels," then the o's going into the next stanza, with the w's of "watch . . . with . . . waiting . . . weeks" and the off-rhyme of "cut out," and the third stanza's chiasmus of w's and b's in "wet brown bag of a woman." Notice how the cadences vary but at intervals coalesce into the adjacent stresses of "wrapped up . . . too old . . . old man's shoes . . . toe cut out . . . next week's grocery . . . wet brown bag," how the quasi-stanzaic units lengthen and grow increasingly emphatic, while the masculine endings are increasingly softened by feminine ones. The object of the gaze, the wasted woman, woman-as-garbage, is like the "ruin" of Shakespeare's sonnet, that makes him "ruminate." Beauty decays. Only what time destroys for Shakespeare is for Clifton destroyed by time and poverty joined.

Clifton's closing triplet, like a Shakespearean couplet, throws the poem into another gear. We move abruptly from sitting to standing. You to me. Destruction to survival. Clifton's whiplash has a tightness like Shakespeare's paradoxical sonnet endings: "To love that well which thou must leave ere long." "This thought is as a death, which cannot choose / But weep to have that which it fears to lose." But can we define Clifton's tone? Grief, shame and compassion govern this poem, we might say, and resolution governs its close. Yet the poem is cruel as well, and I do not think it is simply a matter of facing, confronting, the cruelty of age and poverty. The speaker keeps her distance in the poem. She watches, doesn't touch. Neither is it a protest poem. What of the pivotal preposition "through?" Difficult to pin down, it can mean "despite." Though you fail, I endure. Or it can imply duration or submission. I endure your destruction as if it were a storm pelting me. The gesture signals homage, a salute, almost a military standing at attention. I stand up for you, for your rights, in your honor. Yet "through" can also mean "because of." Your destruction precipitates or causes my survival, my will to survive. I do this for (or instead of) you. I do it because you don't, I triumph because you fail, and even in some sense thanks to your failure.

The reader of "miss rosie" need not be aware of the poem's technical subtlety or its emotional and moral ambiguity; in fact, the subtlety and ambiguity speak precisely to what we habitually repress from consciousness. At the obvious level of content, the poem makes us look at what we might prefer not to see: the condition of poverty and hopelessness. At another level it lets us see ourselves—and the awful complexity of our connection to others.

Forster's "Only connect" could be Clifton's motto. Other poets' juvenilia may elaborate the postures of a solitary or romantically alienated self, but Clifton is already maternal, daughterly, a voice at once personal and collective, rooted and relational. The "good times" of her first title poem describe an evening when the family is drunk and dancing in the kitchen because the rent is paid, the lights back on, and an uncle has hit the numbers. The poem urges "oh children / think about the good times" in a voice that could be either rejoicing or begging, and which invites us to the party yet asks us to recognize ("think") how that party is circled by pain. An early ecological poem, "generations," begins by invoking the responsibilities of "people who are going to be / in a few years / bottoms of trees," and ends by warning that "the generations of rice / of coal / of grasshoppers // by their invisibility / denounce us" (36). In her kitchen cutting greens, Clifton observes, "i hold their bodies in obscene embrace . . . and the kitchen twists dark on its spine / and i taste in my natural appetite / the bond of live things everywhere" (149).

Her family poems brim with linkages. Poems to and about her mother proliferate, and spin through yearning, rue, rivalry, and passionate identification. Her father is adored, pitied, rebuked. Her daughters are "my girls / my almost me" and then "my dearest girls / my girls / my more than me" (124). Or, in a rondeau of relation, "lucy is the ocean / extended by / her girls / are the river / fed by / lucy / is the sun / reflected through / her girls . . ." (165). She addresses her heroines Harriet Tubman, Sojourner Truth and her own grandmother, with the refrain "if i be you" (119). In sum, she assumes connection where the dualisms of our culture assume separation—between self and other, humans and nature, male and female, public and private life, pleasure and pain—and what emanates from her mixings, like the wave of energy released when atoms fuse, is something like joy. This is true even when, or especially when, the experience that feeds the poems is of "blood and breaking."

The other side of Clifton's impulse to connect is the almost gnostic impulse to look inward. In the early work the most obvious form this impulse takes is her stress on memory, and the connection to ancestry and to an Africa that "all of my bones remember" (*Good Woman* 73). Less conspicuously, she contemplates mental process itself, wondering what kinds of knowledge—material and spiritual, external and internal—may be available to us, what the difference is between appearance and reality. Her first poem about her mother's early death expresses puzzlement as much as pain:

> seemed like what she touched was hers
> seemed like what touched her couldn't hold,
> she got us almost through the high grass
> then seemed like she turned around and ran
> right back in
> right back on in (16)

Her first poem about her father, describing his work, asks

> what do my daddy's fingers
> know about grace?
> what do the couplers know
> about being locked together? (17)

A poem about an abortion asks

> what did i know about waters rushing back
> what did i know about drowning

or being drowned (60)

The implication is that truth is always somewhere deeper than words or even actions. In sex a husband "fills / his wife with children and / with things she never knew" (87). Knowledge is also "the life thing in us . . . call it craziness . . . call it whatever you have to / call it anything" (120). The female body is her primary teacher: "i entered the earth in / a woman jar . . . and it has made me / wise" (147). The name her mother gave her, Lucille, means "light," and the poet views her own birth as a symbol of light breaking (148). Clifton celebrates the six fingers she had on each hand at birth, her nappy hair and her free hips, her body like a city, her tasty and electric sexuality (166–70). And again and again she uses the key figure of "turning" to express her need for inner life:

turning out of the
white cage, turning out of the
lady cage
turning at last
on a stem like a black fruit (143)

if in the middle of my life
i am turning the final turn
into the shining dark (159)

see the sensational
two-headed woman
one face turned outward
one face
swiveling slowly in (185)

For what the poet discovers within is a woman's epistemology, the radiant life of the spirit.

* * *

The source of Clifton's spiritual strength is black. It is also what she calls, punning on her own name, "the light" (*Good Woman* 185). It comes, as she has her John the Baptist say in the "some jesus" poems, "in blackness like a star" (*Good Woman* 98).

"Some jesus," the first of Clifton's revisionist religious sequences, begins like this:

adam and eve

the names
of the things
bloom in my mouth

my body opens
into brothers (91)

You have to read that twice, I think, before you realize how simply and stunningly androgynous a poem it is—how lucidly it represents what Robert Hass, speaking of Rilke, calls "the pull inward, the erotic pull of the other we sense buried in the self" (253), but represents it as achieved, not merely desired. The poet distinguishes male and female selves, voices, roles, but doesn't separate them from each other or from herself: she is both, they are both she. Casually proceeding then to inhabit the male personae of Cain, Moses, Solomon, Job, Daniel and Jonah, Clifton's voice in the New Testament section of this sequence slides into the voice of a John who could be in Galilee or Philadelphia praising a savior—

he be calling the people brother
even in the prison
even in the jail (98)

then into the voice of a Mary whose annunciation is erotic, a kiss "as soft as cotton / over my breasts / all shiny bright" (99), a disciple who doesn't mind "laughing like god's fool / behind this jesus" (101), a Lazarus whose raising is also a promise of revolution,

whoever say
dust must be dust
don't see the trees
smell rain
remember africa (102)

a Jesus on "good friday" who says "i rise up above myself / like a fish flying / / men will be gods / if they want it" (104), and a final "spring song" celebrating the green rebirth of "delicious jesus" (106). Gloria (Ashaka) Hull has observed that Clifton feminizes, Africanizes, eroticizes and makes mystical the Biblical stories she uses.[3] My own guess is that she is probably recovering and restoring forms of myth and worship which white tradition has all but erased,[4] and that her intimacy or fusion with biblical personae fulfills on the stage of the inner life what her "if i be you" does with the kin of her outer life.

As her career proceeds, Clifton's spirituality grows bolder and more syncretic. In "to a dark moses" of Clifton's third book, *an ordinary woman,*

> you are the one
> i am lit for.
> come with your rod
> that twists
> and is a serpent.
> i am the bush.
> i am burning.
> i am not consumed. (127)

If we take this poem literally, and why should we not, God is a black woman who is also Lucille Clifton. In the sequence of Kali poems (128, 135–40) it is indeed "a woman god and terrible / with her skulls and breasts," who pushes past the poet's fear and resistance, enters her bones, and forces her to say "i know i am your sister." Admitting the goddess of death as a portion of herself—of ourselves—is Clifton's most radical move in *an ordinary woman.* The poet's next book, *two-headed woman,* includes a sequence of eight poems voicing the life of Mary in a dialect that thickens toward Caribbean, implies a braiding of Christianity and Rastafarianism, and emphatically fuses eroticism and spirituality, exaltation and fear, with her increasingly characteristic light imagery:

> joseph, i cannot still these limbs,
> i hands keep moving toward i breasts,
> so many stars. so bright.
> joseph, is wind burning from east
> joseph, i shine, oh joseph, oh
> illuminated night. (200)

Clifton also lets us feel the human pain of this "chosen" woman whose womb blossoms then dies. Mary's mother Anna wants to "fight this thing" (197). Mary in her last poem has become a weary "old creature" wondering "could i have walk away when voices / singing in my sleep," prophetically worrying about another girl whom a star might choose.

At about this time Clifton's spirituality unmoors itself from scripture. "Breaklight" (154) testifies to a visionary synesthesia of inner light and language: "light keeps on breaking" with the spirit voices of "other nations," trees, water, which the poet mysteriously understands—and then the light reveals itself as the hesitant fears of the poet's dead mother. Uncannily parallel to Dylan Thomas's "Light breaks where no sun shines," the poem opens itself to a kind of holy breaking and entering. That process, writ large and terrifying, becomes the theme of "the light that came to lucille clifton" (209, 213–21), the final sequence in *two-headed woman.* These excruciating poems delineate the poet's experiences of incandescent light infused with soft voices which at first make her fear madness. Only gradually does she identify the voices of light as wingless angels, as parents, as the dead: "in populated air / our ancestors continue . . . i have heard / their shimmering voices / singing" (221).

Numerous writers have testified to the force of religion in Afro-American writing. "Mystical longings, a desire to transcend empirical boundaries and material limitations are . . . the entrancing essence of Afro-America," writes Houston Baker (*Poetics* 105). Derek Walcott notes, "I have never separated the writing of poetry from prayer" (quoted in Baker, *Poetics,* 110). Toni Morrison, Alice Walker, Toni Cade Bambara, Paule Marshall and Audre Lorde are a few of the black writers who make visionary sutures of material and spiritual existence. Yet I think no other writer approaches Clifton's capacity to carry us from fragmentation to wholeness. Thus in the poem elliptically entitled "I. at creation," in her 1987 volume *Next,* when she begins with "i and my body," we might think of the traditional duality of body and soul, but Clifton draws them coupled instead of adversarial:

and i and my body rise
with the dusky beasts
with eve and her brother
to gasp in
the unsubstantial air

and evenly begin the long
slide out of paradise.
all life is life.
all clay is kin and kin.

The moment of "creation" here is both past and continual; it is inseparable from and contiguous with a departure from (not "loss" of) paradise; it perhaps includes the creation of the poem; it is the trauma and triumph of birth, and all creatures share it. At the same time there are the muted ironies, the understanding that a black woman is to be identified with "dusky beasts," but then again with "eve and her brother," and the tacit argument for kinship made by the assonance of "beasts," "eve," "evenly." The assonance of "i" and "rise" at the poem's opening (rise like bread? like new-made creatures? like the newborn from the womb? like the dead at the resurrection? like any person in the morning after sleep?) returns with the "slide" from "paradise" and is reinforced in the next line, which then yields to the alliteration of the final line, as if an argument were being closed. Isn't it closed? Isn't it obvious? The poem's physicality is one with its logic. As readers we perceive ourselves rising amid a multitude of others, gasping like newborns, sliding involuntarily, and arriving at what feels like certain knowledge. The experience of creation, coterminous with the shedding of safety, is the one touch of nature which unifies the world—and the poet makes it seem the most natural thing in the world.

* * *

Having read and taught Lucille Clifton for years, I need to suggest the myriad ways she delights me, invites me, strengthens and supports me—as artist, woman, earthy visionary. I need also to talk about the shadow that is inseparable from the pleasure I take in Clifton's work. That shadow is, of course, race.

You can walk in another's shoes, the saying goes, but you cannot walk in his skin. So I can identify with Clifton's voice, presence and power despite my whiteness and her blackness. The poems make me do that. By being strong and sweet, the poems strengthen and sweeten me. And of course I've seen the same thing happen to others—seen, for example, a whole classroom of white undergraduates break into smiles when I've read "Homage to My Hair" and "Homage to My Hips," not because these girls had nappy hair or big hips themselves, but because Clifton's self-affirmation was contagious. "These hips are big hips / these hips are mighty hips / these hips have never been enslaved" made affirmation feel possible, made everywoman feel momentarily capable of overcoming our commerce-fueled and misogyny-driven disapproval of our own bodies.

Black writers commonly appeal in this way to white readers: they pull us out of ourselves into the condition of the Other, while their power and courage—as writers, as humans—empowers and encourages us. In a sense, this is the function of all strong imaginative writing, in any language. It carries across boundaries as nothing else can do. Yet we delude ourselves if we think that writing in fact (as well as fancy) eliminates difference. I cannot inhabit Clifton's skin. I cannot in fact share her ancestors or her experience as a black woman in America. The pride and anger that vitalize her work can only vicariously, never actually, be mine. And whether I wish it or not—and I don't, and have resisted the knowledge, trying to remain unaware of what Clifton was finally showing me against my will—the pride excludes, and the anger targets, my whiteness. "Kin and kin" notwithstanding, the poems draw a circle in the sand. I stand hurt, outside.

For the absence of militant rhetoric from Clifton's poetry doesn't mean absence of bitterness. I think of Blake's "Chimney-Sweep" in *Songs of Experience*, an indictment of the complacent London rich: "Because I am happy and dance and sing / They think they have done me no injury." A black person lacking a sense of injury in this country is either a very small child, or a fool, or a traitor. What must it feel like to live in a pool of hatred? To know that you are despised (as well as unconsciously envied) by the majority of your fellow citizens? To have seen your leaders and heroes assassinated, your schoolchildren spat on, your churches bombed? To know that your boys and men can be killed—are killed—by white boys and men who never get punished? That your women are just brown sugar? How does it feel to live in a nation whose laws scarcely intend to protect your life, your liberty or your pursuit of happiness?

Part of what separates white from black America, I suspect, is that if whites actually tried to imagine being black, we'd go mad with pain and rage. To be privileged is to be fragile.

Clifton, on the other hand, defines herself without raising her voice:

> i got a long memory
> and i come from a line
> of black and going on women
> who got used to making it through murdered sons
> (*Good Woman* 32)

She defines, in a tone of patient explanation, what young black males feel:

> they act like they don't love their country
> no
> what it is
> is they found out
> their country don't love them. (*Good Woman* 37)

Clifton's stance toward white culture varies from the wry mockery of the first poem in *good times,* with its double sneer at repression and euphemism,

> in the inner city
> or
> like we call it
> home
> we think a lot about uptown
> and the silent nights
> and the houses straight as dead men
> and the pastel lights (15)

to the scornful pity of "after kent state," written after National Guardsmen shot four students demonstrating against the invasion of Cambodia during the Vietnam War,

> only to keep
> his little fear
> he kills his cities
> and his trees
> even his children   oh
> people
> white ways are

the ways of death (57)

to a bit of acerbic mythmaking:

the once and future dead
who learn they will be white men
weep for their history. we call it
rain. (182)

The book title *good news about the earth* comes from a poem which predicts the destruction of white men by mountains and waters, enabling their bodies to join those of Native Americans broken on the Trail of Tears, slaves melted into the ocean floor of Middle Passage. The celebratory and affirmative Clifton possesses this calm judge at her core, just as the Christian Clifton contains a black and ruthless Hindu goddess.

In *next* (1987), a series of poems on South Africa, and another on the death of Crazy Horse, join poems about Gettysburg, Buchenwald, Nagasaki, Jonestown, and the Shatila massacre in Lebanon, indicting "the extraordinary evil / in ordinary men" (21). These in turn join a set of anguished poems describing a young girl's struggle with leukemia, some luminously elegiac poems about the death of her husband Fred, some communings with her dead mother, a rueful sequence about doing poetry readings "in white america," the "shapeshifter poems" on incest, the "california lessons" on race and karma. Though a book filled with grief and grievances, it makes room for the pleasure of grandchildren; it also makes room for a meditation on the poet's own capacity for cruelty—a poem about killing cockroaches. In one mischievous poem, "my dream about being white," the poet imagines herself with "no lips, no behind, hey" wearing white history—

but there's no future
in those clothes
so i take them off and
wake up
dancing. (36)

Now, to a poem like this, how can I respond but doubly? Lucid, funny, self-loving poem, I think. "If I be you," I want to say to its author, "let me remember to respect my own dreams."

Yet to be mocked for my no lips and no backside grieves me; to be assured that my race has no future grieves me; I don't believe it, any more than I believe that white people's ways are "ways of death" rather than abuses of power which black people would / will abuse too when they have equal opportunity. Hey, honey, I want to respond; I don't demonize you, so don't demonize me.

Yet there is more; and as a white woman it behooves me to think further. What is the "little fear" of which Clifton speaks, the fear which generates "the ways of death" in American foreign policy, domestic policy, economic policy—and how complicit am I in it? It could be the fear of losing control. It could be the fear of empathizing with the Other, the fear of suffering. Three decades ago James Baldwin in *The Fire Next Time* claimed that white Americans do not face "reality—the fact that life is tragic . . . but people who cannot suffer can never grow up" (84). I find that argument rather persuasive.

One wants to feel loved back, by what one loves. It doesn't necessarily happen. Why should it? It won't kill me, comfortable as I otherwise am, to experience now and again the kind of hurt a black person feels every day. Race forms one of the two most basic divisions among human beings—gender is the other—which have stood since history began as excuses for hatred, violence, exploitation. All societies, all peoples are racist. That victims as well as oppressors can be racist is hardly news. No solution in sight, the best we can do is listen to each other, and the privileged need to listen harder.

Clifton has lately addressed the problem of speaking across race explicitly. The sequence "in white america" records a black poet's loneliness and alienation in a town where she's been invited to read—a town where a century ago the Native American longhouses and crops were burned "by not these people here" (*next* 92), and dark women scrubbed the floor of the church where no dark woman could rise to worship. Her lady tour guide means well:

> "this was a female school,
> my mother's mother graduated
> second in her class.
> they were taught embroidery,
> and chenille and filigree,
> ladies' learning. yes,

> we have a liberal history here."
> smiling she pats my darky hand. (73)

Those are not lines I can read without wincing—for the poet's sake and for my own. Am I that innocent and ignorant "she?" Do I too condescend, smilingly appropriate, complacently pat the darky hands of, the black writers I think I'm admiring and loving? At the reading, the poet looks at the audience which is "none of my faces," and does the best she can: "the human hair between us / stretches but does not break" (75). For the time being, that may be the best anyone can expect.

* * *

Quilting: poems 1987–1990, Clifton's boldest book, continues her meditations on history, loss, tragedy. Her affirmation of the body continues in two glorious poems on menstruation, "poem in praise of menstruation," and "to my last period," followed by the hilarious "wishes for sons," which fantasizes for them cramps, the last tampon, one week early, one week late, hot flashes and clots, and gynecologists resembling themselves.

Among the things of the spirit, her largest and loveliest work now is the ten-poem "Tree of Life" sequence, a lyric re-imagining of the role of Lucifer in Eden. "How art thou fallen from heaven, oh Lucifer, son of the morning," cries Isaiah (14:12). Clifton's version of the myth makes Lucifer (Lat. "light-bringer") at once light, lightning, and snake, servant of God, illuminator of mankind.[5]

As in the "some jesus" poems, the poet speaks through plural voices which seem to inhabit her. Hers is the voice of the mystified angels describing lucifer's creation and fall in the first three poems, then woman's sensuous voice in "eve's version" and man's sensually and intellectually desperate one in "adam thinking." Most fascinatingly, her voice is also Lucifer's.

Clifton's possession of and by the spirit of Lucifer, whose name echoes hers, and who is "six-fingered" like her, is an identification with masculine creativity. When the rather neoplatonic seraphim ponder "was it the woman / enticed you to leave us," Lucifer confirms and globalizes his sexuality:

> bearer of lightning
> and of lust
>
> thrust between the

legs of the earth
into this garden

phallus and father
doing holy work

oh sweet delight
oh eden (75)

The trajectory of "Tree of Life" is from heaven to earth, creation to final day, ignorance to knowledge. Part of its charm is its teasing allusiveness, its indeterminacies and uncertainties. When the "shine" of lucifer's birth seems too much for "one small heaven" (72), should we be reminded of the breaking of vessels which in kabbala is the moment of creation? When lucifer leaves heaven in shadow,

    and even the
solitary brother
has risen from his seat
of stones   he is holding
they say   a wooden stick
and pointing toward
a garden, (71)

is the brother (never mentioned again) Death, or Christ, or the original black man? Is the stick the tree of life, the cross, or both? The unidentified speaker of "the garden of delight"—sixth poem in the sequence—invokes possible Edens of earth, air, fire and water "for some," using an alchemical scheme, concluding with the quintessential eden of the poet:

and for some
certain only of the syllables
it is the element they
search their lives for

eden

for them
it is a test (76)

Ambiguities converge here. First, that poets may find eden only in certain syllables (not all of them), or that syllables are the only things they are certain of. Then, that they spend their lives searching, or that they search *within* their lives. Is eden, then, internal or external? Do words lead to it, or is it embodied in them? Is the test finding eden, or living in it?

In the penultimate poem uncertainty moves toward certitude. Eve has whispered her knowledge of names to Adam, and the unidentified voice describes the threesome of "the story thus far." As in Clifton's earlier "creation," the time might be the year zero, or the day before yesterday: "so they went out / clay and morning star / following the bright back / of the woman." (I recall, in this vista, Whitman's Adam with his Eve "by my side or back of me . . . or in front, and I following her" [69].) As they pass the gate "into the unborn world," the imagery grows brighter, chaos falls away, "and everywhere seemed light / seemed glorious / seemed very eden" (79). Again the fall is not a fall but a birth, the light of Eros and knowledge still surrounds the protagonists, or *seems* to. The "seemed," though inconspicuous, is crucial. Not until the final poem do uncertainties crown themselves assured. In the sequence's last poem, "lucifer speaks in his own voice," the light-bringer-snake knows he has done God's will and is

> certain of a
> graceful bed
> and a soft caress
> along my long belly
> at endtime,

but only in the final lines does his voice finally merge with the poet's, as if to summarize her career so far:

> illuminate i could
> and so
> illuminate i did.

That is the simplest possible description of Clifton's work.

Notes

Excerpts from *Good Woman: Poems and a Memoir 1969–1980* copyright © 1987; *Quilting: Poems 1987–1990* copyright © 1991; *Next: New Poems* copyright ©1987 by Lucille Clifton. Reprinted with the permission of Boa Editions, Ltd., 92 Park Ave., Brockport, NY 14420. Excerpts from *two-headed woman* copyright © 1980 by the University of Massachusetts Press and are reprinted by permission of Curtis Brown Ltd. An earlier version of this essay appeared in the November-December 1993 issue of *American Poetry Review.*

1. Lucille Clifton, *Good Woman: Poems and a Memoir 1969–1980* (Brockport, N.Y.: Boa Editions, Ltd., 1987), p. 51. Unless indicated, all Clifton quotations are from this volume. Other volumes of her poetry are *Next: New Poems* (Boa, 1987), *Quilting: Poems 1987–1990* (Boa, 1991), and *The Book of Light* (Copper Canyon, 1993). (This essay was completed prior to the publication of *Book of Light).*

2. The great facilitator here as in so much other work that women poets and Third World poets do is of course the Whitman who was "of the woman as well as the man" (39), not contained between his hat and boots, the Whitman who could joke "I find I incorporate gneiss" (46)—in other words, the Whitman of unlimited sympathies and a fluid "I." But it is important to remember that Emily Dickinson, too, liked to represent herself as male from time to time and to identify herself with biblical figures of both genders. Her rueful poem about going forth like David against Goliath—"I took my Power in my Hand" (540)—has a tone very like Clifton's.

3. From an unpublished paper on Clifton and the Bible.

4. Or maybe not erased at all? Jesus as a version of earlier dying-and-reviving gods may be cultural anthropology to the scholar but living religion to an Afro-American. So may goddesses, priestesses, spirit possession, the sacralization of nature and sexuality, and the collapse of gender polarities during worship. For illumination on the survivals of African religion and ritual in the diaspora, see Robert Thompson's *Flash of the Spirit,* a study of Caribbean voodoo and how it syncretizes gods and rituals from various African cultures; Zora Neale Hurston's *Tell My Horse* (Berkeley: Turtle Island, 1983) and *The Sanctified Church,* Louis Mars, *The Crisis of Possession in Voodoo,*

(Berkeley: Reed, Cannon and Johnson, 1977), and Houston A. Baker Jr., *Workings of the Spirit: the Poetics of Afro-American Women's Writing* (Chicago: University of Chicago Press, 1991). Baker's description of classic Afro-American spiritual performance, in his chapter on Hurston, applies beautifully to Clifton. See also Karen McCarthy, *Mama Lola: A Vodou Priestess in Brooklyn* (Berkeley: University of California Press, 1991).

5. Barbara G. Walker in *The Women's Encyclopedia of Myths and Secrets* (San Francisco: Harper & Row, 1983) traces Lucifer to Canaanite myths in which he represents heavenly masculine fire fertilizing the abyss, notes that he "continued to be linked with both lust and lightning during the Christian era," and claims that Gnostic Christians down to the fourteenth-century mystic Meister Eckhart interpret him as a bringer of enlightenment, a hero, savior, and revealer of sacred mysteries (551–54). I am grateful to Gloria (Ashaka) Hull for noticing Clifton's use of Walker and for many other insights into the poet's use of biblical material.

Works Cited

Baker, Houston A., Jr. *Afro-American Poetics: Revisions of Harlem and the Black Aesthetic*. Madison: University of Wisconsin Press, 1988.

———. *Workings of the Spirit: the Poetics of Afro-American Women's Writing*. Chicago: University of Chicago Press, 1991.

Baldwin, James. *The Fire Next Time*. London: Penguin, 1964.

Clifton, Lucille. *The Book of Light*. Port Townshend, Wash.: Copper Canyon Press, 1993.

———. *Generations: A Memoir*. New York: Random House, 1976.

———. *Good Woman: Poems and a Memoir 1969–1980*. Brockport, N.Y.: Boa Editions, Ltd., 1987.

———. *Next: New Poems*. Brockport, N.Y.: Boa Editions, Ltd., 1987.

———. *Quilting: Poems 1987–1990*. Brockport, N.Y.: Boa Editions, Ltd., 1991.

Dickinson, Emily. *Complete Poems*. Ed. Thomas H. Johnson. Boston: Little, Brown, 1960.

Forster, E. M. *Howards End*. New York: Vintage, 1954.

Hacker, Marilyn. "A Pocketful of Poets." *Women's Review of Books* 5:10–11 (1988): 24.

Hass, Robert. "Looking for Rilke." *Twentieth Century Pleasures*. New York: Ecco Press, 1984.

Hurston, Zora Neale. *The Sanctified Church*. Berkeley: Turtle Island, 1983.

———. *Tell My Horse*. Berkeley: Turtle Island, 1983.

Mars, Louis. *The Crisis of Possession in Voodoo*. Berkeley: Reed, Cannon and Johnson, 1977.

McCarthy, Karen. *Mama Lola: A Vodou Priestess in Brooklyn*. Berkeley: University of California Press, 1991.

McCluskey, Audrey. "Tell the Good News: A View of the Works of Lucille Clifton." *Black Women Writers*. Ed. Mari Evans. New York: Doubleday, 1984.

Moore, Marianne. *Complete Poems*. New York: Macmillan, 1967.

Thompson, Robert. *Flash of the Spirit: African and Afro-American Art and Philosophy*. New York: Random House, 1983.

Walker, Barbara G. *The Women's Encyclopedia of Myths and Secrets*. San Francisco: Harper & Row, 1983.

Whitman, Walt. *Complete Poetry and Selected Prose*. Boston: Houghton Mifflin, 1959.

Shakespeare's Naylor, Naylor's Shakespeare: Shakespearean Allusion as Appropriation in Gloria Naylor's Quartet

Peter Erickson

> We've finally, thank God, stopped that nonsense in this country where the ideal concept was a melting pot. Now we're saying, "No, it's a patchwork quilt, not a melting pot." Because—guess what?—nobody was melting. It wasn't happening. The novel [*Linden Hills*] was a sort of cautionary tale about that, about attempting to do the impossible—especially for the black American, because we're also a racist society.

> My quibble is with people who construct literary canons . . . and how we determine what is real writing and what is fringe writing. Those are all political decisions. I don't back away from saying that I'm a political being. I think, as a black American, I'm more political than others. My existence in this country was an act of politics. My continuing existence is such.[1]

The attempt to rewrite the Renaissance has been a major strand in criticism through the 1980s and into the 1990s. At least four renaissances are being vigorously reinterpreted. The current reconsideration of the English and European Renaissance of the sixteenth and seventeenth centuries is exemplified by the collection *Rewriting the Renaissance,* whose title articulates a much wider effort. Three American versions of renaissance are also being reconstructed. F. O. Matthiessen's classic *American Renaissance* has been challenged by a series of critics.[2] Gloria T. Hull's study reassesses the Harlem Renaissance.[3] In conversation with Gloria Naylor, Toni Morrison applies the term renaissance to contemporary black women writers: "It's a real renaissance. You know, we have spoken of renaissance before. But this one is ours, not somebody else's."[4] Yet work by critic Hazel V. Carby suggests that this most recent Renaissance is being rewritten even as Morrison formulates it.[5]

My specific concern here is points of contact between the first and fourth of these Renaissances as represented by Gloria Naylor's use of Shakespeare. No longer is *Othello* the exclusive or even primary focus for the consideration of race and racism in Shakespeare.[6] Two related lines of feminist criticism have opened up a much more comprehensive discussion of the meanings of race in the Renaissance. The first is the emergence of new studies that view race not as an "unhistorical" category but as a central issue for the early modern period.[7] As a result, the topic of race is not confined to instances of black characters in the plays but involves a much wider cultural context and a more subtle sense of racial discourse and symbolic patterns. The second development is the recent emphasis on responses to Shakespeare by authors, including black women writers, from later historical periods.[8] Comparative studies that cross period divisions provide another perspective from which to assess the question of race in Shakespeare's work.

* * *

Gloria Naylor's four novels, conceived from the outset as a quartet, are linked by a set of internal cross-references to characters and places.[9] Shakespeare, however, provides a second set of connections, for he figures in all four novels. My starting-point is this question: what is Shakespeare doing here? Why does Naylor so consistently evoke the Shakespearean reference point?

As an epitome of the literary master and as a representative of the main line of the inherited literary tradition, Shakespeare provides Naylor with a counterpoint to the emergent tradition of contemporary black women writers. The presence of Shakespeare allows Naylor to explore the relation between these two traditions, which she experiences not only as distinct but also as split, divided, opposed:

> The writers I had been taught to love were either male or white. And who was I to argue that Ellison, Austen, Dickens, the Brontës, Baldwin and Faulkner weren't masters? They were and are. But inside there was still

> the faintest whisper: Was there no one telling my story? ("Conversation" 568)

Because of the absence of her story, it was "a long road from gathering the authority within myself to believe that I could actually be a writer" (568). In Naylor's development, this authority comes crucially from her immediate predecessor Toni Morrison: "But for me, where was the *authority* for me to enter this forbidden terrain? But then finally you were being taught to me" (575).

The perception of two traditions—one that omits black women, one that focuses on them—creates for Naylor an irreducible gap. The new tradition produces stories that are "'different but equal'" (Mills 17), with the stress falling on both terms. They are equal and not minor or second-rate, but they are also still different. Naylor resists the pressure of the logic that if they are truly equal, then they cannot be fundamentally different since all works of the first rank are judged by a single standard and thereby incorporated into a single canon.

Naylor's energies are directed rather toward preserving and dramatizing the signal differences between the dual traditions of which Shakespeare and Morrison are emblematic. Naylor's bond with Morrison as the originator of an alternate, non-Shakespearean tradition makes Morrison a more important resource than Shakespeare; Morrison provides an identity and a voice, which Shakespeare is powerless to do. Yet Naylor's primary allegiance to Morrison does not lead to the exclusion of Shakespeare. If, sustained by Morrison, Naylor need not approach Shakespeare with disabling reverence, neither does she simply reject him, as her evident attraction to Shakespearean language testifies. Naylor's involvement and negotiations with Shakespeare occur in an intermediate zone that conveys a delicate tension in Naylor's double perspective on Shakespeare: she appreciates Shakespeare while at the same time she is determined critically to rewrite him.

Naylor's attention to Shakespeare serves to raise the question of Shakespeare's changed status when seen from the vantage-point of the emergent tradition in which Naylor is a participant. By putting into play and testing both positive and critical attitudes toward Shakespeare, Naylor's work dramatizes with particular fullness the conflict between established and emergent traditions.

* * *

In Naylor's first novel, *The Women of Brewster Place,* the Shakespearean moment is located in the "Cora Lee" story, the fifth of seven sections. The moment exemplifies the delicacy of tone with which Naylor approaches Shakespeare: her humor is too finely textured—too sympathetic and poignant—to be merely satirical.

Cora Lee, overwhelmed by her sole responsibility for her children, takes refuge from her burden in a heavy dose of TV soaps. This pattern is temporarily disrupted when she and the children are invited to a black production of *A Midsummer Night's Dream.* Shakespeare as cultural event inspires in Cora Lee an unprecedented outburst of energetic determination: "It would be good for them. They need things like Shakespeare and all that" (121); "They would sit still and get this Shakespeare thing if she had to break their backs" (124). The specific incentive is defined by Cora Lee's association of Shakespeare with school, career aspiration, and upward mobility: "Junior high; high school; college—none of them stayed little forever. And then on to good jobs in insurance companies and the post office, even doctors or lawyers" (126).

Naylor matches the comedy of *A Midsummer Night's Dream* with her own mischievous comic mood. She builds up the Shakespearean motif of the dream by linking Bottom's and Puck's references to dreaming (126) with allusions to Mercutio's set piece on Queen Mab (107, epigraph for "Cora Lee" section) and Prospero's "We are such stuff as dreams are made on" (121). Using this Shakespearean background, Naylor plays off two meanings of dream—genuine hope and futile fantasy—against each other in the immediate context of black urban poverty. Though Mercutio's apparently genial speech comes from an early moment in *Romeo and Juliet* before the tragic current has taken hold, Naylor does not ultimately block out the tragic implications of Cora Lee's situation. The "night of wonders" (127) that Shakespearean comedy creates for Cora Lee proves to be only an interlude. The evidence of "hopeful echoes" she finds upon her return home is summarily cancelled: "Then she turned and firmly folded her evening like gold and lavender gauze deep within the creases of her dreams . . . " (127).

The discrepancy between hopeful dreaming and dead-end finality is abruptly brought into focus by her child's questioning: "'Mama,' Sammy pulled on her arm,

'Shakespeare's black?'" (127). Naylor's gentle ironies become painful ones as she directly poses the issue of the relevance of Shakespeare's pastoral to black urban landscape. We are forced to acknowledge not only that Shakespeare is white but also that, even when "'brought . . . up to date'" (119), his translation into a black cultural idiom is neither automatically assured nor unambiguously benign. Moving up from the low culture of white-produced TV soaps to the high culture of black-produced Shakespeare no longer seems an answer.

The problematic aspects of Shakespearean inspiration are intertwined with the paradoxical position of Kiswana Browne, who issues the invitation to Cora Lee to attend the Shakespeare play produced by her boyfriend Abshu. Unlike the others "who came because they had no choice and would remain for the same reason" (4), Kiswana, having rejected her middle-class family situation in Linden Hills, is the one woman in Brewster Place who is there by choice. Kiswana's renunciation is subsequently vindicated by Naylor's own condemnation of Linden Hills in her second novel. Yet there is pointed irony in Kiswana's being the intermediary who arouses in Cora Lee a Shakespearean dream of upward educational mobility when Kiswana herself has already deliberately rejected it, having dropped out of college: "'Those bourgie schools were counterrevolutionary'" (83); "'What good would I be after four or five years of a lot of white brainwashing in some phony, prestige institution, huh?'" (84). When she does take courses again at a community college, Shakespeare is not in her curriculum (161).

Kiswana's appeal to come to the performance of *A Midsummer Night's Dream* is her second invitation to Cora Lee; the first is a request that she attend the meeting of a tenants' association that Kiswana is organizing (115–16). Naylor does not so much reject Kiswana's political commitment as show its limits. Kiswana, too, is compromised by the double meaning of dreams as hope and as lack of realism: "She placed her dreams on the back of the bird and fantasized that it would glide forever . . . she watched with a sigh as the bird beat its wings in awkward frantic movements. . . . This brought her back to earth" (75).

When the well-attended meeting in Kiswana's apartment is disrupted over an objection to the participation of Lorraine, a lesbian, Kiswana is unable to respond effectively. Her belated apology still expresses this inadequacy: "'I should have said something—after all, it was my house—but things got out of hand so quickly, I'm sorry, I . . . '" (160). Kiswana's politics fail to include the political issue of lesbian relationships. Even in Mattie's dream sequence at the end of the novel, Kiswana is represented as hesitant to acknowledge the consequences of the hostility to Lorraine's lesbian identity. Confronted with blood-stained bricks that body forth both Lorraine's violent rape and her retaliatory murder of the defenseless man who befriends but ultimately cannot protect her against male aggression, Kiswana initially responds with denial:

> She tried to pass a brick to Kiswana, who looked as if she had stepped into a nightmare.
>
> "There's no blood on those bricks!" Kiswana grabbed Ciel by the arm. "You know there's no blood—it's raining. It's just raining!"
>
> Ciel pressed the brick into Kiswana's hand and forced her fingers to curl around it. "Does it matter? Does it really matter?"
>
> Kiswana looked down at the wet stone and her rain-soaked braids leaked onto the surface, spreading the dark stain. She wept and ran to throw the brick spotted with her blood out into the avenue. (187)

Kiswana's weeping during this act of symbolic identification marks the final separation from the comic note struck by *A Midsummer Night's Dream*. The "Cora Lee" section containing the Shakespearean episode is strategically placed because of its sharp juxtaposition with the section that follows on "The Two," the lesbian couple. The humor, shifting to a different register, now serves as a medium for releasing and partially transforming suspicion and uncertainty about lesbian sexuality. The attack on Lorraine at the block meeting is defused through humor, but it is a strained, ambivalent humor that conveys tentative acceptance without completely dispelling the underlying discomfort and anxiety:

> The laughter that burst out of their lungs was such a relief that eyes were watery. The room laid back its head and howled in gratitude to Ben for allowing it to breathe again. Sophie's rantings could not be heard

> above the wheezing, coughing, and backslapping that now went on.
>
> Lorraine left the apartment.... (146)

The humor escalates in the wildly comic moment when Lorraine's lover Theresa puts on an angry display with food for the benefit of a disapproving voyeur:

> Theresa's sides were starting to ache from laughing, and she sat down in one of the kitchen chairs. Lorraine pushed the bowl a little further down the table from her, and this set them off again. Theresa laughed and rocked in the chair until tears were rolling down her cheeks. Then she crossed that fine line between laughter and tears and started to sob. (159)

The phrase used to express the way humor gives access to hurt aptly characterizes Naylor's harsher comic action: in moving from "Cora Lee" to "The Two," the novel has "crossed the fine line between laughter and tears."

This crossing can be described as a shift from Shakespeare's rendering of the dream motif to that of Langston Hughes in "What happens to a dream deferred?," the politically charged poem that Naylor uses as the epigraph for the novel as a whole. Naylor's break with the evanescent atmosphere of *A Midsummer Night's Dream* is particularly appropriate because the play's design undermines female bonds: the intimate connection between Hermia and Helena is severed by the marital demands imposed by comic form.[10] Setting aside a comic pattern that cannot be accommodated to her focus on female bonds, Naylor answers Hughes's final line "*Or does it explode?*" with her own word "exploded" (188). Naylor's explosion dismantles the wall that maintains Brewster Place as an isolated ghetto. By contrast, the removal of the wall in *A Midsummer Night's Dream* occurs within the concluding play-within-a-play, a carefully circumscribed entertainment that observes firm class distinctions between the lower-class artisans who perform and the aristocratic audience whom they serve to amuse.

Naylor's fantasy is fiercer, enabling a glimpse of black female action across differences in class and sexuality. Middle-class Kiswana, moving beyond her earlier evasiveness about Lorraine's lesbian identity (160), participates in a protest she did not plan that honors Lorraine's sacrifice. Theresa, Lorraine's partner, joins in: "She grabbed the bricks from Cora and threw one into the avenue . . . " (187–88). Naylor makes clear that this unified action occurs in imagination only, not in reality, by articulating it as Mattie's dream preceding the actual block party. But the dream vision is so intensely imagined that the daylight reality which succeeds cannot displace it; this achievement belongs to Naylor's, not Shakespeare's, imagination.

* * *

In *Linden Hills,* Naylor's second novel, the main reference point from Western literary tradition appears to be Dante's *Inferno* (Mills 17). However, in a penultimate moment, the two black friends, Lester and Willie, the latter a struggling poet, discuss Shakespeare. The terms have modulated from the humorously innocent query "'Shakespeare's black?'" in *The Women of Brewster Place* to the more pressing issue of "'why black folks ain't produced a Shakespeare'" (*Linden Hills* 282).

In these first two novels, the dominant typography is the splitting of black urban landscape into separate poor and middle-class areas. The novels' views of Shakespeare are correlated with this internal class division. From the perspective of Brewster Place, Shakespeare belongs to Linden Hills and the rising middle-class expectations associated with that privileged space: at the play, Cora "looked around and didn't recognize anyone from Brewster so the blacks here probably came from Linden Hills . . . " (124). But, on closer inspection in *Linden Hills*, Shakespeare is not to be found there either, as the exchange between Willie and Lester testifies:

> "You'd think of all the places in the world, this neighborhood had a chance of giving us at least one black Shakespeare."
>
> "But Linden Hills ain't about that, Willie. You should know that by now." (283)

Shakespeare's location with respect to black society remains elusive and hence the shift from the relatively playful tone in the first novel's representation of Shakespeare to the more frustrated note in the second.

The phrase "one black Shakespeare" expresses the highest artistic desire as the replication of the Shakespearean model. But to shape one's desire in this way may be to create a self-defeating dependence; Shakespeare comes to symbolize a quest for black recognition that is unattainable within the narrow terms of imitation suggested by the uncomfortable echo effect that ties Willie's name to Will Shakespeare's. Naylor's third novel will move outside this framework through a decisive turn to a wider geographical exploration. The earlier counterpoint between poor and middle-class is subsumed by a larger structure of tensions between Northern urban and Southern rural that gradually emerges into prominence over the course of the three novels.[11] The increasing emphasis on the North-South contrast leads, I shall argue, to a different kind of engagement with Shakespeare because the Southern terrain of *Mama Day* makes possible a literary mapping wherein Shakespeare can be not only emulated but also outmaneuvered.

The Women of Brewster Place dramatizes its Southern origins through Mattie Michael, whose story both begins in the South and begins the novel. Though left behind in the move northward, the South has a powerful residual presence because a crucial part of the network of female bonds is formed there: Mattie's friendship with Etta Mae Johnson (section 2) is established before their arrival in New York as is Mattie's relationship with Ciel (section 4). Partly because of this Southern connection, Mattie can be seen as a prototype of Mama Day in Naylor's third novel. While lacking Mama Day's specific knowledge of magic, Mattie nonetheless has a maternal force and communal authority that parallel Mama Day's. Mattie's care of Ciel after the death of Ciel's child is analogous to Mama Day's concern for Cocoa: "The black mammoth gripped so firmly that the slightest increase of pressure would have cracked the girl's spine. But she rocked" (*The Women of Brewster Place* 103).

Mattie differs from Mama Day in two crucial respects: she remains permanently in the North with no prospect of returning to the home base in the South she has been forced to leave; and her reunion with Ciel is fulfilled only in a dream—"Mattie pressed Ciel into her full bosom and rocked her slowly" (177). But Mattie's dream organizes the women of Brewster Place in a manner that anticipates Mama Day's more potent art. In so doing, Mattie holds out the possibility of a black alternative to the Shakespearean imagination, an alternative to be realized when Naylor's Mama Day supplants rather than duplicates Shakespeare's Prospero.

The central line of development from Mattie to Mama Day can be traced in *Linden Hills* through the figure of Roberta Johnson, who, as grandmother to Laurel Dumont, is "'the closest thing to a natural mother you got'" (223). Remaining firmly based in the rural South, the grandmother sponsors the Berkeley education that separates them: "Because all Roberta knew was that she had cashed in her life insurance to send a child she had named Laurel Johnson to the state of California, and it sent her back a stranger" (226–27). Laurel's engulfment in the "emptiness" (238) of middle-class achievement places her beyond the grandmother's power to rescue her:

> "Why did you come, Laurel?"
>
> There was a long pause, and then her voice was barely a whisper. "When people are in trouble, don't they go home?"
>
> Roberta covered her clenched hands gently. "But this ain't your home, child." (231)

Yet in reversing the one-way northward migration, Laurel's attempt to reconnect with a Southern rural landscape in *Linden Hills* prefigures Cocoa's return from New York City to the South in *Mama Day*.

The resource from which Laurel has been cut off involves tradition: "She was taking in the sight of an old woman, the sound of old stories, and the smells of an old tradition with nothing inside her to connect up to them" (239). Roberta evokes the saving power of this native tradition by opposing it to the European art to which Laurel is habituated:

> "You can hear the hurt in Bessie or Billie and I just kinda wish that I'd come here and found you playing their stuff, 'cause that man you seem to like so much—that Mahler—his music says that he ain't made peace with his pain, child. And if you gonna go on, that's what you gotta do." (235)

The motif of conflicting Afro-American and Western traditions extends, by implication, to the vexed homage Willie pays to Shakespeare as formulated in the need for "'one black Shakespeare'" (283). Shakespeare, like Mahler, may be the wrong place to seek artistic salvation.

* * *

Mama Day picks up where *Linden Hills* leaves off by greatly intensifying both the North-South cultural contrast and the Shakespearean motif. Before turning to *Mama Day*'s treatment of the latter, I want to examine the former through a comparison of *Mama Day* with Paule Marshall's *Praisesong for the Widow*.[12] The correspondences between the two novels suggest a common pattern with four steps.

The first step in this sequence is the protracted struggle to achieve middle-class security. This driving upward mobility is recounted in Part II of *Praisesong for the Widow* in the story of the Johnsons' move from Halsey Street in Brooklyn to North White Plains. The counterpart to Jerome Johnson's rise as an accountant is George's successful New York-based engineering career in *Mama Day*. For Kiswana Browne in *The Women of Brewster Place*, the ultimate proof of "middle-class amnesia" (85) is the existence of black Republicans, a condition she vows to avoid: "'But I'll never be a Republican'" (88). George in *Mama Day*, viewing his Republican affiliation as a necessary component of his business success, experiences only occasional regret: "Meeting his type always made me ashamed to be a Republican" (56).

A second phase begins with symptoms of malaise after the hard-won attainment of middle-class status, with a growing awareness of the emptiness of arrival. Avey Johnson's perception of being stuck in an impasse propels Marshall's novel forward. George's more muted dissatisfaction with the limitations of his constricted identity is implicitly expressed by his desire to reach out and to incorporate Cocoa's very different background:

> And I wondered if it was too late, if seven years in New York had been just enough for you to lose that, like you were trying to lose your southern accent . . . That's why I wanted you to call me George. There isn't a southerner alive who could bring that name in under two syllables. (33)

This turning-point leads to a third stage, the counter-project of recovering what has been lost in middle-class achievement. The project takes the particular geographic form of leaving behind New York City in order to reclaim a living connection with a self-contained Southern black culture symbolized by an island community. In the case of *Praisesong for the Widow*, the specific locale is Tatum Island, where, as a child, Avey Johnson visited her great-aunt Cuney, who is responsible for Avey's name Avatara (42).[13] Avey regains her connection with this heritage by literally enacting the meaning in her name—incarnation—in the ritual dance during the festival on the Caribbean island of Carriacou. Not only are Tatum and Carriacou both directly connected with the African origins of their black inhabitants, but also Avey's participation in the Carriacou festival is matched point for point with her recollections of Tatum.

In *Mama Day*, George too "crosses over" (165, 177) onto the Southern island of Willow Springs, a move which for him is equivalent to "entering another world" (175) and which for Naylor marks the boundary of the novel's second half. Both for Avey Johnson and for George, the new realm is governed by a set of beliefs that demand faith and challenge skepticism. Avey manages the process with relative ease: "she had awakened with it [her mind] like a slate that had been wiped clean, a *tabula rasa* upon which a whole new history could be written" (151). George's test of belief is more involuntary and more stressful: "How could I believe?" (288).

Mama Day denies, or fulfills more stringently, the affirmative answer *Praisesong for the Widow* gives to Avey's question:

> Would it have been possible to have done both? That is, to have wrested, as they had done all those years, the means needed to rescue them from Halsey Street and to see the children through, while preserving, safeguarding, treasuring those things that had come down to them over the generations, which had defined them in a particular way. . . . They could have done both, it suddenly seemed to her. (139)

In Marshall's novel, the tragedy—the death of Avey's husband—has already occurred, leaving the novel free to concentrate on transcendence for Avey. *Mama Day*, however, dramatizes the tragic cost through its focus on George's crisis and sacrificial death.

Yet this difference between the two novels becomes less pronounced when the fourth stage of resolution is considered.

Whatever George's deficiencies, the novel more than makes up for his inability to believe with its own decisive investment in the character of Mama Day. Despite Naylor's rejection of happy endings on page 119—"Grown women aren't supposed to believe in Prince Charmings and happily-ever-afters. Real life isn't about that. . . ."—*Mama Day* conveys a strongly positive sense of completion through Mama Day's epilogue. With Mama Day's help, Cocoa finds the peace that eludes Laurel in *Linden Hills*: Cocoa's is "a face that's been given the meaning of peace" (312). Although the transmission of heritage passes through the female line from Mama Day to Cocoa, George is included in this resolution. In spite of his failure, George initiates and shares the peace: "there was total peace" (302). As Mama Day predicts, his bond with Cocoa is maintained after his death through her ongoing communication with him: "whatever roads take her from here, they'll always lead back to you" (308).

A similarity between Marshall's and Naylor's respective endings is reinforced by the way their recovery of the distant past is accompanied by studied neglect of more recent political history. Avey's change in *Praisesong for the Widow* is measured symbolically by the reversal of her initial refusal to sell the White Plains house she has achieved with her husband (26):

> Sell the house in North White Plains as Marion had been urging her to do for years and use the money to build in Tatum.
>
> It would be a vacation house, and once she retired she would live part of the year there. . . .
>
> And Marion could bring some of the children from her school. . . . The place could serve as a summer camp. (256)

By this decision, Avey responds to the "mission" bequeathed by her great-aunt Cuney (42); at the same time, this triumph is partly undercut by the way her language suggests a real-estate transaction.

The resolution is romanticized because it is a substitute for a direct confrontation with the images of political conflict in the sixties that Avey has "conveniently forgotten" (31):

> Hadn't she lived through most of the sixties and early seventies as if Watts and Selma and the tanks and

> Stoner guns in the streets of Detroit somehow did not pertain to her, denying her rage, and carefully effacing any dream that might have come to her during the night by the time she awoke the next morning. (140)

This spirit of denial remains in force; Avey's plan does not undo the repression of her anxiety over political struggle.[14] A similar dynamic is at work in *Mama Day*, where preoccupation with the deep time of the ancestral past squeezes out contemporary political issues from which Willow Springs is portrayed as fundamentally immune. The sixties are by-passed, treated peripherally as high comedy in the tale of outwitting the abrasive white deputy (79–81).

Both Marshall's Tatum and Naylor's Willow Springs take on an aspect of pastoral refuge that makes them subject to Hazel V. Carby's analysis of black folk tradition as a romantic avoidance of the present political crisis whose primary focus is urban.[15] In Carby's persuasive view, recent literary criticism has privileged the folk line as the authentic tradition, excluding or minimizing the other, equally authentic black urban mode and thereby participating in the evasion to which folk genres are prone. Like *Praisesong for the Widow*, *Mama Day* abandons New York City without regret: "It was a relief to leave for good" (305). I want to acknowledge the force of Carby's powerful critique, but at the same time to argue that *Mama Day* is not simply escapist because it enacts another drama—the cultural political struggle with the Shakespearean past. Though Naylor's presentation will not permit disbelief in Mama Day, her skepticism remains active in relation to Shakespeare.

Much in *King Lear* and *The Tempest*, the two principal plays evoked in *Mama Day*, seems merely to aid and abet the sentimental pastoral tendencies in the novel. Both plays assume the salubrious value of pastoral space—the exposed heath in Lear's case, the magically controlled island in Prospero's. Both plays employ the rhythm of the tempest followed by the restorative calm after the storm; in Naylor's final line, "the waters were still" (312). Moreover, the generic progression from *King Lear* as tragedy to *The Tempest* as late romance serves to reinforce a romanticized version of pastoral.

These congruencies between Shakespeare and *Mama Day* do not tell the whole story, however. Naylor's sustained engagement with Shakespeare cannot be explained by the image of Shakespeare as an exclusively positive resource, nor is Naylor's action limited to the harmonious adaptation and recapitulation of Shakespearean motifs. Rather, the effect of *Mama Day*'s exploration of Shakespearean heritage is critically to revise and decenter it.

* * *

Naylor's reassessment of Shakespeare in *Mama Day* is carried out on two levels. On the first, George's attachment to *King Lear* is probed; on the second, more pervasive level, associations between Willow Springs and *The Tempest* are tested. This twofold approach is correlated with the novel's overall geographic movement from North to South since George's *Lear* is situated in the former while *The Tempest*'s connections are with the latter.

George's adoption of Shakespeare serves as a badge of his upward mobility. His successive editions of *King Lear* both mark the increasing value of the play as a material object and cultural status symbol and also measure the progress of his relationship with Cocoa. He begins with a "worn copy" (60) that he prefers to Cocoa and ends with "the calfskin and gold-leafed copy" (304) that Cocoa gives him as a birthday present. *King Lear* specifically provides the medium for negotiating George's seduction of Cocoa: "The games people play. I wasn't coming to your apartment the following Tuesday night to talk about *King Lear*" (104).

The chief point of emotional connection to the play is George's identification with Edmund: "It had a special poignancy for me, reading the rage of a bastard . . . " (106). Edmund's soliloquy—"Now, gods, stand up for bastards"—speaks to George's desire to make it against the odds. George smugly notes Cocoa's naive reading, though he withholds his commentary so as not to impede the seduction:

> And you were so glad I'd turned you on to this. It showed you how hard the playwright tried to convey that men had the same feelings as women. No, that was not true. No way. Along with *The Taming of the Shrew*, this had to be Shakespeare's most sexist treatment of women—but far be it from me to contradict anything you had to say. I didn't want to waste any more time than necessary for you to work yourself up to untying the strings on that red halter. (106)

But George's own misinterpretation is just as bad, for Shakespeare does not stand up for bastards any more than for women. Edmund is defeated by Edgar in the end, and George chooses to neglect his fate.

George's relatively superficial attachment to Shakespeare comes nowhere close to his passionate commitment to football. If Shakespeare's images of women are restrictive, football excludes women entirely. In Cocoa's detached view of football's male bonding: "They line up, bend down, and all of a sudden they're in a pile, smelling each other's behinds" (126). Since Naylor herself shares Cocoa's resistance to George's love of football,[16] one might say that Naylor has paid George back by imposing on him her own fascination with Shakespeare. After the tempest hits Willow Springs, she puts into George's mouth a phrase derived from Prospero's revels speech: "this was the stuff of dreams" (258). But George's understanding of the cue proves inadequate. While his attitude toward football approaches the religious—"And I'm not talking in metaphors—it could create miracles" (124), his response to Mama Day conspicuously denies that this attitude could apply to her female arena: "'Well, you're talking in a lot of metaphors'" (294). Ultimately his approach to Willow Springs remains on the same order as his treatment of "the symbolism" (105–6) of *King Lear*.

The novel's second Shakespearean strand, the interplay between *The Tempest* and Naylor's representation of the Southern island of Willow Springs, involves a much more active encounter with Shakespeare. Naylor rewrites the exchange between Prospero and Caliban concerning ownership, in effect honoring Caliban's accusation—"This island's mine, by Sycorax my mother, / Which thou tak'st from me"—and reinstating his legitimate, female-derived possession. The black islanders of Willow Springs oppose the trend in island development that would reduce them to Caliban-like servility:

> Hadn't we seen it happen back in the '80s on St. Helena, Daufuskie, and St. John's? And before that in the '60s on Hilton Head? . . . And the only dark faces you see now in them "vacation paradises" is the ones cleaning the toilets and cutting the grass . . . Weren't gonna happen in Willow Springs. 'Cause if Mama Day say no, everybody say no. (6)

Their attitude toward real estate contrasts sharply with that represented by the black developer Luther Nedeed in *Linden Hills*; where Nedeed imitates the white model, Willow Springs rejects it. Nedeed's obsessive concern with the empty ceremony of a traditional family Christmas is replaced in *Mama Day* by the non-Christian observance of the winter solstice that signifies cultural independence: "old Reverend Hooper couldn't stop Candle Walk night. . . . Any fool knows Christmas is December twenty-fifth—that ain't never caught on too much here. And Candle Walk is always the night of the twenty-second" (108).

Naylor's depiction of Willow Springs's resistance to white corporate and cultural control parallels her own resistance to Shakespearean colonization of her art. However, although Naylor teasingly alludes to Caliban—"some slave on a Caribbean island" Cocoa recalls "from her high school Shakespeare" (64), the main line of Naylor's resistance lies elsewhere. As a recent survey shows, twentieth-century attempts to revise *The Tempest* have concentrated on reversing the Prospero-Caliban relationship by imagining a newly empowered Caliban.[17] Naylor's special contribution is her focus on women characters, a focus that adds a reconfiguration of genders to the issues of race and class associated with Caliban. Largely ignoring Caliban, Naylor's subversive strategy is to create a black female equivalent to Prospero.

The force of Naylor's project is implied by the central character's double name: both Miranda and Mama Day. If the former suggests the tie to Shakespeare, the latter breaks it by indicating the possibility of escape from Shakespearean entrapment in the subservient daughter role. The age and experience of Naylor's Miranda not only contrasts with the youth and innocence of Shakespeare's Miranda; Mama Day's scope also encompasses and outdoes Prospero himself. In 1999 at the novel's close, Mama Day, having been born in 1895, is 104 years old and even then her epilogue is not quite ready to seek release: "and when she's tied up the twentieth century, she'll take a little peek into the other side—for pure devilment and curiosity—and then leave for a rest that she deserves" (312). The hyperbole of her age establishes that Mama Day is more than able to compete with Prospero, whose "Every third thought shall be my grave" seems pinched and feeble next to the splendor of her approach to death.

Naylor not only has Mama Day usurp Prospero's role but also redefines that role by altering the prerogatives that go with it. The moral structure of *The Tempest* is carried over into *Mama Day* only in a residual way. Ruby, for example, is an embodiment of evil against whom Mama Day is allowed a Prospero-like spectacular punitive display (270, 273). However, Naylor's main stress is on the differences between Prospero's and Mama Day's magical powers. The storm at the outset of *The Tempest* is Prospero's concoction, as he reveals with paternal reassurance and pride in act one, scene two. By contrast, Mama Day is powerless to prevent the storm's destruction of Little Caesar, the child whom she had helped Bernice to produce. As Mama Day reflects, "she ain't never tried to get *over* nature" (262). While Prospero may belatedly accept the limits of his magic, Mama Day is mindful of her limitations from the beginning.

The contrast between Prospero and Mama Day is especially sharp with respect to gender politics. Though the relationship between Mama Day and her father Jean-Paul is portrayed as a positive resource, it is nonetheless subordinate to the primary emphasis on strong female bonds—bonds that Miranda's isolation makes impossible in *The Tempest*. Mama Day's central drama concerns the recovery of connections with three women: Sapphira, the slave woman who originated the Day line; Ophelia, Mama Day's mother who, distraught over the death of her daughter Peace, drowned herself; and Cocoa, her grandniece, who has left Willow Springs and now works in New York City.

Like Mama Day, Cocoa has a double name that operates to deny Shakespearean expectations. Cocoa is named Ophelia after her great grandmother, whose death by water recalls the destiny of Shakespeare's Ophelia in the male-dominated world of *Hamlet*. Cocoa's alternate name aids the process of exorcising the burden both of her great grandmother's demise and of the potential Shakespearean connotations. Mama Day's comment about tradition can be applied to the novel's general stance toward patriarchal political structures in *Hamlet*, *King Lear*, or *The Tempest*: "'Tradition is fine, but you gotta know when to stop being a fool'" (307).

It is true that in its own way *Mama Day* is as determined as any Shakespearean comedy in its marital and reproductive drive. Like Prospero, Mama Day orchestrates generational continuity: "I plan to keep on living till I can rock one of yours on my knee" (35). This parallel does not mean, however, that Mama Day derives after all from a Shakespearean analogue. Mama Day is shaped rather by the figure of the black mother as artist described by writers such as Paule Marshall, Alice Walker, and June Jordan,[18] and it is within this distinct tradition that the Mama Day-Cocoa relationship has to be considered.

In Paule Marshall's *Praisesong for the Widow,* the unattributed poetic phrase "my sweetest lepers" (16, 256) comes from Gwendolyn Brooks's "the children of the poor," whose first line chillingly observes: "People who have no children can be hard."[19] This assertion has a resonance with Toni Morrison's *Tar Baby* (1981), where the unattached and childless Jadine is presented not as an opportunity but as a problem.[20] In the 1985 conversation with Naylor, Morrison comments: "That's another one of those unreal, I think also fraudulent, conflicts between women who want to be mothers and women who don't. Why should there be any conflict with that? You could, first of all, do both" (573). But Morrison's idea of choice modulates into the imperative of doing both: "No one should be asked to make a choice between a home and a career. Why not have both? It's all possible" (575).

Morrison's comments suggest some of the emotional charge behind the novel's procreational pressure, a pressure exemplified by the quilt Cocoa receives from Mama Day and her sister: "I also knew they hadn't gone through that kind of labor just for me. . . . They had sewed for *my* grandchildren to be conceived under this quilt" (147). Cocoa begins as a potential Jadine, but through Mama Day's intervention ends by carrying on the family line, on which the inheritance of land and the survival of Willow Springs depend. The novel's conclusion leaves no room for doubt about Cocoa's commitment to Mama Day's legacy. Yet their bond is not completely idealized; a slight prickliness and tension flicker around the edges. Cocoa's original departure from the island signals her need for psychological separation; she vigorously rejects George's notion of settling in Willow Springs (220); even when she relocates, she maintains some distance by living in Charleston instead of returning to the island itself.

We have in the end to see Naylor's work in relation to two different contexts, both of which are important for a full view.

Naylor's departures from Shakespeare—especially her rejection of the absences and restrictions imposed by Shakespearean images of women—are substantial.[21] By countering Shakespeare, Naylor demonstrates the degree to which Shakespeare does not author us, the extent to which that role has irreversibly passed to others. New problems indeed arise, but they are not Shakespeare's problems nor does his work contain the materials needed for exploring all the possible options.

* * *

In *Bailey's Cafe,* the fourth novel, Gloria Naylor again uses two devices to create a sense of linkage from one novel to the next. The first is to develop a character or situation referred to in a previous novel; the second is to continue a pattern of allusions to Shakespeare. In this final novel of the quartet, however, Naylor teases us by deferring fulfillment of these expectations for so long that we have just about forgotten or given up. For example, *Mama Day,* the third novel, has planted George's reference to his birth at Bailey's Cafe (130–31). Yet Naylor makes us wait until the last three pages of the novel *Bailey's Cafe* before mentioning George and revealing who his mother is and where (unbeknownst to George) he fits in the overall scheme. The comment of one of the characters—"in this business you could use a sense of humor" (91)—applies to Naylor's role as novelist.

Initially, the strongest connection *Bailey's Cafe* demonstrates with Naylor's previous work is to her first novel, *The Women of Brewster Place.* Like the earlier novel, *Bailey's Cafe* presents a series of stories of down-and-out women. The resemblance is sufficiently close that the basic approach now seems routine, predictable, at times even trite. Having delayed almost too late until the last third of the novel, Naylor springs a surprise. The last, longest, and most important story is devoted to a man. This is where Naylor breaks new ground. The legacy from the first three novels in the quartet is a line of failed, incomplete, or uncertain male characters: from the negative instances of the brutal young rapists and the helplessly alcoholic Ben in *The Women of Brewster Place* to the shaky efforts of Lester and Willie in *Linden Hills* and George in *Mama Day* to break out and to seek alternative modes of masculine identity. In *Bailey's Cafe* Naylor provides a positive model of masculinity. It is a sign of

Naylor's humor that the man capable of this masculinity bears the name Miss Maple and wears women's dresses.

However, Naylor emphasizes that Miss Maple represents a case neither of sexual ambiguity nor of gender indeterminacy. Sugar Man, the epitome of traditional manhood, demonstrates the false perception created by anxiety: "And it does no good to tell him for the thousandth time that Miss Maple isn't a homosexual. Sugar Man has had to cling onto that or he would just about lose his senses when Miss Maple is around" (163). In order to reach a different definition of manhood, Miss Maple, then Stanley, has had to overcome the same anxiety: "Manhood is a pervasive preoccupation when you're an adolescent boy, and you tend to see a fairy under every bush" (175). This fear is concentrated on his father, whom the son regards according to convention as "a coward" (170) for his refusal to fight back against white racist harassment: "I didn't see him as a man at all" (173). Eventually the boy's view is reversed: he breaks out of the impasse in which his resentment towards his father has trapped him and comes to realize that his father is instead the model for an alternative manhood: "how to be my own man" (173). How Naylor brings about this transformation is testimony to the brilliance of her comic imagination.

In the funniest moment in the book, Naylor has father and son stripped naked and locked in a storeroom by four uncouth white brothers, whereupon the two black men put on female clothing, break out of their prison, and take revenge by summarily dispatching each of the four whites in turn. The scene could not be more cartoonish, slapstick and farcical, yet the secret of Naylor's comic inventiveness is that its effects are both hilarious and deeply moving at the same time, as though the hilarity gave access to deeper levels of feeling. Under the duress of their imprisonment, Stanley's angry outburst against his father suddenly gives way to the physical contact he had earlier shunned: "Papa reached out to me in the darkness and I jerked my shoulder away from his hands. Don't you touch me. My teeth were clenched. Just don't touch me" (180):

> You don't even amount to the ape they [the white men] called you—you're nothing. And you've always been nothing. Nothing . . . nothing . . . noth. . . . My whole body started vibrating, my teeth chattering, my hands and leg muscles moving with a will of their own. He

> caught me in his arms before I fell to the floor. And then he placed me down gently to hold me as I cried like the child I was.
> My flesh against his flesh.... (181–82)

Forced by the occasion, the father for the first time expresses his hope that his son "identify yourself as a man" and the son begins to have a new understanding of what—from his father's perspective—it means "to become a man" (182).

Of course this reconciliation of father and son is confirmed by the father's abandonment of passive resistance and his recourse to violent retaliation. Ironically, what finally provokes his heroic attack is the white men's desecration of the complete set of Shakespeare volumes the father has purchased as a "legacy" (174) for his son: 'They had gotten to the books. The silk cover was gouged with holes, the spine busted and bent over double. They'd torn out handfuls of pages, crushed what was left between their fists, and then urinated on the whole thing. The stench of *The Tempest* was quickly filling the whole room" (183). The entire network of Shakespearean allusions through the previous three novels is compressed into one image—the Shakespeare corpus represented in the most literal way possible as a set of books, physical objects shipped in a crate. The image illustrates the complex multiple effects of Naylor's comedy. On one level, the educated, self-confident black man is moved to defend the Shakespearean heritage against ignorant whites. Yet on another level the humor turns in a different direction to make the Caliban-like gesture of destroying the books a magnificent act of exorcism. As a fitting conclusion to her long engagement with Shakespeare over the course of the quartet, this farewell is a riddance ritual that announces the end of Naylor's artistic apprenticeship. The moment is not only unaccountably funny but also satisfying. The taboo surrounding Shakespeare as sacred icon is broken; we are allowed to experience Naylor's outrageous comic violation as a release.

The final section of the novel that follows Miss Maple's story continues the focus on male identity and enters what might be considered non-Shakespearean territory: the relationship between blacks and Jews. The problems of black anti-Semitism and Jewish racism have recently received new attention.[22] Naylor's contribution to this discussion is deeply affecting because she is able to use the medium of fiction to convey the possibility of cooperation. The black male proprietor of Bailey's Cafe and Gabe, the Jewish owner of the pawnshop, are brought together specifically to bless the baby boy to whom Miriam, an Ethiopian Jew, has given birth. The festive response by the novel's three key male figures to "the baby's first thin cry" is touching: "Then Gabe grabbed me, whirled me around, and we started to dance. He could kick pretty high for an old goat. Miss Maple took his other hand and the three of us were out in the middle of the floor, hands raised and feet stomping" (225). The same three men preside over the formal ceremony of circumcision: "I had to stand in as the honorary *sandek,* the godfather. And Miss Maple took the role of the other male guests to help me respond to the blessing. Don't worry, Gabe said; God will forgive you for not being Jews" (226). Through this cross-cultural nurturant concern, the novel provides a final suggestion of a new male identity. At the risk of sounding ungrateful in the face of the genuine gratitude I feel, I must also register the negative side of this positive outcome. Political and ceremonial discourse is made to seem a largely male affair. The one explicit protest against this state—that of Miriam's mother (157)—is not fully or clearly stated.

* * *

The conclusion of this analysis of Naylor's use of Shakespeare is that Shakespeare's cultural reach is diminished, not extended. Shakespeare's work can no longer be conceived as an infinitely expanding literary umbrella, the ultimate primary source capable of commenting on all subsequent developments no matter how far historically removed. Faced with apparently limitless possibilities for interpretation, Shakespeareans have tended to romanticize their critical quandary by investing it with an existential myth of Shakespeare's inexhaustibility, by means of which Shakespeare already anticipates every possible future situation or response. This notion of Shakespearean anticipation amounts to a denial of history, of change, and of our own agency.

Naylor's work provides a valuable test case for how we are going to formulate a multicultural approach to literary studies. Naylor's interest in Shakespeare neither translates into kinship nor supports a model of continuity; the main note is rather one of conflict and difference. As Gloria T. Hull remarks, "Black women poets are not 'Shakespeare's sisters.' In fact, they seem to be siblings of no one but themselves" ("Afro-American Women Poets" 165). *Mama Day* owes less to Shakespeare than to a separate tradition of black women writers. Shakespeare does not assimilate Naylor; Naylor assimilates Shakespeare.

The result is that we must give up the assumption that the literary curriculum revolves around Shakespeare. The habits of a Shakespeare-centered universe may inspire ever more elaborate and farfetched attempts at "saving the appearances" comparable to the calculations devised to defend a geocentric system against the encroachments of a heliocentric view. The cultural act of naming newly discovered moons—most recently those of Uranus—after Shakespearean characters may seem to provide confirmation of old patterns; new moons cannot talk back and disconfirm. But new authors like Gloria Naylor can. Her fictions encourage us to direct our energies toward investigations of Shakespeare's place in a reconstellated cultural situation in which his work, while still significant, is no longer the all-defining center of things.

Notes

This essay combines and revises two earlier pieces: Chapter 7 in *Rewriting Shakespeare, Rewriting Ourselves* (Berkeley: University of California Press, 1991) and the section on *Bailey's Cafe* in "Canon Revision Update: A 1992 Edition," *The Kenyon Review* ns 15: 3 (Summer 1993): 197–207. Copyright © 1991 University of California Press and 1993 Kenyon College.

1. The epigraphs are drawn from the interview with Gloria Naylor in Donna Perry's *Backtalk: Women Writers Speak Out* (New Brunswick: Rutgers University Press, 1993), 217–44. This interview is hereafter cited as Perry.
2. Recent work on Matthiessen includes Jonathan Arac, "F. O. Matthiessen: Authorizing an American Renaissance," in *The American Renaissance Reconsidered: Selected Papers from the English Institute 1982–83*, eds. Walter Benn Michaels and Donald E. Pease (Baltimore: Johns Hopkins University Press, 1985), 90–112; Sacvan Bercovitch, "The Problem of Ideology in American Literary History," *Critical Inquiry* 12 (1986): 631–53; Donald E. Pease, "F. O. Matthiessen," in *Modern American Critics, 1920–1955*, ed. Gregory S. Jay (Detroit: Gale, 1988), 138–48; William E. Cain, *F. O. Matthiessen and the Politics of Criticism* (Madison: University of Wisconsin Press, 1988).
3. Gloria T. Hull, *Color, Sex and Poetry: Three Women Writers of the Harlem Renaissance* (Bloomington: Indiana University Press, 1987). See also *Shadowed Dreams: Women's Poetry of the Harlem Renaissance*, ed. Maureen Honey (New Brunswick: Rutgers University Press, 1989).
4. Gloria Naylor and Toni Morrison, "A Conversation," *Southern Review* 21 (1985): 589, cited hereafter as "Conversation." Morrison's use of the term Renaissance is repeated in *Wild Women in the Whirlwind: Afra-American Culture and the Contemporary Literary Renaissance*, eds. Joanne M. Braxton and Andree Nicola McLaughlin (New Brunswick: Rutgers University Press, 1990).
5. The revisionist argument can be seen in two recent essays by Hazel V. Carby: "In Body and Spirit: Representing Black Women Musicians," *Black Music Research Journal* 11 (1991): 177–92, and "The Multicultural Wars," in *Black Popular Culture*, eds. Michele Wallace and Gina Dent (Seattle: Bay Press, 1992), 187–99.

6. Naylor glances only briefly at Othello in *Mama Day* (64), where she finds other points of entry into Shakespeare more useful. In her passing reference to Othello in *The Temple of My Familiar* (San Diego: Harcourt Brace Jovanovich, 1989), Alice Walker emphasizes what Shakespeare's play omits: "'But did you never wonder why, in the little bit of the story the whites could not prevent Shakespeare, at least, from trying to tell . . . , that there are only Moors (defined as men) and no Moor*esses*?'" (195). In shifting her focus to the missing black female, Walker implicitly notes the play's limitations as an imaginative resource.

7. Three recent examples of the renewed investigation of race in the Renaissance are my "Representations of Blacks and Blackness in the Renaissance," *Criticism* 35 (1993): 499–526; *Women, "Race," and Writing in the Early Modern Period*, ed. Margo Hendricks and Patricia Parker (London: Routledge, 1994); and Kim F. Hall, *Things of Darkness: Race, Gender, and Power in the Early Modern Period* (Ithaca: Cornell University Press, 1995).

8. These cross-period studies include my *Rewriting Shakespeare, Rewriting Ourselves* (1991), *Cross-Cultural Performances: Differences in Women's Re-Visions of Shakespeare*, ed. Marianne Novy (Urbana: University of Illinois Press, 1993), and Marianne Novy's *Engaging with Shakespeare: Responses of George Eliot and Other Women Novelists* (Athens: University of Georgia Press, 1994). Each contains commentary specifically on Gloria Naylor: the chapter on Naylor in *Rewriting Shakespeare*; Valerie Traub's "Rainbows of Darkness: Deconstructing Shakespeare in the Work of Gloria Naylor and Zora Neale Hurston," in *Cross-Cultural Performances*, 150–64; and the section on "Gloria Naylor and Nadine Gordimer" in Marianne Novy's *Engaging with Shakespeare*, 168–78.

9. The concept of a quartet is mentioned in Bronwyn Mills's interview article, "Gloria Naylor: Dreaming the Dream," *Sojourner* (May 1988): 17, hereafter cited as Mills. In her prefatory note to an excerpt from *Bailey's Cafe* in the Summer 1992 issue of *Southern Review*, Naylor begins, "*Bailey's Cafe* finally completes the quartet of novels I dreamed of creating while I was working on *The Women of Brewster Place*."

10. A full analysis of this aspect of the play is given in Shirley Nelson Garner's "*A Midsummer Night's Dream*: 'Jack

shall have Jill;/Nought shall go ill,'" *Women's Studies* 9: 1 (1981): 47–63.

11. The resonance of the Southern location is increased when its autobiographical dimension is added: though born in New York City, Naylor "returned to the town of Robinsonville, Mississippi, where her family originated, to research folk medicine for *Mama Day*" (Mills 17). See also Perry, pp. 218–19, 232.

12. Marshall's third novel, *Praisesong for the Widow* (New York: G. P. Putnam's Sons, 1983), precedes *Mama Day* by five years.

13. In her Introduction to her 1967 short story "To Da-duh, In Memoriam," in *Reena and Other Stories* (Old Westbury: Feminist Press, 1983), Marshall links the character Aunt Cuney with Da-duh, Marshall's grandmother. The balance of forces between New York City and black island culture to the south is quite differently portrayed in the two cases. The granddaughter's triumph in the short story is reversed sixteen years later in the novel, which awards power to the grandmother figure.

14. This criticism of *Praisesong for the Widow* is not intended as a generalization about Marshall's work as a whole. Her previous novel about Barbados, *The Chosen Place, The Timeless People* (1969), exhibits an acute political awareness; there is nothing inherent in a Caribbean island location that automatically excludes sensitivity to political questions. *Daughters*, Marshall's fourth novel, recovers this political perspective, as I indicate in my review in *Callaloo* 16: 1 (Winter 1993): 268–71.

15. Carby's argument is presented in "The Quicksands of Representation: Rethinking Black Cultural Politics," the final chapter in her *Reconstructing Womanhood: The Emergence of the Afro-American Woman Novelist* (New York: Oxford University Press, 1987), 163–75, and elaborated in "Ideologies of Black Folk: The Historical Novel of Slavery," in *Slavery and the Literary Imagination: Selected Papers from the English Institute, 1987*, eds. Deborah E. McDowell and Arnold Rampersad (Baltimore: Johns Hopkins University Press, 1989), 125–43. Critical reassessments of Zora Neale Hurston's *Their Eyes Were Watching God* considered as an epitome of the black folk mode include: Mary Helen Washington, "'I Love the Way Janie Crawford Left Her Husbands': Zora Neale Hurston's Emergent Female Hero," in

her *Invented Lives: Narratives of Black Women 1860–1960* (Garden City: Doubleday, 1987), 237–54; Michele Wallace, "Who Owns Zora Neale Hurston?: Critics Carve Up the Legend," in her *Invisibility Blues: From Pop to Theory* (London: Verso, 1990), 172–86; and Hazel V. Carby, "The Politics of Fiction, Anthropology, and the Folk: Zora Neale Hurston," in *New Essays on* Their Eyes Were Watching God, ed. Michael Awkward (Cambridge: Cambridge University Press, 1990), 71–93.

16. Naylor comments in her own voice on football in the boxed inset, "Keeping Up with the Characters," accompanying the review of *Mama Day* in *The New York Times Book Review* (February 21, 1988): 7.

17. The survey is Alden T. Vaughan's, in his two articles "Caliban in the 'Third World': Shakespeare's Savage as Sociopolitical Symbol," *Massachusetts Review* 29 (1988): 289–313 and "Shakespeare's Indian: The Americanization of Caliban," *Shakespeare Quarterly* 39 (1988): 137–53. See also: Alden T. Vaughan and Virginia Mason Vaughan, *Shakespeare's Caliban: A Cultural History* (Cambridge: Cambridge University Press, 1991).

18. The mother is identified as an artist in Paule Marshall, "Shaping the World of My Art," *New Letters* 40: 1 (October 1973): 97–112 (subsequently incorporated in "From the Poets in the Kitchen," *New York Times Book Review*, [January 9, 1983]); Alice Walker, "In Search of Our Mothers' Gardens," *Ms.* Magazine (May 1974); and June Jordan, "Notes of a Barnard Dropout (1975)," *Civil Wars* (Boston: Beacon Press, 1981), 96–102.

19. Just as Toni Morrison acknowledges Paule Marshall as a predecessor ("Conversation," 589), so Marshall names Gwendolyn Brooks as a precursor: see Marshall's contribution to "The Negro Woman in American Literature," *Freedomways* 6: 1 (Winter 1966): 23–24.

20. For a detailed analysis, see my "Images of Nurturance in Toni Morrison's *Tar Baby*," *CLA Journal* 28: 1 (September 1984): 11–32; reprinted in *Toni Morrison: Critical Perspectives Past and Present*, ed. Henry Louis Gates Jr. and K. A. Appiah (New York: Amistad, 1993), 293–307.

21. In "The Woman in the Cave: Recent Feminist Fictions and the Classical Underworld," *Contemporary Literature* 29: 1 (September 1984): 369–402, Margaret Homans suggests a parallel in *Linden Hills* between Willa Nedeed's relation to her husband and the quality of Naylor's recourse to Dante.

Homans, moreover, praises Naylor's tacit admission of her literary containment or entrapment as an acknowledgment of "the limits of feminist revisionism" (371). But two points need to be made. First, Naylor's dependence on the model of the *Inferno* is excessive and stifling; the cumbersome apparatus derived from Dante constitutes a structural weakness in the novel. Second, Naylor's situation in *Linden Hills* is not a fixed, final position. *Mama Day* reconsiders the conflict between male literary tradition and female author in very different terms, the difference being made not by the replacement of Dante by Shakespeare, who, like Dante, offers patriarchal forms that efface women, but rather by Naylor's more actively critical manner of negotiating her relations with the established tradition. *Mama Day* is the better for providing what Homans does not find in *Linden Hills*—the "countertradition of strong womanhood to oppose the destructive legacy of patriarchy" (396). A more recent, general statement of Homans's position can be found in "'Women of Color' Writers and Feminist Theory," *New Literary History* 25 (1994): 73–94.

22. Examples are: Henry Louis Gates Jr., "Black Demagogues and Pseudo-Scholars," *The New York Times* (July 20, 1992): A15; Andrew Hacker, "Jewish Racism, Black Anti-Semitism," *Reconstruction* 1: 3 (1991): 14–17; Michael Lerner, *The Socialism of Fools: Anti-Semitism on the Left* (Oakland, Calif.: Tikkun Books, 1992); Cornel West, "Black Anti-Semitism and the Rhetoric of Resentment," *Tikkun* 7: 1 (Jan./Feb. 1992): 15–16; West and Lerner, "A Conversation between Cornel West and Michael Lerner," in *Bridges and Boundaries: African Americans and American Jews*, ed. Jack Salzman with Adina Back and Gretchen Sullivan Sorin (New York: George Braziller, 1992), 141–51; Paul Gilroy, *The Black Atlantic: Modernity and Double-Consciousness* (Cambridge: Harvard University Press, 1993), 205–17; "The Rift between Blacks and Jews," *Time* magazine (Feb. 28, 1994): 28–34; Nell Irvin Painter, "It's Time to Acknowledge the Damage Inflicted by Intolerance," *Chronicle of Higher Education* (March 23, 1994): A64; Henry Louis Gates Jr., "A Liberalism of Heart and Spine," *The New York Times* (March 27, 1994): E17.

Works Cited

Arac, Jonathan. "F. O. Matthiessen: Authorizing an American Renaissance." *The American Renaissance Reconsidered: Selected Papers from the English Institute 1982–83*. Ed. Walter Benn Michaels and Donald E. Pease. Baltimore: Johns Hopkins University Press, 1985.

Bercovitch, Sacvan. "The Problem of Ideology in American Literary History." *Critical Inquiry* 12 (1986): 631–53.

Braxton, Joanne M., and Andree Nicola McLaughlin, eds. *Wild Women in the Whirlwind: Afra-American Culture and the Contemporary Literary Renaissance*. New Brunswick: Rutgers University Press, 1990.

Cain, William E. *F. O. Matthiessen and the Politics of Criticism*. Madison: University of Wisconsin Press, 1988.

Carby, Hazel V. "Ideologies of Black Folk: The Historical Novel of Slavery." *Slavery and the Literary Imagination: Selected Papers from the English Institute, 1987*. Ed. Deborah E. McDowell and Arnold Rampersad. Baltimore: Johns Hopkins University Press, 1989.

———. "In Body and Spirit: Representing Black Women Musicians." *Black Music Research Journal* 11 (1991): 177–92.

———. "The Multicultural Wars." *Black Popular Culture*. Ed. Michele Wallace and Gina Dent. Seattle: Bay Press, 1992.

———. "The Politics of Fiction, Anthropology, and the Folk: Zora Neale Hurston." *New Essays on* Their Eyes Were Watching God. Ed. Michael Awkward. Cambridge: Cambridge University Press, 1990.

———. *Reconstructing Womanhood: The Emergence of the Afro-American Woman Novelist*. New York: Oxford University Press, 1987.

Erickson, Peter. "Canon Revision Update: A 1992 Edition." *The Kenyon Review* ns 15:3 (Summer 1993): 197–207.

———. "Hard Work: Paule Marshall's *Daughters*." *Callaloo* 16:1 (Winter 1993): 268–71.

———. "Images of Nurturance in Toni Morrison's *Tar Baby*." *CLA Journal* 28:1 (September 1984): 11–32.

———. "Representations of Blacks and Blacks in the Renaissance." *Criticism* 35 (1993): 499–526.

———. *Rewriting Shakespeare, Rewriting Ourselves*. Berkeley: University of California Press, 1991.

Ferguson, Margaret W., Maureen Quilligan, and Nancy J. Vickers, eds. *Rewriting the Renaissance: The Discourses of Sexual Difference in Early Modern Europe.* Chicago: University of Chicago Press, 1986.

Garner, Shirley Nelson. "*A Midsummer Night's Dream*: 'Jack shall have Jill; / Nought shall go ill.'" *Women's Studies* 9:1 (1981): 47–63.

Gates, Henry Louis, Jr. "Black Demagogues and Pseudo-Scholars." *The New York Times* (July 20, 1992): A15.

———. "A Liberalism of Heart and Spine." *The New York Times* (March 27, 1994): E17.

Gates, Henry Louis, Jr., and K. A. Appiah, eds. *Toni Morrison: Critical Perspectives Past and Present.* New York: Amistad, 1993.

Gilroy, Paul. *The Black Atlantic: Modernity and Double-Consciousness.* Cambridge: Harvard University Press, 1993.

Hacker, Andrew. "Jewish Racism, Black Anti-Semitism." *Reconstruction* 1:3 (1991): 14–17.

Hall, Kim F. *Things of Darkness: Race, Gender, and Power in the Early Modern Period.* Ithaca: Cornell University Press, 1995.

Hendricks, Margo, and Patricia Parker, eds. *Women, "Race," and Writing in the Early Modern Period.* London: Routledge, 1994.

Homans, Margaret. "The Woman in the Cave: Recent Feminist Fictions and the Classical Underworld." *Contemporary Literature* 29:1 (September 1984): 369–402.

———. "'Women of Color' Writers and Feminist Theory." *New Literary History* 25 (1994): 73–94.

Honey, Maureen, ed. *Shadowed Dreams: Women's Poetry of the Harlem Renaissance.* New Brunswick: Rutgers University Press, 1989.

Hull, Gloria T. "Afro-American Women Poets: A Bio-Critical Survey." *Shakespeare's Sisters: Feminist Essays on Women Poets.* Ed. Sandra M. Gilbert and Susan Gubar. Bloomington: Indiana University Press, 1979.

———. *Color, Sex and Poetry: Three Women Writers of the Harlem Renaissance.* Bloomington: Indiana University Press, 1987.

Jordan, June. "Notes of a Barnard Dropout (1975)." *Civil Wars.* Boston: Beacon Press, 1981.

Lerner, Michael. *The Socialism of Fools: Anti-Semitism on the Left.* Oakland: Tikkun Books, 1992.

Marshall, Paule. *The Chosen Place, The Timeless People.* New York: Harcourt Brace, 1969.

———. *Daughters*. New York: Atheneum, 1991.

———. "The Negro Woman in American Literature." *Freedomways* 6:1 (Winter 1966): 8–25.

———. *Praisesong for the Widow*. New York: G. P. Putnam's Sons, 1983.

———. "Shaping the World of My Art." *New Letters* 40:1 (October 1973): 97–112.

———. "To Da-duh, In Memoriam." *Reena and Other Stories*. Old Westbury, N.Y. : Feminist Press, 1983.

Mills, Bronwyn. "Gloria Naylor: Dreaming the Dream." *Sojourner* (May 1988): 17.

Naylor, Gloria. *Bailey's Cafe*. New York: Harcourt Brace Jovanovich, 1992.

———. "Keeping Up with the Characters." *The New York Times Book Review* (February 21, 1988): 7.

———. *Linden Hills*. New York: Ticknor & Fields, 1985.

———. *Mama Day*. New York: Ticknor & Fields, 1988.

———. "Mood: Indigo, from *Bailey's Cafe*." *Southern Review* 28 (1992): 502–36.

———. *The Women of Brewster Place*. New York: Viking Press, 1982.

Naylor, Gloria, and Toni Morrison. "A Conversation." *Southern Review* 21 (1985): 567–93.

Novy, Marianne. *Engaging with Shakespeare: Responses of George Eliot and Other Women Novelists*. Athens: University of Georgia Press, 1994.

Novy, Marianne, ed. *Cross-Cultural Performances: Differences in Women's Re-Visions of Shakespeare*. Urbana: University of Illinois Press, 1993.

Painter, Nell Irvin. "It's Time to Acknowledge the Damage Inflicted by Intolerance." *The Chronicle of Higher Education* (March 23, 1994): A64.

Pease, Donald E. "F. O. Matthiessen." *Modern American Critics*. Ed. Gregory S. Jay. Detroit: Gale, 1988.

Perry, Donna. *Backtalk: Women Writers Speak Out*. New Brunswick: Rutgers University Press, 1993.

"The Rift Between Blacks and Jews." *Time* Magazine (Feb. 28, 1994): 28–34.

Traub, Valerie. "Rainbows of Darkness: Deconstructing Shakespeare in the Work of Gloria Naylor and Zora Neale Hurston." *Cross-Cultural Performances: Differences in*

Women's Re-Visions of Shakespeare. Ed. Marianne Novy. Urbana: University of Illinois Press, 1993.

Vaughan, Alden T. "Caliban in the 'Third World': Shakespeare's Savage as Sociopolitical Symbol." *Massachusetts Review* 29 (1988): 289–313.

———. "Shakespeare's Indian: The Americanization of Caliban." *Shakespeare Quarterly* 39 (1988): 137–53.

Vaughan, Alden T., and Virginia Mason Vaughan. *Shakespeare's Caliban: A Cultural History*. Cambridge: Cambridge University Press, 1991.

Walker, Alice. "In Search of Our Mothers' Gardens." *Ms.* Magazine (May 1974): 64–70, 105.

———. *The Temple of My Familiar*. San Diego: Harcourt Brace Jovanovich, 1989.

Wallace, Michele. "Who Owns Zora Neale Hurston?: Critics Carve Up the Legend." *Invisibility Blues: From Pop to Theory*. London: Verso, 1990.

Washington, Mary Helen. "'I Love the Way Janie Crawford Left Her Husbands': Zora Neale Hurston's Emergent Female Hero." *Invented Lives: Narratives of Black Women 1860–1960*. Ed. Mary Helen Washington. Garden City: Doubleday, 1987.

West, Cornel. "Black Anti-Semitism and the Rhetoric of Resentment." *Tikkun* 7 (Jan./Feb. 1992): 15–16.

West, Cornel, and Michael Lerner. "A Conversation between Cornel West and Michael Lerner." *Bridges and Boundaries: African Americans and American Jews*. Ed. Jack Salzman with Adina Black and Gretchen Sullivan Sorin. New York: George Braziller, 1992.

On Stepping into Footprints Which Feel Like Your Own: Literacy, Empowerment, and the African-American Literary Tradition

Reggie Young

> The only phenomenon with which writing has always been concomitant is the creation of cities and empires, that is the integration of large numbers of individuals into a political system, and their grading into castes or classes.... [I]t seems to have favored the exploitation of human beings rather than their enlightenment.... My hypothesis, if correct, would oblige us to recognize the fact that the primary function of written communication is to facilitate slavery.
>
> Claude Levi-Strauss, *Tristes Tropiques*

> The black can never be the subject of [white] culture, only its object.
>
> Abdul JanMohamed, "Negating the Negation as a Form of Affirmation in Minority Discourse: The Construction of Richard Wright"

> It was slavery again, all right. No such thing as colored troops, colored politicians, or a colored teacher anywhere near the place. The only teacher to come anywhere near the place was white; the only time he came was in the winter when the weather was so bad the children couldn't go in the field. You didn't need a pass to leave like in slavery time, but you had to give Colonel Dye's name if the secret group stopped you on the road.... Yankee business came in—yes; Yankee money came

in to help the South back on her feet—yes; but no Yankee troops. We was left there to root hog or die.

Ernest J. Gaines, *The Autobiography of Miss Jane Pittman*

While an intrinsic ardor bids me write
the muse doth promise to assist my pen

Phillis Wheatley,
"To the University of Cambridge, in New England"

As a writer and teacher of African-American literature, I have found that no other works of literature have been as influential to the continued development of the African-American literary tradition as the narratives of former and escaped slaves. Slave narratives are so important to African-American writers that they are still being composed in various forms today. I became aware of the extent of their importance only after I began to prepare to teach courses in African-American literature, and at that time I found that my own efforts at creative writings were no more than an extension of the slave narrative tradition; in fact, the novel that I wrote for my doctoral dissertation turned out to be a *contemporary slave narrative*. I came to realize that slave narratives are important to the continued development of the literature and to me as a writer because they are works of self-affirmation by individuals who have been denied their own humanity and confined to a state of intellectual darkness through a process that restricts their access to literacy. The writers of slave narratives, however, acquire literacy skills for themselves in various ways and from a variety of sources which they use to encode the stories of their human experience on the printed page as a testimony of their being. In studying the narrative expressions of escaped slaves, it becomes apparent that acts of writing by peoples of African descent since their enslavement in this country have been, *and still are*, acts of liberation, because the path African Americans must take toward freedom is one paved by the acquisition of literacy.

Frederick Douglass's first autobiography was the first slave narrative that I read, but at that time, during the late 1960s, texts such as Douglass's were generally considered historical writings. Few by this time had studied them as literary works.

The circumstances of my reading Douglass were different than those of most people: I first read *The Narrative of the Life of Frederick Douglass, an African Slave* for a *freedom school* class that I was to lead as a peer-teacher. I was a high school student at the time and lived in a section of Chicago—the West Side—that was made up of recent migrants from the South. One of our history teachers suggested that I use Douglass's book, especially since what we were doing was similar to what Douglass did when he taught classes for his fellow slaves. Our "school without walls" was organized by myself and other students after we staged a walk-out to protest the inadequate conditions of our facilities and instructional services. Although most of the students in the school walked out, few found it worth their while to attend freedom school classes; they did not think it made much sense to walk out of school if all they were going to do was to attend school anyway.

Although I knew back in high school that I wanted to become a writer—teaching is something I found myself called to do later—most of the students in my poor, inner-city high school knew very little about the existence of something called *black literature*. I was fortunate to have had developed an interest in books because of my family's early influence and nurturing. While in high school, I found a job as a page at the downtown branch of the Chicago Public Library, which gave me an opportunity to expose myself to past and present titles by African Americans as I stacked books onto the shelves of the humanities and social sciences departments. Although I found the concept of black people writing books to be exciting, most of the people living in my community were still under the domination of Booker T. Washington's ghost: they felt there was a stigma attached to reading books, especially since the time spent reading could be better spent learning a trade that *might* lead to a job. They believed that the stories, novels, plays, poems, and autobiographies written by African Americans were no more than historical documents and relics. No one was expected to actually read "that stuff," and few of us actually did. Since we knew virtually nothing of literary value, these works, as literature, had little meaning.

My interest in the writings of escaped slaves developed years later when I was allowed to design a concentration in African-American literature for myself in preparation for my graduate exams in English. In my graduate program, there were no specialists on the faculty in African-American literature, which denied me the opportunity to take courses in that area. Therefore, I used my exams to start an intensive study of African-American literature and its criticism. Although I had already read much of what was available by twentieth-century African-American writers, I had not had a chance to study many of the critical works on African-American texts in my graduate school curriculum. During my exam studies, I discovered the depth of critical work being done by scholars in explicating the texts of the African-American literary tradition (*literary tradition*—I had never given much thought to the works by African-American writers as being a part of a tradition) and that a great amount of energy was being spent in reading the writings of escaped slaves as literature.[1]

Since then, I have worked to establish myself as both a creative writer and literary critic in the academy, even in this day of academic specialization,[2] because in my dual role I see myself following in the footsteps of many of the African-American writers who came before me. Throughout the course of African-American literary history, especially in many of its developmental stages, the writers and critics have often been one and the same.[3] When there have been few others to do the crucial chores of defining the literature, paying critical scrutiny to the works composed by African-American writers, and promoting the writers and placing their works in print, the writers have acted to help perform these tasks themselves. Evidence of these efforts can be found in many of the anthologies of African-American writing published earlier in the century which were arranged and edited by the likes of James Weldon Johnson, Langston Hughes, Arna Bontemps, and Countee Cullen; in the magazines such as the NAACP's *Crisis* and the Urban League's *Opportunity*, which featured Jessie Fauset and Countee Cullen among their editors; and even the short-lived *Fire!!*, a literary magazine organized and published by a group of writers and artists, including Wallace Thurman, Hughes, Zora Neale Hurston, and Gwendolyn Bennett. The tradition's writers are individuals who were forced to wear many hats, and some, including Frederick Douglass, Frances Ellen Watkins Harper, and W. E. B. Du Bois, were social activists, political spokespersons, and scholars (even if self-taught) who ventured into the area of creative production because they realized that it was there that one could best advance the cause of the race.[4] In so doing, as Bernice Johnson Reagon has said, these leaders had to be "cultural artists of great power," since African Americans have always tended to respond best "when information is heard and felt" (McCaskill 96). In their spoken and written narratives, the cause they rallied African Americans to respond to was that of their humanity, something that had been denied peoples of African descent from the time of their enslavement, because it was the very denial of their humanity that was used to justify the trade in slaves.[5] Peoples of African descent from the beginning were aware of the stacked game of intellectual denial that was being played against them, a game used to justify their victimization. Almost immediately, it seems, if we consider the legacy of the various types of narratives left behind by former slaves, they took it upon themselves to challenge the intellectual rationale behind their enslavement by placing their stories into writing.

It is no wonder, then, that Lucy Terry, a native African who was kidnapped and sold into New England slavery at an early age, would compose an important poem in New England colonial history,[6] as evidenced by the inclusion of her "Bars Fight, August 28, 1746," in Josiah Holland's *History of Western Massachusetts* (*Heath* 654), which was published in 1855, over one hundred years after the poem's composition. Terry's race was not a factor in her poem's inclusion in Holland's *History*, since the work was published a century before issues of multiculturalism surfaced in this country. Although the historical information available on Terry is limited, we know that she not only composed one of the first poems by an African in the English colonies, but that she also gained her emancipation during her lifetime, got her son admitted into Williams College, and successfully argued her own case in a land dispute against a white male—remarkable achievements for a woman born in Africa and raised a slave during the colonial period (Stetson 3). She *read* the game of literacy and human denial that was being waged against the people kidnapped from Africa, challenged it, and ultimately won, as indicated by her literacy, literary achievement, eventual emancipation, and her assertion of rights in a racist and patriarchal system, making her black America's first literary activist. In doing so, she helped to lay the foundation for the path of the tradition that African-American writers would soon follow.

Phillis Wheatley, like Terry, was also taken from her family in her native Senegal while still a young girl; nevertheless, she composed some of the most important verses *by anyone* in North America during the colonial period.[7] According to June Jordan, Wheatley was "the first Black human being to be published in America," as well as "the second female to be published in America" (24), and "the first decidedly American poet on this continent, Black or white, male or female" (29). Early American racism denied her the opportunity to issue a volume of her poems in the land of her captivity, making her go abroad to England to publish her *Poems on Various Subjects, Religious and Moral*. While in England, the young slave woman was celebrated for her poetic achievements in the country that produced Shakespeare, Milton, Donne, and Pope. Back in the colonies, however, the leading intellectuals, including the future third president, argued against the quality of her poems and the significance of her poetic works.[8] Those who still insist upon belittling the enormous scope of Wheatley's intellectual achievements generally ignore the fact that the number of poets in the colonies in the years before they separated from England were few, and that even fewer attracted the attention that Wheatley did—not because she was a slave who wrote poetry, but because she was a gifted poet despite her captivity. Although the justifications for denying Wheatley's humanity, as well as the humanity of all African peoples, were grounded in the invention that one of her nature could not read, write, or reason, with the highest form of intellectual reasoning defined as creative expression written in verse form, Wheatley challenged the intellectual arguments used to deny the humanity of the peoples who were brought from Africa and relegated to the status of American slaves (Gates "*Race*" 7–9). In doing so, she not only became the first African in America to publish a book of verse, but also one of black America's first freedom fighters, since the battle for black humanity was something that could not be won by physical insurrections and violent revolts.

Douglass, a century later, by composing the narratives of his life, retraced Wheatley's footsteps along the path of this still-emerging literary tradition and went beyond hers, leaving footprints of his own. Douglass recognized the importance of African Americans placing their narratives in writing so much that he wrote the story of his life in three different yet remarkable versions. But Douglass wrote more than his autobiographical narratives and the great speeches that he composed which are still being studied today—he also wrote a novel, *The Heroic Slave*. Although his effort at fiction was not as successful as those of some of the other early African-American novelists who followed (notably William Wells Brown's *Clotel*, Martin Delaney's *Blake*, and Harriet Wilson's *Our Nig*),[9] Douglass recognized that the novel, following the publication of Harriet Beecher Stowe's *Uncle Tom's Cabin*, held tremendous potential as a form of creative expression in the struggle for black humanity, one that had been untouched as an area of intellectual expression by former slaves. He placed his footsteps there. As the most important African-American intellectual figure of his time, Douglass's venture into that area of expression, which was both *creative* and *intellectual* in nature, paved the way for other African Americans, and, in fact, invited and encouraged them to retrace his footsteps so that they could add their own.

What Douglass accomplished through his struggle to achieve literacy skills and in recording his experiences in writing anticipates what African Americans, to varying degrees, have accomplished—increasingly—in each subsequent generation, and what I have been able to achieve on a much smaller scale. For me personally, because of the relationship I developed with writers and their works while living in a community where too many of the inhabitants lived in a state of blindness regarding the value and importance of the written word and by writing a novel in the process of earning a Ph.D., I read and wrote myself, like Douglass, from a state of virtual slavery to one of relative freedom: from a condition of intellectual and spiritual darkness to one of self-value, self-realization, and self-empowerment. My literacy skills allowed me to escape from a life of confinement in the streets of the *'hood*, just as Douglass's provided him a means to overcome a life of chattel slavery in the ante-bellum South.[10] As I have written elsewhere, especially in "Literacy, Literature and the Liberation of the American Bluesvilles: (On Writing Our World into Being)," the majority of peoples of African descent in this country still endure conditions of bondage inflicted by their lack of educational resources and opportunities.

* * *

The acquisition of reading and writing skills has been one of the greatest obstacles faced by African Americans in their struggle for humanity in the context of Western idealism, especially since the inexperience of their African ancestors in reading and writing printed letters was used by European and American colonial spokespersons to justify the trade in African slaves and their continued forced bondage well into the nineteenth century. In fact, I would argue that certain aspects of American slavery did not end with the legal abolition of slavery as specified in the Thirteenth Amendment in 1865 and that the lingering effects of bondage are still felt by many of the descendants of the former slaves who dwell in poor and marginalized communities today.

During the slave trade an ideological rationale was developed to reduce the beings who were taken from Africa to a dehumanized state of chattel property. This process of reverse enlightenment, or *disenlightenment*, was necessary because Africans during the time of their initial contacts with Europeans lived in anything but cultural and spiritual darkness, even if their lives were not centered around the printed word and manufactured text. Curiously, the rationales constructed to justify slavery were conceived during the so-called "Age of Enlightenment" in Europe, a movement that promoted the "light" of "*man's* reason as adequate to solve [the] important problems and to establish the essential norms in life" (Abrams 50, emphasis mine). One of the most important accomplishments of the enlightened thinkers of the Western world, at least in economic terms, was the philosophy they devised to classify the victims in the trade in human flesh as less than fully realized beings. Since Africans lacked experience in the printed word and manufactured texts, they reasoned blacks occupied a much lower rung than whites on what they conceived of as the "Great Chain of Being" (Gates, *Signifying* 130). By using their own cultural practices and values as the standard to define the rest of humankind, they declared that Africans were not only fit to be slaves but that slavery would ultimately benefit them because it would give them exposure to what they considered to be the light of knowledge and reason due to the contact they would have with whites. No matter what these so-called enlightenment thinkers stated in their various treatises, what evolved in practice was the restricting of African slaves to lives of cultural and intellectual darkness. They were denied both access to the print literacy of their enslavers and the practices of their former native cultures (although we know that some slaves learned to read and write, while many others adapted aspects of their former cultures to their lives as slaves). In this sense, the very nature of American slavery can be seen as the process of disenlightening and dehumanizing human beings.

Ending the practice of legal slavery was not enough to overthrow the bonds of slavery, since the process of disenlightenment continued long after emancipation from the work place of the plantations and small farms of the South was granted. Although the lives of most slaves during the ante-bellum period revolved around the tasks of labor that they were required to perform, their status as non-waged laborers is not what made them slaves; therefore, liberating them from the workplace was not enough to truly liberate them from their conditions of slavery. Just as scholars have diagnosed and studied how the ideological effects of racism often linger and result in racially hostile conditions that are felt by its victims even in the absence of the consciously racist, the institutional practice of slavery in this country has yielded similar results: once the process of disenlightenment had been set up and perfected, especially after it had become an integral part of the American mind set, there was no longer a need to have individuals serve in the roles of slave owners, masters, overseers, and sympathizers to keep the system of human bondage in operation. This helps to account for why in less than two decades after the pseudo-emancipation of black slaves went into effect, many of the so-called freedmen and women, along with their offspring, found themselves faced with conditions similar to the ante-bellum period of their confinement: only now, instead of being ruled from the "Big House" of the plantation, their realities were dictated by the commissaries that lorded over the feudal system of American sharecropping. An excellent illustration of the continued cycle of enslavement after legal emancipation can be found in Ernest Gaines's *Autobiography of Miss Jane Pittman,* where the protagonist and other characters are depicted living in a state of bondage for nearly one hundred years after their legal emancipation.

Although many former slaves and their descendants migrated to the North in the decades after the Civil War, especially in response to the growing climate of Jim Crowism in the South, their movement resulted in little more than a change of location and conditions of bondage for the vast majority of the migrants. Although the people of African descent who migrated to the North were no longer confined to lives as rural, agrarian sharecroppers, they found themselves quickly transformed into the equivalent of urban, industrial sharecroppers, being both under- and unemployed due to the menial labor positions they were limited to hold. Allen H. Spear, William A. Tuttle Jr., St. Clair Drake, Horace R. Clayton, and other historians and sociologists have studied the transition to urban life in the North faced by the descendants of Southern slavery.[11] They have shown how the new black city dwellers found themselves bound in a never ending cycle of debt due to their lack of wages and the high rates of interest they incurred. They were forced to buy food, clothing, furniture, and other material goods on credit from ethnic stores that functioned in the new urban black belt ghettos in a manner similar to the commissary stores in the South.[12]

An examination of the educational policies in the nation after the Civil War and after its quickly deconstructed Reconstruction period shows that most efforts to provide education to the former slaves did little more than to prepare them to exist in a more modern form of bondage, one that would marginalize them to the point of invisibility so that the greater society would no longer have to bear the stigma of its slave past. In "'Knowledge is Power': The Black Struggle for Literacy," Thomas Holt discusses the educational policies in the nation regarding the former slaves. He shows how these policies emerged through a collaborative process involving political and civic leaders from both the North and South; their aim was to do everything *but* enlighten the descendants of American slavery in the South, something Ralph Ellison's protagonist discovers still in effect decades later in *Invisible Man*.[13] The objective of the kind of educational schemes they devised was to make freedmen and women less desirous of intellectual knowledge and critical thought, further perpetuating the process of disenlightenment that was never eradicated after the end of legal slavery. Very few of the policies enacted concerning the education of the former slaves and their descendants—from the end of Reconstruction to the Civil Rights movement—were designed to rehumanize them; that is, to truly liberate them through a process of reenlightenment, either in instructing them to master the literacy of printed letters, or in revealing to them the truth about their historical and cultural pasts. Nor did the policies of either the South or the nation as a whole ever incorporate into the curricula of its white citizens, either native born or immigrant, the truth concerning the former slaves' humanity. As a result, the country's official *but unspoken* literacy gave credence to the myth that the descendants of Africa in this country were not fully realized beings and, therefore, did not deserve the rights, privileges and status of such beings.

If the true bonds of slavery have never been fully broken, the struggle and process of slave liberation continues: it has been the dominant theme in the struggles of African Americans throughout their history, and issues of bondage and freedom are still major areas of exploration for African Americans, whether in literature, film, music, or other types of narrative expression. In the tradition of earlier writers such as Terry, Wheatley, Harriet Jacobs, Harper, Paul Laurence Dunbar, and numerous others who found themselves faced with the erasure of their being, and of having their very status as inhabitants in the human community wiped away in a society whose de facto practices declared them objects at birth, African-American writers are still writing themselves into being. Contemporary African-American writers are continually retracing the legacy—the footprints, so to speak—of the writers who cleared a path for others to follow headed toward freedom.

From this perspective, it is easy to see why the majority of literary works by the descendants of African slaves in this country, virtually the entire black canon, should be viewed as slave narratives of varying types—and works from other types of narrative expression must also be included. Acts of writing and reading by African Americans in this country beyond a basic functional level have been and are subversive: they bind the black writer and reader as one in the quest for mass African-American enlightenment (enlightenment in this sense meaning empowering forms of literacies, including but not limited to print). This includes virtually every form of text of creative/intellectual expression since each form of African-American cultural expression is informed by, or, to borrow from Gates's *Signifying Monkey*, *signifies* on all other forms in the expressive culture.[14] Such a perspective opens up new ways of understanding works as diverse as Hurston's *Their Eyes Were*

Watching God and Wright's *Native Son*, despite the many differences between the two authors and their conflicting views on race, culture, and the representation of the black experience in literature. One possibility offered in approaching the works from this perspective is the opportunity to examine them as studies in the struggle for literacy and self-empowerment, with literacy defined, as Jacqueline Jones Royster, Barbara McCaskill, and others have argued, in a much broader sense than the act and process of reading and writing. In these novels we can see the characters' struggle for literacy as a quest to find voice. Janie finds the voice of self-realization and personal growth, which she uses to enlighten her friend Pheoby, who will, in turn, be able to school the rest of the members of her community.[15] Bigger Thomas, in Wright's novel, through his process of self-realization and personal growth, changes, by the end, from a destructive non-being to one who has been able to achieve enough self-understanding to find value in himself as a person, despite his incarceration and impending execution. Although various groups of scholars extract from or exploit the tradition according to their own theoretical approaches to literary studies, the tradition can be looked upon as one continuous developing body, with each work sharing in common its quest for the affirmation of the African-American being.

* * *

Since the publication of Margaret Walker's *Jubilee* during the early stages of the Black Arts Movement in the mid-1960s, African-American writers have returned to the slave past as a focus of their creative/critical explorations. Before the publication of Walker's neoslave narrative, ante-bellum slavery had been largely ignored by twentieth-century African-American writers.[16] In revisiting the era of African-American enslavement in the South, these writers have explored various concepts of literacy in their works. In Sherley Ann Williams's *Dessa Rose*, for example, an illiterate slave (illiterate in the sense that she cannot read and write printed letters) who escapes to the West *knowing* that the Fugitive Slave Act has made the North a dangerous place for self-emancipated slaves repeatedly recites her story to her young son because she reckons he will someday possess the necessary skills to put it in writing for her. In teaching him her story, and, in so doing, teaching it to us, she embeds the tale of her enslavement and the act of her reacquisition of self in both his and our collective memories. In

Morrison's *Beloved*, Denver's fascination with her mother Sethe's tale about her sojourn away from the Sweet Home plantation and to the free states with the white woman named Amy Denver is fueled by the fact that the ultimate product of the story is her own birth. It is important to her because she can *see herself* as the subject of the tale—at least when, from her point of view, Sethe *tells the story right*. It is a tale that offers proof of her substance and being, and helps her define her own subjectivity in a world that would deny her those things.

Besides exploring the ante-bellum slave past, contemporary African-American novelists have continued the tradition of investigating current aspects of the disenlightening bondage faced by the descendants of African slaves. I have elsewhere discussed my novel, *Crimes in Bluesville*, for example, as a *contemporary slave narrative*, a name that I use for works of literature and film which focus on the plight of African-American youths whose lives are confined to states of urban bondage.[17] June Bug, the central character, owes much of his literacy—which is the key to his survival, his escape from urban bondage, and his spiritual salvation—to a box of books by African-American writers from Wheatley and Douglass to Ellison and Brooks. The books had belonged to his father, who died as the victim of racial violence before June Bug's birth. By leaving the books behind he was able to provide his son with the gift of literacy as an inheritance. It is partially due to his access to these relics of black enlightenment that June Bug is able to overcome the shackles of urban black bondage in the mid-1960s when others around him are falling victim to the various forms of social and cultural *miseducation*.[18] Although the Black Arts Movement had begun by then, many African Americans residing in the more recently settled urban black belts—or bluesvilles—[19] even during this era of "art for the people's sake," never knew there was a black arts movement taking place. In his autobiography *The Big Sea*, Langston Hughes describes a similar relationship between the residents of the Harlem community and the renaissance that was supposedly taking place in their midst (228). Before he is able to escape, even June Bug succumbs to some of the manifestations of social and cultural bondage which affect the lives of those around him in his bluesville community, including alcoholism, drug addiction, lack of employment opportunities, black-on-black classism, neo-racism, intraracial crime and economic exploitation, and the destructive effects of mass cultural misogyny. He overcomes these oppressive forces not only by reading the texts of former slaves and descendants of slaves but also through the nurturing and schooling he receives from several women, who expose him to some of the kinds of literacies not available in books. Through June Bug's process of reenlightenment, he better learns to understand other signs and texts produced by the culture, which enables him to produce a tale of his own flight from bondage. Thus, he is able to join the ranks of those before him who have transcended the conditions of virtual slavery to that of a conditional freedom due to his literacy skills. At the end of the novel, he is able to practically write himself out of his Northern urban ghetto to, curiously enough, a college in the South.

Jess Mowry's *Way Past Cool* is one of the most interesting narratives of African-American urban bondage produced in the early 1990s, a narrative about urban youths attempting to cope with their conditions of slavery. Like many other slave narratives, it examines literacy and violence as methods of revolt in the effort to achieve liberation. Due to the language of the text, including that of the narrator and the characters, which is informed by the idioms of today's African-American urban youth, the novel can be effectively labeled a "rap" novel, although its intentions are clearly set on "increasing the peace" by educating inner-city "boyz" and "girlz" to the dangers of their conditions of bondage. In this way it distinguishes itself from the commercialized forms of rap music promoted on video shows such as *Yo MTV Raps* and BET's *Rap City* and from the self-destructive and misogynist forms of "gangsta" rap, which are often more intent on producing glorified images of violence than offering substantive contributions to community peace or in any way furthering the struggle for black enlightenment. Mowry's intentions are to create a modern day version of Gates's "trope of the talking book."[20] Mowry's text is geared towards urban youths who do not read literary works because few books are published that they feel are relevant to their struggles for enlightenment and most are much too expensive for them to afford. By creating a narrative that they can hear, one that speaks their language, and one that addresses their plight in a way that is meaningful to them and their struggles, Mowry has offered them a text that they can call their own. The novel's orality is important because the slave narrative form, since its inception, according to Bernard W. Bell, has served as a bridge between the oral and literary traditions in African-American expressive culture (28). This bridge or link between the spoken and written texts of the culture is important in that it offers a connection between those descendants of African slaves who have previously escaped their conditions of dis-enlightening bondage in this country and those who make up today's urban youth culture. It offers urban youths access to the types or forms of litera*cies* which are dominant in the greater society outside of the bluesville communities where they live, literacies necessary for them to master so that they will be able to do more than merely survive in their current conditions of bondage. These literacies, the ones associated with the printed word and information technologies, are the ones that they will have to master in order for them to eventually effect their escapes away from disenlightened bondage and their bluesville realities. The fact that African-American urban youths are often limited to the use of oral expression links the reality of their being to that of the ante-bellum slave of the South in that they have either no access to relevant and enlightening educational opportunities, or those opportunities are very limited. Although the characters we find in contemporary African-American urban youth narratives, as well as the people in the culture itself, are often in bondage due to addictions to alcohol, drugs, and gang involvement, it is not the booze and the drugs that are the sources of their enslavement: their addictions only serve to disguise the true condition of their slavery and to blind them to the asset that they need the most for eventual escape—the tools of literacy.

Although literacy is an important theme in Mowry's novel, his characters are hindered from acquiring so much as the basic reading, writing, and informational skills usually gained in educational institutions to survive the violence of their urban bondage; therefore, they must master different types and degrees of literacies. For example, there is the education that takes place in the family, which in the communities made up of the descendants of African slaves are families that are extensions of the nuclear family or families headed by a single parent. The experiences for children growing up in disenlightened and economically depressed households can be more destructive than constructive if they are not stable and nurturing environments that prepare their young to function in the outside world, something that is often not the case in marginalized communities. There is also the schooling of the streets, which one must master, to some degree, and then hope for an ample amount of grace and/or luck—what the kids in Mowry's novel call *magic* (101)—in order to merely survive. Then there is book learning, and this is the most important element in taking a step *beyond* surviving, and to actually escape the conditions of one's bondage in a society that privileges the printed word. Unfortunately, this is the literacy that is most inaccessible, since instructional educational opportunities are less available to those who need them the most.

In *Way Past Cool*, a drug dealer's bodyguard named Ty is an autobiographical figure representing Mowry's experiences growing up in the Oakland community referred to as "Oak-town." Ty manages to survive the intraracial, intracultural, and intracommunity violence that he encounters as he attempts to provide better material means for his brother and the rest of his family, but he does little to escape not only his physical enslavement but also the disenlightening, dehumanizing, social and psychological nature of his bondage. His failure to do so is largely the result of his lack of schooling, which, among other things, limits his ambitions and hinders his ability to fully understand the circumstances of his being.

In John Singleton's *Boyz in the Hood*, one of the characters, Tre, escapes from the physical and intellectual bondage of South Central L.A. as a direct result of the various types of schooling that he receives, but the difference between merely surviving and actually escaping are his past educational background and academic achievements, combined with the strong support that he receives from his family. Without a strong support from his estranged parents, including his father, who is both street-wise and politically conscious, and his self-sacrificing mother, Tre might have suffered a fate similar to those of his best friends, who both die violent deaths in the streets. But because of the literacy skills he possesses due to his institutional schooling, it becomes possible for him to virtually compose the terms of his own pass to freedom from ghettoized bondage: an admission letter to college, one ironically located, as in *Crimes in Bluesville*, in the South. In Mowry's novel, however, few of the characters have the advantages from which Tre and June Bug benefit, and we see them struggling merely to survive past the age of 14, which Mowry considers to be the critical age in the lives of black urban youths (MacRae 97).

In *Beyond the Veil,* Robert B. Stepto states that "the broad enduring issue of the African American's search for freedom [has been] . . . the quest for freedom and literacy." According to Stepto, "freedom occasions literacy and . . . literacy initiates freedom" (x). For Stepto, it appears, the specific type of literacy necessary to engage in a successful liberation struggle is that of the written word. He finds that over-privileging the spoken word can result in a form of entrapment, using Ellison's *Invisible Man* as an example, and that one can extract oneself from such circumstances only through writing (xi). From this perspective, the streetwise ways of the protagonists in *Way Past Cool* will ultimately be of only limited value; by the novel's end they will have no more than survived the threats imposed on them by a vicious drug dealer, his bodyguard (Ty), and two corrupt and brutal cops, because they do not gain the tools necessary to overcome and escape their urban bondage.

As with the characters in *Boyz in the Hood,* violence, especially in the form of gunshots, is a part of their day-to-day existence, as they try to survive the bluesville-type environment of their Oaktown community. For example, they have to duck bullets from drive-by shooters on their way to school, and they have to face rival groups of boys when they arrive there. (I hesitate to call the boys a gang—they refer to their group as "The Friends" in the novel—because of the stereotypical implications of the term's usage in reference to African-American youths.) Without strong family bonds, the boys are family to each other, a clan whose members have come together to aid each other's survival, and to protect the three square-block area that they consider their turf. For them, protecting their turf means keeping drug dealers and junkies off their streets, and the novel's central plot deals with their efforts to do away with the dealer by banding together with a rival group of boys. Throughout the novel, the boys learn and teach each other the ways of the street, but the book's mood is one cast in darkness, despite the fact that much of the narrative takes place during daylight hours. The narrative conveys this mood because Mowry's characters exist in an unenlightened setting, one where young boys must fight for daily survival, and where many of them suffer a fate similar to what Gwendolyn Brooks depicts in her poem, "We Real Cool":

We real cool. We
Left school. We

Lurk late. We
Strike straight. We

Sing sin. We
Thin gin. We

Jazz June. We
Die soon. (331)

By the end of the novel, the Friends and their allies, with the help of Ty—who rebels against the dealer—and Ty's girlfriend, succeed in "smoking" the drug dealer and surviving a gun battle with some corrupt cops who were being paid by the dealer for protection. For their efforts, they wind up with nearly five thousand dollars of the dealer's cash and three new automatic weapons to replace the "K-Mart Specials" that they had owned before. But they realize the money will do them little good since their parents would be suspicious of it, and rival groups of boys would try to rip them off if it were known that they had so much cash. Therefore, they give the money to the former bodyguard so that he can buy himself a used dump truck and start a new life, doing the same kind of urban menial sharecropping that his father had done before him. The novel's conclusion illustrates the insufficiency of money, violence, and guns in the quest for empowerment.

Mowry's intimate depiction of the environment in which urban youths find themselves confined not only illustrates the conditions of their bondage for readers who have never investigated the realities of the most marginalized areas of United States society, but it also shows the futility of life among the descendants of African slaves who have little access to, or even awareness of, the empowering aspects of printed-word literacy, since educational opportunities and resources within their communities are so limited. Since the characters in his work are only fictional, it would be nearly meaningless to spend much time debating their possible fates, but based on the evidence available regarding black males in inner-city communities today, the ones who do survive past their youth, such as Ty and the Friends in Mowry's novel, would find their options in life severely limited. But since the novel is written in a language that *speaks* in a manner that urban youths can both relate to and fully understand, it is a text that not only has the ability to encourage them *to think*, but to think critically about their circumstances of living in a virtual state of bondage. In composing his urban youth narrative, Mowry places his footprints in the path of the African-American literary tradition by offering a novel pointed in the direction of the North Star.

* * *

According to Barbara McCaskill, the African-American struggle for literacy has a threefold purpose: "to communicate the importance of liberation, self-definition, and the preservation of community spirit and history" (77). Since so many of the professional critics, whether black or white, who are now working on various African-American writers and texts intend to fulfill their own individual goals and concerns—with theoretical approaches to literary texts in the academy regarded by some to be more important than the literature itself—and not necessarily to contribute to the struggle for the further enlightenment of those who have been confined to the darker margins of our society, the contributions of African-American writers in formulating, evaluating, and promoting the printed word amongst those who have been confined and limited to conditions of slavery should not be ignored. Since the beginning of the tradition forged by the likes of Terry, Wheatley, Douglass, and those who followed, African-American writers have engaged themselves in the process of overcoming the intellectual rationales used to justify the enslavement of the people taken from Africa and brought to this country, rationales which were later adjusted and used to keep the former slaves and their descendants relegated to a state of disenlightening bondage even after their pseudo-emancipation.

I can attribute my own literacy and escape from bondage to the fact that the writers of the tradition left behind works which were available for me to discover, works which, by their very existence, encouraged me to read books. For much of my early youth, growing up in my own personal bluesville, I had little interest in reading because I had no idea of the existence of books that were especially earmarked for me, books written by African Americans about the plight of being black in this country. But after I discovered the texts of the tradition, I began to see my own experiences as the potential subject of creative exploration—I could see myself as more than an object that was hidden away in the impenetrable dark regions of society. After discovering that there was such a thing as *black literature*, and that African Americans have a long tradition of recording their narratives on the printed page, I found myself encouraged to read, but that meant that I had to first learn how to read: not just functionally, but with critical perception. Becoming a reader, however, was not a problem, because I was motivated; besides, the tradition's texts helped me in my efforts to become a reader since they spoke to me in a language that I could actually hear and understand, about people whose histories and experiences were closely related to my own. Although I grew up in a world which, through a process of disenlightenment, made me feel like a non-entity because *I* was a descendant of African slaves, I eventually discovered my own self-worth, a result of becoming cognizant of the fact that I did have a literature that I could call my own. As a result, I learned that the stories of my own life, and those of my family, community, and others in our culture were of value because they did have a place in books, even those that originated in oral expressive forms. That was all I needed to stimulate my own intellectual development; the ensuing relationship that I developed with the texts of the tradition was enough to motivate me to believe that I too could place my footprints in the path forged by the writers of the African-American literary tradition, to further extend it in its quest for literacy and empowerment of all of the descendants of African slavery.

As a child of the Black Arts and Black Aesthetic movements, which is when my personal creative nurturing began, in a period that gave root to my intellectual being—a time when, out of necessity, the black writer and the black critic were often one, whether as one person, or two people working hand-in-hand—I cannot lose sight of the necessity of my work being geared not for the sake of the work itself, but for the people and the tradition I represent. In both my critical and creative work, I am doing no more than responding to a calling: a calling which echoes out of the tradition's texts to all the descendants of African slaves, an echo that must be *read* to be *heard*. As a teacher, my goal is to make students aware of the literature's affirmative nature, and to encourage those who feel called to help continue the literature's tradition—to assist them in placing their footprints on the path that is moving toward the enlightenment of all the descendants of African slaves.

Notes

1. Henry Louis Gates Jr. surveys some of the significant developments in the post-Black Aesthetic era of African-American literary studies in "Tell Me Sir, . . . But What Is Black Literature?" the introduction to a *PMLA* special topic issue on African-American literature. See Dexter Fisher and Robert B. Stepto, eds., *Afro-American Literature: The Reconstruction of Instruction*; Houston A. Baker, "Discovering America: Generational Shifts, Afro-American Literary Criticism, and the Study of Expressive Culture," in *Blues, Ideology, and Afro-American Literature*; and Baker and Patricia Redmond, eds., *Afro-American Literary Studies in the 1990s*. For a debate by African-American scholars on Black Aesthetic-type approaches to the literature versus more recent theoretical approaches, see Joyce A. Joyce, "The Black Canon: Reconstructing Black American Literary Criticism" and "Who the Cap Fit: Unconsciousness and Unconscionableness in the Criticism of Houston Baker and Henry Louis Gates"; Gates, "What's Love Got to Do With It?"; and Baker, "In Dubious Battle."

2. In graduate school, I specialized in creative writing: I wrote a volume of poems for my M.A. thesis, and a novel for my dissertation. Working in creative writing offered me a greater opportunity to both write *black* literature, and engage myself in a study of works by African-American writers than I would have had in a literature option.

3. In the early Black Studies Programs, many universities hired black writers, especially poets, to teach black literature courses because English departments had never trained scholars in African-American literature. With the exception of the few critics already working in the field, black writers were only ones available who knew the literature. Those writers inspired many of their students to seek careers as writers and teachers of African-American literature. (Sterling Plumpp, the Chicago poet and current Professor of African-American Studies at the University of Illinois at Chicago, served as both my role model and mentor.) Today, it is much more difficult for black writers to gain jobs teaching African-American literature in the academy. Many of the old Black Studies programs have been either eliminated or merged into the traditional departments. For those wanting to teach African-American literature, more specialized training is now required, especially in critical

theory. Among many African Americans, however, there is a resistance to what they see as white and Eurocentric forms of critical theory; therefore some African Americans, especially creative writers, feel discouraged from seeking university jobs teaching African-American literature.

4. Just as many African Americans have ventured into the area of creative expression to advance the causes of the race, there are many examples of individuals who became social and political activists after establishing careers as writers. This includes Langston Hughes, Richard Wright, James Baldwin, Lorraine Hansberry, LeRoi Jones/Amiri Baraka, Nikki Giovanni and Alice Walker.

5. In "The Word in Black and White: Ideologies of Race and Literacy in Ante-bellum America," Dana Nelson [Salvino] discusses the attempts made to legislate away the humanity of the peoples brought to this country as slaves. See also Gates, "Writing, 'Race,' and the Difference It Makes" and my "Literacy, Literature, and the Liberation of the American Bluesvilles": (On Writing Our World into Being)."

6. In "Black Women Poets from Wheatley to Walker," Gloria T. Hull points out that the poem, which survived orally until its initial publication, is remembered today only because of its historical importance.

7. Before the recent trend of close reading and in depth study of texts by African-American writers, some critics, including a number of important African Americans, dismissed Wheatley's importance as a *black* writer, citing what they believed was the absence of racial awareness and social protest in her work. Several scholars in recent years have reexamined the details of her life and have provided new insights into her work. See William H. Robinson, *Phillis Wheatley and Her Writings*; Gloria T. Hull, "Black Women Poets from Wheatley to Walker"; June Jordan, "The Difficult Miracle of Black Poetry in America or Something Like a Sonnet for Phillis Wheatley"; Henry Louis Gates Jr., *Figures in Black: Words, Signs, and the "Racial" Self*; and Frances Smith Foster, *Written By Herself: Literary Production by African American Women, 1746–1892*.

8. For more information concerning the arguments made against the intellectual capabilities of Wheatley and other blacks, see Gates, "Writing, 'Race,' and the Difference It Makes"; *Figures in Black: Words, Signs, and the "Racial" Self*; and

The Signifying Monkey: A Theory of Afro-American Literary Criticism.

9. Information about Harriet Wilson's background, race, and authorship of *Our Nig* was recently uncovered by Gates. His research proved that the 1859 publication of her novel made it the first by an African-American woman. Previously, Frances Ellen Watkins Harper's *Iola Leroy* was considered to be the first novel published by an African-American woman. See Gates, *Figures in Black,* and Gates's introduction to the Vintage edition of *Our Nig.*

10. Even after Douglass escaped to the North, due to the Fugitive Slave Act he was still technically a slave. He could have been captured and taken back into slavery at any time. From the revenues he generated through his speaking engagements at abolitionist meetings and from the sales from the publication of his first narrative, he earned enough money to pay for his own freedom.

11. Each of these studies examine the lives of black migrants from the South who settled in the black belt area of Chicago's South Side during the first half of this century. See Spear, *Black Chicago: The Making of a Negro Ghetto, 1890–1920;* Tuttle, *Race Riot: Chicago in the Red Summer of 1919;* and Drake and Clayton, *Black Metropolis: A Study of Negro Life in a Northern City.*

12. In discussing the "great migration" of African Americans moving from the South to the North in the late nineteenth and early twentieth centuries, Spear, Tuttle, and other scholars, list among the factors that agents recruited Southern blacks to move to the North to serve as strikebreakers in labor disputes with white immigrant workers. These black "scabs" were paid less wages than the white strikers had been and were often fired after the strikes ended or were forced into even lower-paying unskilled positions.

13. In "'Knowledge is Power': The Black Struggle for Literacy," Holt discusses how little was done in either the South or the North to provide a level of instruction that would be of use to the ex-slaves and their offspring in the process of social acclimation and elevation. Marita Bonner offers several illustrations of how educational deficiencies affected the lives of recent Northern migrants in *Frye Street and Environs.* For example, in the story "One True Love," she portrays a young African-American woman who discovers that her elementary

and secondary schooling has done little to prepare her for classes in a community college. Disillusioned by her failure, she becomes ill and dies. I must note, however, that Holt, in his essay, does offer examples of the "self-help" efforts made by slaves and their descendants to educate themselves. In my reading of the African-American literary tradition, I see the texts composed by black writers as an important part of this continuing process of self-help education.

14. In referring to Gates's *The Signifying Monkey*, I am interested in the ways that various "black" texts are related to the production of different "black" texts, especially in other forms and genres, through a process of intertextual exchange. For example, sampling in rap music is an act of this kind of intertextual signifying, because it not only borrows lines, notes, and rifts from other musical recordings, but also the voices of poets reading from their works, passages from speeches given by famous personalities such as Dr. Martin Luther King, Malcolm X, and Nelson Mandela, and even various sounds taken directly from the streets of the *'hood*. African-American film makers such as Spike Lee and Julie Dash signify on works of African-American literature. For example, Lee's first movie, *She's Gotta Have It*, is an example of extended signifying on Hurston's *Their Eyes Were Watching God*. According to Stephen Henderson, in his introduction to *Understanding the New Black Poetry*, black poets often attempt to make their poems sound like musical instruments in a jazz performance, while jazz artists try to make their instruments rap like black poets performing their poems. During the Black Arts Movement, a number of writers and critics, including Henderson, Hoyt Fuller, Larry Neal, Baraka, and Haki Madhubuti, discussed the interchange between the texts in various forms and genres in the process of black creative expression, especially between poetry and music. Although they discussed in detail some of the various concepts of literary signifying, they did not use that term: Gates was the first to use the expression "signifying" in a critical discussion of intertextual influence and exchange.

15. In *Beyond the Veil*, Robert Stepto argues that Hurston only "creates the essential illusion that Janie has achieved her voice," because of Hurston's use "of an omniscient third person, rather than . . . a first person narrator" to have Janie relate the tale of her experiences. In using a third-person voice, he claims that Hurston fails to give "Janie her voice outright" (166). In her

introductory essay to an excerpt from the novel in *Invented Lives,* Mary Helen Washington concurs with Stepto's reading. Although they find Janie's use of a third-person voice problematic, I see it as inventive—I do not believe Hurston's creative approach for having Janie recite her story in a third-person voice, using what Gates calls "free indirect discourse" (*Signifying* 208–9), "undercuts the development of Janie's 'voice'" (Washington 244) nor does it diminish her ability to realize and express her own subjectivity.

16. Bernard Bell coins the expression "neoslave narratives" in his study, *The Afro-American Novel and Its Tradition* (285). According to Deborah E. McDowell, in "Negotiating between Tenses: Witnessing Slavery After Freedom—*Dessa Rose*," these novels are mainly a "post-sixties phenomenon." McDowell says that "Margaret Walker's *Jubilee* (1966) might be chosen arbitrarily as something of a catalyst, for since it was published, novels about slavery have appeared at an unstoppable rate" (144). Neoslave narratives published since *Jubilee* include Ernest Gaines, *The Autobiography of Miss Jane Pittman*; Alex Haley, *Roots*; Octavia Butler, *Kindred*; Charles Johnson, *Oxherding Tale*; Ishmael Reed, *Flight to Canada*; Toni Morrison, *Beloved*; and Sherley Ann Williams, *Dessa Rose*.

17. See my "Literacy, Literature, and the Liberation of the American Bluesvilles." In that essay, I call the novel a "quasi-slave narrative."

18. This term is borrowed from the title of Carter G. Woodson's study, *The Miseducation of the Negro.*

19. I first used the term "Bluesville" as a name for the West Side of Chicago, where I grew up, knowing that the South Side African-American community once referred to itself as "Bronzeville." In fact, Gwendolyn Brooks titled her first book *A Street in Bronzeville.* (The volume has since been republished in her collected works, *Blacks.*) The South Side "black belt" was settled by African Americans in the decades of the late nineteenth and early 20th centuries, and after it developed into an autonomous black enclave in the middle of the city, it gave itself the honorary name "Bronzeville" in demonstration of racial pride. For a number of years, Chicago's South Side even held elections for the mayor of Bronzeville (Drake and Clayton 2: 383). As a result of its history of involvement in electoral politics, Bronzeville eventually saw one of its residents, Harold Washington, elected as mayor of the entire city. The greater

West Side was settled by African Americans much later, in the decades after World War II. During much of its history, the West Side's African-American community has had no better than an estranged relationship with the South Side. The South Side has a larger base of political and economic power, and possesses most of the city's African-American cultural institutions and civic resources. In comparison, the West Side exists in a virtual state of desolation, best known for its poverty and gangs. As the home of the most recent African-American migrants from the South, especially from the Mississippi delta regions, it was once known as Chicago's "home of the blues." In *signifying* on the South Side, I felt that "Bluesville" was a very appropriate name for the West Side. In "Literacy, Literature, and the Liberation of the American Bluesvilles," I apply the term "bluesvilles" to all of the similarly underdeveloped and marginalized communities made up of African Americans in this country: peoples whose lives, to borrow Houston A. Baker's expression from *Blues, Ideology, and Afro-American Literature*, are still dominated by the *economics of slavery* (23–31).

20. In *The Signifying Monkey*, Gates discusses the "trope of the talking book" as "the paradox of representing, of containing somehow, the oral within the written, precisely when oral black culture was transforming itself into a written culture" (131–32). In a sense, Mowry and many other writers in the African-American literary tradition have reversed the process in creating African-American talking books: they, in essence, contain the *written* within the oral, in an act of creating "speakerly texts" which "privilege the representation of the speakerly black voice" (Gates, *Signifying*, 112).

Works Cited

Abrams, M. H. *A Glossary of Literary Terms*. 5th ed. New York: Holt, 1988.

Babb, Valerie. "Liberation Literacy. Literacy and Empowerment in Marginalized American Texts." *Multicultural Literature and Literacies: Making Space for Difference*. Ed. Suzanne M. Miller and Barbara McCaskill. Albany: State University of New York Press, 1993.

Baker, Houston A. *Blues, Ideology, and Afro-American Literature*. Chicago: University of Chicago Press, 1984.

———. "In Dubious Battle." *New Literary History* 18 (1986): 363–69.

Baker, Houston A., and Patricia Redmond, eds. *Afro-American Literary Studies in the 1990s*. Chicago: University of Chicago Press, 1989.

Bell, Bernard W. *The Afro-American Novel and Its Tradition*. Amherst: University of Massachusetts Press, 1987.

Bonner, Marita. *Frye Street and Environs*. Boston: Beacon, 1987.

Brooks, Gwendolyn. *Blacks*. Chicago: Third World, 1993.

Brown, William Wells. *Clotel*. *Three Classic African-American Novels*. Ed. William L. Andrews. New York: Mentor, 1990.

Butler, Octavia. *Kindred*. Boston: Beacon, 1988.

Delaney, Martin. *Blake, or The Huts of America*. Ed. Floyd J. Miller. Boston: Beacon, 1970.

Douglass, Frederick. *The Heroic Slave*. *Three Classic African American Novels*. Ed. William L. Andrews. New York: Mentor, 1990.

———. *The Narrative of the Life of Frederick Douglass, An American Slave*. *Classic Slave Narratives*. Ed. Henry Louis Gates Jr. New York: Mentor, 1987.

Drake, St. Clair, and Horace Clayton. *Black Metropolis: A Study of Negro Life in a Northern City*. 2 vols. New York: Harcourt, 1970.

Ellison, Ralph. *Invisible Man*. New York: Vintage, 1989.

Fisher, Dexter, and Robert B. Stepto, eds. *Afro-American Literature: The Reconstruction of Instruction*. New York: MLA, 1979.

Foster, Frances Smith. *Written By Herself: Literary Production by African American Women, 1746–1892*. Bloomington: Indiana University Press, 1993.

Franklin, John Hope. *From Slavery to Freedom: A History of Negro Americans*. 3rd ed. New York: Vintage, 1969.

Gaines, Ernest. *The Autobiography of Miss Jane Pittman*. New York: Bantam, 1972.

Gates, Henry Louis. *Figures in Black: Words, Signs, and the "Racial" Self.* New York: Oxford University Press, 1987.

———. *The Signifying Monkey: A Theory of Afro-American Literary Criticism*. New York: Oxford University Press, 1988.

———. "'Tell Me Sir, . . . What Is 'Black' Literature?'" *PMLA* 105 (1990): 11–22.

———. "What's Love Got to Do With It?" *New Literary History* 18 (1986): 345–62.

———. "Writing, 'Race,' and the Difference It Makes." Intro. *"Race," Writing, and Difference*. Chicago: University of Chicago Press, 1986.

Haley, Alex. *Roots*. New York: Dell, 1980.

Heath Anthology of American Literature. Vol. 1. Ed. Paul Lauter, et al. Lexington: Heath, 1990.

Henderson, Stephen. Intro. "The Form of Things Unknown." *Understanding the New Black Poetry*. Ed. Stephen Henderson. New York: William Morrow, 1973.

Holt, Thomas. "'Knowledge is Power.' The Black Struggle for Literacy." *The Right to Literacy*. Ed. Andrea Lunsford, et al. New York: MLA, 1990.

Hughes, Langston. *The Big Sea*. New York: Thunder's Mouth, 1986.

Hull, Gloria T. "Black Women Poets from Wheatley to Walker." *Sturdy Black Bridges: Visions of Black Women in Literature*. Ed. Roseanne P. Bell, et al. Garden City, N.Y. : Anchor, 1979.

Hurston, Zora Neale. *Their Eyes Were Watching God*. New York: Harper, 1990.

Johnson, Charles. *Oxherding Tale*. New York: Grove, 1982.

Jordan, June. "The Difficult Miracle of Black Poetry in America or Something Like a Sonnet for Phillis Wheatley." *Wild Women in the Whirlwind: Afra-American Culture and the Contemporary Literary Renaissance*. Ed. Joanne M. Braxton and Andree Nicola McLaughlin. New Brunswick: Rutgers University Press, 1990.

Joyce, Joyce A. "The Black Canon: Reconstructing Black American Literary Criticism." *New Literary History* 18 (1986): (335–54).

———. "Who the Cap Fit: Unconscionableness in the Criticism of Houston Baker and Henry Louis Gates." *New Literary History* 18 (1986): (371–83).

Lee, Spike. Dir. and screenwriter. *She's Gotta Have It*. Island Pictures, 1986.

McCaskill, Barbara. "A Stamp on the Envelope Upside Down Means Love; or, Literature and Literacy in the Multicultural Classroom." *Multicultural Literature and Literacies: Making Space for Difference*. Ed. Suzanne M. Miller and Barbara McCaskill. Albany: State University of New York Press, 1993.

McDowell, Deborah E. "Negotiating between Tenses: Witnessing Slavery After Freedom—Dessa Rose." *Slavery in the Literary Imagination*. Ed. Deborah McDowell and Arnold Rampersad. Baltimore: Johns Hopkins University Press, 1989.

MacRae, Cathi Dunn. 'The Young Adult Perplex." Rev. of *Way Past Cool*, by Jess Mowry. *Wilson Library Bulletin* (Sept. 1992): 96–98.

Morrison, Toni. *Beloved*. New York: Plume, 1987.

———. *Sula*. New York: Plume, 1973.

Mowry, Jess. *Way Past Cool*. New York: HarperCollins, 1992.

Nelson [Salvino], Dana. "The Word in Black and White: Ideologies of Race and Literacy in Ante-bellum America." *Reading in America: Literature and Social History*. Ed. Cathy N. Davidson. Baltimore: Johns Hopkins University Press, 1989.

Reed, Ishmael. *Flight to Canada*. New York: Avon, 1976.

Robinson, William H. *Phillis Wheatley and Her Writings*. New York: Garland, 1984.

Royster, Jacqueline Jones. "Perspectives on the Intellectual Tradition of Black Women Writers." *The Right to Literacy*. Ed. Andrea Lunsford, et al. New York: MLA, 1990.

Singleton, John. Dir. and screenwriter. *Boyz in the Hood*. Columbia, 1991.

Spear, Allen H. *Black Chicago: The Making of a Negro Ghetto, 1890–1920*. Chicago: University of Chicago Press, 1967.

Stepto, Robert B. *From Behind the Veil: A Study of Afro-American Narrative*. Urbana: University of Illinois Press, 1991.

Stetson, Erlene. Ed. and Intro. *Black Sister: Poetry by Black American Women, 1746–1980*. Bloomington: Indiana University Press, 1981.

Stowe, Harriet Beecher. *Uncle Tom's Cabin*. New York: Penguin, 1981.

Tuttle, William, Jr. *Race Riot: Chicago in the Red Summer of 1919*. New York: Atheneum, 1970.

Walker, Margaret. *Jubilee*. New York: Bantam, 1975.

Washington, Mary Helen. "'I Love the Way Janie Crawford Left Her Husbands': Zora Neale Hurston's Emergent Female Hero." *Invented Lives*. Ed. Mary Helen Washington. New York: Anchor, 1987.

Williams, Sherley Ann. *Dessa Rose*. New York: Berkley, 1986.

Wilson, Harriet E. *Our Nig*. Intro. Henry Louis Gates Jr. New York: Vintage, 1983.

Woodson, Carter G. *The Miseducation of the Negro*. Trenton: Africa World Press, 1990.

Wright, Richard. *Native Son*. New York: Harper and Row, 1969.

Young, Reggie [Reginald Scott Young]. *Crimes in Bluesville*. Diss. University of Illinois at Chicago. 1990. Chicago: UMI, 1990. 9107659.

———. "Literacy, Literature, and the Liberation of the American Bluesvilles: (On Writing Our World into Being). *Multicultural Literature and Literacies: Making Space for Difference*. Ed. Suzanne M. Miller and Barbara McCaskill. Albany: State University of New York Press, 1993.

[redacted] UNIVERSITY